AQUA SULIS TO CALIFORNIA

CW01655180

By Brian J. Walters

Case ID: 1-12913534121

ABOUT THE AUTHOR

He was born in south London a few years before the start of the Second World War. He was the youngest in the family, with four older sisters.

As a boy and young man, he participated in track athletics and made a name for himself in running, jumping, and throwing events. At the age of 18, he was rated number 17 in the world at the high jump.

Amongst his many other interests was music, although he failed miserably at the piano unlike his sisters, two of whom were talented pianists.

Among his lifelong interests are oil paintings of which he has created hundreds. Several of his grandchildren have had lessons with him and created their masterpieces. One grandson is currently a successful artist. Also, for 54 years he has sung in church choirs. To this day, at 88 years of age, he has a strong baritone voice, often singing solos as required.

The author and his wife had 5 children, (4 sons and one daughter), and now have 11 grandchildren and 21 great-grandchildren. This book was started 30 years ago, to record life the way it was, for them. It includes many interesting changes in technology, the way of life, and also the story of a family of seven, successfully starting again in a new country.

The author and wife currently live in their beloved home of 47 years, overlooking a lagoon and beach in Southern California.

DEDICATIONS

To My Wife,

My love and friend of 68 years, who also contributed greatly to this story.

Prologue

Several thousand years ago, before the Romans arrived in England, the area currently known as the counties of Somerset and Gloucestershire, was occupied by an iron-age Celtic tribe known as Dubunni. The Celtic tribes were barbarians and fierce warriors known for painting their faces with a blue dye called "wode".

The Celts captured Rome in 390 BC and attacked Greece a century later. They went on to establish a presence in Asia Minor. Rome was taken back sometime later, but the Celts remained in control of Northern Italy and many other areas in Europe. When Rome became more powerful, there were many skirmishes with the Celts in mainland Europe, but the Romans prevailed when England was attacked in 430 AD.

Many areas around Aqua Sulis (Bath in Somerset) show evidence of settlements from this period, in the form of stone, wood, and earth, and surrounded by ditches. Later, with the peace brought by the Roman occupation, most families lived in farming communities.

The topography of the area is largely the result of the last ice age, 12,000 years ago. Many millions of years before that, the area was below sea level, which accounts for the deep layer of underlying limestone rock, the main building material used in modern-day Bath. You can actually see tiny shells and grains of sand and other debris in the limestone.

The ice sheet generally carved the area into a valley surrounded by hills. There were many landslides even up to recent times, and as recently as the seventeen hundreds. The weather and the River Avon sculpted and smoothed Aqua Sulis to its present form. The vegetation was some grassland and dense woodland.

The weather in Aqua Sulis is more temperate than the rest of England. With plenty of grass and woodland and with a river running through the valley, Aqua Sulis must have been a nice place to live. Obviously, the Romans agreed as it became a very popular Roman city.

Table of Contents

Chapter 1 - The Beginning

2000 years ago, Aqua Sulis was a regional capital and a very important city to the Roman occupiers of South Western England. It was a spa city with a virtually unlimited source of mineral-laden, boiling spring water coming out of the ground. This foul-tasting water continues to run to this day. There were hot water baths, swimming pools, steam rooms, and all the latest facilities for the Roman elite to relax, under the mistaken belief that if the water tasted and smelled bad then it had to be good for you. And taste bad, it does.

Aqua Sulis, which is now known as the beautiful City of Bath, also known as the Queen City of the West, is in a valley, almost completely surrounded by hills approximately 700 to 900 feet high, with small openings on the east and west ends. These openings allow the River Avon to flow westward through Bath to the Bristol Channel, which separates Western England from South Wales, on the way to the Atlantic.

In recent years, Bath has won the "The Britain In Bloom" contest many times and it is generally acknowledged as the most beautiful city in the South West of England. In addition, during the Georgian era, under the influence of a rich playboy named Beau Nash, Bath became the fashionable place to go for anybody who was anybody or wanted to be somebody. All the fashionable people had a place in Bath, which is full of beautiful Georgian buildings with spectacular circular and semi-circular crescents of large 4 and 5-storey houses. The names of many famous people can still be seen on tiny plaques, as former occupants of some of the buildings. All buildings are built of off-white limestone, quarried from the surrounding hills, and known as, would you believe it, Bath Stone. This stone is comparatively soft, lending itself easily to decorative carving, a feature that has been used to the fullest. However, it doesn't wear well, needing much maintenance and cleaning which is an ongoing activity. The burning of coal fires is no longer allowed, and the buildings should stay cleaner than they did years ago. The city can boast of many beautiful churches, including the Bath Abbey, over 600 years old, built on the foundations of another abbey going back 700 years before that.

Today, Bath is a bustling city of approximately 100,000 people, in the center of a large rural farming area, and is the nearest big center for many thousands of country folk.

Bath is 30 miles from Stonehenge, and 20 miles from the village of Cheddar, the home of the original Cheddar cheese and also famous for its deep gorge and limestone caves with magnificent stalagmites and stalactites. Castle Combe, one of the most picturesque of the surrounding villages, where the movie "Dr. Doolittle" was filmed, is about 15 miles away. Lacock, another picturesque village about 12 miles away, has several old cottages going back as much as 700 years. Bath itself has a small church at Charlecombe (a small village within the Bath boundary) which is over 1100 years old. London is 100 miles directly east of Bath. Bristol, a port made famous as the starting point for journeys to the New World, and literary works such as "Treasure Island", is 12 miles to the west.

Chapter 2 - The Characters Appear

On a rainy day in 1934, on the 11th of June, at 11 am, Elaine Newton (nee Osman), of 18 Seymour Road, Bath, in the county of Somerset, England, gave birth to her first child and named her Muriel Joy. The birth, a difficult one, took place in Clairemont Nursing Home. As was usual in those times, Elaine stayed in the nursing home for 14 days. The baby weighed in at 8lbs 8ozs. It may be significant that later in the day that Muriel was born there was a very heavy thunderstorm. Muriel's father's name was Harry Frederick Arthur John Newton.

110 miles to the East, and 11 months later, (namely on May 23rd, 1935), at 9 Upper Grove Road, Belvedere in the county of Kent, in England, another momentous happening took place. In the early hours of the morning, Lilian Evelyn Walters (nee Smith) presented her husband, Arthur Edward, with a son, named Brian John, the fifth child after 4 daughters. He weighed in at 9lbs 6 Oz, and was remarkable for being 24 inches long. He was also described as "skinny".

Belvedere was a smallish town of about 5,000 people, a few miles east southeast of and 10/12 miles from central London. Belvedere was in a large apple-growing area with many apple orchards. It was set between two larger towns, Woolwich and Erith, on the south side of the river Thames. Greenwich, known for the Zero Longitude point was right next to Woolwich on the London side. Woolwich had what was called "The Arsenal" at least during the Second World War, where all sorts of explosive devices were manufactured and stored, and this was where the local first division soccer club got it's name, "Woolwich Arsenal".

Chapter 3 - Muriel's Early Recollections, by Muriel.

Among my earliest recollections are of living in a 3-storey house, with my parents, my mother's unmarried sister, Auntie Cecelia, also known as Celia or Cissie, my mother's unmarried brother named Horace Wilfred (thereafter known as Jack for obvious reasons), and their mother, my widowed Grandmother Alice. My Grandmother's maiden name was "Wise" and her married name was "Osman", a name, we always supposed, came from a past ancestor from Turkey. (I visited Turkey 60 years later and was treated like royalty when I announced that my mother's maiden name was Osman). The "Wise" family was well known in Bath as bakers with a large store in the center of the city. Other close relatives in the area were my mother's brother, Uncle Stan (Osman) a tall slim kindly man for whom I had great affection. He was married to my Auntie May. She was my Godmother. They had two children, my cousins, Sybil and Tony. Sybil was 12 years and Tony was 4 years older than me. Uncle Stan and Auntie May were very kind to me, taking me to functions like tennis matches etc. Uncle Stan, who was a bigwig in the Bath Fur & Feather Club, (rabbits, pigeons, canaries etc.) would take me along, and later on, when I was 12, when there was a show, he would have me fill out the winner certificates as he liked my writing. Another relative, and somebody who was very dear to me, was Great Uncle Frank, (Francis Palmer), who was a frequent visitor to the house. He was married to my Grandmother's sister, another Aunt Cecelia (Cissie), who died before my birth. Uncle Frank worked for the leading jeweler in Bath, and he gave me several small pieces of jewelry when I was young. However, my most favorite uncle was Uncle Jack. He was an Internal Revenue Inspector, and gave me two pence a week pocket-money, and would take me on local work trips in his government-provided chauffeur-driven car. The car was equipped with a drop-down table in the back seat, and I would stay in the car with the chauffeur and draw, etc. whilst Uncle Jack would do his audits. I was extremely fortunate to have so many nice uncles.

Although my first given name was Muriel, it was not completely favored, and sometimes I was called Joy, my second name. I say this to avoid possible confusion later in this chronicle.

My mother was born in Bath in 1911 and was the baby of her family. She is 5'4" with dark hair, hazel eyes, and is quite tough in a quiet ladylike fashion. My father was born in Calne, in the county of Wiltshire, in 1906, at the family's farm, Hale Farm. He was one of six children. He was 5'10" and always very slim. He had blue eyes and dark hair. He had a hard younger life, and was hard on everybody around him but mostly on himself. He didn't mince words and had a tendency to speak his mind regardless of the consequences.

Before long I had a baby brother, John, and sisters named Susan, Dawn, and Phyllis. The 2nd World War had started just before Dawn was born, and soon after, my father went to war in the Royal Signals. He rose to the rank of Captain, and the story goes that he was demoted to the rank of private for insubordination. He again rose to the rank of Captain and managed to hang on to it this time.

Sister Dawn was a beautiful child, and when she was about 15 months old, she was having a bad time cutting her back teeth. She had a teething convulsion, which left her paralyzed down her right side. From that time on for a few years, she had to wear a leg caliper and special shoes.

Somebody who had a great influence on my life was my mother's sister, Auntie Celia. As stated above, she lived with us and always watched our manners and corrected us. Often, she would take the eldest three of us out to posh cafes, etc. One time she took all three of us to Lynemouth in Devon, on a day bus trip. On the way there, the door would not stay shut, and as she was trying to shut it, it slammed on her finger and almost severed it. She had to spend the whole day with this. She was quite faint and ill.

Another time she took me to Shaftsbury to visit her school friend, Olive Hardey. When we returned we brought back two golden Labrador retriever puppies, Bruce and Rover. As they got bigger it became too much for us and I had to take Bruce to the RSPCA, and he was adopted by somebody. A week later he arrived back with us and I had to take him back to the RSPCA.

At one time I shared a bedroom with Auntie Celia, and she had dozens of pairs of shoes. I remember having a great time trying them on and tottering around in them.

One of the things I enjoyed was her playing the piano. I especially liked her playing The Grand March. She was an excellent pianist and was the accompanist in local shows.

Bath was not a high priority on the German's list for bombing raids, only receiving a few bombs until suddenly over two days in April of 1942, the might of the German air force was unleashed on Bath all at once over 2 nights. It was referred to as "The Bath Blitz". In the early part of the war The Admiralty, (British Navy) decided to move out of London to a country area. They chose Bath and in a couple of places on the top of the surrounding hills, they constructed widely spaced single-storey "hutments" as they described them. The Admiralty, which employed as many as 15,000 people, was probably the target for the Blitz although little damage was done to Admiralty buildings. The city sustained major devastation with whole blocks being flattened. A few of the old churches were hit, but strangely, most of the really historic places came through OK. Over 400 people were killed in the two nights. The original Wise bakery in Julian Road was completely demolished. Before this, during the few air raids, we stayed in the house away from windows, etc.

However, on the day before the blitz, we were warned to find shelter. Our whole family took shelter in the arched cellars of a local brewery

Numbers 8 through 12 in our road, Seymour Road, were demolished along with most of the glass windows in the area. Somehow the plan to hit Bath must have been known beforehand.

Immediately following the Bath Blitz in April 1942, my mother and us 4 children (Phyllis was not quite ready to be born yet) and Grandmother were evacuated from the city supposedly out of fear of continuing serious air raids. There was very limited public transportation, and only around the city. There were no private cars for the whole duration of the war. There was no petrol (gasoline) available except for essential vehicles. We were transported to my Auntie Margaret's farm, (Hare Street Farm) at East Tytherton, near Chippenham in the county of Wiltshire. Our transportation was our coal merchant's lorry (truck). I can assure you that there are cleaner vehicles than those used for coal deliveries, but there were limited choices.

Hare Street Farm is about 25 miles from Bath, but seems so much further as the last 8 miles is by way of narrow (7 feet wide) twisting country lanes where 10 miles per hour is speeding. The farmer was my Uncle Stan, (Stanley Martin), married to my father's sister Margaret. Auntie Margaret had been widowed with one child, Cousin Anne, and the new marriage produced a son, Christopher Martin. Anne is one year younger, and Christopher is about 9 years younger than me.

On May 4th, 1942 at the farm, Sister Phyllis was born.

My father served in India and Burma, and was captured by the Japanese, but was liberated 18 days later by the overtaking British army. Everybody else in his unit was executed. During Dad's army service, he served as a dispatch rider and was mentioned in dispatches. When he returned to England, I remember Dad coming into the house late one wet and stormy dark night, soaked to the skin after being on his motorbike. He opened up one of his big overcoat pockets from which he took a very tiny ginger kitten which had been wandering on the road miles from anywhere. We kept the kitten and called him Ginger. My mother was fond of cats and we always had one. The first one I remember was a tabby called "Chummy". All it seemed to do was sleep as far as I could see.

Once Dad must have been ill and I remember him wearing a blue uniform. This color uniform meant that he was excused from active duty until healed or got well.

When Dad was in India he used to write blue pre-stamped airmail letters which came with coal black censor markings blotting out some of the message. Obviously, great pains were taken to prevent any information from getting into the wrong hands. I know my mother found this quite annoying. Dad called us children his mucky pups when referring to us in those letters. There was quite often a passage to be read out to us. It would contain promises of things he would bring home for us when the war was over, such as a baby elephant and so on. We eagerly awaited his homecoming and the elephant, but of course, it was only a silly promise on which children hang hopes and dreams. Dad did bring presents from India. Mine was a lovely leather handbag with exquisite embossed scenes of Indian life and a blue beaded necklace which I will mention again later on.

Because Dad was always making promises which never came to pass, we stopped believing the stories. Some of the wonderful things promised were: "We are going to buy a fish and chip shop in Marshfield and you will all have to help". "We are going to buy a pub in the country and you will all have to help". "We are moving to the country and have a small-holding (small farm), and you'll all have to help". There were countless others but I have forgotten them.

I cannot really pin down my very earliest memory, but I remember certain random things. Some of these I will detail as I go along. My favorite childhood song was "The Teddy Bear's Picnic" which was sung with gusto by my mother to us children and never failed to enthrall us. Other favorites were, “Babes in The Woods" . . . . "My dears do you know how a long time ago, two poor little children named Minnie and Joe, were stolen away on a fine summer’s day, and were lost in the woods so I've heard people say" etc... We also loved "The March Of The Toy Soldiers". Mum would also relate the long poem about cats. It started "A cat once to her kittens said come listen prim to me, your Pa and I have both agreed to have some friends to tea. So hurry off and wash yourselves and put your whiskers straight, and hurry off and tell the guests, be here at half past eight. But tell them not to venture out if bad or stormy weather, but if its fine upon the roof we all shall meet together", and so on.

I had a much-loved Teddy Bear which became absolutely bald as the years went by due to me absent-mindedly pulling his fur out one or two hairs at a time. This was a habit I unconsciously continued, using my eyebrows when I had no Teddy Bear. (I continued to try this on my husband’s eyebrows, but had some opposition from that quarter). I also had a black doll which I called Mary, and an actual baby-size doll named Peter. Peter was broken by my brother John, and I was heartbroken. My Uncle Frank took him to the doll's hospital and he was mended as good as new. I had a book titled "The Eskimo Twins" which I read over and over. Auntie Celia gave me a book of poems by Walter de la Mare, and I learned several by heart.

Learning poems and Bible passages by heart featured quite a bit in my school and Sunday school life. I know my mother was quite amused (largely, I believe, because I was the eldest, it being novel to her). It probably paled as more children joined the learning path, and recitations became more frequent. She would make me repeat the latest piece of learning over and over. My first song at infants school was “Snowdrops and Crocuses, Heralds of Spring", which my mother can recite to this day (60 years later), so often did she make me recite it! Then my first poem was "A Smile". “A smile is such a funny thing it wrinkles up your face, so when it's gone you'll never find its secret hiding place. But far more wonderful it is to see what smiles can do, you smile at one, he smiles at you, so one smile makes two”. Both of these were learned at Christ Church Infants School which I attended from the age of five. Miss Chase was the headmistress and she had teeth that were quite prominent and made indentations in her bottom lip. This always fascinated me and when looking at her, this is where my eyes focused. I tried pressing my adult teeth (which also stick out a bit) into my lip, but now I can't think why. My teeth, being a bit prominent were the cause of great distress to me and sometimes I would stand with them pressed into my bedroom wall, hoping they would become straight and pretty. What misery we go through as children over the silliest things. Great Uncle Frank's son Albert was a dentist and I begged him to do something to straighten my teeth but he said it was impossible, and that was that.

At Christ Church School, on wet days we did not go out into the playground, but did exercises in the cloakroom. I remember hurting my little finger and having it strapped up. I was excused from these exercises until it had healed. I remember my brother, John, being at this school with me. It was a co-ed school.

After 3 years of infants' school, I went to Harley Street Girls junior school. I really don't remember too clearly the early days of going to school. I know we walked everywhere. We did not have a car and there was no other way. Since my mother had so many children, she did not accompany us much of the time, and we were all used to getting ourselves there and back. Sometimes I would meet up with John, my younger brother, and we'd go to Hedgemead Park on the way home and play. John has never forgiven me because Miss Chase gave him a message for Mum that the next sister down, Susan, could go to school starting immediately. John says that I took off like a deer in order to reach home before him and make the announcement to Mum. Sorry, John if I stole your thunder.

Once on the way to Harley Street school, I fell down on the road close to where my Aunt Maud (Mum's cousin, Maud Weston, nee Wise) lived. A large piece of gravel got embedded in my right knee, and it was bleeding badly. I ran home, and my mother took me to a neighbor, Ben Bath who was a fireman and trained in first aid. He advised a visit to the doctor, and we saw Dr. Lane who wanted to stitch it but I had other ideas and would not let him near it. The scar is still there and has never bothered me. An interesting note about my Auntie Maud. She never had any children and was married to a rather domineering man. Maud was an excellent pianist and was a lot of fun. Consequently she was always in demand to play at parties and gatherings. Unfortunately, she used to drink alcohol and very often had more than she could manage. The story goes that one night after an evening of celebrating when she got home her husband got her to sign some documents. What she didn't realize was that she had signed away all rights to her house and property. Maud had inherited both money and property from her parents. Although she tried to contest the signing when she sobered up, the documents were legal and she never regained control. Her marriage was not a happy one. When her husband died, he had willed everything to a niece on his side of the family and Maud had financial problems until her death.

Christmas was very special in our house, and preparations started in September with the making of pickled onions, piccalilli, and chutney. The best shallots had to be topped and tailed and washed and salted and for years I had to do my share of the preparation.

Christmas puddings and the Christmas cake were made about that time because they had to age. I absolutely detested having to remove the seeds from the raisins for the Christmas cake and puddings.

On Christmas day we had all kinds of special food and confections that were only available at Christmas in wartime, and, we had to save up all kinds of food ration points to be able to buy it.

About a week before Christmas we put up a few decorations in one room, (largely paper chains and garlands) we made ourselves with glue made from flour and boiling water. We always had a small Christmas tree, with a few lights on it.

On Christmas Eve we all went to bed after hanging one of Granny's stockings on the end of each bed. Miraculously, on Christmas morning we found these stockings filled with goodies. We always had an orange, an apple, a tangerine, 2 walnuts, a sugar mouse, and a few other goodies like a pencil, or eraser, and sugar cigarettes. Good things were in very short supply due to the war.

Our Christmas day began with the opening of our stockings, and eating an enormous English breakfast consisting of bacon (English type), English sausages, fried eggs, fried tomatoes, fried bread, and mushrooms. Followed by toast and marmalade if you had room. Amazingly, the tree was covered in tiny presents labeled with our names, but not to be touched until later.

By the time we were up for breakfast, Mum had already stuffed the goose, and it would be already cooking. This was always the English traditional meat for Christmas Day. My Dad always collected the goose grease which was used as a cure for every ill, and as a lubricant and preservative for shoes etc... Dad swore by it.

We usually had our Christmas Dinner at about 1.30 pm. The table was elegantly laid with all the best china, and Christmas crackers, with funny hats and little toys in them. Dinner would consist of goose, roasted potatoes, roasted parsnips, roasted onions, and roasted butter beans, carrots, Brussels sprouts, leeks, and stuffing and homemade red-currant sauce, and gravy. Following this, we would have Christmas pudding with custard and cream with castor sugar (fine grain) sprinkled over it.

When dinner was eaten and all dishes done we would have our main presents. At about 4.30 pm or 5.00 pm, we would have Christmas Tea (meal). This consisted of blanc-mange, jelly, trifle, and the piece de resistance, the Christmas cake. It would have a Christmas frill and a snow scene on the top, in white icing with little figures and trees on it. Also, we always had an edible Christmas log, a Swiss Roll covered in chocolate, filled with cream and decorated with a sprig of holly, and a robin. After this, we would have the presents off the Christmas tree. We saved food ration coupons all year for this Christmas feast.

At about 8.00 pm we had supper, consisting of cold meats like ham, tongue and goose, cheeses, pickled onions, chutney, and pickled beetroot (beets), followed by mincemeat tarts and sausage rolls. The adults would have sherry and port, and sometimes a glass of homemade parsnip or rhubarb wine. Also, Advocaat (Dutch liqueur) if it was available. All the children were allowed to have a small amount of Advocaat also. Christmas Day was entirely for the children, but the next day, Boxing Day, was for the adults. Children had to amuse themselves while the grown-ups took it easy. Meals were basically cold leftovers.

From the age of about 12, I went to Auntie May and Uncle Stan's house for Boxing Day. They always had a party in the evening, and sometimes played cards, and once, they gave me a shilling for a stake. I won the kitty, about 15 shillings, a huge amount for a young girl.

One Christmas Day, when we unwrapped our presents, we threw the wrapping paper on the fire.

One day a lighted piece of paper went up the chimney. The fire station was across the river and they saw smoke and sparks coming from the chimney, and we had a visit from them. Our chimney was on fire.

The war was just a way of life to us children. I was so young (five) when it started that I didn't know things could be different. At Harley Street School the girls all knitted for the war effort. I made khaki balaclava helmets and scarves. The wool and knitting needles were supplied and always stayed in the school building.

Harley Street had four grades. The top grade was in a classroom at the top of the building and was big enough to house the whole school for morning assembly and prayers to start the day. In this room were large wooden Honor Boards on which the names of all girls who had passed the 11plus exam, (sometimes called the "scholarship exam") were listed. Each year was separated by date. My cousin Sybil was on one of the boards. Eventually my name was added to an Honor Board when I passed the 11plus. (The 11plus was an exam given to all children in their 11th year of age.) If you pass this exam you can go to a higher level of education which is supposed to fit you for a university if this is what you choose to do. Only about 8% of the entrants pass the 11plus, and have this opportunity. It is quite an honor to pass. When I was to take the exam I was promised one English pound note by three of my relatives, Granny, Auntie Celia, and Uncle Jack. The equivalent value in 2004 would probably be about $40 to $50. I passed the exam and all three paid up and I was the proud recipient of three one-pound notes. Of course, this was duly put into the post office savings account for me. About three times during my years at Harley Street we had American candy distributed in the form of jars of sweets. All candy was strictly rationed. We thought it was wonderful. When Dad was in the army, each Saturday morning Mum and I would change the sheets in all the beds. I had some other jobs to do. We had brass stair rods for me to clean. These were decorative items and served no useful purpose. The carpet was nailed in place and the rods fitted into brackets in the crease of each stair. I am not sure of the exact number, but it was about 30. We also had some old steel knives (not stainless) and these had to be cleaned with Vim (like Ajax). Another of my jobs was scrubbing the kitchen table with scouring powder. This table had a wooden top and was scrubbed to whiteness.

The job I hated the most was "slop pail duty". Indoor plumbing was rare. We had a toilet which was attached to the house, but you had to go outside to get to it which was a problem during the night. We were lucky that we had a glass lean-to conservatory, which saved us from getting soaked in the rain during the day.

"Slop pail duty" was visiting all the bedrooms in the mornings with a large bucket, a jug of water, and a cloth. Every bedroom had a chamber pot, and they were emptied into the bucket, and rinsed from the water jug, and dried off with the cloth.

Brother John always chopped wood, but it was often my job to clean and "black" the cast-iron fireplace and lay the fire.

Every Sunday morning was spent helping my mother at the washtub. Whites were boiled up in the boiler. This boiler was built-in and like a giant cauldron. It was filled with cold water and heated by a coal fire lit underneath. When the washing was boiled for long enough (I'm not sure now just how long that was) the hot clothes were pulled out with the boiler stick (a thick wooden pole) and placed in a container to be taken to the sink to be rinsed. Then the clothes had to be put through the mangle to squeeze out all excess water before being hung up on the clothesline to dry. None of these jobs exist in today's world. Mum did not hang the washing out on Sunday as it was thought not proper. She waited until Monday. Of course, I was in school then.

Sunday afternoon was spent at Sunday School.

Once during Miss Heale's Sunday School class, I watched a maggot crawling around in her fur coat. She always smelled of mothballs, but apparently, they didn't work. Miss Heale was a lovely lady who seemed about 100 years old. I expect she was in her 70's. We always had to learn some Bible verses by heart and recite them the following week. Once a year, during the summer months, we had a Sunday School outing to the seaside, organized and subsidized by the parish church. We always went to Weston-Super-Mare by train. It was only a distance of 32 miles but it took about one to two hours.

Once during the journey to the seaside a three-year-old in the same compartment as us accused the rest of us of trying to see his "private parts". For some reason, we all found this very amusing and kept giggling all the way there. None of us had ever heard that expression before and it just tickled us to death.

At the end of each year, Sunday School prizes were awarded for perfect attendance, good study habits and learning of verses, and good behavior. In the first year, the prize was always a Bible. After that it was always a religious book.

My childhood was not a happy one. I was the eldest. There were so many children, so much work to be done, lots of endless shopping, and play-time for me was mostly dragging two or three of the children with me. Dad was away at war.

On one of my many enforced babysitting visits to Hedgemead Park with all 4 of the younger ones, we had a calamity. Phyllis was the baby, about 2 years, in a push-chair (baby carriage). Dawn was in her leg caliper. We all arrived at the park, which was on the side of a very steep slope culminating in railings directly next to the main London Road. John and Susan were playing on the nearby swings in the play area and I was sitting on a park bench and reading a book. Phyllis got out of the push-chair, and was playing on the grass with Dawn.

Without me realizing it, Dawn got into the push-chair and Phyllis was pushing her around, and suddenly the push-chair took off down the slope. I chased after Dawn, but couldn't catch her. A lady passing in the road put her hand through the railings and took some of the impact, but Dawn's head must have hit the railings as she had a cut which was pouring blood. John and Susan appeared and I sent them to find Mr. Fields, the park-keeper, who came flying along in his hob-nailed boots. I was holding the gash closed to stop the bleeding, and got covered in blood. Mr. Fields picked Dawn up with me holding the wound closed, and we climbed up to the top of the park, an extremely steep climb, to the Eye Infirmary, (eye hospital) which happened to be just across the upper road. I had left the other 3 children sitting on a park bench. I was sent home to get my mother to the hospital. On the way, many people asked me what had happened as I was crying and covered with blood.

My mother was shocked at the sight of me and said she would deal with me when she got home, and dispatched me to get the other 3 sitting on the park bench. When I got there they had not moved!

Another incident occurred in the same park when I was going home from school one day. I was walking down the steps to get to the London Road on the way home. At the top section, there was a center wooden handrail. I mostly slid down it with no problem, but now it had suddenly grown a rough jagged section, which ripped my underwear and I got lots of splinters in my bottom. This was one of the most embarrassing episodes of my life as my mother had to pick all the splinters out. I never did that again.

That same summer, in the same park, we found a bicycle in the bushes, and we took it to the police station. We were told that if nobody claimed it in 3 months, it was ours.

John and I went especially every week to the police station in the center of town, to see if anybody had claimed it, and the week before the three months were up, we were told it had been claimed. Now I am older and wiser, and suspicious of what probably happened. It is a fact that if you lose a bicycle you report it immediately. You don't wait 2 3/4 months to go to the police.

During the summer holidays when jobs at home were done, we would be sent to play in one of the many parks in the area. One of the furthest away for us was Alice Park, so if we went there we liked to take a picnic. This meant making lots of jam sandwiches for all of us children. It would be a lot of preparation, but the long walk there made us hungry and the minute we arrived, we would have something to eat. We would get home in time for tea. Sydney Gardens was another nice park. The railway line to London ran through the middle of it. There was a bandstand, tennis courts, lawn bowls, and it was fairly close to our home. Henrietta Park was very small and had nothing for us to do, so we seldom went there. Hedgemead was probably our most used park, it spread out over a large area and had lots of places to hide when we played hide and seek. Usually, we played in the local parks. Occasionally, we would venture to the huge Victoria Park, for which we most certainly would take a picnic.

One incident that I clearly remember was when I was eleven. John and I went fishing for minnows in the river. We had a jam jar on a piece of string and we were very absorbed in our task when an older boy yelled out to John to come over to him. John went over and came back to me and said something about "that boy wants you to be his girlfriend." His name turned out to be Leslie Lawrence. This was the first time that I really was aware of boys as boys!

I had long hair, which I wore in plaits (braids).

John and I were very competitive and we would have all sorts of contests. We had "stare-outs", to see who could stare the longest without blinking. Another time we held our arms in the air to see who could keep the arm up for the longest time. Of course, we had all the usual competitions like spelling and adding up etc.

We did not have entertainment like TV and therefore had to amuse ourselves. We played all kinds of games. Hide and Seek was a favorite. All kinds of ball games. Hopscotch and skipping. We had whips and tops, and hoops. Tag was also a very popular game.

Once a year, always in the summer, we had the chimney sweep. This was a big to-do. The sweep was always dirty looking. He came with his poles and brushes and clothes. He came into the house to the fireplace that was to be swept and put his big cloth all around the fire opening. There was a hole in the middle of the cloth. He put the big round flu brush inside the cloth (so you couldn't see it) and attached a bendy pole through the cloth to the brush. He would push this up the chimney and when the pole ended he would screw another section into it. He would keep this up until the brush poked out of the top of the chimney. Of course, someone had to watch the chimney top and let him know when this happened. One of us children would be assigned to this task and we would eagerly await the first sign of the brush. Once the brush was spotted the descent of the brush was started. On the way up, and on the way down, the brush would be given a good twirl every now and then. Sometimes this would result in clouds of soot coming down the chimney and falling (hopefully inside the clothe) into the hearth. Gradually the poles would be removed and finally, the brush would appear. The clothe would be carefully taken down and the soot gathered up and taken away by the sweep.

We had a lot of door-to-door salesmen. Some were welcome and some were not. There was the rag and bone man. You would hear his calling "Rags and Bones" when he was streets away. He bought exactly that, rags and bones from joints of meat, plus other discarded items. He would load up his cart, always pulled by a sad-looking horse, appearing like it was on its last legs. Then there were the gypsies. They came twice a year and in the spring they would sell bunches of flowers which they had picked in the woods, such as bluebells, cowslips, and snowdrops. They always had wooden clothespins for sale.

They would ring the bell and say "Cross my palm with silver dearie and I'll tell your fortune". Mum always bought flowers and the pegs and gave them a sixpence. Most people would buy from them because they were afraid a curse would be put on them as gypsies were rumored to do. They were always on the move. They lived in horse-drawn caravans and would park in farmer's fields, where they were not welcome because the farmers always believed that they stole their chickens etc. Then there was the Fuller Brush man. He sold hair brushes, scrubbing brushes, and assorted household items. Mum always bought a couple of things from him.

Then there was the tinker who sharpened knives, and fixed pots and pans etc. People would line up in the street with everything they wanted to be sharpened, knives, scissors, hedge-clippers, etc. He did quite a trade when he came.

Once or twice I remember an umbrella salesman.

Every day we had our milk and bread delivered to the house. If you wanted something special, you had to order it ahead if you wanted it delivered. This was normal for everyone and the way things were done.

One of the big rituals in our house once a year was the washing of all the best china and crystal glassware that only saw the light of day on high days and holidays. We had a sitting room which was almost like a shrine. We seldom used it. The piano was in there, and you had your piano lesson there and practiced there. It was always so cold and lonely, so you practiced as little as possible. However, once a year after the big wash of the best stuff and cleaning of the silver, a very posh tea would be prepared. Trifle, blancmanges of several different colors made in fancy shaped molds, a couple of jellies (jello), jam tarts, sponge cakes, fruit cakes, chocolate biscuits, and assorted goodies such as canned peaches (when the rationing allowed) or whatever fresh fruit was in season. We had scones with clotted cream, and finger sandwiches. This posh tea was served in the sitting room and we thought this was absolutely fabulous.

One year we were all in the sitting room eating our posh tea and there was a ring of the front doorbell. Dad answered the door, and it was three of his snooty relatives, the Carringtons, who had never visited us before and were not expected. They were invited in and they were astonished and said "do you always eat like this"? And Dad said "oh yes". We never saw them come to the house again. Mum was thrilled to bits. It couldn't have worked out better.

On one of our nightly rituals in the winter, for at least 6 months of the year, we children had to line up and have a spoonful of each of the following, (no vitamin pills in those days):

Cod Liver Oil (lovely)

Parrishes Chemical Food

Rose Hip Syrup

Luckily I was the eldest and got the clean spoon for each one.

Another winter custom; if Mum thought we had a cold, she would warm a bottle of Camphorated Oil in front of the coal fire, and we'd have our chests rubbed with it. We all smelled very lovely. When we came home from school, the first one home would find Mum in a coat to keep warm. Then she would light the coal fire which was the only way to warm the house. Every ordinary person was too poor to burn fires all day, and also, coal was rationed through the war years. We wore thick underwear, vests with sleeves, and fleecy lined bodices. Otherwise, we'd have frozen, but for some strange reason, our legs went virtually bare. We used to get chapped knees from the cold and rain on our legs.

There was always a big black kettle on the hob at the side of the fire. It was used for tea, for washing, and anything that needed small amounts of hot water. Twice a week, the coal boiler was fired up for boiling up the white linens on Sunday, then Saturday for bath night in a galvanized tub in the kitchen.

Our bedrooms never had heat. We would take hot water bottles, filled from the black kettles, and put them in the beds a little before getting in.

I remember making dozens of pieces of toast by the fire. We used to get bright red faces and slightly scorched hands, but it tasted so good. We used a special long fork, about 2 feet long. Granny always cut the bread slices. There was no such thing as sliced bread in those days. Sometimes, granny would whisper "Shall we have Granny pieces"? It was a real treat. The loaf was buttered then a paper-thin slice was cut, then it was sprinkled with sugar. If you didn't butter it on the loaf, it was too thin to butter afterward.

Another tea-time treat was a soft-boiled egg in an egg cup, with "soldiers". These were made from a slice of buttered bread and cut into 1/2" wide strips for dipping into the egg. Only 1/3 or less of the eggshell was removed. You must remember that it was a real treat in those days. If you could get the eggs (rationed from 1939 until 1951), you may not have been able to afford them.

One of my favorite winter foods was to put potatoes in the ashes of the fire and let them bake until they were flowery and soft inside. We would put our whole butter ration on one, and eat with relish. But best of all were my mother's boiled suet puddings. There were different varieties. Some were done in basins, wrapped in a cloth, like treacle puddings, and some were just wrapped in the cloth in a sausage shape. These were made with raisins, crystallized fruit, and glace cherries.

One day we'd been fighting and arguing while we waited for the pudding to cook. Mum got the pudding out of the cloth and said as we'd been so bad we would have none. She threw it down the garden. We all went after it, and picked up pieces. When she realized what we were doing she came after us with the wooden spoon. We all ran, but she got in a few good whacks.

The wooden spoon figured very large in our lives, especially at the time that Mum was poking the fire and stood up a bit sharpish, and banged her head on the mantle-piece (shelf above the fireplace).

We had all been arguing when we heard this thump. We all froze and didn't make a sound for 20 minutes for fear of the wooden spoon. At last, I said to Mum, "Can I talk to you now"? She burst out laughing.

Meal times at home were a big production because of the large numbers. 5 children, Mum, and Granny. Uncle Jack had just left as he had got married to a nice lady called Auntie Joyce. Auntie Celia worked in Bristol, leaving early, and returning late, and eating elsewhere.

It seemed to always fall to me to lay the table, clear the table, wash the dishes, etc., and I got a bit fed up with it, so decided to get some help, and made up a chart that rotated the jobs between John, Susan, and me. We stuck to this arrangement for years.

Some early memories of Granny (my mother's mother), include her reading to me, and then me reading to her. I'm told that when I was very young, I used to say "reader, reader, reader", and call it reading. Then one day, I remember her saying to me "Listen to mouthy", meaning the rag and bone man who was out in the street yelling his "rag and bones", and I remember saying "Show me mouthy Granny". They all thought this was very funny.

She had some funny expressions which she used. One of her favorite animals was a Mangeroo Pheasant. One day I was looking in a mirror and she scared me to death by saying "If you look in the mirror too much you'll see Old Nick". Granny always wore black dresses to the floor, like all older ladies of that era, and her hair was braided (plaited), and twisted into a coil at the back. On special occasions, she wore her best dress which was silver/gray and then her hair was in an elegant loose up-do which made her look quite different. My clearest memory of her is sitting by the fire darning an endless pile of our socks. This was before the introduction of nylon socks. If you wore the normal woolen socks for two days, you would have holes to darn. In the war years, they were more darn than the original socks.

Granny was not well. Mum didn't have much time for us and life seemed quite miserable. We were not wealthy and indeed were led to believe that we were very poor. Poorer than we really were. Mum seemed to me to be a very hard and rigid person always ready to wield the wooden spoon. Every meal was placed with the wooden spoon on the table ready to lash out at anyone who stepped out of line. It must have been very hard for Mum with no husband to help out, but the children don't understand. Mum had a great voice and used to sing all manner of opera and popular songs of the day at full throttle. I loved to hear her sing and tried to copy her, but alas my feeble attempts in no way matched the splendor of her voice. Some of the songs from The Desert Song and Rose Marie were the most often sung, but the most frequent rendering was, "Vilia, the Witch of the Wood", which I loved with a passion.

There was a BBC radio program each morning called "Housewives Choice". Listeners could write in to request any piece of music or song to be played and their name would be read just before it was played. I wrote in once and asked for "Rustle of Spring" to be played for my mother Elaine Newton etc. It must have been during the school holidays because I couldn't believe my ears when they played my request. Mum was thrilled to bits.

I used to spend most of my money on gifts for Mum. I would go into Woolworth's and buy brooches quite often. The stuff that appeals to a child, and what a child can afford is not really up to much quality. Looking back I don't know why Mum didn't take me aside and thank me but tell me not to spend any more of my money on that kind of stuff. I didn't have much money and it was something that I wanted to do. When I got a bit older I would buy earthenware tea sets. We seemed to break a lot of cups and crockery. This meant that we often had all manner of non-matching dishes on the table. I hated odds and ends and liked everything to match. Hence, my buying of the tea sets.

When I had my own 2 eldest children, Christopher and David, they gave me a present one day. It was quite lovely a painted heart locket which I have to this day. However, I did not want them to repeat this kind of thing and spend their precious money on me, so I told them that I loved the locket and especially the thoughts of love that brought it to me, but I had other lovely things to wear and to save their money.

My brother John was a choir boy in our parish church, Walcott church. He was paid for singing in the choir and received his money either once a month or quarterly, I really can't remember. However, I was very jealous that he had the opportunity to earn some money. Money was scarce and there were no jobs for children in those days. One choir rehearsal night (rehearsals were held at the home of the organist who was the choirmaster) I went to his home. His name was Mr. Hart and he lived in Belgrave Crescent, which was right across the street from Seymour Road and the back gardens faced the front of our houses. I was quite used to going into his house because his wife was my piano teacher. Mr. Hart was very surprised to see me. He knew who I was and I told him I wanted to join the choir. He was dumbfounded. He told me girls didn't sing in the choir. I asked why not. He said because they didn't. I told him I thought it most unfair that my brother, simply because he is a boy, could earn some money by being in the choir and I would like to do the same. By now he was a little amused and told me he had never had such a thing happen to him before, but I COULD NOT SING IN THE CHOIR. And that was that.

I did not play the piano very well. Every time Mrs. Hart presented a new piece for me to play I asked her to play it through for me first. Consequently, I somehow managed to struggle through each new piece well enough for her to start another piece. Eventually, she refused to play the new piece through first so I decided I had had enough of piano lessons.

In my experience, most school teachers were not very nice to children in those days, and school was far from pleasant. At Harley Street school, the first year was taught by Miss Hills. A large lady with hair drawn severely back and she had a mustache. She often made me stand behind the piano as a punishment, once for getting an ink blot on my paper. Actually, I didn't mind this in the winter because there was a large black pot-bellied stove close by and it was warm and cozy. The second year was taught by Miss Hill (no “s” on the end, and no relation to the other teacher). She was younger and a bit nicer to me. She had been a school friend of Auntie Celia. We did more mental arithmetic in her class than any of my other classes ever. Mental arithmetic is when you do it in your head. It could be addition, multiplication, division, and so on.

Miss Hill was big on this and I became fairly good at it. (Later on at senior school I was always good at arithmetic, but algebra and geometry were not good subjects for me, to put it mildly). The third year was taught by Miss Goldstein, who was also the headmistress. Close to retirement (she actually retired at the end of the year she taught me) she was a real misery. One day she asked what I was looking at in class. It was a ring on my finger, made for me by a friend of the family, out of airplane glass. This was glass from planes that had been shot down, and to me, it was a real treasure and I was so proud of it. We were not allowed to wear any jewelry of any kind to school, and so Miss Goldstein confiscated my ring. I never got it back. I asked at the end of the day if I could have it back and was refused. At the end of the school term, I asked again and the ring could not be found. Amazing! At the time I was in the third year, and Miss Tanner taught the fourth year. When Miss Goldstein retired Miss Tanner became headmistress and from then on taught third year. I never had her as a teacher, but she was very nice and I liked her. We had a new teacher at the school for my fourth year, Miss Ace. She was lovely and it was a happy year for me. During this year, I took the 11plus exam (or scholarship exam) mentioned earlier in this book.

During the war years, all manner of strange things became the norm. We, children, did not realize that things had not always been so. There were static water tanks (reserve storage for water to put out fires caused by incendiary bombs). These were an open invitation for child drownings and occasionally there were such accidents. They were open and not guarded in any way. At the top of the next street, Arundel Road, there were foundations and partly built walls of houses, the completion of which was abandoned when the war started. This is what we heard. We children used to climb and walk all around these skeleton walls, which were two-storeys high in some places. We were fearless and I never heard of anyone falling off or getting hurt. These walls had all kinds of weeds and things growing all around them. Years later houses were erected in those spots. Whether the original foundations were used I have no idea.

In this same time period, at the right season, we would go into an orchard higher up the hill where we lived, and steal apples or rhubarb, gooseberries, or cherries. This orchard was a scary place. It was really a large garden surrounded by a high wall, and we always felt we were being watched so we didn't stay long. We didn’t take very much at a time and never got caught. It was just a daring thing to do. We did NOT tell our mothers either, they would have killed us.

A couple of times we went into Camden Woods, higher up the hill again. Someone had a box of matches. We cut creeper vines in four to six-inch lengths and lit one end. Now we were smoking! This was a really grown-up thing to do. Just about every adult smoked. The big snag with the creeper was that it was full of bugs and they couldn't exit from the lit end, so they just had to come into your mouth. You had to keep spitting them out. I only did that twice, that was enough for me.

For two or three years I was a Brownie, the name given to young girl scouts. In my last year as a Brownie, I went to camp for a week, in a tent at Timsbury. It was a first for me and I thought it was fun.

Later, I was in the Junior Red Cross. We studied first aid and home nursing and maternity care among other things. One Christmas, during a flu epidemic, when many nurses became sick, the Red Cross was asked for help. We went on duty on Christmas Day to St. Martin's Hospital to do whatever we were asked to do. Because I was quite young I wasn't allowed to do a great deal and spent most of the day rolling bandages and that sort of thing.

Eventually, I became a Girl Guide, the English name for a girl scout. I got a couple of badges, health was one of them and I had to drink 8 glasses of water each day and Mum had to sign a sheet to say that I had done this. This is an enormous amount of water to consume daily. It was not easy for me to do. I went to camp with the Guides, to Lyme Regis, which is on the coast in Devon. I don't ever remember going on holiday with my family. When I was young it didn't happen, but as soon as I went to work they went on a family holiday, without me. I was working and I was sent to stay with Auntie Margie for two weeks. She lived close to the railway, and the first night when the train thundered by, the whole house shook and I thought I would never get to sleep with that racket. After a couple of days, I scarcely paid any attention. It is amazing how quickly you adapt to that sort of thing.

One other group I belonged to was the church youth. We did not call it that. We called it "Crypt". We met in the crypt under the church. The cellar rooms were quite creepy and not fun in which to be alone. Sometimes before the meeting began, if we got there early, we would play games in the cemetery that adjoined the church. We would jump from gravestone to gravestone until we were shouted at and told to stop.

Our daily lives were not easy. As you probably know, it rains a lot in England and the winters were very cold indeed. We did not have a bathroom in Seymour Road, only the toilet, the entrance to which was outside. On Saturday nights the big galvanized bath was brought in and placed in front of the fire. As I said before, it was filled with hot water from the boiler (like you see in cowboy movies) and we all took a turn in the water. This was a weekly occurrence whether you needed it or not! When my parents bought 17 Seymour Road we had our first inside bathroom/toilet put in. This was heaven indeed.

When we used to come home wet in the winter, the only way to get the coats and things dry was to hang them around the fire on a clothes horse. This meant the only means of keeping the house warm was obscured from both view and comfort. Clothing was mostly wool or cotton. None of the present-day non-iron materials were available. Everything had to be ironed. Most weeks there were enormous amounts of mending to be done. Socks were made from wool and always had to be darned. It was a never-ending mending pile. Granny was always busy with it. Later, with more children in the family, and an increase in quantities of mending, Auntie Margie was enlisted to assist. She came every Tuesday for that.

Another misery for me was dogs. No one controlled their animals and they roamed unleashed. Sometimes when I went home from school I could not pass because the street was blocked by a neighbor's nasty dog. There were three ways we could go home. From Bennett's

Lane, often blocked by Mr. Savage's dog. From Bunkers Hill, often blocked by Rex, an Airedale belonging to Mrs. Stonestreet. From Thomas Street, or via "the slip" mostly blocked by Baddams dog. I have often walked all three ways to the house before finding a dog less way home. It would have done no good to complain, this was the way it was and you kept peace with your neighbors and said nothing.

I used to do the majority of the shopping for Mum. This meant walking to the shops, being served, one person at a time by the shopkeeper and then carrying all you had purchased, home in the shopping bag or basket that you took with you. It is a wonder that my arms do not touch the ground with all the heavyweights that I have carried. Everything was rationed and I knew the value of all the points and was a very good shopper indeed. In all of the shops you were registered and known by name. Everyone knew everyone else in my area. This is good and bad. You certainly could not do or say anything amiss. It would be reported back to your mother almost immediately.

The war was coming to a close. I was in my 11th year. My cousin Tony had left school and would start work. During the school holiday, Eileen's Flower shop had a new delivery driver who did not know his way around Bath. Eileen's owners were friends of my Auntie May and Uncle Stan and I was asked if I would like to earn a couple of shillings sitting in the delivery van with the driver to guide him on his rounds. I did this for 3 days and quite enjoyed myself, and being paid. I thought I was in seventh heaven.

The war was over. First VE day (Victory in Europe), then VJ day (Victory over Japan)). The whole country held local celebrations. Seymour Road and Belgrave Crescent held a combined celebration on our road. We had food and games and competitions and races. I came in second in two races. One of the races was won by Valerie Smith and the other by a girl named Thelma (visiting from Plymouth, a town on the south coast). Both girls were older and bigger than me. I got second place in the fancy dress competition as Little Red Riding Hood. Sister Susan went as a nurse. There were a lot of nurses, so it wasn't considered original. I have no idea what the prizes were. We all had a great time and the children all sensed the relief in the adults.

Now begins a new stage of life, a new Senior school. I had passed the scholarship exam (11plus) and was to attend The City of Bath Girl's School.

Chapter 4 - Brian's Earliest Recollections, by Brian

Amongst my first recollections is being pestered daily by my 4 older sisters for me to participate as a student in their play "Schools", and take part in backyard dramatic productions, being "the baby" when required to be. After 4 daughters, my mother tended to be over-protective of me, which restricted my freedom, but I was the cat's meow with my mother's two sisters.

My mother's younger sister was Auntie Dolly (Dorothy), who married Uncle Leslie Saxton when I was 4. I was Pageboy at the wedding and wore a smart light green homemade (by my mother) satin suit with short trousers. I can see it now. The other aunt, Auntie May married Uncle Fred Smith when I was 5, but I don't remember much about the wedding, probably because the light green satin suit was not a novelty this time.

Uncle Fred was a policeman and seemed enormous to me. He was 6' 2" tall and reputed to be at least 15 stones, (210lbs). Anybody who was 15 stones was looked upon as a giant in those days. Something I do remember is that Uncle Fred once spent 15 minutes teaching me how to comb my hair with a nice parting etc. Other relatives that were close were my mother's brother, Uncle Ron (Ronald) who lived in a close-by town, Dartford, an industrial town like Woolwich, again on the south side of the River Thames. He had recently divorced and had a girlfriend named Margery, who had a young daughter named Pamela. Also, close by lived my mother's father, Harry Baldwin Smith, a tough hard-seeming wild man, who was well over 6 feet tall and heavily built, at least 15 stones or more. He had a broken nose. Apparently, he had been a boxer of local fame and was not averse to taking on the world, including three policemen outside the local pub (public house) according to my father. My father swears he actually witnessed it. Apparently, my grandfather won.

One other relative was an occasional visitor to the house. It was my father's older brother, Bert (Bertram) Walters. He was married to Auntie Winnie (Winifred). He was a part-time professional ventriloquist, and conjurer (magician). He often put on shows for us in the evenings. Auntie Winnie was a real comedienne also. She kept me in fits of laughter as a child. One day I was out shopping with her and we saw a lady with a tall feather sticking up from her fancy hat. She said, "See that feather, that is an aerial (antenna) through which she talks to her husband". This was typical of the way she talked all the time. She was always fun to be with, at least for somebody of my age. She was present once with me when a real tragedy occurred. I was given a lovely Bakelite mug. (Bakelite was one of the first types of plastic and was accepted as almost unbreakable). This mug was pink and it was decorated with Disney animals. I loved it and used only this mug for drinking. One day I dropped it and Auntie Winnie said, "Be careful or you'll break it". I said, "No I won't, look" and slammed it against the floor where it shattered into dozens of pieces.

Every Sunday we went to church 3 times. We belonged to the Plymouth Brethren, a very strict church where make-up, radios, smoking, drinking, going to movies, and anything which was fun and enjoyable was against the rules. My father smoked like a chimney and would light up as soon as he got around the corner from the church. It was a long walk to get there. We had to go through the village, cross the main Woolwich to Erith road, walk down the slope through the chestnut woods, and there it gets a bit fuzzy. I know that the last bit included walking down these strange steps which had a 4" drop every 3 or 4 feet, with small houses on one side, then there was a cinder path between some garden allotments to the church on the corner across the street. From the cinder path you could see in the distance, the industrial area along the banks of the Thames River. Sometimes you could see the superstructure of a big ship on the river.

We were friends with several church families. The only ones I remember are the Armrots and the Hartleys. Jack Armrot had this funny name that amused me no end, and I think this is why I remember them. The Hartleys were quite well off and lived in a nice house. I remember they had two sons who were very nice, but a bit like nerds. One of them was named Horace, and he used to sniff around my sisters quite a bit if my memory serves me right. Horace showed up at our house in Bath later on during the war that was brewing.

I can see Horace now, smiling with his big teeth. I remember being fascinated by the large bumps he had at the side of his face at the bend of his jawbone.

My father was born in 1900 and was around 5'11" tall, and of average weight. He was said to be a good-looking man. Deep down, I believe, he suffered from a lack of confidence. I always felt it was through having a very limited education as was common in the early 1900s. However, he was extremely intelligent and could hold his own with most people. He learned fast. His handwriting was beautiful and he could compose the best letters worthy of a highly educated person. He was generous and quite easy to get along with unless you crossed him. He was a comedian and could entertain you with stories for hours. Unfortunately, he married the wrong woman, which made home life a bit of a pain. Neither of them was to blame really, they were just unsuited. They both spent most of their lives angry and unhappy. Although he was not lazy in the true sense of the word, he left things to my mother, which he should not have done and he often was dissatisfied with the result and complained loudly. In the right circumstances, he would work tirelessly, and in some things, when he put his mind to it, he did excellent work. He would spend many hours repairing our shoes and making an excellent job of it. "Snobbing" was the name for shoe repairing in those days.

I remember his snobbing knife. It had been sharpened so much that the blade was tapered toward the point down to 1/8" wide for the last 1½".

Every spring he would dig the garden, rake it to a fine "tilth" (his word) until it was like a billiard table. Then he would plant vegetables and tend them like a loving mother. He was known for his large parsnips. He had this metal rod that he would pound into the ground about 3 feet, then wiggle it around in a circle and make a row of cone-shaped holes about 4" diameter at the top. Then he would sift a pile of fine earth, and fill the holes. In the center of the fine dirt, he would place 5 parsnip seeds.

When they germinated, he would select the best little seedling and discard the rest, and the chosen one grew and grew. He always left the parsnips in the ground until we had at least one frost, and this is where they stayed for the whole winter until they were used up. The frost was supposed to make them sweet. Now came the hard part. You had to dig around the top to a depth of about 6" to get a handhold, then pull with all your might. Eventually with a crack, and you may well go flying backward, the parsnip would break 2 feet into the ground, and you'd have 2 to 3lbs of my favorite root vegetable. The bottom end was about 1 1/2" diameter where it broke off. The bit left in the ground was larger than most gardener's parsnips.

I think I was the apple of his eye as the only boy, but he didn't show it and seemed to not have much time for me when I was young but his pride in me showed up many times later on. When he was old he loved to visit and would have lived with us if he could. He was regarded as a giant in knowledge and understanding of the Bible as I found out at his funeral.

He died on 25th September 1982 at the age of 82, of liver cancer. At his funeral, to my surprise, 2 church ministers from different churches spoke saying that he had a better knowledge and understanding of the Bible than any other person they'd ever met including the professionals. I feel he would have risen to greater heights if he had married a woman of a different type and had a better education.

My mother had a tough life from the time that her mother died when she was 7. She was the eldest, and “mother” to the other 3 children. She always talked about her father as a good man, but her stories convey the fact that he was a selfish, neglectful man, who spent money on alcohol and let the children virtually starve at times.

She was impetuous and brave. Tough and tempestuous. Just like her father, she would take on anybody, but also lacking in confidence to the point that she would not complain when it was warranted. She would delay complaining, but eventually violently explode and alienate people and receive little sympathy as a result. I remember her taking some over-ripe bananas back to Rogers greengrocery, (produce) in Belvedere village, and throwing them at the owner when a quiet talk would have gained her some replacements. (I was probably about 3 when this happened as bananas weren't available after 1939 when I was 4).

Our mother worked very hard, making all my sister's clothes. Every night she would tie up their hair in what was called rags, short strips of cloth, and in the morning undo the rags and brush the hair into ringlets. She cooked good meals all the time with meat when you could get it, and vegetables. She would often go without when there were shortages. She made sure we all had Parrishes Chemical Food (a tonic heavy in minerals), cod liver oil, and sometimes rose hips syrup. We always had two bottles of milk at school each day, had all the love we could handle, and really lacked for nothing in spite of lack of money and severe shortages of everything.

During the years before the war started we would always go on holiday (vacation) for a week. Sometimes we would have a caravan, (trailer in the US), and once I remember we rented a house sharing it with the Jack Armrot's family, friends from church. I remember the house holiday. The house was in a large open area, all grass and a few bushes dotted about, on the top of a cliff, overlooking the English Channel. Jack Armrot had an air rifle, and he and my father used to shoot at rabbits in the bushes. .I don't remember the caravan holidays except I've seen photographs with me in the front being held by my sisters. (The name "Armrot" always fascinated me and I have often wondered how the name originated. Did somebody, way back in time, actually have an arm with rot)?

Every year all children in England had a medical examination at school. The school doctor was a venerated person, and would see us one at a time usually in the area we called the "cloakroom". This was an open space near the entrance to the school, where we hung our coats. Our mothers were welcomed at the examination, but only a few would show up. My mother always did, and every year she would argue with the doctor to the effect that I was delicate and should have Minadex. This was a green, gray liquid, a tonic provided for delicate children. It was distributed by the teachers. Every year, the doctor would say that there was nothing wrong with me, and that I didn't need it, but my mother insisted that I was delicate. Later on, she called me frail. Actually I never quite made it down to puny in her eyes.

The young readers probably cannot imagine life without television and computer screens. When I was young, the only thing even like it was "the magic lantern", usually a treat at church or school. This would be a bit like the home projector of color slides, except this was in a sepia shade of black and white. Nobody owned their own projector then. The only thing we had at home was the radio. It was a large box and ran off what we called an accumulator, really a 6 volts, rechargeable battery in an upright rectangular glass container, full of acid. About once a month or every 3 weeks we had to walk to the local radio store for a recharge. Then go back the next day to pick it up. It used to cost four pence. The job of transporting it fell to one of my sisters, and I often went with them, up the alley creeping past Gilbert's dog, then down Barnfield road to the village. Being glass and full of acid gave the job a certain amount of reverence and we were always glad when it was over. In the early part of the war, radios arrived which could plug into the wall socket.

One day, when I was probably about 3 1/2, the field in front of our house was being dug up and men started to build houses. I was very interested in all of this and supervised them for hours from a window at the front of our house. The walls were going up. The bricklayers built scaffolding out of wooden poles tied together with wire rope. However, one day when the brick walls reached halfway up the second storey, we had a freak storm which grown-ups called a whirlwind, and I remember my mother carrying me to the front door after it had passed and the scaffolding was all down, and so were some of the walls. (I couldn't have been any older than 3 or 3 1/2 because all building stopped when the war started in 1939, and my mother was still able to easily carry me around, also I wasn't going to school).

When I was a child I spoke with a London, near Cockney accent like everybody else. A true Cockney is said to be born within the sound of Bow bells. The Bow bells are in a large church in the London borough of Bow. Real old-time cockneys spoke in a sort of slang where they have a phrase that rhymes with what they are trying to say. Then they cut that rhyming phrase to the first word like: “Apples and pears”, which means stairs, but they only say the word “apples”. “Trouble and strife” is cut to “trouble” and means wife, and so forth. When spoken quickly to the uninitiated it can make your head spin. As a very young kid, I had no difficulty with any words, except I would mix up "shoulder" and "soldier". I couldn't get those right for a couple of years.

A few other slang words I remember are: “eighteen pence” cut to “eighteen” which means “sense”. “North and South” cut to “North” means “mouth”. If you wanted to say something like “Have some sense, shut your mouth and go upstairs and talk to your wife”, it would come out like: “Use some eighteen, shut your north, go up the apples and talk to your trouble”. Truly, unintelligible to the uninitiated.

One of the happiest times was a period when I would go to the end of the road and wait for the United Dairy's milk delivery cart. It was pulled by a gray horse named Razor. I used to go with the milkman all around, helping him make deliveries and sometimes he even let me hold the reins. He would pay me quite handsomely as I saved him a good deal of legwork. The horse was a light gray, but when you looked closely, most of the hairs were dark gray, but about every third hair was silver. One day when I was placing a pint of milk on a doorstep, a big dog came up behind me and went crazy barking and growling. This scared me to death. For the rest of the milk delivery, I sat high up on the cart, drinking milk. I think my enthusiasm waned after that.

Another thing that I enjoyed was going to see my Auntie Dolly. After she married, when I was 4, she lived diagonally across the large square of houses where we lived. There was a field in the middle until the building started. She made a great fuss about me as the only boy in the family. She never did have children, and she continued to "mother" me for many years. Her husband, Uncle Les, was a cabinet-maker and loved carpentry. He had spent years at sea as a ship's carpenter and made perfect and detailed 16" to18" miniatures of freighters and tankers. Every feature was painted in its proper color. He made operational model sailing boats for me, which I enjoyed for years. My Grandfather lived with them as he had never re-married and was in his 70s.

I thoroughly enjoyed Auntie Dolly's Christmas Boxing Day parties. All the relatives including the children had a great time. We would play all the old English games that families passed down to the children. My father, Uncle Fred, and Uncle Ron were all very funny and kept us laughing. There wasn't much drinking, just good fun. I remember one game that I was not allowed to play, called "murder". All lights were turned out and then it became like hide and go seek, but in total darkness. The person selected to be the murderer would creep around the house and "murder" somebody who then became the next murderer. From all around the house would come screams and whispering as people bumped into each other in the dark, and of course, this tipped off the real murderer. There was one game I remember, when Uncle Ron had not arrived as he had to work late. I was sitting on my Auntie Dolly's best couch while the game was on. I sat very still as I was a bit scared sitting alone in the dark. Suddenly the game was over, and the lights were turned on. To my complete surprise, Uncle Ron was sitting beside me. He had arrived and realized what was going on and was able to creep in and take a seat. I think he was as surprised to see me as I was to see him. He could just as easily sat on me on the other end of the couch.

I also remember being dragged along with my 11-year-old sister Brenda's adventures with her 28-year-old friend Topsy Tibbel. Topsy had Downs Syndrome and had the intellect of an eight-year-old, but she was game and tough, as was Brenda. (By the way, Brenda was the family's chief scrumper, apple stealer). Their favorite place was the "static water tank" that had been built just down the hill from Topsy's house. These tanks, I assume, were built as a supply of emergency water as part of the preparation for war. They were circular, about 40 feet in diameter with sides about 5 feet high. Just ideal for having kids fall in. The water was always green and there was all sorts of junk in them.

I remember going often with sister Sylvia to her friend Violet Standon's house just up the road. Sylvia was an excellent pianist as was my eldest sister Christine. I could watch their fingers for hours when they were playing. Every Sunday evening we would all stand around the piano, and either Sylvia or Christine would play while we all sang. My best friend lived next door but one. Her name was Barbara Highland, and we played together most days. She was a few months older than me... The sister just above me in age was Daphne, and we also spent lots of time together. One time, we went down to what was called the Village, and she apparently knew that the corner general store, Jones's, had a back room, and when the store was empty the assistant went into the back through a door with lace curtains. If you crept in bending below counter height you could not be seen through the door, and you could reach up and help yourself. We did just that and got some chewing gum. Now, at our ages of about 5 and 7, chewing gum was a no no. If you accidentally swallowed it, as everybody knew, it would wind around your heart and kill you, but we didn't care, and off we went with our ill-gotten gains. Our triumph was short-lived. We got home to be told to sit up the table and eat lunch. I had my very first mouthful of chewing gum and was not experienced in hiding it. I was sure my mother would know all about our caper if she saw it, so I palmed it and it stuck to the handle of my knife in a big clump making eating very difficult for a 5-year-old.

My favorite store in the village was Dorman's. They had a very prominent position in the middle of a fork in the road. They had a whole window of toys and I would spend time gazing at them at every opportunity. Auntie May and Uncle Fred lived almost opposite on the left fork. Just around the corner from Dorman's on the right side of the fork, Uncle Fred's parents lived, next the wood yard. Beyond that was the Co-op food store where everything you spent was noted against your account number, and twice a year you would get a dividend. Many a kid owed his winter coat or shoes to the Co-op dividend.

Every Wednesday or Thursday, I can't remember which. My mother would walk with me through the village and catch the bus to Woolwich. The weekly street market was held on that day and we always bought fresh fish. The market was held in a wide cobbled area immediately on the bank of the River Thames. At this point, the river was about 400 yards wide as it was nearing the North Sea. There were probably 12 hand-carts with 5 selling fish and the others selling a variety of other items. Sometimes there was a fishing boat tied up with fish being unloaded and occasionally a basket of fish would be tipped onto a hand-cart. There were all sorts of fish and other types of sea creatures like cockles, whelks, winkles, crabs, eels, etc. My mother would buy herrings and kippers mostly, and then we would do a bit more shopping and then go home. The best fish came from the North Sea, being a very cold sea. On one of these trips, my mother bought a bottle of our tonic, Parrishes Chemical Food, and gave it to me to hold. Before we left the shop I dropped it and the bottle smashed on the marble tiled floor. I was not popular. I remember that the floor was made up of black and white 6" tiles. The shop assistant spread sawdust on the mess before sweeping it up.

I always enjoyed the bus ride home the most, and would always try to sit in the front downstairs seat right behind the driver's window. I watched with great interest as he changed gears all the way home. All too soon the ride was over. These double-decker red London Transport buses had Daimler engines and they had a very singular engine sound. It was a soft soothing sound to me and I loved the long climb out of Woolwich as they seemed at their best and smoothest at the speed they climbed that hill.

One of my favorite things to do was to visit Mrs. Akroyd who lived alone right next door. I would go around the front of her house, and up the side alley trying to not disturb the next neighbor's big black dog which always rushed to the fence to bark and growl at passers-by. I'm not completely sure of their name but I have the feeling it may have been "Gilbert". Anyway, I would open Mrs. Akroyd's side gate and then go into the back door after knocking. All of us children were welcome in Mrs. Akroyd's house. She would be sitting by the fire all day, every day, in warm or cold weather. She was the oldest person in the world to me. I would sit down quietly and wait as she read the newspaper, and before long would come the bit I enjoyed so much. She would cough with the wheeziest, most gurgly cough you ever heard, and tear off a square of the ever-present pile of newspapers, spit into it, wrap it, and throw it on the fire. It would almost immediately start to bubble, and I couldn't take my eyes off it, until, in a moment or two it would dry up. However, by this time, she would be about ready to cough again and I would wait patiently. I've often wondered what it was that fascinated me about this spectacle.

One day, on my way to Mrs. Akroyd's, a butcher boy on a bike with a small front wheel with a basket above it, came tearing out of the alley and got my feet caught up in his front wheel. Both he and packages of meat went everywhere. It was great, I got lots of sympathy and attention over that.

From about June, all the local kids went off "scrumping". This was the name given to raiding an orchard. We lived in an apple-growing area. It didn't seem to matter that at the beginning of each season when the apples were small and green, all the kids had stomach ache and diarrhea. This went on to a decreasing degree until the apples ripened. I remember the scary tales of kids being chased by farmers and policemen. Of course, this was in the days when youthful offenders got their ears boxed instead of being hauled off to court.

I spent lots of time playing with our gramophone. There were two records that I played over and over. They were "Over my shoulder goes one care" etc., and the other was a rendering by what sounded like a bunch of drunken hill-billies singing "It ain't gonna rain no more no more" etc. Records in those days were 78 revs. per minute, about 10" diameter and they would break if you dropped them which is why I only had two records. My favorite book was "Water-melon Pete", a story about this little black boy who had a liking for watermelon, and he found a loose board in the farmer's fence one day. He crawled through and ate so much watermelon that he couldn't get back through the hole. I don't remember how the story ended. Another favorite book was "15 Rabbits", the life story of a family of rabbits.

My mother was born in Belvedere in 1903, in the same house in which I was born. As related earlier she was the eldest of 4 children. Their mother who apparently was a gentle woman, died giving birth to the fifth child. At the age of 7, my mother became a mother to the other three children as her father was working full time as a plasterer, followed by evenings at the pub. My mother says her father, Harry Smith, who didn't re-marry until he was about 78, was a wonderful father, but the facts tell the opposite story. She also tells of going barefoot in the summer and eating only green tomatoes for weeks on end as that was the only food available. She also tells of a time that a neighbor picked on one of them, and their father went after him. Apparently, the neighbor was digging in his allotment, (a garden space rented out front of the houses), with a garden fork, and he took off when he saw Harry coming. Harry grabbed the fork and continued the chase. When he got closer, the story goes, he threw the fork like a spear, and one of the tines of the fork went down inside the shoe/boot and through the heel, pinning the neighbor to the ground. My mother also tells of the times when all 4 children hid in the coal cellar when bill collectors came. From what I have heard, Harry was an awful father who drank all the money and seriously neglected the children.

In reading between the lines of the many stories my mother told, the fact is that when my mother's mother died, her relatives who apparently were quite financially well off, wanted to take the children. But due to the fact that they had opposed the marriage because of Harry's wild ways, he would not allow it. He said he didn't want to risk them being split up. Harry himself came from a family who had owned a considerable amount of property, and most of the family prospered. It appears that Harry or Harry's father was a black sheep.

My father's family lived in Sutton Veny, a small village in the county of Wiltshire, not more than 20 miles from where Joy's father was born and 25 miles from Bath. He was the youngest of 8 children, 6 boys, and 2 girls. As was normal in the country districts around the year 1900 when my father was born, from an early age he worked on the land, only going to school from the age of 8 until 12. At the age of 14, he was packed off to London to be an apprentice at Vickers Armstrong, a large engineering and civil engineering company. He lived near my mother and was acquainted with Harry and his exploits. His parents died before I was born. His father had been in India in the army and had been bitten by a snake, and suffered for years until he died a premature death. My father's mother also died early. My father's mother was quite old when he, the 8th child was born. The only other ones of his family I knew were his brother, my Uncle Bert, and a sister whose name I can't remember. It may have been Maggie. Most of his other brothers emigrated to Canada.

My mother went into "service" at the age of 14. For the younger readers, this means moving into a rich person's home to be trained as a live-in servant, usually one of many. The family with whom my mother was placed was named Vincent. They owned lots of orchards surrounding Belvedere. She was allowed Sunday morning off to go to church where she met my father. They were both in the church choir.

Back to 9 Upper Grove Road, where the 2nd World War was just about started. I remember the BBC broadcasts announcing the ultimatum to Hitler, to get out of Poland etc., and the subsequent somber announcement that Britain was now at war with Germany. Even though it did not mean much to me at the time, thereafter, when I heard a BBC announcer say in the very formal tones" this is BBC London", it would always send a shiver up my back. I was 4 years old, and I remember going to Beadonwell Hill School with the rest of the family to be issued with gas masks. Everybody got theirs, and then it was my turn. Young children of my age got bright red Mickey Mouse masks with huge red ears. They were grotesque and really scary. Some civil servant had made a very bad decision in the choosing of this design, so after quite a bit of crying, I got the regular type like my older sisters.

Belvedere is in a straight line between Germany and the center of London, a fact which was obvious to the government and so our area was fortunate to be host to several anti-aircraft gun emplacements. The nearest one was about 100 yards up our road, hidden between the trees in our local apple orchard.

Every householder was issued with the materials with which to make an air-raid shelter. There were two types, the Anderson shelter if you had a garden, or a Morrison (table) shelter if no garden. We were issued with an Anderson shelter as we had a back garden. Our issue of materials consisted of 4 sets of two pieces of curved corrugated galvanized metal 2 feet wide, which were all bolted together to form an arch 8 feet long by 6 feet high, and approx. 6 feet wide. These arched sets were placed in a hole dug into the ground, the deeper the better. End pieces, one with an opening, were bolted to the end arched pieces, and the earth taken from the hole was spread over the top. The deeper the hole, the more earth that was available to cover the shelter making it safer. Inside, we had wooden bunks with hessian (sack cloth or burlap) stretched between the supports. We had dirt steps down to the entrance, and had to pass through a short tunnel to enter the shelter. The Anderson shelter did an excellent job in protection but it had one weakness. It rains a lot in England, and water would seep into the hole. Normally there was 3" to 6" of water in the floor of the shelter, in spite of almost daily baling. This necessitated duck-boards to keep feet dry. My father's perfectly manicured vegetable garden was completely ruined by all the work going on.

After the air-raid shelter, it was recommended that all windows have paper sticky tape crisscrossed so as to create less flying glass, and then we had to make window blinds out of black cloth and pieces of wood, all issued by the government. This was to prevent light escaping which might aid enemy planes in knowing where they were. There was a volunteer force of men too old to go to war, who were called ARP wardens. It was one of their jobs to patrol the streets and make sure there was no light showing. "Put that light out" was a very common shout from the street to some careless householder. The ARP wardens were also involved in digging through rubble to find people buried in their destroyed homes. Another change that came with the war was the appointment of a "Special Constabulary". This was a force of policemen who were over retirement age and were drafted to replace policemen who had gone to war. This war, being the Second World War with Germany, drew on the experiences of the First World War, and organizations such as the "Specials" as they were called, quickly fell into place. There was even a Cockney pub song which states "You can't trust the Specials like the old-time copper when you can't find your way home". This refers to a situation when somebody is drunk, and the Special isn't sure of directions to get you home. This song dates from the First World War.

I clearly remember the first siren indicating the approach of German bombers. The "all clear" was a steady note that we'd often heard during testing. The real warning was a varying up-and-down wail. I was almost five. At night, my sisters and I were constantly scared of Germans suddenly appearing at our bedroom doors, and I remember going to bed at night and laying rigid, too scared to move at the thought. The hallway light was left on for scared kids. Suddenly we heard the siren start with a low groan, the spinning inner wheel working its way up to full-wailing speed. And this time for real, with 5 children erupting on the upstairs landing and falling down the stairs before it had barely started. Our mother got blankets and we hurried barefoot down the wet cold garden to the air-raid shelter. We had 3 bunks on each side with mine (the shortest) across the far end. Candles were the only source of light. There was no way of heating. We could hear the anti-aircraft guns in the distance, and gradually coming closer. Suddenly it seemed like the very earth had erupted. The ground shook with explosions from the guns just 100 yards away. We could hear the crump of bombs detonating and the sharper thump of the guns. Eventually, the "all clear" sounded and we went back to bed.

For the next few months, this was the pattern. In addition to guns, there were searchlights at night and what were called barrage balloons. The barrage balloons were huge and looked like fat silver bombs with 4 ears or fins. Sometimes I thought they looked like inflated silver gray Elephants. They were filled with hydrogen. They must have been 100 feet long, and were tethered around strategic targets at varying heights with long cables hanging from them to catch unwary enemy planes.

It was about this time that I started school. I was now 5 years old and clearly remember carrying my gas mask in its box with the string over my shoulder like all the other kids. My mother took me to school on the first day and gave me a penny. I remember sitting at a double desk with another boy beside me, and all the mothers are behind a glass partition at the back of the classroom. I showed my neighbor my new penny.

I believe it was late 1941, when Hitler got really serious about bombing London, and the Battle of Britain began. He was going to break the British spirit. He forgot that adversity makes people stick together and get strong. Everybody who had them took up permanent residence in air-raid shelters to survive the around-the-clock bombings. For those less fortunate such as people living in the middle of London without room for shelter, the underground railway system, like a honeycomb beneath the streets, was a godsend. It was turned into a mass shelter with hundreds of bunk beds filling the platforms at each station. People who could stayed 24 hours per day and gradually created makeshift homes. Even babies were born there. For the rest of us, when a lull occurred we were able to go to school occasionally, and we'd pass piles of rubble where previously there were houses. I was lucky in that I had older sisters to take me to and from school.

When we were at home we would be mostly in the shelter and would go to bed in the air-raid shelter. Altogether we lived in the air-raid shelter for many months. Sister Sylvia was a bit scared, but the rest of us were either too stupid or too young to be scared. We used to play games such as Noughts and Crosses (Tic Tac Toe), or "I Spy". Another of our favorite pastimes was to hold our folded elbows up to our mouths and blow hard in the crease, make disgusting noises, and announce "That was Hitler" or" Mussolini" or any other German name that was in the news. The problem with playing I Spy in the shelter was the limited items, which made guessing correctly very easy. My sister Daphne and I used to draw pictures by candlelight. We would get a sheet of paper each and have drawing competitions. We divided the paper into 9 or 12 squares and then one of us would suggest "Let's draw a house", or a dog or a tree, etc. We would fill all the squares with drawings, then swap sheets and assign marks (grades). I would watch what marks she gave each of my drawings and then I would give her a lower mark. If she reads this she will find out for the first time how I got to be the best artist. Actually, Daphne was pretty good and both of us oil paint pictures to this day.

There was a problem with the Anderson shelter concept which was annoying. With a number of people inside, and the cold of England, our breath would condense on the metal, and it would collect on the ceiling and run down the slope until it met an imperfection at which time it would drop onto the top bunk or occupant. In time all the bunk fabric became damp and we all know what damp sackcloth smells like. Coupled with this, the candles used for illumination left smoky trails on the ceiling which colored the droplets black, and the smell of candle smoke completed the picture. To this day, the smell of candles or damp sack cloth brings a very graphic picture to my mind.

About this time there was a scheme to evacuate children out of the London area, and some of my sisters were involved for a time. I don't remember the details but I faintly remember that they were sent to a couple of farms in the country to the northeast of London. I remember that my mother would not let me go.

We did pay them a visit, and they were at neighboring farms. One thing I remember clearly was the fact that I was taken to a barn and shown this massive bull, which seemed to me to be the most enormous animal I'd ever seen. One farmer's name was Houston. However, my sisters were soon back with us at home, and life settled into a routine which included sleeping in the air-raid shelter at night and dodging back and forth during the day when sirens sounded.

One of our exciting past-times was collecting shards of shrapnel immediately after the raids. Sometimes it was still hot. If you were really lucky you found a piece of an airplane, which brings to mind the thrill when my father would let me peep out of the shelter in daytime raids. You could watch "dog fights" between British Spitfires and Hurricanes and German planes. I remember them glinting in the sun and the zooming noise they made as they twisted and turned and machine-gunned each other. One day when the "all clear" had sounded and we thought the raid was over we were on the road looking for shrapnel, and suddenly there was an ear-splitting roar as a German fighter at rooftop level, trailing smoke, roared up the road over us. We could clearly see the pilot, almost close enough to touch. Seconds later there was a terrific explosion.

One sunny day, there was an extra heavy raid, and the sky became filled with smoke. It got worse and worse with huge earth-shaking explosions. Apparently, the raid had concentrated on the Woolwich Arsenal. The smoke got so bad that it was dark at 3.00 pm and for the next 24 hours, the explosions and smoke continued. Sleep was impossible even for me a 5-year-old. The noise wasn't so bad, but the shaking of the ground was very disturbing.

It was a dangerous time. One day we were in the shelter and my father went out to chat to Mr. Hayer the neighbor on the opposite side to Mrs. Akroyd. Suddenly, Mr. Hayer was felled by a piece of shrapnel which whizzed between the two men, hitting Mr. Hayer in the shoulder.

Of course, everything was rationed, clothes, food, coal, although you couldn't spend long enough in your house to even think of lighting a coal fire. Nobody had any glass left in their windows from the concussion of the bombs. You could go to a government depot and get a free issue of tarpaper, wooden strips 1" by 1/4", and nails to cover your gaping empty window frames.

Everybody was continually cold, from lack of food and heating. A pat of butter like that used in restaurants today was one week's butter ration. On a good week, you might be lucky enough to get 1 egg per week per person, but this happened rarely. Cooking was a rare treat. It was done by running into the house in the lull of the bombing, and if the gas or electricity was on you were in business, but very often the bombing had disrupted the service. One interesting note is the fact that we didn't see bananas for about 6 years, and only very occasionally, oranges, but the local greengrocer (produce) store had displays of several bunches of wax or artificial bananas, and you would often see small kids who had never tasted one, standing and gazing at them. Fyffes Bananas was a major banana supplier before the war, and every store had artificial bunches of their product. Our sweets (candy) ration was usually 2oz per week. We bought a Mars bar, between Daphne and me. Then we cut it in half and then ¼" vertical slices. Each slice would be cut into vertical ¼" pieces, and we'd spend the next couple of hours eating one piece at a time.

At this time my father worked for the Admiralty in London. He was over the age when he could go into the services so he was required to stay in London 2 or 3 nights a week and do fire watching. He had to stay on the roof of the building in which he worked, with a partner, watch for fires, and report to the authorities. They had water, and buckets of sand to pour on incendiary bombs. This apparently worked if you got there quickly enough. Some of these fire watchers were machine-gunned by the airplanes, or trapped on the roof of burning buildings. Some went home to find their homes and families gone.

One day, great excitement. My father was being transferred out of London to a place I'd never heard of except when I needed a bath. The day came and my mother and us children took the underground (subway) to Paddington Station where we boarded a GWR (Great Western Railway) train to Bath. I can't quite remember where my father was at the time. The train was jam-packed with all sorts of service people. There were air force, army, and navy personnel from all over the world. Of course, there were British, Canadian, New Zealand, Australian, Polish, and a few Americans. There were WAFS, WACS, and English land army girls. Their kit bags were bigger than me and filled the aisles. Their rifles kept falling over with a clatter. There was nowhere to sit, and the train stopped at every station taking 5 hours to reach Bath 100 miles away. In Bath, we were met by an army of WVS ladies. They were the Women's Voluntary Service of Britain. They were older ladies who had time to do a whole variety of good deeds to help the war effort in any way. They visited the wounded, wrote letters, and took care of refugees (which we were for the moment).

We were taken up the road to the Pavilion, a local dance hall, and were issued temporary ration cards (our ration books were useless until we could register with various local stores), and we were all given a brown carrier bag with a few items of food. I only remember one of the items I received as it was a particular favorite. A can of evaporated milk!!!!

I had a brown label tied to the buttonhole of my overcoat with my name written on it in case I got lost in the crowds of refugees.

The next few weeks were a blur. I have a slight recollection of us staying for a short time with a family named Watkins who lived at Bloomfield Park, Bath. Mr. Watkins was an elder of our new church in Bath. Eventually, housing was provided and we did move into the lower two floors of a large imposing house at 62, Newbridge Road, Bath, which originally had large grounds behind it. However, as part of the war effort, a factory had been built there for light engineering work for the government. The company was called Horstman Gear Co.

In England at that time, when you moved house, you took the curtains and floor covering, which was mostly Lino (Linoleum). You couldn't buy it in wartime, and I remember my father spending hours on his knees cutting it up with his snobbing knife and fitting tiny bits of lino together and nailing them down to cover the floor. He did this every time we moved which was many, as you will find out, and the pieces got smaller and smaller. I was sent to bed at around 7.30 pm at the time of our move to Bath, and I remember the banging as the lino was nailed. I used to lay in bed and sing as loud as possible to cover the noise, which, I believe, gave me a strong singing voice later in life.

Within a month or so of arriving in Bath, my father's brother, Uncle Bert who also worked for the Admiralty, and Auntie Winnie and their two daughters were transferred to Bath and were billeted with us. They occupied the top floor of the same house.

One day we discovered that the tubes sticking out of the walls were speaking tubes used to communicate with the servants who worked in the basement at one time. Boy O boy, did that keep us running up and down for days.

Life settled down to normal, and I went to school regularly for the first time. I went to St. John's Infants School, about a mile away down the main road (The Upper Bristol Road) toward the center of Bath. I had friends that went to the same school and passed our house and they would call for me on the way there, so we 3 six-year-olds walked to and from school together. These friends were Anthony (Tony) Fletcher and David Hart. Tony Fletcher had some glandular problem and was grossly overweight. Everybody else called him Fatty Fletcher. One day when we were 8, we were lining up for the school dinner and he confided that he now weighed 8 stones, 12 lbs. (124 lbs.). David Hart was a bit shorter than me and was a very fast runner. I was also very fast and he was the first one I had ever met who could compete with me. We often used to race each other returning from school, and I can still hear Tony saying "Wait for me".

A sad note: It is mid-2003, and I am re-reading this, making final corrections and changes. In recent months, I have been in contact with a classmate from my old senior school which I left at the age of about 16. His name is Terry Holvey, and he still lives in Bath. Many months ago I asked him if he knew anything about the whereabouts of David Hart and Tony Fletcher. Just two days ago, he finally reported that he had met another classmate who had information. Tony Fletcher apparently died over 40 years ago, in his 30's. This does not surprise me as he was very much overweight as a young person. Apparently, David Hart became a church minister of some sort, and he died a few years ago in his 60s.

My sister Daphne went to the same school as me at first. She is 2 and1/2 years older and we often ran into each other. In those days six-year-olds were quite safe walking along the busy streets. One of the first things you learned at school was the way to cross the streets safely. It's a pity that this is not done today.

I remember the time we were walking home from school and a bad thunderstorm started. There was very little rain but loud and continuous thunderclaps sent all the children into a tizzy. A group of us collected together, Tony and David and my sister plus a few others. We weren't too scared at first, but our fears fed on each other until we were terrified. One of our number in the group was crying and we had to take a turn off the main road and go up Chelsea Road to her home, so we all went with her, too scared to separate. Then we ran and ran until we got home, and then I realized that I really was not nearly as scared and sat in the window and watched the flashes.

Sometimes on the way home, for a change, we would make a detour through the cemetery and look at the headstones and flowers, and go down Chelsea Road to the main road again. It was a very pleasant walk. In those days we would never even think of touching anything, let alone damage or take anything. My, how things have changed!

One large disappointment in my 6-year-old life was that my favorite teacher Miss Fallon got married. I never forgave her for that. I was so upset when she told us this news, that after a lesson in music, without looking I closed the top of the upright piano on which she had placed a small aquarium, and glass and water and fish went everywhere. She did not even grumble at me. I think she realized I was mortified at what I'd done.

By this time we were regular attendees at Manvers Hall, a meeting place for the Plymouth Brethren in Bath. Every Sunday morning our parents and us 5 children would walk into town and go to church. The buses didn't run until the afternoon. The church had what I felt was a strange service. Nobody took charge, and people would just stand up and propose a hymn, or say "Let us pray" and give a prayer, or read a bit from the Bible. Sometimes the silence got to be deafening as nobody spoke or moved for minutes at a time and I remember feeling all tense as I did in bed in Belvedere when I was scared the Germans were coming. Often, on the walk home from church, we would run into a couple of servicemen, and my parents would invite them home to share a meal even though we had little enough for ourselves. This went down very well with my teenage sisters.

Surprise surprise, one day Horace Hartley from our church in Belvedere, showed up at Manvers Hall in his new air force uniform. He had been sent to a camp near Bath. He was very excited to see my sisters. I don't think my sisters were quite as happy.

Sister Daphne and I would catch the bus and go to Sunday school at around 2.00 pm. We would sing hymns and what we called choruses like "Jesus Loves Me" and "Lay Up Treasure In Heaven". Then we'd break off and go into small groups of 5 or 6 with our own teacher. I can see my teacher now, Miss Barrett, a tall slim elderly unmarried lady who always wore fancy hats. She was always very kind and polite. At about 6.30 pm the whole family would get the bus and go back for the evening church service.

At one point, Uncle Bert who lived upstairs, put on a show every week with his ventriloquist dummy on his knee. Then he'd do card tricks and make coins come out of my ear etc. He really was good and entertained us and his own family, plus a few neighbors. By this time, my father had dug the garden and raked it to a perfectly flat surface as he always did in Belvedere. He was an excellent gardener and grew some lovely vegetables. He had just finished his raking in the front garden, and a neighbor had come to admire it, bringing his 3-year-old on a small tri-cycle, when suddenly Daphne, about 8 or 9 years old let out a scream and rushed down the path toward the road and grabbed the 3-year-old just as he was about to tumble down the 6 feet of steps to the road level on his tri-cycle. At the same time, the child's father rushed across the newly raked soil leaving deep footprints. My father didn't say anything. If we as much as put a handprint in Dad's garden, our heads would come off. Daphne was the hero of the day.

There was one funny incident as Christmas got near. I was in McIlroys department store with my mother when she discovered that they had a "Hornby" clockwork train set for sale. This was a rare event in wartime England. It was obvious that my mother was trying to hide from me the fact that she was buying it, so I went along with it and pretended to not notice. I overheard that she was only able to get it as they had no key with which to wind it up. An acquaintance of my parents from our church worked at Horstman Gear company and he was able to make a key. I remember him giving it to my father whilst trying to hide it from me but I was smart enough to know what was going on.

Over the next few weeks I looked for this train set when nobody was around, and one day when Mother was out, I found it in the bottom of her wardrobe, or closet. Auntie Winnie was looking after me from her upstairs rooms, and she happened to find me just as I had the track put together and had the train moving.

The track was an oval about 4 feet long and about 3 feet wide, and there was an engine, a tender, and three carriages. It had to be wound up about every 2 trips around the track, but it was wonderful. I had never played with anything like this before.

Auntie Winnie told me to put it away and she said she wouldn't tell my mother. I'm sure she did, and the next day the train was gone to another hiding place. I finally got it on Christmas morning in my pillow case put out on the bottom of my bed.

Unfortunately, the "Londoners", generally were not welcome in Bath. Our neighbor to the west of us was a miserable old ex-army colonel, and there was an eight-foot wall between the gardens. My sisters were fond of playing their version of tennis, and often a ball would go over the wall. At first, they would go around to the front gate, shaking with fear and ask for the ball back, and he would not give it to them. Then I believe they tried sneaking in to retrieve a ball. Anyway, it was a completely nasty situation, where we were not welcome at all by this neighbor.

Life in Bath was so different from our war experiences in London. We slept in our own beds with hardly any air-raids. If the siren occasionally sounded, there was rarely any action. We could walk a mile or so and be completely in the country, with cows and fields and a boating station where you could rent a punt or a rowing boat on the River Avon. The war seemed far away . . . . . until.

It was a Saturday evening and it had been a nice April day, and the siren was going. To be on the safe side, we all went down to the cellar at 62 Newbridge Road. Uncle Bert and Auntie Winnie and the two girls were with us. The activity in the skies increased alarmingly, with continuous explosions. Within no time, according to my father and Uncle Bert, who were sneaking out to look, the sky was aglow with the fires. Here we go again. The peace was too good to last.

The raid continued until the early hours of the morning, and as the sun came up the sky was grey with smoke. We had very few windows left, but otherwise, we had come through OK. I remember the old pump organ which was against an outside wall next to a French window. The heavy curtain over the window had been closed, and glass was laying on the floor all around the left side of the organ and across the width of the window. I remember being worried about the organ being damaged and tried it. It was OK. Apparently, a bomb had fallen on the Horstman Gear Co. behind our house, but on the other side of the factory, and, the story goes that somebody had been blown up and body parts were festooned in a tree. Such is war. We were all set to and cleaned up.

The next day was Sunday, and I don't remember whether we went to church at all, but I do remember in the early evening the siren went again and all hell let loose just like the night before. This time the local Gas Works were hit. The Gas Works had huge tanks which we called gasometers. Each tank must have been 100 feet in diameter and the top would move up and down dependent on the amount of gas in them. They could reach 100 feet high when full.

Well, the two men in the house, my Dad and his brother, Uncle Bert, decided they'd go and look at this fire, so off they went whilst it was still light. They returned rather quickly. Half a mile from home they had been machine-gunned by a German plane. Bombing Bath was like shooting fish in a barrel. No guns, no fighters, and no barrage balloons, but the Admiralty, which was probably the real target had hardly any damage.

On the Monday morning immediately following the second night of the bombing we had a surprise visitor. The neighbor from beyond the wall paid us a visit and returned all the tennis balls. Apparently, we were now more welcome. Isn't it amazing how sympathetic people become when they get a dose of the same medicine and this was after only 2 nights of bombing?

In the late afternoon of the next few days, we all set out, my mother and children, to walk out into the country, a couple of miles beyond the river to a tiny village named Newton St Loe. We were allowed to use the church and with several other families, we slept between the pews. I remember the smell of the dust even today. After a few days of this, with no further raids, we stayed home.

For the record, even though I have no definite recollection, my eldest sister Christine must have been working. I know that she worked at one time as a typist in the Admiralty.

A few days after the bombing, I was either chasing or being chased around a corner of the house, and fell over a pile of broken glass, and got a bad cut on the palm of my hand. It poured blood, and my mother wrapped it in a towel and hurried me off to the local doctor's house. He cleaned it and patched it up, after removing a piece of glass. We were almost home when I realized that my leg was hurting more. I had a half-inch diameter piece of my leg missing with blood going into my shoe. It had not been noticed before.

About 10 days later, my mother and I were going to London. I can't remember the reason. My hand was not healing, and still hurt. In the London area, we visited a lady, my mother's lifelong best friend who I called Auntie Gladys. She was a large woman with a strangely deep voice, but very nice and friendly. She had two adopted children around my age named Diane and Ronnie. I remember having a good time playing with them and later, I was placed in a bathtub along with them. I remember being most indignant as I had never been in a bathtub with a girl before nor another boy for that matter. Anyway, Auntie Gladys felt that I still had a piece of glass in my hand, and so she put a poultice of Epsom salts and glycerin on it. Lo and behold a few days later a piece of glass came out sticking up like the sail of a sailboat. Auntie Gladys' husband was Uncle Reg. He appeared to me to be the tallest person I had ever seen, but since I've been grown up I've been told he was shorter than I am.

It was probably about this time that we heard that my mother's father, Harry Smith, had got married at the age of approx. 78. Apparently the bad thing about this, according to everybody, was the fact that the woman he married was in her 50s, not much older than my mother.

It was about 10 years later that I heard that Harry had caught his wife with another, younger, man, and had beaten him up. My best recollection of the story I picked up from overhearing conversations, was that at 85 they didn't want to put him in jail, so they confined him to a hospital where he went on a hunger strike for many months. He was not allowed out, so the story goes, and he gradually sank to 70 lbs. from over 200 lbs., when he finally died. This final sad chapter of his life was completely unnecessary according to my Auntie Dolly with whom he had lived. It was said that if he had stayed with her, he would have lived much longer as he was a very strong, active, and fit older man. His refusal to eat was exactly in line with what I've heard of his normal behavior. But now back to the story in chronological order.

We had been in Bath a year or so when the news came that Father was being transferred back to the London area and we moved to accommodation provided by the Admiralty at 24, The Broadway, Stanmore, in the county of Middlesex, a few miles north of London. The lino pieces got smaller. My two eldest sisters, Christine and Sylvia were both working as typists for the Admiralty and I believe that they stayed in Bath in a lady's hostel in Pierpont Street. One thing I remember from that time is a blouse that Sylvia wore. Due to a shortage of fabric, this blouse had no back except for ribbons to hold it on. She wore it with a cardigan or jacket. It made me laugh.

The Broadway where we lived, was a busy road that led to Watford. We had a small frontage road with tall trees between us and the main road. Our living quarters were above a store in a block of stores. The store was not in use but had a name above it "Leopold Farmer" with no indication of what Leopold's business had been. We had a Morrison Table Shelter delivered, and we built it in the room just to the rear of the store itself, on the ground floor. The shelter was 8 feet by 5 feet, with 2 sheets of about 1/4" thick steel as the top, with corner legs of right angle steel 6" on each side, with center legs and several cross support beams. There was a strong mesh floor 3" above the house floor and side panels of the same mesh. If a bomb hit your house, the table would support the debris without you being hurt, or that was the theory. We had padding on the mesh floor, but I never remember the shelter being used. Hitler had by that time mostly given up trying to beat the RAF and the British people and was using his resources against Russia.

After we left Bath we never did go to church anymore. I think that the strict Plymouth Brethren applied too much pressure on life when added to the pressures of daily survival in wartime.

I think it is timely to mention a story that was in a newspaper or magazine and I remember my parents talking about it. Apparently a bunch of what I would call "crazies", broke away from the regular Plymouth Brethren, and formed the "Strict Sect". One of their rules was that if your wife or child doesn't believe in and agree with the Strict Sect, then they should be cast out and thrown into the street. So much for the love and understanding of their Christianity. This is a prime example of the way man has ruined the name of Christianity, bearing in mind that most wars in history have been over religious differences. At least Hitler was straightforward about it and made it clear that he hated some people and wanted to take over the world for good old avariciousness. If I was God I would be thoroughly ashamed of some people who professed to be pious Christian people, causing wars over religion.

The Stanmore area was great for us children. I went to school about 300 yards away. This was the closest school in my whole life. This school was different in one thing. At every school, children received 1/3 of a pint (a pint is 20 oz. in England) of milk in the morning and your parents could pay extra for the same in the afternoon. Well, at this school we had mugs, and the school caretaker would pour the milk from a big jug. Many of the children asked for less and he would always say "Tell me when", and then they would yell "Stop" and he would go on pouring until the mug was full. When they complained that he didn't stop, he told them "I said tell me WHEN". They never learned, and I thought (at about 8 years old) that he was very clever.

At the end of our block, there was an opening between the buildings for a wide paved alley. If you followed the alley back, it turned into a completely different world with a tiny old-style one-man bakery, with a lean-to cover for his cart and a field with a pond for his horse. The pond was full of newts, and tadpoles in the spring, and beyond were allotments which people rented to grow food. There was lots of rhubarb which came a close second to apples if scrumping was of interest. In the middle of the allotments was this huge mulberry tree, and silkworms were the most popular interest for the local kids. (I'm sure everybody knows that silkworms live on mulberry leaves). This tree was very large and spread out into thick branches about 10 feet from the ground making it close to a bowl shape, and a great place for kids to congregate.

The baker was a genuinely kind man and all the kids knew him and would drop in to see him if they were up early enough before he left on his rounds. He allowed children to have fun in the field with the pond and the horse, but that was a different time when people were kinder and considerate of other people's property. Now, sadly, the few bad ones spoil it for everybody.

Sister Daphne and I had a routine every Saturday morning at about 8.00 am. We would run over to the bakery and wait for the bread to be done. The smell and the warmth were wonderful, and we would get one of the first loaves out of the oven, almost too hot to hold, and run home. Of course, everything was rationed including bread. We were registered with this baker, so it just saved him from delivering to us.

When we got home which was just a few yards, we would cut off each end of the loaf, and spread our whole ration of butter on our own slice. This was heaven indeed, and the memory of this time warms me still. Later I realize how lucky I am in having experienced such hard times. Very small and simple things make me happy, whereas those who have always had everything can get little joy out of the small everyday delights.

About 300 yards away on the main road, there was a large house with armed guards outside. We found out that Mr. Clement Atlee lived there. He was a bigwig in the government and became Prime Minister some years later.

Then there was a time when a terrible racket came down the road. It was 2 very large tanks which parked on the frontage road about 100 yards away. A couple of tank crew were there and they set up shop. You can imagine that the tanks were like a magnet to the kids. You could get into a tank and look around if you bought a savings stamp. (Children could buy these stamps and stick them in a book provided. The book held 15 shillings worth in six penny stamps). Invariably when the book was filled they were redeemed and spent. An amount of 15 shillings was a princely sum in those days. Anyway, when business was slow at the tanks, which was nearly the whole time, the soldiers would let the kids crawl all over them and inside, etc. until one day there was a deafening roar of a tank engine and a plume of black exhaust smoke and about 6 boys tumbled out of the tank as if the devil himself was after them. They must have fiddled with controls and happened upon the way to start the engine. The tanks left the next morning.

Soon after this, we moved about 8 miles to a very nice house at 718, Kenton Lane, Harrow Weald. I had never heard of a house number being so high. The house stood alone with lovely trees in the front garden including a cherry apple. The fruit was about 1" to 1 1/4" and bright red. It was said that they made good jam, but we didn't try it for shortage of sugar. The backyard was quite large as backyards go. We had 6 apple trees. No need to go scrumping now.

For school, I had to walk several miles almost into Harrow, the home of one of the famous schools like Eton, etc.

I remember one day that at the afternoon playtime, I left and walked home thinking school had ended for the day. It was only when my mother asked me "What are you doing home so early" that I realized what had happened.

My school was on the main road into Harrow and the traffic was continuous and fast. The school entrance was up a short driveway at the side of the school to save kids from running out into the traffic. I had to go the other way and I used to climb over the wall and save about 100 yards walk.

One memory of this school lingers. There was a girl there (we were all about 8) who, if you asked her to would hold her skirt up so you could see her underwear and even more if you pushed it. Funny thing, I remember her name; Phyllis. There was one negative to that school. The route to and fro was full of dogs laying around which caused many a kid to make detours or start praying that the dogs would stay put while they crossed to the other side of the road. Many times people would say "he won't hurt you", but did the dog know that? There is one interesting worthwhile note here. 40 years later in America, I ran into somebody who went to the same school and used to climb over the same wall. He was a bit younger so we did not know each other before.

It was while living at this house that one of the kids found this thin piece of brass tubing. It was about 18" long, and we cut it into 5 pieces as there were 5 of us there. We had a place where we could light a bonfire, and we stuffed a piece of stick into the hole in one end of a wooden cotton reel. With a piece of iron rod which we made red hot, we hollowed out the other end of the cotton reel to make a bowl. Then we got the brass tubing hot, too hot to hold with bare hands and forced it through the side of the bowl to make a smoking pipe.

We had previously noticed that every day there were dozens and dozens of cigarette butts outside the pub, and we regularly collected them and reclaimed the tobacco. I suppose that when the pub cleared out at closing time, the patrons would stand outside gossiping and finishing their cigarettes before leaving. In a few days, we had a good amount of tobacco. When our pipes were finished we filled the bowls with tobacco as we'd seen adults do, and lit up.

All was fine for a few minutes with us puffing away then holding the bowl and removing the pipes to talk as adults did. Then suddenly, as the tobacco really got going, we put the pipes to our lips to a chorus of yelps of pain. The brass tubes were quite short at about 3" to 4" and the heat traveled up to the end, and we all got little blisters on our lips.

It was about this time I learned to ride a bike. It was a friend's bike and he was good enough to let me try it. Before long I was wobbling around and doing OK.

My eldest sister Christine had a Rudge (the make) bike when we lived in Belvedere, but after that there were no more bicycles bought. Actually, I had a very nice 3-wheeler in Belvedere also, but the peddle assembly which was clamped around the central frame tube, broke after a couple of months and it was never repaired even though it was transported everywhere for years.

Back to Christine's Rudge. It was in a terrible state of repair, but I recollect stuffing the flat tires with grass, and off I went. Brakes were questionable and I was too small to sit on the saddle but it was a girl's bike so I could straddle the frame easily.

Stopping with my feet was full of risk but workable. There was only one problem, I had to fight Daphne for it.

At times, when my father was home, his bike would be seen leaning against the fence. It was a huge bicycle, with a 28" frame and 28" wheels. I remember the saddle was higher than my head, and the crossbar level with my nose. I realized that I could ride this bike with one shoulder under the crossbar and one leg peddling through the gap under the crossbar. The whole bicycle tended to slope because the weight was all to one side which made precision steering a bit more guesswork than design, but it worked for me. I don't believe my father ever found out that I recall.

Some notable things about that house, were: it was about 5 miles from the place that was the main British intelligence facility. It was where the captured German enigma code machine was held and used. Of course, we didn't know about the enigma until after the war. Apparently, a submarine was captured and the crew didn't sink it and the machine was found. The Germans didn't know the machine was captured and went on using it for the rest of the war and every message was deciphered. The name of the place where the Intelligence building comes to mind is Bentley Priory, a large estate in the area between Harrow and Harrow Weald. 718, Kenton Lane was also notable for it being the address where I drank the famous 1/2 cup of cod liver oil. Did I mention this before? In case I didn't, I will relate it again. My sister Daphne made such a fuss over taking a spoonful of cod liver oil, that I said I could drink a cupful. She bet me I couldn't. We compromised on half a cup, and I was as sick as a dog for a week.

This was the place where I first felt the urge to be a bit independent.

For a week all the local kids had been planning a Saturday trip to catch some tiddlers at a big pond a couple of miles away. We got canes and bits of wire and old stockings and created workable fishing nets. I had a jam jar with string around the neck and a carrying loop, and I was all set for the big day. On the day, the kids were congregating a few yards down the road, but I couldn't find my shoes. (Shoes like everything else were rationed, and you only had one pair and were glad at that). Off they went without me.

Later I found my mother had taken them so that I couldn't go. She was afraid I would get hurt, which doesn't make sense in view of some exploits when I was so much younger. But that is women for you.

The tide of war was turning in favor of the Allies. But Hitler had a few tricks up his sleeve. The first Doodlebug or flying bomb or V1 arrived and as time went on they became more numerous. They were designed with just enough fuel to reach London. Any part of London would do. A true terror only, vengeance weapon. Hitler's army had been destroyed in Russia, and his raw materials supplies were running out. His Rumanian oil fields were in the hands of the Russians and he was beaten in North Africa. He was down to distilling fuel from vegetable peeling and rotting vegetation, but not ready to give up.

The war dragged on, and guess what. We were in London for the Battle of Britain and left for Bath just in time to get settled in for the Bath Blitz and now we were back in London in time for the Doodlebugs, (flying bombs). The Doodlebugs were equipped with ram jet engines. They work on the principle of catapulting them to about 200 miles per hour. The forward motion filled a cylinder, open at the front end, with air under pressure, then fuel was added, the front closed and the rear opened as ignition took place. The resulting explosion pushed the bomb forward in a series of rapid pulses. Primitive but effective. However, the RAF had a good time shooting at them as they traveled quite slowly and in a straight line.

It was reported that RAF fighters used wing tips to turn them around and send them back to Germany. There were fewer sirens. The Doodlebugs announced themselves. The put... put... put... was warning enough, and people carried on as normal unless the put... put... put... stopped when everybody ran for cover.

When the engine stopped the bomb would glide down. The Doodlebugs sort of died out as the launch sites in Peenemunde, Holland were bombed repeatedly and largely destroyed, but Hitler had a further cunning plan.

In the meantime, the BBC news announced every morning the number of bombers that had hit Germany and how many had been lost. It was not unusual to hear something like 600 bombers, perhaps 400 Super Fortresses, and 200 British Lancasters bombed The Ruhr, the heart of German Industry, and often hundreds didn't return. And this was every night 7 days a week. Suddenly the losses dropped. There had been no fighter planes with range enough to accompany the bombers, but the American Mustang fighter appeared. It had range enough to go with the bombers and the tables turned. The end was nearing.

Britain was fast becoming one vast arms storage area. In Southern England every bit of land with any trees sheltered tanks, trucks, guns, and every other piece of war equipment. All towns and military bases were overflowing with military personnel from all over the world. American forces were the most popular, and "Got any gum chum" was a popular greeting. British ladies had dates with all sorts of foreign men, again mostly American. A pair of American silk stockings got many an English girl in over her head. My sisters dated Americans and they were able to get all sorts of food which we hadn't seen for ages.

Now the V2 rockets started to rain down on London and we were again sent back to Bath. There was no warning about the rockets. It was traveling faster than the sound of its coming. Air raids were occurring occasionally but nothing like on the scale of a few years earlier.

We were assigned housing at 11, St. James Street, Bath. I was about 9 at the time and went to East Twerton Junior School which must have been 4 or 5 miles away. It was such a long walk. There was one consolation. My old friends Tony (Fatty) and David went to the same school, although we could not walk together as we went on a completely different route. Again this accommodation was over a tiny general shop selling some grocery items, fruits, and vegetables, and best of all they had a machine which made Tizer.

Mrs. Lodder was the proprietor and sat in the shop from 9.00 am until 5.00 pm, with an hour for lunch. I believe it was more for social purposes than anything. Tizer was a fizzy soft drink made with this machine, and Mrs. Lodder would pour in a jug of water, add bright orange essence, and turn on carbon dioxide from a big tank in the corner. I loved Tizer and spent lots of pocket money on it although I doubt it would pass health restrictions now. Mrs. Lodder lived about 50 yards down the road, Julian Road, in a house with a big gate 8 feet high by about 10 feet wide with a small door set in one side. The house was U shaped around a courtyard, and behind the gate, Mr. Lodder kept his posh car which he drove as a poor man's limousine.

Mr. Lodder was an interesting man with lots of stories. I remember that his chin stuck out quite a bit. It wasn't a big chin, just prominent, and he always looked as if he needed a shave. The chin made it more noticeable.

My mother tended to be a bit disorganized and always seemed to arrive at the point when she would need to go shopping just before the time I was due to arrive home. It got so bad that I stopped even trying the door, and would just sit on the step to await her. Once it was almost dark, and I was frozen, and I heard a noise behind the door and I tried the handle and it was unlocked. She had been in all the time. It happened twice at this house and a few times at others.

It was approaching Guy Fawkes Day, 5th November. For those not familiar with the gentleman, he was a rebel in England, I think, in the 16th century and was caught loading up the basement of the Houses of Parliament in London, with gunpowder. His objective was to blow it up. He was caught, tortured, and burned to death for his sins, and thereafter on the anniversary of his death it became the custom to build a bonfire with an effigy of Guy Fawkes on the top. Also, fireworks are on sale and every kid has some. Anyway, my sister Daphne and I ran down to the shop many times and bought some every time we got any money. I well remember going along Julian Road to Victoria Park, and under the huge horse-chestnut trees I placed a banger in an empty whisky bottle and we ran back about 40 feet. The result shocked me. Fragments of glass peppered the trees, and we could hear the flutter of the leaves as pieces of glass came down. I realize that we could have been hurt, and never did that again.

We were not long for 11, St James Street. We moved to 39, Avon Park, Bath, a regular house this time.

At 39 Avon Park, there were lots of kids to play with. Not only that, the River Avon was just 200 yards away. There was a small park right on the river bank, with swings, roundabouts, and a slide, also room to play football which is now commonly called soccer. (Question: Why is American football called football when it is mostly played with hands? I resent the fact that English football has to give up the correct descriptive name and use "soccer" which is in no way descriptive of the game, in fact, I have never met anybody who even knew where the word came from). To the right of the park, there was an area devoted to allotments, but a large part of it was wild with weeds taller than I was. This was where our gang den was built. These gangs were not the same as today's gangs with shootings and drugs. We used to squeeze into these tiny structures of sticks, cardboard, and brush. We always had a campfire and we used to tell questionable stories and smoke stems of weeds which had pithy centers. As soon as the fire was lit we'd often put potatoes in it. Unfortunately, we were impatient, and we would pull them out, cinders on one side and virtually raw on the other. However, we ate them with gusto and invariably we would be constipated. What a pity we could not have combined the effects with scrumpimg green apples as they would have cancelled each other out.

I clearly remember friends that lived there and went to school with me. There was Teddy Boswell, an unremarkable person but OK to pass the time with, and William Bird and his younger brother Richard Bird, always referred to as Dicky Bird. Dicky Bird was remarkable in that he was the same age as me but a tiny skinny little kid with the thinnest legs, just like a dicky bird, which was the term for a bird in baby talk in those days. (I sometimes think that God has little jokes with us like this).

William Bird was a couple of years older than most of the children and had a mean streak, and was a bit of a bully. Bobby Wallace was a redhead, one of a family of about 8, all girls except Bobby. Now the Wallaces were all very nice people and painfully poor. Most of them had carroty red hair. Their mother was memorable because of her thick eyeglasses, like the bottoms of a Coke bottle, but a kinder woman would be hard to find.

Bobby had a young sister, Suzy, who was about 5, and she was renowned for wetting her knickers, and she always smelled like wetted knickers. One time Bobby was in the hospital, and they had borrowed pajamas from me. They were returned nicely washed except they must have been laundered in the same water as Suzy's knickers as they smelled like Suzy. My mother immediately washed them again.. Other names I remember were a girl named Joyce, and another one named Paddy both completely unremarkable, but they hung around with us boys.

I didn't realize what a beautiful view it was from the park until I look back. Just 40 yards to the left the river and canal joined up, with the river tumbling over a weir (man-made waterfall) of about 5 feet high. The canal was necessary with locks so that barges could bypass the weir. On the island between the forks of the two water-ways was an old-fashioned mill building surrounded by trees, which was very picturesque. On the far side of the river was a line of willows right down to the water's edge.

To the right again was a small piggery, which, by the smell must have contained 1,000 pigs, although there was only room for about 20 to 30. One feature of wartime England was the "pig bin" placed at every corner for citizens to put all their peelings and vegetable waste, for use in feeding pigs to supplement meat supplies.

One day I was walking down the river bank where there were willows on our side of the river, when I spotted this branch that was straight, and of an almost consistent 1"diameter for about 6 feet in length. I got out my trusty pen knife and in a few minutes, it was mine. I made a bow, and with some thinner willow branches for arrows, I became the new Robin Hood. However, there was one little problem. At about 9 years of age, I was not strong enough to pull it back too far. I persevered and in no time I could get a reasonable amount of oomph behind my arrows. Of course, by this time all the kids went for this latest craze and had bows and arrows, but none as good as mine. We held target and distance competitions and my bow could outdistance the others by far. The other kids used to line up to try my bow.

One day I saw two of the local kids carrying a piece of wood about 2" x 4", about 10 feet long. This was a very valuable find, and it was winter with snow on the ground. All the kids were moping because they didn't have toboggans, this was a chance too good to miss, and somehow I was able to talk them out of it. I suppose I was meant to have it. In no time I straightened some rusty 3 ½ " nails, and with a few cross pieces of wood, I had a toboggan. However, it didn't run well on the snow. I needed some steel on the runners, and within no time at all I found some thin strips of hard springy steel, 1 1/4" wide which had been under the coil springs of a discarded bed. Only one problem. I could not drill holes through it with a hand drill. I finally talked to my father who did it for me. This was before the days of electric drills. I now had a super toboggan. After a bit of wear each year, you could see yourself in the steel.

There was what struck me as a strange situation involving Tony Tandy, the class wimp. He was the smallest and the quietest, and really very nice. We had just returned from the summer vacation and this new kid, Michael Collins joined the class. He was what we called a rough kid, always looking for an argument. He was a loudmouth bully, and he wore boots! This always labeled kids as "rough", which meant to most kids, poor class or inferior, and a troublemaker. In addition, like a lot of rough kids, he always had a stream of mucous from his nose on his upper lip. It is hard to believe now, but this was common in those days. Sometimes they would sniff it back up, or run their tongue over their upper lip when it got too much. It fairly makes your stomach turn now but in those days we took no notice. I was always the biggest or nearly the biggest and I rarely had problems with other kids, but for the rest, Michael Collins, who was quite small really, took the class by storm, and in no time, most of them were intimidated by him all except . . . . . you guessed it, Tony Tandy. He, in fact, took great delight in bullying Michael in front of everybody, and there was no doubt that Michael was afraid of Tony.

This bothered me and I asked Tony the reason for this strange thing. He told me that Michael had moved into the house next door to him during the vacation time, and they had gotten into an argument and fight. Tony wiped the floor with Michael. Here was living proof that the loudmouth bully is often only so much hot air. It's a lesson for all.

At school, we were working on posters for a safety first competition. This competition was city-wide and the winners would receive an award from none other than The Lord Mayor of Bath. You'll never guess who won 2nd prize. I received 7 shillings and 6 pence, a princely sum indeed for a boy my age.

There was a time when my mother got a bee in her bonnet about going out to work. Finally, she did something about it and got a job with the Admiralty. The Admiralty was the biggest employer in the Bath area. The hours she worked were 9 am to 3.30 pm, which was fine for school days but no good for the 6 weeks of school summer holidays.

She would not leave me home as she said I would get into some (mysterious) mischief, which only she seemed to know about. (I wished at the time that I knew about this mischief because I know I would have enjoyed it if it was that bad). Anyway, when wc first arrived in Bath we had registered with The Maypole food store. The manager's name was Bill Horsefield, and my mother was quite friendly with him, which helped in getting a bit extra food occasionally. For the school holiday, she asked Mr. Horsefield if she could leave me at the store on the way to work and pick me up on the way home. He agreed to this, and so that is what happened.

There were about 4 or 5 young lady assistants and they made a fuss of me, and I was allowed to sit in the basement and weigh up 1lb bags of sugar and rice, etc. After a bit of this, and after I had sampled virtually every item of food that looked interesting, I poked around and found a door that opened into a small area under the metal grill set in the surface of the sidewalk outside the store. Most older places of business in England have a metal grill or metal door set into the pavement so that deliveries can be made directly into the storage basement. I looked up, and guess what. Lots of ladies were walking past oblivious to me and I could see their underwear. This was not of great interest as I had 4 older sisters, and there were no mysteries there, but it was something I knew I should not be doing and that was fun. I don't expect that I was the first and certainly not the last to do that.

However, a 9-year-old around the Maypole must have been a bit wearing, and one day either Mr. Horsefield or one of the girls yelled at me, and I was upset and left the store and awaited my mother outside the shop. For days and days, my mother dropped me off, and I spent the whole time standing around in the street until she came back. To give Mr. Horsefield his due, many times he tried to get me back into the store but I always refused.

The next year my mother dropped me off at the Parade Gardens. This was a botanical garden, a small park right in the middle of Bath. She would give me entrance money and money to buy food from the snack bar and there I would stay until she returned. I have a faint recollection that sister Daphne was going to stay with Auntie Dolly during these long school holidays. I have no idea where Sister Brenda was during these times. Maybe she was now working as they started at 14 years of age and she would have been close to that age.

At first glance experiences like the above seem callous and cruel. But we are a sum total of what we have seen and suffered and enjoyed. My mother, from 7 years of age had it very hard, and it made her tough. She is currently 98 years of age, and her toughness maybe is what keeps her going when her younger siblings who were protected by her, have all passed on. I sometimes worry that in this modern time of 2001, when young people have everything easy, and done for them, will they be able to cope? I expect, knowing the resilience of the human spirit that if they can't handle it, that very fact will be enough adversity which will strengthen them.

I know that in some ways my mother was over-protective and tried to make me a sissy, but that was balanced out and toughened me by the way she inadvertently exposed me to adversity.

One day my eldest sister Christine announced that she was getting married to Flt Lt. William Dexter from Calgary, Alberta, Canada. He flew Mosquitos in the Canadian Air Force. The Mosquito was a unique machine. It was a twin-engine fighter bomber and one of the fastest planes of the war. It was unusual in that the engines stuck out ahead of the nose, but it was unique in that the air-frame was mostly made from wood.

The wedding ceremony was, I believe, held in Manvers Hall, which had been our church, and the wedding reception was at the Pump Room. The music was provided by Mr. Louis Field and his ensemble. The Pump Room, is a grand building, a remnant from the time when Bath was the fashionable place to be and the Pump Room was the fashionable meeting place. It has many meeting rooms, high ceilings, and chandeliers. Also, it is built partly over the historic remains of the Roman Baths, mentioned in the first paragraph of this story.

The wedding reception was held in the evening when the Roman ruins were closed to the public, but sister Daphne and I found a way in, and I remember whizzing around and having a grand old time.

Mr. Louis Field knew most of the family, even me, having taught some of us piano and singing. His drummer allowed me to play the drums for a time whilst the adults danced. I was at the drums later in the evening when it was time for the ensemble to close with "God Save the King", and I let loose at an appropriate spot with a loud thump with the big drum and a bang on the cymbals. Apparently, this was a no no, and I was promptly removed from the drummer's seat.

I had a very satisfactory evening over all, and Christine and Bill went off on a honeymoon to a tiny little village named Dunster, in the county of Devon. I approved of Bill Dexter, I thought he was OK.

He took me to a few places. One memorable day he took me to a public swimming pool, the Royal Baths. Unfortunately, the drawstring in the waist disappeared inside my bathing suit, and we had no safety pin to re-thread it. Bill painstakingly worked the string back to the opening, taking about 20 minutes to do it.

At school, I was in Miss Thomas's class and I was 9. She was a tiny 5' 2", and a skinny 35-year-old spinster, although she wasn't bad looking. She had exhibited a mean streak on many occasions. We sat at double desks and my partner was Geoffrey Auten. He was a bit thick and survived by copying almost everything I did.

One day during the afternoon milk break he was craning his neck to copy my work just as I finished my milk, so I blew through my drinking straw and he got a small spray of milk on him. Miss Thomas saw me and without letting me tell her why, got me out the front, and she rapped my knuckles with the edge of a wooden ruler. He got away scot-free. I thought it was unfair, and using the edge of the ruler? However, she really paid about 13 years later. It was unlucky for her. Read on.

One day we woke up to hear that the Allies had crossed the English Channel in the dark and early hours of the morning. Many thousands of small boats had been commandeered to assist in getting everything and everybody over. Hitler had been tricked by a feint, which led him to believe that the invasion was going to occur somewhere other than the real target of Normandy. For some days the Germans insisted that the main invasion was going elsewhere and held back reinforcements giving the Allies the foothold they needed.

It was around this time that sisters Sylvia, Brenda, and Daphne got to know Eric Fennel. Eric seemed very tall with fair wavy hair. He had a car and was one of the few people we knew who could get petrol (gasoline). He lived in a small village named Corston right next to Newton St. Loe, where our mother had taken us to avoid raids after the Bath Blitz.

Eric Fennel put together shows at Military camps all around Bath. Sylvia had a particular talent for hearing a new piece of popular music on the radio and within a few moments, she could play it perfectly. Then off she would go and buy the sheet music. She became the music for Eric's shows, and Brenda would dance, and Daphne at about 13 years of age would sing the new songs to the troops. I'm sure there were other people in the shows but I never heard anything about that.

The three sisters would spend hours making costumes and practicing for the shows which were held every week. Daphne continued her singing lessons with Louis Field, and I remember that she entered the Mid-Somerset Arts Festival. I laughed when my mother made her swallow a raw egg under the belief that it improved the voice. Daphne argued and carried on something awful but my mother prevailed. I don't believe it would do a thing for you but she did OK. I cannot remember the exact result.

Now at last the war was over. Within hours a street celebration was put together and our black ebony upright piano was wheeled/carried down the street, the beer was flowing, and everybody was deliriously happy. My mother was angry. Somebody put a beer glass on the open top of the piano and the beer got tipped inside. I personally believe it sounded better than before. The kids were happy as they were looking forward to being able to buy all the sweets (candy) they could eat. But, not so fast, it was 5 years before rationing stopped.

After rationing finally ended, for about a month, all the candy went off the store shelves as fast as it was put on them, then sales dropped to less than before rationing ended.

I was now in Mrs. Allen's class at East Twerton Junior School with 46 other 10-year-olds.

I don't know why nowadays there is so much discussion about class size because we learned OK. I think it is more a matter of children being taught to behave properly and having respect for people and things, in short, being taught and having discipline. If parents abdicate their responsibility and don't teach the children and expose them to discipline, teachers cannot make up the gap, and the children pay eventually.

Mrs. Allen was an excellent teacher and everybody knew that they had to behave or else. This was the big year because in early summer we had to take the "scholarship" examination. My Father got so excited in the discussion about the scholarship examination that he took a pound note (about $20 & in the year 1999 dollars) and pinned it to the wall and said that if I passed, the pound note was mine. However, within a month, the pound note mysteriously disappeared, and I never saw it again even though I passed the examination.

During this year in Mrs. Allen's class, a new pupil joined the school. His father was in the Admiralty and had been transferred from Plymouth, Devon, to Bath. By lunchtime, he had revealed that he had a tendency to be a bit of a pushy type of kid, and although he was a lot smaller than me, we had a pushing match in the playground on his first day. To get ahead a bit in time, he passed the scholarship after going for a special interview, and he remained in the same class as me throughout our school years. We were never too friendly, there was always a level of tension between us, but we got by. His name was Brian Winter. Remember this name.

Addendum

In looking back and reading the earlier part of our story, I find that I missed many details of every-day life during World War II.

At the risk of much repetition, I have decided to enlarge on this subject as an addendum, and create a separate "book within a book". Please excuse the duplication of material already covered.

My first memories on the subject of World War II was the talk of "War". A new ominous sounding word to me, a 4 year old boy. It drew a picture, (or maybe it was the tone of voice) of something harsh, threatening and awful. It was 1939.

Adults were paying much more attention to the BBC news, and the newspapers appeared to have large headlines, unreadable to me at my age. However, I distinctly remember hearing the BBC announcement that we were now at war with Germany, and me thinking that Germany had something to do with things that caused illness, i.e. germs. I thought that Germany was where germs came from.

The next recollection was being fitted for an ugly and scary bright red child's gas mask, details of which I know I have spoken of in the book. I ended up with an adult gas mask, just the same as my older sisters and parents.

Shortly after, large lorries (trucks) appeared, slowly moving up our street, delivering the components to each house for the construction of our own air raid shelters. These were Anderson shelters made by bolting together 3 or 4 pairs of 2 feet wide curved corrugated and galvanized iron sheets, to form a 6 foot high arch. Then you joined the 3 or 4 arches together to make a "tunnel" about 6 or 8 feet long with two end pieces. This arch was to be erected in a hole in the garden at least 4 feet deep, with the removed dirt to be spread on top and sides of the arch. One of the end pieces had an opening for an entrance, the top of which would be about ground level. These shelters were no good against direct hits but gave benefits in the case of a near miss. It was certainly safer than staying in a house that would collapse on you if it was hit.

We were also issued with lengths of 2" x 3" of wood, and sacking or burlap for making bunks in the shelter, and in a couple of weeks we were all set with our shelter and sleeping bunks.

Names heard on the radio and seen in newspapers included Neville Chamberlain, (famous for his supposedly successful meeting with Hitler, and his announcement afterward, "peace in our time". However, Hitler invaded Poland almost immediately), Mussolini, Rippontrop, Goering, and Goebbals to name a few. Lord Haw Haw was the name of a traitorous Englishman who collaborated with the Germans and would interrupt BBC broadcasts with propaganda messages. Apparently the Germans had this very powerful transmitter that could break into the BBC programs for short announcements. He would be cut off in a matter of a minute or two. Some of his messages would include actual names of British politicians and even individual servicemen, so their spies must have been very active.

There were many changes. We were issued with tarpaper, wood slats and nails to cover windows blown out by bombs. Also everybody had to make black window drapes (curtains) to keep all light from showing. We had to apply for ration books for food, clothes, coal etc. Sales of petrol (gasoline) for private vehicles were halted. All metal railings around cemeteries, private houses etc were collected and used in the war effort. Windows were reinforced by strips of sticky paper stretched across them to reduced splintering from explosions. Large water storage tanks were constructed at strategic points to provide water for fire fighting. These tanks were circular concrete structues and about 35 feet diameter with 5 foot walls. They accounted for many young kids drowning. At most cross streets you could find "pig bins," placed there for all waste vegetable items such as potato peelings, outer cabbage leaves etc. and it was used to feet pigs to add to the meat supply.

All young men were conscripted, including the younger policemen. New, older policemen, possibly retired men (called "specials") appeared wearing flat caps instead of the well known British police helmets. (I'm reminded of a popular song from the time of World War I, which had a line: "you can't trust the specials like the old time copper when you can't find your way home"). I believe it refers to the fact that the regular police always gave good directions to find your way when you were drunk or lost, but the specials didn't know their way around so well. All signs giving travel directions were removed to confuse any enemy, so finding your way was an important factor.

More and more people in military uniforms appeared on buses and trains, and military vehicles became a common sight. A whole new group called ARP wardens was formed. They patrolled the streets and often we'd hear at night, a shout "put that light out" as a result of light showing around the black curtains. They also fought fires and dug out people trapped in bombed houses. I believe that ARP stands for Air Raid Patrol.

Another group was formed called WVS, (women's voluntary service) for older capable ladies who took care of all emergency human needs for all ages from babies to elderly.

All able bodied men, too old to join the services were encouraged to join the Home Guard. This was exactly what the name implies. They behaved like the military in all ways, being issued with rifles and other light armaments, and had local barracks and a training ground. Their uniforms were army khaki, and it was a common sight to see them marching through the town. The main differences to the regular army was the fact that they lived at home and maintained regular jobs, only participating in the home guard in the evenings and weekends. Their officers were retired army officers.

Other activities of note were the Land Army and the young knitters. Young ladies who wished to help the war effort were sent away to farms to work the land. In some instances they worked alongside German prisoners who were also working on the land. Younger girls, school girls, were drafted into knitting groups to make Balaclava helmets and woolen scarves and socks for the fighting men.

Red brick rectangular little buildings began appearing around the towns. They were usually about 20 feet by 15 feet and about 10 feet high with flat concrete tops. They had no windows but had one small heavy steel door with a protective wall around it to save bomb blasts getting inside. These were the new public air raid shelters. The outer walls were also a place for the posters that appeared in all public places, warning that "walls have ears", and "careless talk costs lives" or "loose lips sink ships" etc..

Alternatively, in the larger cities, building basements were often co-opted as public air raid shelters. In the London area the subway system stations were used as shelters for thousands. At the time of the Battle Of Britain, in 1940, we endured months of air raids all around the clock, and 57 nights of continuous bombing without a break. People lived almost permanently in these stations for months at a time. Many babies were born there and some elderly died there from natural causes. Apparently the continuous bombing was Hitler's effort to break Britain's will to keep fighting. This was when the Royal Air Force was stretched to its limit, and unknown to Hitler, if it had continued a bit longer, there may have been a different outcome.

As expected, one day, the air raid sirens sounded in earnest for the first time and we made for our shelter in the back yard. My father had fitted ours up with 3 bunks each side and a small one across the back wall for me. All 7 of us, 4 sisters, my parents and I fitted in nicely if a little bit crowded.

I don't remember what happened with the first raid, but there was not much going on in the first few weeks of raids. But soon it heated up to the point where bombs were dropping all over the place and fires were started and people were killed and injured.

Something I remember vividly is the smell of damp burlap and candle smoke. An unfortunate feature of an air raid shelter made of metal in a cold climate and with lots of people breathing in a confined space, is the formation of condensation. It would run down the curved side of the metal arch until it hit an imperfection, and then drop on the top bunk or the occupant. Added to the mixture was the soot of candle smoke which also collected on the high points of the shelter causing the condensation to leave a dirty, smelly residue. If I smell candle smoke or damp burlap, I immediately recall the months spent in an air raid shelter as a small boy.

Just a couple of hundred yards up the road from our house was an orchard and there was an anti-aircraft gun emplacement among the trees. When the guns fired it shook the ground violently which made sleep difficult. Around strategic targets were large gas filled "barrage balloons" tethered, with long cables hanging down from them. The idea was to discourage enemy aircraft from getting too close

I was enrolled in school shortly after the bombing started, and like everybody else, I had had to carry my gas mask with me. At school we had to practice getting under our desks if bombs started falling. I'm sure there was an air raid shelter at the school, but I don't remember anything about this.

Once or twice when going to and from school, we passed collapsed (bombed) houses that had been there the day before, and I remember that the older kids used to climb around on them. In fact, bomb sites eventually became a popular play area for most kids

As time went on into 1940, the intensity and frequency of air raids increased to the point that we children went to bed expecting to have to get up and run for the shelter. I remember laying in bed, rigid with fear, watching the doorway for Germans coming to get me. Nearly every night, we would hear a low growling sound indicating the start up of the siren, warning of an impending visit of German bombers. Instantly my sisters and I would erupt bare foot to the top of the stairs on our way down to the shelter. We'd race up the garden path, in the dark and often in rain or snow, to the shelter. We tumbled down the shelter steps, into the dark, followed by our parents who were struggling to light candles as we climbed into our bunks. The dirt floor of the shelter was several feet below ground level in wet and rainy England, and of course there was seepage. In spite of continuous baling, there was always water underfoot.

The raids became more frequent and long lasting to the point where we went to bed and virtually lived in the shelter without attempting to use our beds. By this time there was little glass left in the windows and electricity and gas services were spasmodic due to the bombing. Cooked food was a rarity, and normal daily activities such as school, work and shopping became extremely difficult. Sleep was very disturbed by the continuous crump of bombs and the rumble of anti-aircraft guns.

In the middle of the months of this continuous bombardment, the Arsenal at Woolwich, just about 6 miles away, was badly hit, and for 24 hours there were continuous explosions that shook the ground. The fires and smoke were so intense that it was still dark at 3.00pm the next afternoon. This period lasted many months and became known as the Battle of Britain.

Often, during the quieter moments, my father would get out of the shelter and gossip to Mr Hayer, our neighbor, over the garden fence. I remember one time when I was allowed out on a sunny day to watch several shiny aircraft way up in the sky in a dog fight. They were very high, but you could clearly hear the zooming of their engines and rat tat tat of their guns. One day Mr Hayer was hit in the shoulder by shrapnel whilst talking to my father.

Often during daytime, when the "all clear" sounded, my sisters and I would go out and look for shrapnel. We used to find lots of large splintered metal shards some as long as 6 or 8 inches. Occasionally we found pieces of brass and other metal parts lying around. One day we were busy shrapnel hunting after a raid, when there was a deafening roar from just down our road. A German fighter plane roared diagonally toward us at rooftop height trailing smoke. In the second or so that it was in view, we could clearly see the pilot and rivets in the wings. Within another second or so there was a loud crash and explosion with a pall of smoke rising up from the direction of the apple orchard up our road.

My father worked in central London for the Admiralty, and had to do his share of fire watching all night from the roof of his office building. He was equipped with buckets of sand and water in case of incendiary bombs. He was lucky in that his brother was assigned to do the same shift which made it a bit more pleasant.

Our food ration books came in a variety of colors. Green ones were for very young children, blue ones for older children, gray ones for expectant mothers, and off white or light tan were for everybody else. Typical weekly rations (it varied slightly according to supply) were 2 ounces each of lard, sugar, cheese, bacon, fresh meat, corned beef, and candy, 1 ounce of tea and 1 egg. Milk, bread, and potatoes etc were also rationed but I can't remember amounts. Oranges were only available for Christmas, and we saw no bananas for the whole duration of the war. Most vegetables other than potatoes were not rationed, but were scarce and a little bit hard to find.

Green blue and gray ration books earned slightly more than the regular rations. Occasionally, we could buy Australian frozen rabbits, and sometimes whale meat. I remember the one time we were served whale meat at a school lunch. It was very good.

To supplement food supplies any little area of land not being used was turned into what was called "allotments", and individuals were able to rent them for the purpose of growing vegetables. My father had an allotment and also grew vegetables around the air raid shelter in our back garden.

Eventually the almost continuous raids slackened, and in 1941 my father was transferred to Bath, a city 100 miles west of London. My mother with me and sisters traveled by train. It was full of servicemen from all over the world. There were Americans, Canadians, Australian, New Zealanders, South Africans and Polish soldiers. They all carried rifles which were propped up, and fell over with a clatter with each lurch of the train. We stopped at every station and the 100 miles took almost 4 hours to complete. We were met in Bath by WVS ladies who took us to The Pavillion, a large function building, where I had a name label tied to the buttonhole of my overcoat.

I suppose it was to know who I was if I got lost in the crowds. We all received brown paper bags with items of food, and then issued with temporary ration cards to allow us to buy food until permanent ration books could be supplied. We were provided with housing in the 2 lower floors of a large house, and my father's brother also in the admiralty was transferred and had the top floor of the house. My father joined us in about a week.

Bath had received no bombing at all up to this point, but within a matter of a few weeks, the sirens started going again, and we endured two nights of concentrated bombing. Bath, being a smaller area was hit pretty hard. There were no shelters and people congregated in basements. After this for the next couple of weeks our whole family walked about 3 or 4 miles to a small village named Corston where we could spend the night in the village church laying on the floor between the pews. The floors were wood and very hard, and I remember the smell of the dust that would rise up every time you moved. However, after the 2 nights of bombing there were no more serious raids on Bath.

During the evening of the second night of bombing, with bombs still falling, my father and his brother went to see the local gas works that had been seriously damaged and was on fire. On the way they were spotted by a German fighter plane which dived at them firing its machine guns. They were lucky to be by a high wall of a large house and could dodge around the corner for shelter. The plane turned and came back so they dodged back again. The large house had a famous occupant named Haile Selasse, the Emporer or King (can't remember) of Abysinia, now known as Ethiopia. He had left his country to avoid capture by the Italians when they invaded.

My father returned home without seeing the gasworks

An engineering company situated close to our house, was bombed and as a result we lost all the glass at the back of the house. My father had swept it into a pile and I was being chased by a sister and fell on this pile. I had a deep cut on my hand and a chunk out of my leg.

Life in Bath was pleasant, without the constant air raids. We were in a valley surrounded by grassy hills with the river Avon flowing through it. Unfortunately, with the influx of lots of people from London, the locals felt a bit put on and were unpleasant at times, until after the 2 nights of bombing. When they had experience of what we had lived with for many months they suddenly became much more friendly.

I was attending a small school about 2 miles from home and struck up a long friendship with 2 boys of my age who lived along the road from my house. We walked to and from school every day together.

After a couple of years in Bath, my father was moved back to the London area. I'm guessing it was about 1943 and air raids were spasmodic. We were provided a home with two floors over a store, and it was a wonderful place for kids. My school was about 300 yards away. I had never had a school this close.

There were fields and woods, and at the back of our house was a small bakery and next to it was a field for the horse that pulled the baker's cart. In the fields was a pond with frogs and newts, and of course, in the spring we caught tadpoles and small newts. I think I enjoyed this place more than any when I was young. We were issued with a Morrison air raid shelter. These were called table shelters and were huge steel tables with massive legs, solid steel tops and wire mesh sides. They were for assembly inside the house, and were designed to help you survive in the case of a house collapse.

I know I recited in the main book, one of the highlights of living there, but it is worth repeating. My sister Daphne and I used to get up early on Saturday morning and run over to the bakery and await the first loaf of bread to come out of the oven. The place was warm and cozy.

We would get the bread and run home, and cut an inch think slice off each end of the loaf, and slather on our whole butter ration and slowly eat it. Heaven!

Eventually we were sent back to Bath and were assigned living accommodation over another store. It was a general store run by a lady named Mrs Lodder. Just a quarter of a mile down the road was Victoria Park, a huge area of grass, ponds, trees and children's areas. Air raids in Bath were a thing of the past now. I had to walk many miles to school, but there was a compensation. My two old friends with whom I used to walk to the school in our previous time in Bath, were now going to this new school.

It wasn't very long before the news came that my father had been transferred back to London area, and we went to live in Harrow Weald, near Harrow, in a very nice house. We had no shelter, but we did have 6 apple trees in the back garden. This house was near to a large estate called Bentley Priory, where the German Enigma Code Machine was taken. This item was on a submarine that was captured. The standing instruction was for all machines to be destroyed before they could fall into Allied hands. This machine was not, and it was duplicated and used all over to interpret all German coded transmissions for the rest of the war.

Soon, the flying bombs started falling all around London. Nobody took any notice of them whilst they putt putt putted along, but as soon as the motors stopped everybody ran for shelter, because down they came. In a matter of months, the V2 rockets started raining down. This was different, they came at all times without warning. There was no sound because they were going faster than sound. You knew when a rocket had arrived by the huge explosion.

Soon after this we were off back to Bath. The war was winding down a bit. Bath was full of foreign and British troops, and all roads which had any trees had tanks, military trucks and large guns etc hidden away under the branches. This was a build-up for the cross channel invasion of France. Eventually it came, and it was the beginning of the end for Germany. The day the war in Europe was over, in 1945, there were huge celebrations. Our piano was wheeled out into the street and dancing and singing went on for hours. My mother was very annoyed as somebody put a glass of beer on the opened top of the piano, and somebody knocked it over and the piano got a half a pint of beer inside. It didn't appear to do any damage as the piano always sounded the same.

Unfortunately, one of my priorities, the candy ration of 2 ounces per week, continued until 1950. Then, the stores emptied within a day or so, but 3 months later, sales of candy were at a lower level than when rationed.

Chapter 5 - Muriel at the Senior School by Muriel

It was 1945, and I started at my new school, the City of Bath Girls School. By some strange chance, there was almost nobody from my old school in my class. Everything was a bit scary, as they did things very differently from my old school. We all looked the same as we had all visited the school-appointed outfitters for the school uniform. It cost a fortune. We had to wear a navy blue gym slip, a light blue blouse, a navy blue pullover, a navy blue and gold tie, a navy blue velour hat, with a hat band to match the tie, and a navy blue gabardine raincoat. We were issued extra clothing coupons to buy this. Then we had to buy a satchel to carry our books and homework etc.

There were 4 houses, like at an old-time boarding school. I was assigned to the Bush House. The prefects would give demerits for the slightest infraction, such as being out without wearing your hat. These demerits counted against your house, and if you had too many you had to stand up in front of the house and explain.

There was another girl in my class named Newton. Mary and Janet were her first two name, same initials as mine (Muriel, changed to Muriel Joy on coming to America). We told some of the teachers we were twins. They made a big thing of it until somebody noticed different addresses, then they weren't too pleased with us.

My homeroom teacher was Miss Michaelson. She was very short, under 5 feet, and with thick glasses. She had a tendency to dwarfism. She taught French and was very nice to us girls.

A month after the start of my first term (semester), a new girl started and she became a lifelong friend. Her name was Audrey Hill, then Audrey Ailes after her marriage. We did everything together in school and out. She lived near me and so we were able to travel to and from school together.

My father came home from the war shortly after I started at the new school. I distinctly remember the next morning. I took cups of tea up to my parents as I wanted to get a good look at him. I hadn't seen him for several years and I barely remembered him. I admired his teeth and looked around for a pot or container for false teeth, thinking that they were too perfect to be natural, and he saw me and asked what I was looking for. He thought it was very funny.

It seemed very strange having a father in the house. Life was changed. Dad appeared to pick on me, but when my brother John got older, he started to pick on him also. However, there were some advantages to having a father at home.

I was bullied and taunted by this local bully, and one day I was walking along with Dad, and there was this boy who had been making my life miserable. I told Dad, who called him over and scared the daylights out of him. I was left alone after that.

After Dad came home, he would help Mum with the laundry on Sundays, and it became my job to cook the Sunday roast dinner. Most Sundays I made a Victoria sponge cake as Dad really liked my sponge cakes.

I don't remember ever having a birthday party. However, once I had Audrey for a friend, Mum suggested that on my birthday, she would pay for Audrey and me to go to town and have tea in a restaurant and then go to the pictures (movies). This became an annual event until I left school.

Whilst we are talking about my father, it is interesting to talk about his siblings, my aunts, and uncles. My father was the eldest in his family and named Harry Frederick Arthur John Newton. I'm not sure of the order, but the others were named Madgewick, Mary, (she died as a child), Gertrude thereafter known as Peg, (she went to New Zealand), May, known as Minky thereafter, and Margaret, married to Uncle Stan at Hare Street Farm near Chippenham in the county of Wiltshire.

Auntie Minky married Uncle Len, who was memorable as a typical native of Somerset County, with a broad accent. They lived in Bath. I was staying at their house for a weekend and one evening when Uncle Len came home, Auntie Minky served him a dinner plate containing nothing but . . . . A chicken's head. He ate it with great relish whilst I looked on in horror. I had an awful vision of a chicken's head being served to me, but they must have run out, and I breathed a sigh of relief.

Uncle Madgewick was a Beefeater, one of the guards at the Tower of London.

Toward the end of my first year at the City of Bath Girl's School, I was sliding down the banister (handrail) at school 2 floors up, and I fell through the stairwell and landed on my knees and banged my head. I'm not sure if I passed out, but don't remember much except the feeling that my head was splitting. The school doctor happened to be there and examined me. She evidently thought I was OK to go home so I was sent in a taxi. The next day, one knee was swollen like a football. The other one was also very swollen. Our family doctor, Dr. Miles came to check me out and said I should stay home for the rest of the week.

Shortly after, my back started to give me trouble, and for several years it was misdiagnosed as lumbago. I had stopped growing by this time, at almost 12 years of age. When I was 15, the pain was severe, and I was sent to a specialist, who prescribed a plaster body cast for 3 months. This was no fun especially as I was in hospital for 3 days in a tent with light bulbs on 24 hours a day to get the plaster to dry. I spent half the time on my back, and half on my stomach. There was no bathing or showering for the whole three months, so every day I had to put a clean gauze tube over my head, attach it to the one I was wearing with safety pins, and pull it down until the old one could be detached and washed. As the pulling was going on, I sprinkled baby talcum powder on the clean one. I had a great deal of itching and had to carry a knitting needle for scratching. At school, I'd go to the toilet to scratch. My friend Audrey would come with me and scratch from the back as I couldn't reach everywhere.

After 3 months, the cast was cut off by a man with garden shears. It was a terrifying procedure. At any minute I expected to be cut open. Also, it was a terribly embarrassing experience for a 15-year-old. After this, I had to wear a custom-made surgical corset, which, I was told, I'd have to wear for the rest of my life.

I wore it until it wore out, probably two years, then I thought I would try going without it. Luckily it worked out OK and still does if I am careful. I always sit carefully with a cushion at the center of my back. I was told I would have major problems if I had any children, but this didn't happen.

It was April of 1947 when my mother gave birth to my sister Pamela. I was in my second year at the City of Bath Girls School and was kept home for two weeks to look after the house with laundry, cooking, and care of the other 4 younger children. There were a couple of mishaps with the laundry. The first week a blue hair ribbon got in with the white sheets, and the second week, it was a red ribbon. We were the first on our road to have patriotic colored sheets. I got into real trouble for that. When I got back to school I had to line up outside the headmistress's office with all the other girls who had been absent. Miss Cook read the note from my mother, and said "If your parents choose to breed like rabbits, they must make other arrangements". This is typical of the mean old maids who were school teachers at that time. They would say this sort of thing to bully children, but they would not say the same to parents. What was the point of telling me? She should have written to my parents.

When my mother brought Pamela home from the nursing home, Father made such a fuss you would think it was the first baby. He said she would be brought up properly, and be the perfect child, and he lavished more on her than he did the rest of us. Also, she was sent to a private school. In spite of everything, Pamela turned out to be completely unspoiled and a completely lovely sister.

In the evenings I often had to babysit all the children. Pamela was a very difficult child and started crying soon after Mum left. I had to give her the 10.00 pm feed, and she would not take it and cry. I would get into trouble because she hadn't been fed. Finally, I would get into bed quite late.

About this time, my parents decided we should all be christened. There were 6 children at this time. Godparents were picked out for everyone except me, so I chose Auntie Celia but was told she had been assigned to my sister Susan. Auntie May (married to Uncle Stan) was the only one left, so I asked her and she agreed. Probably as a result of this, we became quite close and as I've said elsewhere, I visited them often, doing her shopping every Monday.

When I was about 14, I came home from school one day to find that there had been a terrible accident. Like everybody else, we had a cast-iron gas stove, which must have not been turned off, or was leaking gas from the oven. Granny went to light it and was blown across the room and the stove landed on her. She was badly hurt and in bed. We had to creep around for days. I never saw her out of bed again for the next two years until she died. I was 16 years old. She was the first dead person I'd ever seen.

After the explosion, we had all gas appliances removed from the house and got a new electric stove.

Soon after this, my parents bought the house next door. Auntie Celia and Granny were our neighbors. Mum continued to look after Granny during the days.

In this new house, Dad put in an upstairs bathroom and toilet, and that was the end of the slop bucket duty.

After Granny died, Auntie Celia lived there alone until she died at 79.

Audrey and I often went for long walks, and we were walking along Charlecombe Lane, close to Charlecombe Church, which is 1100 years old (Built in the year 900). We decided we would look into the church. It is surrounded by large trees and is in a very creepy place. It is known to be haunted (We have a photo we took in 1974, of an empty church, but in the photograph, a shadowy hooded figure can be seen kneeling at the altar. The developers of the film must have wondered what the apparition was as they enclosed an enlarged copy of that area of the picture).

The main door has an iron ring handle, and I was just reaching out to turn it when it turned and the door slowly opened. We were terrified. A visitor was just coming out.

We were shaken and sat down in the empty church to regain our composure. It was evening and quite gloomy. A voice seemed to come from nowhere, saying "Don't let me scare you", which is exactly what it did. It was a lady who had been in the church, praying. We got out of there as fast as our legs would take us.

After that, we were walking along the narrow country lane, recovering. There were tall hedges on each side, and it was now twilight. Suddenly a donkey put its head through the hedge and brayed at us.

We ran and ran. The blue beads which I have previously mentioned, broke, and scattered, but we did not stop.

Both Audrey and I attended Walcott Church and were currently enrolled in confirmation classes. At the end of the classes, you had an oral examination with the Reverend Coleburn.

All through the classes I had asked many questions, most of which were not answered to my satisfaction. When it came to my turn for the exam, Reverend Coleburn said that because of my many questions, my faith was not suitable for confirmation. In fact, he was just upset that I asked him questions he couldn't answer. Audrey didn't pass either probably because we were friends.

We both left that church. We both started at the Bath Abbey, which we really liked. We enrolled in the next confirmation class taken by the Archdeacon of Bath. During these classes, I asked the same sort of questions, some of which he could not answer.

At the end of the classes, the Archdeacon told me I was a delight to have in his class. He said, "I don't have all the answers, but never stop searching." Both of us passed the oral exam, and were confirmed in the Bath Abbey. We joined the Abbey youth club and found everyone to be much nicer than the Walcott Church bunch.

Every Saturday afternoon at about this period, Audrey and I would go to town, and go into several of the big department stores and try on all the ladies' hats. This was in the time of fancy felt hats with feathers, ribbons, artificial fruit, bows, and occasionally net veils. We must have been known to all the assistants, but we were never bothered even though we could not be serious buyers. We did this for years and knew when new stock came in and when the seasons and fashions changed. When I look back now, this seems like strange behavior, but we enjoyed it.

On one of our walks, we walked to Bathampton weir, on the River Avon, and went into the Old Mill which had been turned into a tea garden and cafe. We ordered tea and scones and were having a grand time. Then it was time to go. Suddenly, we discovered that neither of us had any money, and we panicked. We were about 16 and we didn't know what to do.

Then I spied Paul Morgan, one of the boys at the Abbey youth club, whom we both knew, walking over the bridge. I flew out and called him and luckily he had a half crown which he was willing to loan me until the next youth club meeting. It was at this bridge that I'd seen my second dead body, a year or so earlier. It was being pulled out of the river.

Sometimes, when we could afford it, Audrey and I would rent a boat on the river, and row up and down. I was a pretty good oarsman and could stroke and feather quite well.

One day we heard some exciting news. We were all going to Dad's sister's husband's farm for a couple of weeks while they went on holiday. As you know, he grew up on a farm and knew exactly what was needed. This was the first of what became an annual occurrence once Uncle Stan had completed hay-making. We all enjoyed our stay at the farm.

Some of us had to do jobs. We would have to collect the eggs from the hen houses in the orchard, and put them into special egg crates, and they were picked up periodically. We had to shut the hens in at night because of the foxes, but they ran free all day. We got covered with fleas.

The front of the farm faced the road. If you stood on the road, which wasn't very wide (just a country lane), to the left was a double gate, leading to the cow sheds and cow yard. Immediately to the left of the gate was a large stable big enough for 4 horses, 3 cart horses, and Cousin Anne's pony. The cart horses were Prince, a gray-white stallion, Piebald, a brown and white, and Chestnut, a very spirited light chestnut. They were all very large horses with hooves like dinner plates.

There were three separate cow sheds, all stone built, which housed up to one hundred cows. There was a dairy building where the milk went through the coolers, and beyond that, the bull house.

At one time, there were 5 farm laborers, who would milk the cows by hand. Eventually, this number was reduced when milking machines were installed. During the warmer weather, the cows were out all day except for the two milkings. They seemed to know when and where to come. But when the colder weather came, they stayed in the cow sheds, only coming out twice a day when the cow sheds were mucked out. The cows always knew their own stalls.

The cows were haltered for milking, and some were difficult and had to have their legs tied up as they would kick. A couple of them were very fierce, especially the red cow which had long horns. This cow chased my sister Susan all over a field, and she came back to the farm very distressed one day. Following that we teased her that the red cow was going to get her.

One day I found a cow's tooth in one of the mangers.

One time we were there for the last of the haymaking, and I was dispatched with one of the horses, Piebald. I had a loaded hay cart, to cross 3 fields to the rick-yard, all alone. This meant getting horse and cart through 4 narrow gates. You did this by holding the horse's head and walking backward eyeing the clearance, guiding the horse, with it pulling against you, and snorting and stamping. The horse's head was so high, that I had my arm straight up in the air as high as it could go.

Every year, we had to rake the fields. This was to pick up the last of the hay after the main hay-making. It was done with a horse and rake with wheels, and we walked beside it. Most years our father put the horse in the shafts for us, but one time, when I was about 15, he left it to my younger brother John and me.

We had to go three fields away from the farm, catch 2 horses, and back them into the shafts of the rakes so that we had one rake each. I told John there was no way I was going into the field until the horses were in the shafts, so he got Piebald into one rake and was backing Prince into the other when the horse's leg touched the shaft, and it went berserk, lashing out and rearing. It smashed one shaft and went off galloping around the field. I hopped over the fence out of harm's way. I yelled to John to get out of the field.

I flew back to the farm to get Dad. He came out to the field and caught the horse and controlled it with some difficulty. It was a terrifying experience, and I would have nothing to do with horses after that.

From the road, the farmhouse looked like a square 2-storey building, but on the left side, it went way back to the bull house. Above where the bull was kept was the cheese room. The cheese was not currently made there but all of the old equipment was still in place. However, butter was still made there in a hand-cranked churn. It was hard work, but the reward was the great sound of the plop plop of a blob of freshly made butter. It was pure white and tasted heavenly.

In the cheese room right above the bull house, there was another feature. At some point in the history of this 250-year-old farm, somebody had put up a swing with chains hanging from the roof rafters. It made a horrible squeaking noise as we swung to and fro. This seemed to irritate the bull as it would snort and pull on and rattle its chain. The chain was long, allowing wide movement.

One of John's jobs was to pour a bucket of water into the bull's water trough. I would not go near. It was a different bull every year. I assume this was to save in-breeding. The one which I was most scared of was a white one which had pink rings around its eyes. It looked awful.

I went to the farm on my own a couple of times to stay when I was a bit older. The means of getting there was to walk to the Bath train station carrying a case of clothes etc. and then catch a train that stopped at every station or halt (a train stop without a station or employees). You would have to get off at Christian Malford Halt, in the middle of nowhere, and walk about 5 miles to the farm, still with the case. There was no such thing as a case with wheels in those days.

A couple of times when more of us went, Uncle Stan met us with his tiny car to drive us back. His driving warranted a complete book on its own. He would rarely look ahead and veered from side to side, but cars were such a rarity that we survived. There was a story told that another car did appear from the opposite direction once, and Auntie Margaret jumped out with the car still moving as she was so afraid. This is sworn to be the truth, and I believe it, knowing Auntie Margaret and Uncle Stan's driving.

On one of my lone visits, Cousin Anne and I were sent out to help with the potato planting. The fields were already prepared with the furrows already dug. We had to walk along straddling the furrow, dropping a seed potato every 18". This is backbreaking work as you either have to carry a very heavy bucket or keep going back for refills. I was there again for the potato harvest and we dug up the potatoes, all by hand, and there was a field of them.

One day at the farm, Anne and I rode bicycles to the Cherril White Horse. For those who aren't familiar with this, the white horses of Wiltshire are hundreds of yards wide, dug mostly by ancient Britons. Most of the area is on limestone/chalk subsoil, and if you remove the top bit, you expose the chalk. There are many famous shapes cut out this way, but mostly horses. You can see some of them from 30 miles away as they are mostly cut on the near vertical sides of high hills.

If you leaned out of my bedroom window at the farm, you could reach down and pick greengages from a tree that grew like a vine up the wall of the house. Auntie Margaret loved them, and she would get most upset when she would find them gone.

At Christmas, the geese would be killed and plucked for traditional Christmas dinners. You should remember that the turkey is a Native American bird and was not known in "olde tyme" England when traditions had their start. So it was traditional to have geese for Christmas dinner. The down feathers from the geese were saved, baked, cured, and stored in the cheese room. At the time of writing, we have pillows still in use in our house that I made myself from this farmhouse goose down.

When I look back at those days at Hare Street Farm, they were some of the happiest times of my childhood. Probably the first thing that comes to mind is the stone cream desserts that Auntie Margaret used to make especially for us. It has always been my favorite dessert.

At home, I shared a bedroom for some years with my sister Susan. Susan is four years younger than me and was at that time a bit in awe of me. I was the formidable big sister. Sometimes I would scare her to death by telling ghost stories and then pulling on a piece of wool that I had previously attached to the door knob, making the door move. The wool had to pass under Susan's bed as she was closest to the door. One day her screams caused Mum to come upstairs to investigate. Boy, was I in trouble. However, Susan was pretty gullible and at times I could really get her going with my stories. By and large, we were very good friends and remain so to this day.

At the age of 16, I was due to leave the City of Bath Girls School. Three months before that, my best friend, Audrey Hill had left the school to go to typing school to become a secretary. One of the last things we did at school together was to play hookey, on the day that candy/sweets came off ration. We left school and went into the town to buy sweets. To our horror, we bumped into Miss Harvey, from whose class we had played truant.

She challenged us and asked what we were doing, and told us she would report us to the Headmistress, Miss Cook. The next day was the last one before the Easter holidays so we decided to skip the next day also. However, when I got home, my mother asked if there was anything I wished to tell her. I said "NO". So she said, "Well, I just had an interesting call from Miss Cook, (we'd had a telephone for about 2 years), and she can't wait to see you tomorrow." I replied that we'd decided to not go tomorrow. Mum said, "Oh yes you are."

That evening Audrey and I met and discussed our fate and realized that it looked like we were in for it, so decided to become ill by taking lots of aspirin. We took about 10 each and felt absolutely fine, so off to school we went. We were sent to sit in a room with a secretary to await our fate. We were there for about 2 hours, with talk about expulsion etc., but then a secretary came in to tell us to return to our classroom as we had suffered enough. It was Audrey's last day, so she could not really be punished, which probably saved a greater punishment. Audrey and I remain friends still, in fact, she paid us a long visit a few years ago after her husband died.

When I finally left school, an insurance policy on me, matured, and with the proceeds, Mum bought me a winter coat, a skirt, and a blouse. This was all the outer clothes that I had, other than a couple of cardigans and sweaters that I had knitted myself. My school uniform was worn out and not of any use now.

Everything else I had to buy out of my earnings. Audrey was always well-dressed.

I wanted to be a nurse. I saw an advertisement in a newspaper for probationary nursing students at the London hospital, and I sent for application forms. I was under 21 which required my parents to give their written consent, which they refused to do. I was told I was going to work for the Post Office as a telephone operator. I must admit that I found the possibility of leaving home attractive. By this time my sister Christine was born, making 7 children.

Chapter 6 - Brian at the Senior School by Brian

At the new address, there were new children and new places to get to know. However, at about the same time, Bobby Wallace and family showed up, arriving at a house about 100 yards away. One of the new kids named Walter Hodges, commonly called Bing (after Bing Crosby, the singer, because Walter had a deep voice), had also passed the scholarship and would be going to the same school as me. A staggering piece of information suddenly became apparent. Here I was, now just 11, and the baby of the family for all these years, and my mother was now pregnant at 43 years of age.

My sister Christine had recently gone off to Canada as a war bride, Sylvia was working as a typist in the Admiralty, Brenda was a cashier at Kings of Milsom Street, Bath, and Daphne went to Twerton West Central Senior School. Kings was probably one of the poshest stores in Bath where only the wealthy shopped. During the war, controls were put on clothes (and every other item) to prevent black marketing. When everything is short, there is always somebody who will provide it if you pay more. There was a very limited amount of uncontrolled clothing available for a much higher price, which Kings sold. Now all controlled items had a "Utility Label" sown into them (The utility clothing label was two identical solid black circles with a right angle chunk removed). Apparently, the rich old dears in Bath would not buy Utility clothing and there was limited uncontrolled clothing available, so Brenda had a fill-in job when not busy, of removing utility labels. The rich would pay lots more for it and go off happy. Of course, this was illegal, and the store would have been closed down if it had been revealed.

The City Of Bath Boys' School was at Beechen Cliff. It was on a hill on the south side of the city. You could get there by the winding hill to The Bear Flat, and then, you had to walk up steep Kipling Avenue, about ½ mile. On the north side of the hill, facing the actual downtown area was a steep cliff which gave a magnificent view all over this beautiful and historic city, almost like seeing it from the air. You could climb the cliff by way of hundreds of steps called Jacob's ladder. The school was about 200 yards from the cliff, and on the highest point for miles around.

Everything was different about this school. I had to wear a sort of uniform, a gray suit with short trousers, and a school cap (A suit for me cost one week's wage). I would have lots of homework, and carry books which necessitated what we called a satchel. The decent ones were leather and cost almost 1/5 of a weekly wage! You could get canvas ones for about half price but they didn't last, and there was a certain amount of snobbery at this school, so the pressure was on. (It is interesting to note here that we recently bought small backpacks, made in Taiwan, for $5 each. There were no cheap products from the Orient in those days. That area had recently been under the control of the Japanese Imperial Army). By the way, short trousers were what young boys wore until they were 13 or 14, depending to some degree on their size. In a freezing, damp country like England, short trousers make no sense. We used to walk in pouring rain and freezing damp weather in these short pants, with socks up to just below our knees. In the rain, our legs and socks would be wet and our shoes full of water. The bottoms of our trousers would be wet also and as we walked, the wet trousers would rub against the back of our knees and make them raw. Every boy had nasty red sore patches at the back of his knees in the winter.

All at once the school holiday was over, and the first day at the new school loomed. I had to walk about a mile to catch the number 15 bus which went down Englishcombe Lane to the Bear Flat. Then came the long walk up Kipling Avenue. The Bear Flat was a sea of school caps. They were in groups or singles, some had bicycles. It was most noticeable that the very smallest boys were mostly alone, and seemed somewhat lost. In droves, we walked up the hill until we reached the gate at which there were some older boys asking for new boys to identify themselves. (It was easy to pick new boys out as the new caps showed up so well). These were prefects, and from that moment we understood we were "fags". This did not mean that we automatically changed our lifestyle or sexual orientation. At that time, the word "fag" meant either a cigarette or it was the name given to first-formers or new boys at the school. In the old English boarding schools, boys in the last year or so always had a "fag". They were servants to the older boys and would do shopping, clean shoes, make tea and wash dishes, and generally fetch and carry for them. It was supposed to "build character". All of this was not a requirement for this school, the title of fag was only used as a means of putting us in our place.

We were led to our new classroom to meet our class master or teacher. He was Mr. Prosser. He was short in stature carrying more weight than he should for his height, with slicked-back hair and really thick black frames to his glasses. He was not a warm person by any means. All the teachers wore the old type of black teacher's gowns, similar to those worn by choirs. They did not wear mortar boards as in the days of old.

The first days were continuous new activities. We were given books about several subjects which we had not studied before, such as Latin ugh, French, Physics, Biology, Chemistry, Algebra, Geometry etc. etc. The sports to which we would be exposed were Rugby and football in winter, and cricket and track athletics in summer. The 90 new boys were divided into 3 classes of 30 boys. The teachers for the other 2 new classes, besides Mr. Prosser, were Mr. Anderson, thereafter known as Ghandi, and Mr. Gardner, thereafter known as Spud, the object of my wrath at a later date. Apparently, Mr. Prosser was such a colorless individual that he never did have a nickname. Then the homework started.

There were half a dozen boys from my old school who had also passed the scholarship and were in my class. Also Fatty Fletcher and David Hart were there but in another class. After a few months, Mr. Prosser mysteriously disappeared. He was replaced by Mr. Kirkpatrick, a most miserable human being, completely devoid of any humor or human-type feelings. He was universally disliked by the boys and you could tell, by the rest of the staff alike. He taught mathematics. In the 5 years I was at that school nobody ever saw him smile. It is fitting that just after I left that school he died at about 55, and he could no longer torture small boys. I think he had nothing to live for, which certainly was the impression we got.

The next step in our initiation was to be divided up into "houses". This was purely for competitive purposes and a holdover from the old boarding school days. We were all lined up and the names of the 5 houses were repeated over and over and as the teacher passed you, you got your assignment. I was put in Baker's house. Mr. Baker was commonly known as Doughy Baker, an old-time teacher with real personality and obvious affection for the boys and the career he had chosen. He taught chemistry. The other 4 houses, took the names of other senior teachers. Our house color was green. Every morning the 500 boys of the school met for "Assembly" which was the name for prayers and hymn singing before the day started. If you were late for school you had to line up outside the assembly room and give your excuses to a prefect. Once a month assembly was held as a House, and Bakers house met in Doughy Baker's laboratory.

The chosen methods of punishment were beatings with a tennis shoe with the recipient bent over. 3 strokes were normal, but 6 strokes were for extra evil deeds. Also, prefects meted out detention, where you stayed after school, and just sat and stared at the wall for 45 minutes under the glare of a prefect who didn't want to be there either. Most evenings we had as much as two hours of homework, and it was always a tussle between doing it or playing first. If you played first, there was always this black cloud hanging over you, but if you did the homework first, it was more fun, knowing the homework was done. The truth is that many a morning I would run all the way to school to do a bit of homework before school started or do it between lessons if that subject was later in the day.

The school year had started in September, and the first large function was the annual Cross Country Race. There were the junior and senior races. The junior race included most of the 3rd form or 3rd year, 14-year-olds, which I didn't think was fair with them running against the youngest of 10 years of age. Our PT or Physical Training sessions for weeks before the race were devoted to running around the course, but somehow I avoided doing it at all. I thought I was real smart until the day of the race when I was really out of condition compared with the other boys, and 100 yards down Kipling Avenue I had the most awful stitch or in Americanese, cramps. Historically, there was always a small group of undersized boys who pre-arranged to walk the course and cross the finish line together so they could claim they were not the only ones last. By The time my stitch cleared up, this group was 200 yards ahead of me. I started running. There were prefects at all the corners and gates etc., and at the halfway point out of 270 runners, I was 110th. I was still overtaking boys at the end and I was 55th, and earned points for the house. Now I'm sorry that I didn't practice with the others. I might have done very well. As it was, I really started the race 300 to 400 yards behind the leaders. I remember thinking as the race neared the school that I was amazed at how short the race was. I could have run twice as far and a lot faster. But I've always had a tendency to take it easy if I could get away with it.

Before long it was Christmas. My sister Sylvia had given up work and was staying at home with our mother. On January 17th, 1947, I suddenly had a baby sister named Rosemary Patricia. The winter had started badly and now the weather had really turned mean. We had many feet of snow, which didn't melt before the next lot. It stayed bitterly cold for weeks on end. We lived on the top of one of the highest hills in the city where we got the worst of it. The roads were frozen and virtually impassable. The double-decker green Bath Bus Company buses could not get up the hills meaning we had to walk miles. I was once on a bus that tried, and the driver got a good run at a steep bit but gradually lost traction until we were not going forward, then, we started sliding backward and came to rest crossways on the road. It is a very uncomfortable place to be, on the top of a double-decker stopped sideways on a hill after sliding backward out of control. It's a wonder those vehicles never turn over.

The winter of 1947 went down in the history books as one of the worst winters in living memory, but I was 11 and it was great fun for me. I still had my toboggan! The first time I took it out I was disappointed in its performance, then realized the runners were rusty. Within a short time they were shiny as new and, look out here I came. It would convey me at speed down the slightest slope and again was the envy of all the local kids. By accident, the spring steel of the metal runners was the best steel I could have. A softer metal would not have worked as well.

A few of us decided we would go to Twerton Roundhill with our toboggans as this was a famous steep cone-shaped hill and the very highest point around the south of Bath. Unfortunately, it had parallel roads on the north and south sides, not leaving much "flat" on which to slow down. When we got there we found lots of kids with all sorts of home-made toboggans, and there was one fancy professional model. The surface was like glass. I had my first go from halfway up the hill and got up tremendous speed, and only just stopped a few feet from the road. It was great but left me with a feeling that I was not in control once the toboggan started moving. For the uninitiated, we laid on our stomachs and changed direction by dragging one toe in the snow. If you dragged your left toe you went left etc.

I was approached by the boy with the professional model, toboggan that is, (not a woman), and he wanted a go on mine. I didn't mind as it meant I could use his, but I warned him to only go from halfway. He chose to ignore me and went to the very top, and down he came, and thundered right across the road into somebody's garden finishing in an untidy heap. He returned to where I was standing and had tear streaks down his face. He had been thoroughly scared. As the afternoon wore on, with freezing temperatures and the surface receiving continuing polishing, I was finding myself going further and further toward the street before I could stop. The last straw was when I did go halfway across the street and a huge beer barrel delivery truck skidded to a stop just about 4 feet from me. It was hard for vehicles to stop as they were on a gritty ice surface.

It was about now that my father got into the habit of going occasionally to a pub in the evening. He had not done this before. It would have been very much frowned on, nay, it would have turned them puce at the stuffy Plymouth Brethren. Anyway, he got to know a couple of good old boys namely Johnny Symes and Bill Lord. Johnny was of average height, somewhat overweight, 48ish, and divorced. He was one of the nicest, kindest people you could wish to meet. He loved his beer, and having a good time. Any pub would do. He had a broad country accent and would tell all sorts of tall tales of his exploits when he was under the influence. His business was upholstery, re-covering favorite armchairs, etc. He had this motorbike made about 25 years earlier and had this long half-ton capacity flatbed sidecar attached with which he made pick-ups and deliveries. (More about the motorbike and sidecar later). He did not overwork himself, just did enough to pay for his rent and beer. His sidekick was Bill Lord. He was very tall and slim. He spoke with an accent learned at a fancy British public school and although very courteous and proper, he was not the personality that Johnny was. He was single and could have been somebody, but I believe he liked the sauce too much.

Father would bring these two home sometimes and we'd all have a good happy time. Johnny was funny, and developed a special attachment to my sister Sylvia, although he was too old and run down for her. She was flattered and also enjoyed the company. She was still at home helping with baby Rosemary and didn't get to meet too many people. I always remember that Johnny had his own way of saying “Sylvia”. It sounded like “Sylviawl”. He always put the "L" on the end. One day he told us of the story when he had rented a room at a house at 4 The Vineyards, Bath. This was in an old row of Georgian historic houses near the center of Bath. Apparently, he was woken up several times with hands around his throat but there was nobody there! The obvious thought at the time was that he'd had a few too many, but he swore it happened in that house, even when he was sober. There was no doubt that something strange did happen there.

These houses in The Vineyards were more than 200 years old and little did I think that my life would lead me to situations very close and similar.

These two men visited from time to time for many years. Read on.

About this time sister Brenda, who had always had a few boyfriends around, brought home David Horatio Elliott. He was a draughtsman (US version=draftsman) in the Admiralty. Now, if you remember, I was a pretty fast runner. David, who was a short, somewhat stocky fellow, challenged me to a race and beat me easily. I told him to just wait until I was 12. Anyway, he invited me to go to the annual Admiralty Sports (Track Athletics) and he won the 440 yards easily. David was a keep-fit type, to his credit. He didn't smoke or drink. He was born in Kent, in Gillingham I believe. We were good friends and did some stupid things together. One of them was onion eating contests. It is very simple if you would like to try it. Peel some raw apple size onions, one per contestant, and all start eating together. The one who eats the onion, and opens his mouth first to show it is empty, is the winner. If two people tie, then they have to do it again as a run-off. If one declines then the other is a winner. You also need an impartial judge as contestants cannot see for tears. I used to prepare a saucer of vinegar and salt and dip my onion between bites as this seemed to help in getting it down. This falls within the rules.

David had a nice maroon car when we first got to know him, but soon he turned up with another car, a black scruffy-looking old Jowett Javelin. It was a comical looking two-seater with a dickey. For those who don't know what this is, the car has what appears to be an extended trunk (boot in England), and there is a lid, the front end of which opens and leans back and forms the back of a second row of seats. Why anybody would make a car in England with outside seats or own one is beyond me. It might be nice for the average two days of summer, but for the other 363 days, it was a recipe for pneumonia. The strangest feature of the car was the fact that it had only 2 cylinders and the racket it made brought everybody out to see what it was. Now David definitely had a tendency to be a very careful spender, and 2 cylinders are cheaper to run than 4 or 6, so this was probably the reason for the change, plus the bonus of not having to take the family along. However, David took me out a few times. In this day and age, it is hard to believe that an 11-year-old boy regarded riding in a car as a real treat, but throughout the war, no private cars ran.

There was a subject in which David had a great interest. It was hypnotism. One day he told me he was going to see a friend to hypnotize him to make his hair grow. OK, I was game, so off we went. We arrived at this gentleman's flat, which was the top floor of a 5-storey house on Pulteney Street, one of the magnificent rows of Georgian houses in Bath. The top floor had obviously been for servants as it had low ceilings and the front wall sloped inward with Dormer windows. But it was home when you consider the thousands of buildings destroyed in the war. Anyway, the hypnotism started and to my amazement, the fellow went out like a light. David mumbled on about hair growth and then ended up with a statement to the effect that when the subject woke up he would want some water, but it would taste like wine. So the order to wake up was given and he came around and asked for water. David handed him a cracked dirty old cup with water in it and the subject drank and stopped in surprise. He told us that the water tasted like wine!

Pretty soon David and Brenda got married, moved to the London area, and had a flat in my Uncle Ron's house at 19 Priory Hill in Dartford. Houses or flats were impossible to find. While she was there she entered a local Dartford beauty contest and won. Then she went through a series of bigger and bigger contests and finished up winning the bathing beauty title for the entire county of Kent. Brenda, who had always been interested in dancing, got a job as a showgirl in a review-type show at the London Casino as a result of all this, which was the start of the rest of her life. This show ran for 9 months of the year, and for the other 3 months they had the Christmas Pantomime, so Brenda had that time off. For the uninitiated, nearly all live theaters had a Christmas pantomime. It was a large part of every child's Christmas season. The story was usually a well-known fairy story like Jack and the Beanstalk, or Cinderella, but interspersed with funny skits, and audience participation like singing, one side of the theater against the other, or the children were asked to yell out if a certain performer did something bad (purposely). The hero or Jack or the prince who married Cinderella, were always played by shapely ladies, and Jack's or Cinderella's mother was always played by the show's main comedian. A grand time was had by all, and the discussion was always about whether it was better than last year's.

My sister Brenda related an interesting story, which made me think, and is an insight into the way people operate. Every night after she finished Latin Quarter, near midnight, she would walk to the underground to catch the train home. This particular night her stocking started to come loose from her suspender, and she got into a shop doorway to fix it. A late-night reveler on a bicycle stopped and was making crude comments. She asked him politely to leave, but he wouldn't. Brenda, can be somewhat aggressive when required, got mad, and screamed at him "f.....off you dirty son of a bitch". At this, he fled, which, tells me two things. One, that there are times when assumed or demonstrated anger, and speaking the language of the gutter can be very effective, and the authoritative statement added urgency to the situation. When one gets angry the other can be intimidated. When two are both angry then there can be a fight. This is what I call "wisdom" which you will read more later.

There were two jobs that always fell to me from about the age of 10, which I absolutely hated. They were similar in that Sundays always seemed to come as a complete surprise to my parents. The stores were nearly all closed and my father would run out of his life's blood, cigarettes/tobacco, and my mother with a house full of females, would run out of necessary items for them. With the latter, I would be handed a large shopping bag with a note and money inside, and be told to hand it to an assistant at a chemist's shop (pharmacy) if I could find one open. Of course, I had to act dumb and not know what this was all about, which I carried out very well. The other item for my father, was a bit tougher. Firstly, there were nearly always chemists open for emergency medicines, but there were very few newsagents, or tobacconists open. Also, they were not supposed to sell tobacco or cigarettes to minors under 16. I would cover miles maybe walking or riding Christine's Rudge bicycle, until I got my own bike. His instructions were quite clear. His order of preference was, starting with his favorite tobacco: St. Julian Best, St. Bruno Rough Cut, St. Bruno Flake, (I think he put these three first because it was Sunday and they have religious connotations), Condor Sliced, or A1. Then he would say "If you can't get these, get anything, and don't come back without something". Off I would go, and scour the streets for a shop that was open, but maybe they wouldn't sell to me. However, I always found somebody who would sell to me, but very often they would not have any of the tobaccos he liked, so I'd have to make a decision. Every single time I bought an alternative, I'd get home to, "That stuff is no good, and I'd rather you got nothing rather than that ". Occasionally I did get nothing, then had to go back for "anything".

My father had been occasionally going to the Jubilee Pub. There he met and got to know one Walter Charles Walters. (Same last name, thereafter known as Charles). He had recently been demobilized from the Royal Air Force and had been winding down for some time at the Jubilee, their local pub, with his brother Sydney. Eventually, Father told Sylvia about him and a meeting was arranged. Sylvia was/is a bit different to the rest of us. She is more like me, a gentle soul without the killer instincts of my other sisters. She really needed a more sympathetic type of man and Charles was that type. Things went well and eventually, they got married in about 1948 in the tiny village church in Englishcombe village, just a couple of miles into the country beyond the area of the Jubilee pub.

Charles used to go to watch Bath City football club play as did my father and me. We met Charles and Sydney there most weeks and it was then that I learned that Sydney had a son named Brian Walters!! I met Brian. He was almost exactly my age, and he was a very busy soccer player. He went to a regular school where they played soccer, not the snobbish Rugby like we played at my school. In England at that time, rugby was the game of the elite, and soccer (called football) was the game of the masses. I didn't invent these rules, I just had to live with them. It is interesting to note that at the City of Bath Boys School, we played soccer on the field at lunchtime, which was something that got us all into trouble. The other Brian Walters eventually played for Bath, and as he got older he played for the top teams in England.

In playing on the muddy field at lunchtime we would collect a wedge of mud just in front of the heel of our shoes. Some comedians would roll it into little balls and throw it around the classroom. There was one teacher named Guerrier, commonly called Pop Guerrier, who was a lax disciplinarian, and gradually boys got brave and did it in his history class. This went on for weeks, with an occasional mud ball thudding into the blackboard as he wrote on it. Pop Guerrier must have complained about it as one day, the assistant headmaster, Mr. Matthews, called Marcus, (he taught Latin) got us all out in the corridor and we all got 3 whacks with a tennis shoe for the mud throwing. The walls and high ceilings were covered in little mounds of hardened mud.

It was now spring 1947. I was almost 12 and at school, there was talk about qualifying. What was this qualifying? It turned out to be time and standard trials for all track and field athletic events. However, I had had a series of mysterious pains in my stomach. I was sent home from school twice, then it came on really bad, and I started vomiting. I found myself in hospital for my 12th birthday, having my appendix removed. In no time I was back at school, and in time for the qualifying. I passed everyone easily, and each pass earned points for the house. The next event on the calendar was the school sports day when the best in each house competed for house points. David Hart, my old racing buddy was in Baker's house also, and I can see Doughy Baker asking for volunteers to do their best events. I kept quiet, but there was nobody to do the high jump, and I'd not done this before, but he assigned it to me as he said I was the tallest and should be the best. This was the only event I was in, and now it was time to perform. There were 2 boys from each house making 10 in all in the high jump. We used the scissor style. The outcome was that Brian Arthur George (known as Bag) Weston won and I was second. I thought "Wait 'til I'm 13".

I thought this high-jumping lark was pretty good and I thought I should have another go at this. The annual Bath Co-op fete or carnival was coming up. We all went one fine Saturday afternoon and first off Sylvia won the beauty contest then up came the kids' events. I won the high jump and the 100 yards, and got a couple of prizes. We had a good day. Sylvia's picture was in the local paper the next day, and of course, my name was also. Suddenly, at school, I'm an athlete and could practice the high jump instead of playing cricket and other boring stuff. I even got out of practicing and running in the next Cross Country race and subsequent races for the rest of the time at school.

The rest of the year was quite uneventful, with not much to report. My sisters and I all felt that this "fete" business was a great way of cashing in, so we looked around for more. Daphne was about 15 when we went to the Box fete. Box was a small village east of Bath, on the road to London. Daphne won the beauty contest and I won a whole bunch of prizes for running and jumping. Luckily, I took a small bag to carry my prizes.

I believe it was this year that my mother got a bee in her bonnet about moving again, and the lino pieces got even smaller. We moved again to 16 Moorfield Road, Bath. Our next-door neighbors to the right were the Barretts, and the other side were the Crosby's. Again there were lots of kids to play with and plenty to keep us occupied in the area. The road was not busy and good for games. The Crosby's children were mostly grown up, but the Barretts had 4 children, from the youngest, they were Sean, Josephine, Colin, and Connie. I was about 13 now, Connie was 14 months older than me and Colin was about a year younger. Connie had contracted rheumatic fever when she was young, which had damaged her heart valves. She was supposed to take it easy, but she never did and was up to all sorts of mischief. I spent more time with Connie than anybody else. She was fun. She laughed and joked all the time. We went places together and had a happy time. You would never dream how sick she really was. Her father doted on her and supported her in everything whilst begging her to take it easy. He had a shoe repair store and a license for orthopedic shoe repair and manufacture. On the side, he was a bookmaker and made most of his money this way. He almost openly had a girlfriend. Her husband was almost certainly aware of it, but apparently, the money she received allowed him to turn a blind eye. Mrs. Barrett, a bit of a whiner, made much worse by her situation, was extremely unhappy and let everybody know it. She was very sad and I felt sorry for her, but the moaning and complaining did not help her case. I also feel that she was jealous of her own daughter, Connie, who was great friends with her father and his girlfriend but had little time for her mother. As is normal, Mr. Barrett was surrounded by a bunch of what I called "hangers-on". These were virtually illiterate people who would fall out of the pub and stagger across the street to place bets with Joe Barrett, then hang around to hear results and gossip.

Joe had nobody who could write fast enough to take the phone calls from his runners, (agents who would collect bets for him and phone them in), and he knew that he was being cheated. Then I told him that I could write almost as fast as you could speak, and he gave me a Saturday job. I would scribble down the bets in a book, and he was saved all sorts of money. He knew that the horse gambling business and petty larceny go hand in hand. He rewarded me handsomely and I became almost one of the family.

There was one memorable time. My parents had decided we should go to Burnham on Sea, a small seaside town in Somerset, just up the coast from north Devon. We rented a caravan (trailer) for the week. I remember that Daphne, Brenda, and Sylvia were there also, and a couple of boyfriends, but the exact details elude me.

One lunchtime, we all walked down this little country road and found a pub, and we all sat in the garden and were drinking “hard” or rough cider. This cider is a very strong alcoholic drink, and also very inexpensive which means you can afford to buy a lot. Being a grown-up 13 years of age I was able to keep up with the men and got drunk before my parents knew what was happening. The boyfriends were happy to keep plying me just for devilment's sake. We returned to the caravan, with me trying to walk down the line in the center of the road, egged on by the boyfriends and my sisters. Apparently, I didn't make a very good job of it. That was my first time drunk.

Last year, in the high jump event, Brian Weston beat me at 4' 9" to my 4' 8". But I was now 13, and he jumped 4'10" and I jumped 5'3", and broke the junior high jump record of 4 '11".That was the last time Bag Weston ever did the high jump. This was in the days when the modern Fosbury Flop would have been called diving and so it would have been illegal.

At about this time, I was in a geography lesson with Spud Gardner, a short, fat, and mean teacher. He was so boring that you could always see several boys with books propped up on their stomachs, resting on the edge of their desks with folded story comics inside. This particular day, for some reason, I did not have a comic, and with nothing better to do, I was listening and following the book. The desks were on a series of steps rising toward the back of the room. I was not aware of where he was, but he had walked up an aisle at the far side of the room and walked through some empty desks at the top, and was coming down the aisle to my right. Suddenly, I got an almighty whack around the head and I leaped to my feet with my fist ready to knock the boy behind me into the middle of next week. But it wasn't the boy, it was Spud Gardner. He was on the step above but due to my rapid growth, he was at eye level with me. He flinched, and I yelled, "What was that for?" His stammered answer was, "I thought you had a comic", and he carried on with the lesson. There was no apology, and no request to see me afterwards. For the rest of my school days, he didn't say anything to me or look at me. When we passed in the corridor, he would look down on the ground. I had to wait 6 years before he finally paid. Look for the end of this story years later.

It was not long before Mother got the bee in her bonnet about moving again. We moved to 53 Freeview Road in Twerton, a suburb of Bath. We had fields behind and a field across the road in front, with no kids at all on our road. The round of school and homework kept me busy for a large part of every evening. I was now approaching 6 feet tall and still growing. I drank one pint (English pint = 20 oz.) of full cream Guernsey milk at home and two 1/3 pint bottles at school. I had been eating everything in sight for a couple of years. About this time we saw the last of the rationing, so there was only the cost to worry about. I remember that my mother bought me a very expensive pair of shoes, at about 1/3rd of a week's wages, and in three months my left shoe had worn through. My left shoe always seemed to get all the wear. I high jumped off my left foot, so it is possible that my left leg is the strongest. My clothes were costing the same as a man's.

Twerton was several miles from our previous house and it would take 2 buses to reach there, so I lost contact with the Barretts. The new house was near Bath City football ground, in fact, one corner of the enclosing fence was just about 120 yards away to the right on the other side of the road. Behind the football field and at the end of our road there was a park called Innox Park. It had swings, slides, etc. at the flat lower end nearest the football field, but sloped upwards away from the football field. It is bordered by large Elm trees. Beyond the park was a large housing development with the same name, with lots of children of all ages. I probably omitted to say that anybody who went to the City of Bath Boys or Girls School was regarded as close to God by all the other kids and adults, and there was only one kid in the Innox Park area who claimed that distinction. His name was David Grimm, and he was in my year. He was almost as tall as me, but not too bright, but fun. He was known as Gaffer Grimm, a name given to him by one of the teachers at school who thought he was a busybody.

As related earlier, Bath was built on limestone, the building material of choice in the city. Not only were there quarries all over, the ground was half dirt and the rest was rocks, almost fist size. Our house was at a slightly higher elevation than the near corner of the football field, which was fenced by 10 feet high corrugated galvanized metal. There was a footpath coming from Innox Park along the metal fence, which came into the field in front of our house. On the opposite side of the field were the village's main road and the pub. Most evenings a couple of Andy Capp types would appear on the footpath at the corner of the football field, and walk diagonally down through the field to the pub. Anyway, I think there is always a temptation on the part of kids to throw stones at metal fences. I was no different, and we had thousands of rocks in the flower borders, I had a target and could throw. At first, I couldn't reach the fence, but after some weeks, I finally was able to hit the corner. Both sides sloped away from me so accuracy helped. It was dead quiet, no traffic noise, only birds singing and I was just about to throw a rock one day when an Andy Capp appeared. I waited until he was out of my range, but just a short distance from the fence, and let fly without thinking. The stone struck the fence with a loud clang and the poor man jumped with shock. He stopped and looked around him, but nothing happened. I expected him to come and tell my mother, but he stood for a moment and looked around again, then walked on. Why did he not come and at least yell at me? The only explanation is that he thought I was too far away. Now I had a new game which I kept up for years. I was doing a wonderful job of clearing the rocks, and in time I could follow the poor gentleman's way down the field, what seemed to me to be at least 150 yards, and out of sight. More about this later.

Daphne, my "nearest in age", sister was getting married, much to the wrath of my parents. They said she was far too young, but it went ahead anyway. She married Colin Brain, from Colerne in the county of Wiltshire. Colerne was a pretty village high on a plateau almost overlooking Bath, but just across the county line. Colin was a refrigeration engineer.

To my delight, (I was a mature 14-year-old), Innox Park was absolutely bursting with lovely young creatures, all about 14 years of age. The prize was Kathy Love, a shapely young lady who looked every bit of 16. Gaffer Grimm used to drool over her. The park had park benches spread around, and it was normal to see kids sitting in twos and threes in the evening. Well, to my delight, Kathy Love appeared to seek me out, and we spent many an evening sitting in the park together until long after dark. I was very shy and bashful at this age which I regret to say, but I learned fast. Over the next month or so I spent many happy hours on the park benches with several of the Innox Park beauties.

One evening, in the middle of this, probably some months after arriving at the new house, I was sitting in the park with one of the young ladies when I spotted Connie Barrett sitting on the swings watching us. She had a bicycle propped up close by. I made some excuse and went to talk to her. She was almost in tears and asked me why I hadn't been to see them. I got the feeling she meant "her". I apologized, and we agreed that I would get rid of the other young lady and Connie would leave now but come back in an hour. The complete details elude me as this was 50 years ago at the time of writing. Anyway, Connie came back, and it was now nearly dark, and she made it plain that in her eyes we were not just childhood friends, and that she had been completely torn up by my leaving her neighborhood. She still had the same slim young girlish figure. The outcome was that I was very flattered and continued to meet her for a while, which I found I liked very much. She was very happy and now her old self, although it meant her riding a bike up and down several hills there and back. Suddenly, one evening she didn't turn up. I waited and there was no sign. We didn't have phones, and travel was hard, so I just assumed she was tired of me, and I resumed my rounds of the local beauties. That winter, we had a lot of snow, and Innox Park was on a nice slope, but leveled out at the bottom with swings and slides etc. for the little kids. I got out my toboggan and went to the park with some others of my age, and soon we had the snow packed down and getting icy. It was late afternoon, and freezing again. This toboggan was much too small for me now, but it worked OK as long as I kept my legs up.

A momentous occasion was imminent. As the run got faster with use, it became harder and harder to slow down at the bottom and there was limited room as the fence around the Bath City football ground was in the way. The only alternative was to pass between the swings and the slide, and immediately turn to the right to avoid going straight into the fence. As anybody knows who has ridden a toboggan on icy snow, they sideslip somewhat before tight turns so I had to start the turn BEFORE passing between the swings and slide. The faster the run, the sooner I had to start the turn, but there was a bump and a hollow right between the swings and slide. On the very last run ever for my faithful toboggan, the downhill speed was a little frightening. I started to turn way before the swings and took off from the bump and was airborne over the dip. I, and the toboggan were moving straight but pointing to the right, and then we landed. I came down sideways with a crunch. The runners of the toboggan folded under. The toboggan was a little better than matchwood. It was the final goodbye. My hip bones were badly bruised, also my ribs, and I was aching all over.

It was at this house that I first got interested in making gunpowder, and needed to make charcoal. I found the best way was to slice up some wood into fat slivers and put them in a can, say like a treacle or a cocoa tin, with a hole in the lid, and put it on the coal fire. The heat would drive off the gas, and a little jet of flame would come out of the hole. When the flame stopped, it was done.

One evening I was using a newly emptied treacle tin, and the flame eventually died. My father was sitting by the fire with a newspaper held open. Suddenly there was a pop. The can must have been pointed directly at him as the lid flew right at the newspaper, and he was showered by sparks as the hot charcoal ignited on contact with the air. He leaped up with a shriek, patting himself down to kill the sparks, and I brushed up as many of the smoldering charcoal chips as I could. I believe that the treacle on the lid had got hot, run down and filled the hole, and gone hard, causing the explosion.

Within a week or so of this, I was involved in another similar catastrophe. I was melting lead for something, can't remember what, but I had a tin on the fire with bits of toothpaste tubes (yes, they were made of lead in those days), and other assorted sources of lead. For those who aren't familiar with coal fires, sometimes when the fire is glowing orange/red with no flames, the whole fire will suddenly settle. Sylvia was sitting in front of the fire when the fire settled, and the tin, with molten lead, tipped sideways and a quantity tipped out and dropped onto the tiles of the hearth, and splashed everywhere.

It would have been fine if Sylvia had been sitting back a bit, but she was close to the fire, and some globules of hot lead splashed onto her leg and stuck to her stockings. She also stood up with a shriek, just long enough to scream at me, then fainted. I carried her upstairs to her bedroom, followed by Charles, her husband who was yelling all sorts of threats at me. As I laid her on her bed, she miraculously came around and slugged me, then fainted again. Then Charles wanted to go outside with me to fight, but I had done enough damage by this time and I declined. I was almost a foot taller than he was, and much more agile.

It was about 5 months later when I got a letter. It was from Connie. She was writing from a convalescent home on the south coast of England. It told of her becoming ill on the day she didn't turn up to meet me. She was diagnosed with scarlet fever, and due to her heart condition, she had nearly died. In no uncertain terms, she indicated affection for me, and said she would be going home in the next week, and would give anything to see me, but she was not able to resume the normal activities for a while, so she could not come to me. I wrote and told her I would be there when she came home. She was now 16 years old. I was 15 years old and 6'4" tall, but skinny, and like a coiled spring. I could jump over a bar at 5' 6" with one step and was very strong and vigorous.

Sister Daphne had a baby daughter and named her Christine. I was an uncle for the first time.

It so happened that some months before, my mother had taken me out and succumbed to my insistence that I needed a bicycle. It was a second-hand machine with three gears and drop handlebars. I could now ride to school, saving lots of time. I could get home and do my homework much earlier. So on the appointed day, I got on my bike and rode to see the Barretts. I had no idea what to expect. An invalid in a wheelchair maybe? What I found I could hardly believe. Connie was not the slim slip of a girl I'd known, but a beautiful, filled-out young lady who was deliriously happy to see me. To my surprise, I realized how much I had missed her, not knowing then what little time we had left. It struck me as strange how I always had regarded her as the 11-year-old next door, but now even I could not avoid seeing the change. I quickly forgot the Innox Park crowd. Again, I was welcomed as one of the Barrett family, and it was extremely clear that Joe Barrett wanted whatever made his favorite daughter happy and apparently I was it. Her long-term future was in question and he clearly was ever conscious of that. I resumed my Saturday job and saw Connie virtually every day. I could now travel as I had my bike.

In no time Connie resumed her high rate of activity. The bike that her father bought her was a very light-weight expensive machine, the envy of everybody, including me and she made good use of it.

The end of my career at the City of Bath Boys School was approaching. We were scheduled to take the Oxford School Certificate examination in April, and then if you did not intend to go on to a university, you would leave and find a job. Going to a university in those days cost much more than the average family could afford, and so I was destined to find a job. I had set new high jump records for all 3 age groups at school. Joe Barrett had bought a car, and I was included when he took the family off on day trips. I was increasingly treated as one of the family, except that Mrs. Barrett did not seem to be too enthusiastic about me, but then she was this way about everything. Joe's girlfriend, who lived just a few yards from his store, was a great confidante of Connie's, and she definitely approved of me.

The results of the School Certificate exam arrived a few days after I started work in the Admiralty, in the Engineer-in-Chief's Department. I did about as I expected, but way less than I could have done. They were right. I'd wasted the opportunity. For a little bit more serious effort, (I was going through the motions anyway) I could have done so much better. To all younger readers, please learn from this.

I feel I have only mentioned teachers who fell into the category of ogres and meanies. These were in the minority. Most of the teachers were big men metaphorically speaking. They were friendly and helpful. Encouraging and with the best interests in mind for the boys. In particular, Mr. "Charlie" Eck, mathematics teacher who spent many lunchtime hours and after school, coaching me in the high jump. There was "Titch" Barnet, Physical Training teacher who taught us French as his second subject. I think we were his first class as we knew more than he did at first, but we persevered and he came along real fast. He was Welsh and no more than 5'4", but a giant in our eyes. There were many more like these two who put in extra hours in the boys' interests.

Chapter 7 - Muriel Goes To Work, By Muriel

On the other side of Bath, I, Muriel, went to the Post Office for an interview, and written examination, and was accepted. One week after leaving school, I started my 6 weeks training in Bristol, about 12 miles away. I met an older girl named Mary Bloom, and we traveled together on the bus every day.

Two weeks before the end of the training, Mary's fiancé was being shipped out as the Korean War had just started, so she got married and 4 of us from the class went to the wedding. She became Mary Commons.

When I first went to work and became comparatively affluent in the eyes of my younger sisters. I would pay Susan two pence a night to warm my bed. Susan was sent to bed before me, being younger and still at school. She would lay in my bed until I came up to bed, then I would awaken her, and she would get into her own cold bed. We did not have any luxuries. We had no bedside lamp. There was one light in the bedroom in the middle of the ceiling which turned on and off with a switch by the door. Susan's bed was closer to the switch than mine, but still several steps away. Mostly, I would read when I went to bed. Susan by this time was back in her bed and asleep. When I was ready to go to sleep I would re-awaken Susan to get out of bed and turn the light out. She was also paid two pence a night for doing this service. Of course, the bed warming only applied to the winter months. The poor dear didn't enjoy this in and out of bed but did enjoy the payday each week.

One day I put a little bit of lipstick on, and Dad said "Good heavens Elaine (my mother), she'll be painting her bottom next".

I finished my telephone training and was sent to work at the Bath long-distance exchange. Our normal work week was 48 hours, with varying day-time hours from 8.00 am to 8.00 pm. Men did the nights, 8.00 pm to 8.00 am.

There was another exchange called the toll exchange which handled local calls. Please bear in mind that there were no automatic dialing switchboards. Everything was done by an operator.

There was rivalry between local and long-distance, although the long-distance was by far the most complicated.

As I was only 16, I was paid about 1/3rd of what Mary Commons was earning because she was 22 years old, even though she started the same day I did. This was the system.

It gets worse. When I was 18, and training a lady of 46, I was getting 1/3rd of the money she was getting. I went to the chief supervisor, Miss Carder, and complained. She told me how sorry she was, and said that this was the way it was.

Everything I needed when I started work, other than what Mum bought me I had to buy out of my earnings which was 38 shillings to start with, of which 20 shillings went to Mum for my keep. From the remainder, I had to pay for bus fares and lunches and everything else that I needed. Life was very tough.

All telephone workers under 18 had to go for further education one day per week. My day was Friday, and I went with a friend from my exchange, Heather Toone. It was an easy day and was like a day off work.

I completed my first year at the exchange, and unfortunately, there was no school on Fridays as it was the school holidays. However, in early September, the Friday school would start again. I was 17 years old.

That summer I went to Weston-Super-Mare, the nearest seaside town, for the day. Audrey came with me, and I made up my mind that I was going to get nicely tanned and look like Audrey who tanned very easily. I remembered my Uncle Jack's advice "If you want to get a tan, smother yourself with olive oil". I applied the olive oil and lay in the sun all day, and it was a really hot sunny day. We traveled home on the train, and I removed my sunglasses, and Audrey burst into laughter. I had two white rings around my eyes in a bright red face. My face began to throb, and I didn't realize it but I was severely sunburned.

During the night, I became very ill with sun-stroke and spent the next three days in bed, hardly able to bear the weight of the bedclothes. Mum was worried to death. My skin bubbled off in patches and people edged away from me as I looked so bad. It was three or four weeks before I looked and felt OK. I have never done that again.

When Friday school resumed, Heather and I were happy to get this easy day again. During this session, I first saw the new people in the classes. Obviously, they were a year younger and just starting their first year. Amongst them was a new student whom I felt was rather nice looking, but a very shy young man. For several months there wasn't any occasion or reason to speak to him, but one day, I was a bit late getting to a chemistry class and came in the door to find only a few seats left, one by this nice young man. I decided I would sit by him. For the rest of the school year, we sat together for the chemistry lessons. We became friendly, and during breaks, we often walked to Woolworths and bought peanuts and cashews. Although we were very friendly, he never did ask me for a date.

Too soon the school year came to a close, and that was the end of my two years of extra education. I felt that I would not see this nice young man again. I was 18.

Meanwhile, at the long-distance exchange, a group of about 10 of us had become firm friends. We collected as a group for birthdays.

This year, for my gift I selected camera films, as many as the money would cover as Audrey and I were going to the South of France for 8 days. At this time nobody of our age and in our circumstances ever went abroad for a vacation, and it caused somewhat of a sensation.

The next problem was that I didn't have a camera, and arranged to borrow one from a neighbor, Mrs. Stonestreet. I borrowed this camera many times and eventually, Mrs. Stonestreet told me to keep it. 45 years later it sits on a shelf in son Nicholas' house as part of his camera collection.

The day of our trip to France arrived, and Audrey and I walked the 2 miles to the Bath train station carrying our luggage, and caught the train to London. From Victoria station, London, we met our group and by bus, we traveled to Newhaven. There we boarded a ferry to Dieppe in France.

From Dieppe, we went to Paris by bus, where we caught the overnight train to the Nice. We broke our journey at Digne and went on the funicular railway to the highest point in the French Alps. Then we traveled on to Grenoble where we saw the towering granite cliffs. We had lunch and then went on to Nice on the south coast. I should add that we did not have sleeping accommodation, and were exhausted when we arrived.

In Nice, there were a couple of included trips. We went by bus to Monte Carlo and went into a casino, but we were too young to gamble. Another trip took us along the beach road to Mentone. The beach was disappointing. We expected nice sand but it was pebbles. However, the area was beautiful, and the weather, wonderful.

We stayed at a brand new hotel and had a funny incident. Audrey and I were on the elevator and it refused to stop. We went up and down several times, and we could not get out. It was an open elevator with a grill instead of a door, and other guests were getting upset, thinking that we were doing it. Finally, the manager got it to stop at the top floor.

There was an unpleasant incident. We were in a cafe where we bought orange juice, and when we came to pay the server appeared to shortchange us. I called to a lady who appeared to be in charge and made her understand the problem, and she went to a dish, took money, and gave it to us. Then she went to the server and yelled at him, and slapped him.

The next day, we were walking along the Promenade Des Anglais, when I received a violent kick in the back of my knee, and I fell to the ground. It was the server from the cafe. Overall though, we enjoyed the trip immensely.

Very soon after returning, Audrey's family moved to Exeter. They wanted me to go and live with them, but I was not allowed to go.

Without Audrey, my sister Susan became a close companion, and we did things together.

For my 18th birthday, Mum gave me a 9-diamond ring. I thought I was the bees-knees. I gave this ring to my daughter Helen, on her 18th birthday.

Auntie Celia was ill with influenza, and Mum asked me to go to her house and take food.

Whilst there she asked me to change Rover's (the dog) big bowl of water. I had known Rover since a puppy, and had no fear. I picked up his bowl, and he leaped at me and pinned me to the wall, growling and snarling. I dropped the bowl and water went everywhere. I couldn't move. Finally, I was able to work my way to the back door and slip through. I slammed it and ran upstairs to tell Auntie Celia what had happened. I had to leave. From that point, I have not trusted dogs anymore.

Soon after this a notice was circulated at the exchange offering an opportunity to work in Kenya, and 3 of us applied. June Waller, June Bristow, and me. Only one of us was accepted, June Waller. June Bristow failed the physical, and I was rejected as I was under 21.

It turned out to be a nightmare. You could get nowhere without a car, and June Waller had no money and couldn't drive.

We would get notices at the exchange about dances at military camps, and I would go with a group of telephone operators. I had a couple of nice taffeta dance outfits which I made myself. I looked pretty good. Later on, Susan borrowed these clothes, and told me she felt like the bees-knees.

This year my parents bought a large house on London road, which took several weeks to fix up before we could move in. My sister Sheila was born, which caused a sensation at the exchange because nobody ever had a sibling that young.

A distant cousin of Dad's, about 20 years old, was attending a local university and made a habit of dropping in for tea all the time, which got on our nerves a bit. One Sunday afternoon, Mum and Dad were out, working at the new house when she rang our doorbell. We hid and finally thought she had gone away, but she appeared at the back door. We told her we didn't hear the bell. We sent for Mum and Dad at the new house and had to get all the best china etc. out.

Television was in its infancy, and some Saturday nights I would go to Elaine Bussell's (from work) house to watch TV. They were the only ones I knew who had a TV. This was a big thing. Susan always came with me.

Things were not happy at home, and I was buying all sorts of things in preparation for moving out at some point. I also belonged to a book club as I loved to read.

I gave Susan her first Toni perm, the first home perm available. I regularly cut and set her hair.

Elaine Bussell wanted me to go to Austria with her the next year and so we made all arrangements and paid a deposit. This was not to be.

One day I happened to look at the Bath evening paper and saw a photograph of Brian Walters who had won the high jump at some athletic meeting. This was the name of the nice young man from school.

I pointed this out to my brother John, and I said that I had sat next to him at school. He said he knew Brian from school, in the class above him.

In the next couple of years, I bumped into Brian a couple of times. Once when he was taking his little sister somewhere, and then, outside the GWR railway station. I was returning from my Aunt's farm. We talked for over an hour, and I felt it was not seemly to stay any longer, so I finally left.

It was a couple of years later. I had just returned from 3 weeks at Shepton Mallet where I had been sent to train operators in the use of new automatic switchboards when I was handed a letter by my mother. It was from Brian. He was asking me if I wanted to go to the theater, which was a hoot as I now know he hates the theater. He asked me to call him at his office at work. The letter had been written weeks before.

I was very pleased to hear from him, but I was not able to call him until late afternoon the next day. He seemed surprised to hear from me but then it had been a couple of weeks. He wanted to meet me that evening, but I had promised to set and cut Susan's hair. Finally, I weakened and agreed to meet him.

Chapter 8 - Brian Goes to Work, By Brian

The day I started work in the Admiralty, I was asked by Jock Breckenridge, the union representative, and social organizer, if I did any athletic events, and of course I volunteered my high jump capability. I was hurriedly entered in that event in the upcoming annual Admiralty sports day which was a couple of weeks away. The day arrived and my mother accompanied me, I won the high jump at 5' 10" and a man named Barlow who had been winning for years was 2nd at 5' 3". Our whole department got 6 points for the day. I got 5 of them for the high jump. The winning team was from my father's department. They got something like 150 points. Apparently, there was also a throwing the cricket ball event, always won by Mr. Barlow at about 90 yards, which I would have entered if I had known about it. It is probably as well that I didn't enter it as it might have destroyed him. This event was replaced by the discus in following years. Mr. Barlow crossed my path some years later when throwing a cricket ball was involved.

My immediate supervisor for the first few months was Bill Hurford. He was a Welshman and it showed. He was soon transferred to an Admiralty depot in Singapore. A nice ordinary guy. The only thing that really stood out about him in my memory was the fact that he pronounced "Air Freight" as "Air Fright", which used to get some chuckles. Then came Laurie Sheldon, another Welshman who hated other Welsh people. He had tried to lose his Welsh accent and had some success. His earnings were seven times mine. Also in our group was a retired English (Mr. Plod) policeman, Stan Wells. He had been a constable all his life, which speaks highly of his mental capability. He was the ultimate old-time copper, and "thick" is the word that comes to mind as the nearest description of him. He did everything so slowly and deliberately but he was very nice. He did all the copying of documents by hand (there were no copy machines), and earned about 4 times what I did because he was at the top of the age/wage scale and I was at the bottom. The last one in the group was Ada Babbage. She was a 48-year-old spinster, painfully thin, who moved her skinny legs like lightning. She always reminded me of a sparrow with her long nose and oversize spectacles. Here was a woman who could out-talk anybody in a high-pitched, penetrating voice. If you tried to get a word in she seemed to change gear, with the pitch of her voice going up half an octave, and the volume increased. She would not stop for anything until she ran out of words. I used to bait her a bit by continuing to talk getting louder and louder, instead of stopping like everybody else. She did filing and made the tea for everybody, and earned about 4 times what I got.

In the same large room, there was a separate group that employed a Miss Clooke. She was the filing and tea making person for this other group. Miss Clooke was the exact opposite to Ada Baggage. She was huge, slow, and almost exactly a female version of Stan Wells, the retired policeman. She was a middle-aged spinster, had a deep voice, and a hairy chin. Strangely, Ada and Miss Clooke were the best of friends. They would chat for ages about various pills for some unnamed physical problems, and at least weekly they would swap different pills. It was 50% of their conversation. Nobody ever knew what their problems were, but they used to have a thoroughly enjoyable time talking about it.

I sat next to Laurie and we were good friends. We sat in a group of 4 desks put together. Across from me was a girl, Audrey Walker, equivalent to me in age. She worked for and sat next to Catherine Stratford, who, of course, sat opposite and was equal rank to Laurie. They were both 36ish, and Audrey and I were about 16 or 17. Laurie was married and had twin girls around 10 or 12 years old. They were fantastic swimmers and won every award going on at the time. I often wonder how they got on later. Laurie and I did the creative work together with Stan and Ada doing the grunt work. Catherine Stafford and Audrey were remarkable in that they were about as ugly as each other. Audrey carried on as if she was gorgeous, and as if I was after her and she played hard to get, which kept Laurie and me in stitches. Cath Stratford was Scottish, and also looked like it, you know, like a haggis. She was playing around almost openly with one of the married engineers in the section, Frank Gage. At least he was English. He certainly must have had a strong stomach. The whole section boss was Reg Dadswell. He was of medium height, with a huge stomach, bald, with a steeply sloping forehead, and a huge curved nose. He was never without his pipe which he had in his mouth all the time like a part of his face. He was an ugly man, but extremely nice to me. He sat at a desk in the middle of the room of about 20 people, facing Ted Scrivener, who was the engineering section boss. They used to argue all the time and hated each other.

At about that time there were advertisements showing a toucan with a glass of beer on its long curving beak, advertising Guinness. I was immediately struck by the likeness of the toucan to Reg Dadswell and made a drawing of a toucan with a pipe in its beak and it looked exactly like Mr. Dadswell. Everybody thought it was hilarious, and it was passed around the office. Ted Scrivener was the greatest admirer. I never got it back, but Cath Stratford, slightly senior to Laurie, was in charge when Dadswell was on vacation and found it weeks later in Dadswell's "in" tray. I did all the posters and drawings for the department and he would be in no doubt who drew it, and it was obvious that Mr. Scrivener had put it there out of spite.

It would have been early September when I was sent to the Technical College one day per week for further education. Apparently, all under 18 civil service employees did this. My day was Friday, and as all sorts of education levels were represented, it was stuff I'd done years before, and an easy day for me. We did mathematics, English, chemistry, and we had a session in the gymnasium, mostly games like basketball. I don't remember the other courses. I became friendly with Bob Fox, who was very athletic. There were a few girls in the class, but I was not interested.

A few days before Christmas, Connie and I were visiting a flat rented by Brenda, in Catherine Place, Bath. Brenda was on her annual leave from the show, “Latin Quarter”. The weather had been warm and rainy. When it was time to go, it had turned dry and frosty. Connie had only a plastic raincoat, and we were both frozen on the walk to Connie's home. By the next day, she was becoming unwell, and within 24 hours she was in hospital with pneumonia which was a killer in those days. My last picture of Connie was through a plastic oxygen tent at 10.30 pm on Christmas Eve. By 5.00 am Christmas day, she was gone. It was only then that I realized how big a part of my life had gone also.

That evening, I was in bed at the end of the hardest day of my 16 years. The light was off, and there on the wall was a brightly lit, girl-size patch of light. My mother was worried. We adjusted the curtains, mirrors, etc. but it did not change. We could not find a source of light and never could find an explanation for it. It appeared the next night but then disappeared. The Barretts gave me Connie's lightweight bicycle.

There is one more very mysterious event. Shortly after Connie died, I was riding the bike along Brock Street, up a very slight rise, and suddenly I realized that I was being pushed along. I wasn't pedaling, but was going along at a good pace. I didn't have to pedal once all the way along the road. There was no feeling of pressure on me, and there was little wind, and no plausible explanation for this.

55 years later, I have visited Connie's grave every time I go to England which must be 10 times at least. She is in the same spot as her father which is what she would want. Mr. Barrett died many years ago, but I have visited Mrs. Barrett every time I'm in England, and she has stayed with us twice in America, but now at 90 years of age, she is in a nursing home. During a trip to England in May/June 2001 I visited her on two separate occasions and each time she was out of it but she squeezed my hand when I asked if she knew who I was. I have one more thing to accomplish. Many years ago she asked me to be her executor although she has 3 living children in England. I will carry out this function at the proper time. I think at last I have gained her approval.

It took me many months for me to pull myself out of the dumps after Connie left us, but gradually the clouds lifted. I went to work and to school on Fridays and that was all. There was one particular young lady at school that stood out, but she seemed too perfect and at the same time, humble. Her name was Muriel Newton. She was about 5' 6" and tended to be on the slim side although not thin. She wore no make-up and didn't need it. Her hair was in a tidy bun at the back and was very friendly to me but at the same time gave the impression of being untouchable. None of the other 16-year-old boys teased and kidded with her as they did with the other girls. I don't think they dared. I discovered that I knew her brother, John Newton, who was at the City of Bath Boys School. He was a year younger than me.

I had limited contact with just an occasional polite conversation with Muriel as you would expect from two young people in the same class, until the beginning of the last term (semester) of my first year. We were just finding seats for our first chemistry lesson, and I had an empty seat next to me, and Muriel came in the door with her friend Heather Toone. I remember thinking that I hoped she sat next to me, and, she appeared to make a bee-line for the seat as if she knew exactly where she was going to sit. How stupid I was. How could I think all this was an accident? We sat together in Mr. Axfords chemistry class for the rest of the term. One funny thing that happened was that at the final end-of-term examination, Muriel got exactly the same score as I did. Mr. Axford made a sarcastic comment about this coincidence. So, this was why she wanted to sit next to me. I was disappointed. She must have known I was good at chemistry. Muriel was almost a year older than me, so she did not come back for the next year, and so that was that. Yeah, right.

I bought an old 1932 motorbike (older than me) from Bill Lord, one of my father's acquaintances from earlier in this chronicle. I spent lots of time working on it. It ran very rarely, but I had some fun. I paid 7 pounds for it. About $50 in today's money. The tires and tubes were no good, but I stuffed the tires with grass, and that worked OK.

I was now 17 and made the effort to re-involve myself in athletics. I joined the Bath and County Athletic Club, which met at The Glass House Track, just along the road from where I worked. Mike Sawyer was secretary, and Dennis Amor President. They were the club and did everything from arranging matches to getting transport, to recruiting. (I was already a member of the Admiralty club which really didn't do much). The first thing was that they pushed me into entering the county championships. This I did and went off to Taunton, the county of Somerset's capital town.

I remember that day. It was warm in England, maybe 70 deg. F. The grass was very thick and must have been mowed only hours before because it had the strongest smell of new-mown grass that I have ever smelled.

I was very nervous, away from my home turf, but I won easily, which I did again and again for the next 5 or 6 years. In that time I set the county record at 6' 2", just 6" above the previous best. Every summer until I finally gave up high jumping my photograph was in the newspaper virtually every week, because I won every match.

My sister Brenda had divorced David Elliott, and brought Alfie (don't remember his last name but he looked Italian) from London to see us. He was nice enough but I had nothing in common with him. The usual bee showed up in my mother's bonnet and we moved again to Winsley Hill, Limpley Stoke, a small village 15 miles from the center of Bath if you traveled through the valleys, but if you wanted to hill climb it was only about 7 miles. Luckily it was not too far from my workplace which was on the top of the hill nearest to Limpley Stoke. I could walk down Winsley Hill, through Limpley Stoke, climb Brassknocker Hill, and a mile along the top of the hill and I was at work. I still had Connie's bike and eventually used that.

It was while we were living at this house that my younger sister developed asthma. She would have a bout of it every other week or so. She was very ill at times, and would keep my mother up at nights. The House was a long way from anything, sort of way out in the boonies to use a modern expression. There were times when I was a bit bored, and I'd get up to all sorts of tricks. I made gunpowder, and experimented with it. One day I made a bomb with the purpose of removing a big old dead branch from one of the apple trees in our garden. With a loud boom, the branch flew off, and almost immediately my mother came out yelling at me. I didn't know it but the doctor was there seeing my sick little sister, and it had made him jump saying "no wonder she's sick with that sort of thing going on". So now it was my fault that she was sick. This was in the days when doctors were close to God in the average people's minds.

I had a glass fruit bowl in which I used to mix the gunpowder, using an old dessert spoon. These were my mortar and pestle. I would sit and grind it in the evenings, and I had about a pound weight of finely ground gunpowder. As you probably know, gunpowder does not explode until it is confined. Then it explodes as it bursts its confining container. However, unconfined it does burn extremely quickly, especially if it is finely mixed. I had a use for this fine powder. I would have great fireworks. I put a lighted candle under an apple tree and then climbed up with the bowl of gunpowder. When I was 15 feet off the ground I got to one side so as to not be above the candle, and tipped the powder out. I was not accounting for two factors. One, the powder was finer and lighter than I thought, and it spread out in the air into a large cloud. The other factor was the wind which blew the powder in my direction. The bottom of the cloud reached the candle, and it became a huge ball of fire that surrounded me. I had the good sense to not breathe as this massive pall of flame and heat violently rustled the leaves and branches. I lost some of my eyebrows and the tips of my hair were singed, but otherwise, there was no damage. After that, I developed my own black powder that was cheaper and easier to make and more effective.

One funny thing that happened and made Rosemary laugh. At night our father would place the half-smoked remains of his last cigarette, on the mantle-piece. In the morning he would immediately light up.

One morning, with a pin, I dug out a little bit of the tobacco at the burning end and poured in a little bit of gunpowder, and replaced most of the tobacco. I was not there when he got up, but I asked Rosemary what happened. She said, "It burned all the way up to his mouth and made him really jump". It seems that it went a bit further than I intended, but she was amused. He never did give me the satisfaction of knowing it worked because he said nothing to me, although he would have had no doubt who was the culprit.

Not long after this, my sister Brenda, who was worried about Mother being home alone in this remote house, arrived from London with what seemed like a small horse. It was a Borzoi, a Russian wolfhound that she decided would be good company and protection for Mother. She was right about the protection, but who was going to protect us from the dog? The dog settled in and became part of the family, but did nip the mailman's hand once, but that was all. When on his hind paws he could put his forefeet on my head.

One night at about 9.00 pm there was a knock on the door and some giggling from outside. It was my father's old friends Johnny Symes, Bill Lord, and two other men. It was obvious they were drunk. They came into the house and we had an impromptu little party. You had to admire these fellows, they really did enjoy life. Anyway, they left at about 10.30 pm on Johnny's motorcycle and sidecar. They had with them a bell tent, and camping gear, all in his big old flat-bed sidecar with two of them traveling on top of the folded tent. They were even more drunk when they left.

It was about 3.00 am when the door knocker got us all out of bed. The rain was teeming down, and the 4 of them were drenched. They had put their tent up in the space in front of a gate into a field, just up our hill, and rainwater that ran down the side of the road did a sharp turn into the field and ran right through their tent. It took lots of hot tea to warm them up, and at last, they laid around on the floor and chairs, and it was peaceful again. This escapade was typical of the things they got up to.

One day I was walking in the town (Bath) down by the Railway station when I walked into Muriel Newton, just returning from a visit to her aunt's farm about 20 miles away. We must have talked for at least 1½ hours. As I've said before I was somewhat shy and did not have the nerve to consider any moves with this untouchable young lady. She gave mixed vibes. Extremely friendly but still with this aloof-seeming aura. She finally said she had to go, and I reluctantly said goodbye.

I was appointed by the Engineer-in-Chief of the Navy, Admiral Parker, as the organizer of the department team for the 1953 Admiralty sports day. I made the effort, and with the authority he gave me, an 18-year-old, I put a creditable team together. We were 2nd in the team ratings with 132 points. A great improvement over the 6 points we earned two years before. My father's dept. won again. Of course, I was a hero, but it didn't put another shilling in my pay packet.

There was a bit of a fuss from the boss, Reg Dadswell, while I was working on getting the team together. In the week before the sports day. He told me that I had to get caught up with my work. He was right, I was a bit behind, but I made a phone call to Admiral Parker's secretary, giving her the message that I couldn't do it anymore and told her why. Within a few minutes, Dadswell came to me all nervous and upset saying, "Why didn't you tell me what you were doing?" He told Laurie to do my work and get me caught up. I felt a bit mean afterward. Some months later, he returned from lunch, and I was at the drafting table making a poster for some departmental function. It was way past the lunch hour, and suddenly I realized somebody was looking over my shoulder. I turned, it was Dadswell. Neither of us spoke as he read it. He turned and walked on. He wasn't about to risk getting yelled at again.

It may be of interest to share my method of making large posters freehand. I could make excellent posters with lettering as large as 6" tall. I used italic-style lettering and made the pens myself. We had available what we called cartridge paper in large pieces, as large as 3' by 5', which called for large bold lettering. Also available was a variety of colored inks called Indian ink. My posters were famous in this department of about 400 people, and I was kept quite busy.

One day, I discovered that if the Indian ink dried on a folded piece of cartridge paper, it became stiff. I made my first pen by making a roll of this paper, taping it and crushing it, then dipping it in the ink and allowing it to dry flattened. I made them up to ¾" wide. They lasted quite a long time.

By this time I was spending more athletic training time at the civil service track. Maybe it was because a small blonde young lady named Haydee Pamela Anne Walters, same name again, known as Anne, who was in my department, had encouraged me to help her with her sprinting. I had spent so much time around track athletics that I couldn't help picking up know-how, and being the organizer for the department I felt some responsibility. She was cute and sexy, and we saw a lot of each other, both at work and outside. I got her to the point where she could run the 100 yards in 11.2 seconds, but I could still catch her. She was wiping the floor with everybody except Ethel Turner, a member of the Bath and County Club. Ethel's best time was 11.1 seconds. She had attended school with my sister Daphne and was a bit older than Anne and at her prime.

Anne lived at Midsomer Norton, which was about 15 miles from work and my home, and a very awkward place to get to from my home. However, I discovered a route through the tiniest little country roads, which ran up and down hills between high hedges. It seemed to go on forever. I used to ride my bike in the dead of night to and from on these roads. There was no lighting and no people. One night I was barreling down one slope to keep up speed to go up the other side when I saw this faint moving light in the road. I jammed my brakes on and just came to a stop. There was a cow lying across the road completely blocking it. There was a railway line nearby and one of the railway workers had walked into this cow. He was carrying an old oil lantern and saw my bicycle lamp coming, and saved me from having what could have been a nasty accident with nobody around to help.

One evening I was practicing jumping alone at the civil service sports field. The only other people on the field were three cricketers practicing at the nets at the very far side of the 440 yard track, about 250 yards away. I heard a loud crack of a bat on ball. I saw the ball had escaped the net and was curving toward me. It landed 50 yards away and rolled in my direction. One of the cricketers started to run to get the ball, then slowed to a walk. I ran a few yards to the ball and threw it back as hard as possible. It went over the head of the man coming to collect it, and I went on paying attention to my jumping. Then, I saw that all three cricketers were walking in my direction. When they got near, I called out to them and asked what the matter was, knowing that I could outrun them if they were looking for trouble. I wondered if they were angry that I threw the ball over their man's head. Their answer was "Do you realize what you just did?"

They told me that they had approx. 50 years of cricketing experience between them and they had never seen anybody throw a cricket ball as far as I threw it. One of the men was . . . . . . You guessed it, my old friend Mr. Barlow who used to win the Admiralty high jump and throwing the cricket ball. They asked me if I would go with them to the 100 yards track, and they would attempt to get some idea of how far I could throw. We did the experiment and as expected the ball flew way beyond 100 yards. They got a tape from the clubhouse and agreed on a distance of 132 yards. I was surprised even more than they were but then I was older, bigger, and stronger than when I threw rocks. One of them wrote to the News of the World, a Sunday garbage newspaper, and they advised the previous best record was 115 yards.

My sister Brenda went off to New York to join the Ringling Bros/Barnum & Bailey Circus as a showgirl. She was to ride an elephant. We saw her off on the brand new ship USS United States. I believe this ship broke Queen Elizabeth's record for crossing the Atlantic. What happened to the USS United States and the USS America? Haven't heard of them for ages.

I was busy for years with athletics. I did weight training in the winter at a school in the city and jumping training 3 evenings a week in the summer at the track. I represented the county at the White City Stadium in London. I didn't do very well because I had to travel by train the same day and I was always cold and tired when I got there. It was usually won at lower than my best at 6'2". I won a competition at the civil service national championships in London, but most of this is a blur for some strange reason. When I was 18, I was listed in the world's best high jumpers at #17 and I was years from my best, but did not stay in it for many more years.

One night when I was about 19, I was doing weight training with my friend John Dolman, when he suggested I go to a movie with him afterward. We were sitting in the Forum Cinema, Bath, with the lights out watching a movie when somebody sat in the seat beside me. In the interval, the lights went on and I discovered that it was John Newton. We chatted about school, and a bit about Muriel. It was about 2 years since Muriel and I had talked by the train station. John suggested that I write to Muriel, and I said OK. We walked through the town and to the place from where my bus started. There was the driver having a cigarette before starting the trip, and we stood talking across the road. The driver looked at his watch, stubbed out his cigarette and got into the driver's seat, and started the engine. I could run as fast as a deer and knew I could catch the bus, and said goodbye to John and ran and jumped on the platform at the back of the double-decker and climbed the stairs to the upper deck. I was halfway up when I stopped and ran back down. I yelled to John and he heard me and turned. I yelled, "Where do you live?" There was noisy traffic and a noisy bus engine, but I thought he said "4 Walcott Terrace", but it could have been anything close to that.

The next day at work was busy in the morning but in the afternoon I was completely caught up. This was unusual. To fill the time I thought, "Ah, I'll write to Muriel and just see what happens". I thought that if I don't hear back it is probably because I've got the wrong address. It won't be because she doesn't like me. I remember chuckling about that.

I was right, I did have the wrong address as it was two weeks later, and no word. I had put my office telephone number in the letter to make contact easier, but nothing. That was that.

It was another week later about 3.30 pm when I answered my phone and . . . . . . the address was correct. There was Muriel saying hello and not a bit unapproachable. We talked but then, suddenly, she did become unapproachable when I suggested we meet that evening. She said it was not possible. WAS THERE SOMEBODY ELSE? DID SHE NOT LIKE ME? She told me she'd been away for some weeks, training telephone operators at Shepton Mallet, way down in Somerset, and had only got my letter the night before, and that was the reason for the delay. I finally thought there was nothing to lose so I asked her why we couldn't meet that night, and then she told me the bad news. "I have promised faithfully to set my sister's hair tonight, but .... I can meet you every night after tonight for the rest of our lives". I'm not sure she said those exact words, but I know that was what she meant. Now at 67 years married, we are meeting in, the morning, noon, and night.

Chapter 9 - Muriel's bad news for Susan. By Muriel

When I got home on the evening that I had agreed to meet Brian, I had to break the news to Susan that I would do her hair the next night. Mum said to me with a smirk, "How did it go my dear"? She was referring to the fact that I'd told her I was going to call Brian. I told her I was meeting him that very night.

We went to a movie, but can't remember the details. We agreed to meet a few days later. This pattern continued for some months.

Shortly after getting to know Brian, the owner of the house next door had a vacant basement flat, and Susan and I moved into it. It was below sidewalk level at the front, and garden level at the back, but it was all ours. Brian was able to come there and we didn't go out and about much anymore, and were able to start saving a bit.

A funny incident happened one evening. Our landlady had a mentally deficient son of about 60, and he would come down into the basement for coal. This did not involve our space, but he used the passageway alongside of our rooms to get to the coal cellar.

Brian was sitting on my bed and I was counting our savings which I kept in a drawer. The bedroom door was open, and we heard Ernest (the landlady's son) moving around. Brian laid back on the bed, and his head was toward the door, and looking back, he saw a pair of beady little eyes watching us through the crack between the door and the door jamb on the hinge side. He jumped up with surprise at meeting eyes looking back at him, and poor little Ernest must have nearly died with fright as he scurried away.

We had a good laugh, but we moved the hiding place.

Susan was now working for Lawleys, purveyors of fine glass and china in Milsom Street, the posh street in Bath. We teased her that she would marry Ernest one day. He appeared to like Susan.

The story continues, by Brian with input from me, Muriel.

Chapter 10 - Brian and Muriel. By Brian

It must have been my irresistible powers of persuasion that delayed the sister's hair-do for a few days. Muriel and I met that evening for our first arranged meeting and went to see a movie. She was in no way unapproachable, in fact, I couldn't understand how I had misunderstood her before. Afterward, we walked almost to her home, and stopped at a bus stop for me to go home, where she advised that I would meet her at the same spot the next Thursday. It sounded like she was used to people doing exactly what she told them, and that was our first difference of opinion.

The next year continued, with me going to the city from work to meet Muriel, and walking home at a very late hour. It was at least 7 miles. A mile to Bathwick Hill, then a mile climb up that long hill, along the top for a mile or more then down Brassknocker Hill and along through the Limply Stoke Valley, and then up Winsley Hill. I did this journey in rain, thick snow, and ice, seeing the same policeman halfway up Bathwick Hill every night. Looking back, I question my mental state, or maybe I was under the influence of hypnotism.

One of the first social events with Muriel was a Christmas party at her Uncle Stan's and Auntie May's house. There I met Auntie Celia, Cousin Tony, and a few other people, including Roy, a lodger of Uncle Stan's. Apparently, unknown to me, Roy and a few other people there, were big in the Bath Operatic Society. Somebody was playing the piano and there was a bit of singing going on when suddenly, Roy let forth with this horrible strangled, high-pitched loud singing. I burst out laughing because it was really an awful noise and I felt it could only be done as a joke. It couldn't be serious . . . could it? But serious it was. Roy was serenading us!

I got the dirtiest look from Auntie Celia, and I shrank out of sight.

It was about this time that my mother's bee got active in her bonnet again. We moved house and bought new lino. The old lino was in such small pieces, and now you could buy it, as the effects of the war were receding. The new address was 17 Camden Crescent, really close to the center of the city and to where Joy lived. In fact, when Joy went to work at the telephone exchange, she caught a bus 100 yards from our house. By this time, as you know, Muriel had moved out of her parent's house into a semi-basement flat right next door, due to continuous friction with her father. Sister Susan joined her. By this time Muriel's brother John had gone off to join the Rhodesian police.

I would leave work, and go directly to Muriel's flat most nights. Muriel would cook dinner for the three of us. We were saving a little money, and sharing expenses somewhat.

The Christmas of that year was a big one for my family. Brenda came to England with her new husband Frank McCloskey. They met at Barnum and Bailey/Ringling Bros' Circus. Brenda rode an elephant and Frank was the General Manager. They lived in Winter Park, near Orlando in Florida. Whilst they were in England Frank had some phone calls from the US and he had to go back all in a hurry. He returned and by that time he had acquired Clyde Beatty's Circus, the largest 3-ring traveling circus in the world at that time.

I always remember that when it came time to do the dishes after Christmas dinner, we decided to draw lots for the lucky ones. I volunteered to arrange the names for drawing from a hat. I put Brenda's name on every ticket except one, on which I put my father's name. The drawing took place and the first name out for dishwashing was Brenda's. The second one out was my father's, for wiping the dishes. It was lucky that Brenda's name did not come out twice. Brenda paid my father for doing both jobs, but Muriel helped him. Over the next few years, Frank acquired Kings Circus, and Cole Brothers Circus, the oldest traveling circus, which was combined with Clyde Beatty's.

Do you remember my earlier story about Spud Gardner, teacher, coming up behind me and whacking me around the head for absolutely nothing? To compound it he offered no apology. I remembered it also.

Bath and County Athletic Club did not have its own track, and had to scrounge around and use school tracks where we could get permission. This particular year we got permission to use the City of Bath Boys School facility. My old school. One summer evening, I was walking back from the high jump area on my way to the changing rooms at the far end of the school. I stopped on the top of the bank in front of the main entrance, and teacher's entrance, to watch a cricket match being played. To my delight, my short fat friend, Spud Gardner was batting, and facing my direction. I was no longer a defenseless 14-year-old.

My photograph was in the local newspaper every week, and everybody knew me by sight. Within seconds Mr. Gardner was bowled out, and . . . . he had to walk straight at me to get into the school. My smile was from ear to ear. This little squirt was still 5'4" with a fat stomach, but now I was 6'4" and 20 years old, ready to take on the world. I stood in my tracksuit (or sweats) with my hands on my hips and tried to make it obvious that I was waiting. He stumbled a bit as if he wasn't sure which way he was going then made a sharp left turn toward the boys' entrance. I walked slowly along the top of the bank, keeping pace with him. He was watching me, and suddenly he turned back toward the main entrance again, and now I left him in no doubt. I turned back also. He stopped halfway off the field and I could almost see his mind working. He turned back to his diagonal path to the boy's entrance again where there were several people around, and again I tracked him. I suppose he thought it is better to die with people around than to die alone. I was cracking up with laughter inside and he appeared terrified. At last, he arrived at the bottom of the wide steps, with me standing at the top, looking at him and waiting. He, slowly, like an old, old man climbed toward me. His head was down, and I moved closer to him. He passed within 3 feet of me still looking down. I also was looking down but at him. I followed him into the school 3 feet behind him, breathing down his neck. I'm sure he expected a whack around the head at any second, but as he turned right to go down the main corridor, back to the staff rooms, I turned left into the changing rooms. I could do no more, but I'm sure he learned a hard lesson, i.e. make sure you are right, as you never know how nasty young boys might become when they grow up. I felt that I had leveled the score with him in the best way open to me.

As the year went on, I was jumping at my best, and Muriel accompanied me in all matches. She got really upset with Russel Colville, (a sprinter whom Muriel had known as a child), on a bus ride to a match. I mentioned to him something about doing dishes and he said, "You do dishes when you've got Muriel? That's like having a dog and barking yourself". Muriel got mad with him, but I thought it very funny and have trotted it out quite a few times over the last 50 years.

Chapter 11 - We're Married, By Brian

We had a very quiet wedding. Both of us tend to be a bit shy and the thought of a fancy wedding with lots of people was quite scary. The only people present were our parents and my sister Daphne. There was no money for any frills. If we had money we would have chosen to hang on to it for more important things. We are just about the same today.

Both of us went to work the next day. Muriel was the center of attraction when the news got out at the telephone exchange. She had not told anybody of the plans. I only told Audrey Walker, who sat opposite me at work, but she put the word out really fast.

With strange perfection of timing, Muriel's parents had decided that they could turn their third floor into a flat for rent, and we had priority. Somewhere to live was a major problem in those days. Money was extremely tight, and in the 10 years since the end of the war, with economies in Europe in shambles, the thousands of bombed buildings had not been replaced. Children, to a great extent, when married, moved in with parents, with a view to trying to save a little money with which to branch out on their own.

It was a bit of a nightmare moving Muriel's furniture from the basement flat next door into the third floor of Muriel's parents' house, and some of it had to remain as Susan was still there. However, in a few days, it was decided that Susan would move back in with her parents, and this allowed the move to be complete.

The gas stove was a big problem. They were mostly cast iron in those days, built to last a lifetime. We decided, (Muriel, Muriel's mother, and me), that getting it over the garden wall was the best way, and that's what we did. I don't remember the details, but I do remember balancing it on the top of the wall whilst I climbed over, then getting it down the other side to the garden level. Now we had to get it up 4 flights of stairs.

We had made it to about 2 ½ flights up, and tempers were getting frayed. I was getting angry. We had stopped making progress. Finally, to Muriel's tearful consternation, I yelled at them to get out of the way and picked up the gas stove, and staggered up the rest of the stairs. I arrived in the kitchen, and now I had the largest problem of all. How was I going to put down 130lbs or 170lbs of gas stove without it going down with a crash enough to send it through the floor? It slithered down me as I bent my knees, and the crash was enough to make the building shake, but the floor held.

Muriel and her friend Sylvia Knowles now started selling from a mail-order catalog to their workmates at the telephone exchange. Sylvia came every Monday evening to dinner, and they would work on their books, and arrange to send in the weekly payment. This went on for at least a year. Sylvia came from a dysfunctional family and was a bit pathetic within herself. She showed outward confidence, but despair seemed just below the surface. She was an attractive girl but must have put men off somehow because she seemed to have limited choices where men were concerned.

One day Sylvia announced she'd met this young man named Roger. We met him and he was small and slight of build, and softly spoken, but very nice. He started coming to dinner Monday evenings also, and we would talk together as the girls worked on their books.

Roger appeared to enjoy my company very much, which I regarded as a great compliment. But, there could have been another reason.

SPECIAL NOTE; Throughout this book, there are many small stories related, and in order to complete them, facts get out of chronological order. I beg your forgiveness.

I have to get chronologically ahead somewhat and finish this little story now that I've started it. Sylvia and Roger's relationship matured, and she told Muriel that he came to see her at the weekends, and stayed overnight. She rented a couple of rooms in a large house.

"He was such a gentleman", she boasted, "that he would not touch me at all because we were not married, even though we were in the same bed!!!" It seemed to me that there was something strangely wrong here, but Muriel did not agree with me, her being pure romantic that she was, and it was not for us to get involved.

Eventually, we went to their wedding, and they moved to Gloucester, about 30 miles away. We had a motorbike by this time, and one Saturday we were invited to their flat in Gloucester for a Saturday afternoon. Whilst there we were told that Roger's friend came to stay every weekend, and because he was so very tall he could not sleep in the small 3-foot bed in the spare room, so Sylvia used that bed and left the big bed to the men.

We had a nice time, and we were leaving at around 6.00 pm. We were outside when Roger's friend arrived. He was not tall at all. I could sleep very well in a small bed and he was much shorter than me. My feet would stick out a bit but not enough to create a real problem. Everything fell into place now. Muriel stayed in touch, and she found out that 6 months after the marriage, Roger was still being a "gentleman", and now Sylvia was a little worried. A LITTLE worried? Muriel felt it appropriate to advise her friend, and a visit to Muriel's lady doctor was arranged for a Saturday morning. Muriel had begun to see the world in a different light.

On the appointed day, our doorbell rang. It was Sylvia. She had come to tell Muriel that Roger would not let her go to the doctor. He stayed out on the road with their motorbike. That was the last we saw of Sylvia for several years.

It was about 5 years later that Muriel received a call from Sylvia out of the blue, to say she was now living in Bristol, about 10 miles away. She was divorced, and she wanted to come and pay us a visit. We were now living in our own house after a few years of very hard savings, and Muriel suggested she consider staying for the weekend. Muriel was to regret that.

Sylvia arrived and with her was a very strange creature. They came on a motorbike driven by her companion, who was about the same height as Sylvia, about 5'2". This person had on a man's leather motorbike jacket, with huge leather gloves and boots up to the knee, and strutted like a Hell's Angel.

The voice that came out was a "near female" voice but strangled to sound gruff and deep. We were embarrassed and then mortified when they proceeded to sit on the floor with their backs against a sofa, snuggled up with their arms about each other. Muriel soon took Sylvia aside and pointed out that staying overnight was not an option now. That, finally, was the last we saw of Sylvia. We often wonder what sort of a sad life she finally found.

Whilst on the subject of Sylvia, there were a couple of strange things worth telling...

One day early in their friendship, Sylvia took Muriel to see her father. He lived in a small attic flat with a woman, not Sylvia's mother. There was no furniture that Muriel could see except a table, and 4 wooden orange crates on end, and obviously used as chairs. There was one other very strange thing spread around the room. On the floor were at least 50 empty milk bottles.

Later on, Sylvia took Muriel to see her only sister. She was married and lived in the Royal Crescent in Bath. This crescent is one of the Georgian Crescents for which Bath is famous. The houses are very large, with 5 floors. Sylvia's sister and husband lived on the ground floor in one large bed-sitter.

There was some furniture including a bed and a table. .and . . . some orange crates on end . . . and. . . . about 50 empty milk bottles spread around the floor.

It seems that orange crates and milk bottles must have some serious significance for Sylvia's strange relatives.

Sylvia offered no comments, as if collecting milk bottles and sitting on orange crates was the thing to do. The subject never came up again.

To complete the above story, it was necessary to get out of the correct time sequence, so now we turn back a number of years to the time we were first married.

Muriel's father seemed to get along with me pretty well, and I think that Muriel's relationship with him improved. Muriel's younger sisters were always upstairs with us, visiting and we were very happy. Muriel's sister Phyllis was about 12 at the time and she attached herself to me. She was there when I did dishes, peeled vegetables, and hung around every day, until one day I playfully flicked water at her. Inexplicably, she ran off and complained loudly to her mother that I threw water over her. She was very upset, and she never came back after that.

Within a few months, there was great excitement, we were going to have a baby. Muriel carried on very much as usual, in fact, we have a photograph of her playing soccer 3 weeks before

Christopher was born. She is shown jumping for the ball with both feet off the ground! Hardly the behavior of a respectable pregnant lady.

My sister Brenda sent a large package of baby clothes and muslin diapers from America. (They were a godsend as they dried much quicker than the English toweling diapers).

A month or so before our baby was due, my mother and youngest sister, Rosemary went off to Canada. As you learned earlier in this story, Rosemary suffered from asthma, and it was decided in those days that the best thing to do was to leave England's damp and cold. The modern idea is that asthma is an allergy and cold and dampness do not affect it, but she never had a recurrence all the time she stayed out of England. She came for three weeks' vacation when she was about 14 and spent most of the time sick with asthma, the first since she left, which proves that the English climate has something to do with it.

Susan, Muriel's next younger sister, had met this nice young Scottish fellow named George. We invited him and Susan to dinner, and things were going fine.

A funny thing happened one evening. Susan was going to a dance with George and was wearing a newly bought bra. She appeared at our flat all dressed up ready to go, but a bit worried about this new bra, a padded form bra. She felt it was a bit too pointed and hard. She asked Muriel to check it/her out. They stood in the middle of the room with Muriel groping away saying "I don't think it's too bad". They both turned to me asking me to come over and give my opinion.

I don't know if they really wanted me to go and grope Susan or not, but they were insistent, and didn't seem to realize what they were asking. They waited, and my embarrassed reluctance finally caused the penny to drop. Susan blushed bright red, and Muriel giggled.

We were lucky in that the Post Office (which ran the telephones systems) paid employees whilst they were off having a baby, so our income continued, thank goodness.

I can remember the early morning that Muriel woke me up saying the bed was wet and that she thought her bladder had burst! She actually said that. We soon realized when pains started that it was time to think about getting to St. Martins Hospital where Muriel had booked. To our horror when we arrived at the hospital, they announced that they were full up, and they said that the other local hospital, the Royal United Hospital was also full and they had been sending people to Bristol, a half-hour journey. Time was getting close, and they finally suggested a small private hospital, Forbes Frazer, which was just the other side of Bath. They offered this, saying that there would be a charge and not completely free as the other hospitals. That is where we went, arriving at about 6.30 am. This was in the days when men had no part in having babies. The farther away you kept them the better. There were no buses running at this early hour, so after Muriel was admitted, and she was settled in, I was sent away. I walked home and then went to work. The nurse in-charge told me to call back at 3.00 pm to see if there was any news.

The day dragged, and at 3.00 pm I decided I would not use the office phone. I walked about 300 yards to a public phone on the main road of the Admiralty installation where I worked. I got the news that Christopher had been born within minutes of my phone call (at 3.05 pm) and weighed in at 7lbs 15ozs. It was Thursday 7th June 1956. I was 21, and Muriel was 21 until the 11th of June.

I remember the incredible run back across the grass to the office. I don't think I have ever run so fast before or since. It was as if my feet barely touched the ground. I've heard people describe this feeling before, and now I had experienced it for myself.

The Forbes Frazer was a small hospital with all private rooms. Each room had a rose-covered patio with French windows. Meals were served with silver and china, not chrome and earthenware as in the other hospitals, which were run by the socialized medicine system in England. The additional charge was not much, and Joy took a liking to be treated with importance. She was in there for 12 days which was normal in those days. The last thing they said to Muriel was, "See you again next year". They were only just right with 9 days to spare.

In the hospital Muriel had commented on how tanned Christopher looked, saying maybe he'd been put in a sunny spot in the nursery, only to be told that he had a touch of jaundice, apparently common with newborns.

Just after Muriel came out of hospital, my mother returned from Canada and their decision was made to emigrate permanently as soon as it could be arranged.

Chapter 12 - We Are Now Three

Christopher seemed a beautiful baby to us. Muriel made everybody look at photographs, and he was surrounded by all of Muriel's adoring younger sisters. We didn't lack for people to cuddle him, especially in the first few weeks. Soon it was time for Muriel to go back to work, and as arranged, my mother agreed to have Christopher during the day for as long as she was in England.

However, it wasn't very long before my mother went off back to Canada, and Muriel's mother took over caring for Christopher. My father was to follow to Canada some weeks later when he had sold up everything, but he became ill and he came to stay with us for the last 3 weeks. In the evenings, Muriel's mother would join us and we played card games around my father's bed, which he seemed to enjoy very much. When his luck was bad, he would turn over in bed, which he equated with walking around his chair to change his luck. The big day came and off he went to Canada. By this time, I was the only one of my immediate family still in England. Daphne, Colin and daughter, and Sylvia and Charles had emigrated to Florida in the preceding few years, to live near Brenda. As related earlier in this story, my eldest sister had gone to Canada as a war bride at the end of the Second World War.

It was time for me to look around for higher-paid work, and an opportunity came up which included living accommodation. This was very attractive as housing was very valuable and costly, and free rent was part of the job. We vacated the flat at Muriel's mother's house and a very nice young couple moved in. I became the manager of a shop that sold newspapers, magazines, sweets, chocolate, all sorts of candies, stationery, books, tobacco, cigarettes, cigars, greeting cards, and had a lending library. There was only one snag, most of the newspapers were delivered by delivery boys who had to come at about 6.00 am to get the papers delivered on time. Also many people would pick up newspapers, cigarettes and magazines on the way to work, so I had to be there to open up at 6.00 am. The store stayed open until 6.30 pm, and this was 6 days a week, which made a very long week. I was tired nearly all the time, and our ability to have any other sort of life diminished. Muriel would leave very early for work and take Christopher to the town on one bus, catch another to her mother's, then walk about a mile to catch a third bus to work. Then, of course, did the reverse to get home quite late. I kept up the high jumping, but with so little time, I didn't have much enthusiasm and didn't make any progress.

While we were at the shop, we saw this very attractive motorbike for sale at the local dealer, and we lashed out and bought it. It was stretching our finances to the limit, but we felt it would make life a little easier. It was a Douglas, Dragonfly model, and unique in England in that it had horizontally opposed cylinders which stuck out each side just in front of the footrests. It kept your feet warm which was a bonus. The motorbike I got at the age of 15 from Bill Lord was also a Douglas, with the same horizontally opposed cylinders, but one pointing to the front and one to the rear. This new model attracted admirers everywhere. It was such a different-looking machine. However, it had a problem, the big end bearings, (where the bottom of the connecting rods meets the crankshaft). It had needle roller bearings, instead of the more common white metal bearings, and they would fail after a short time.

Sure enough, after a while, I started to hear a slight tapping sound, and it got gradually worse. I had to face up to the problem, and took the engine apart. The bearings were quite loose, and I had the crankshaft taken apart by a local company to see if they could repair it. In the meantime, the Douglas Co had gone out of business because of the crankshaft problem. With the crankshaft in pieces, the cause of the problem was very obvious. Sand from the mold was filling the oilways, so that no oil could get to the bearings. In my opinion, this was near criminal behavior on the part of some worker or workers who destroyed a company and caused all sorts of trouble for owners simply through laziness and not doing their job. The motorbike was a wonderful machine. It was very comfortable to ride, and economical on petrol. I used to do 120 miles to an Imperial gallon, or 96 miles to the American gallon. It had excellent acceleration, but not a very good high speed. I suspect it was under-geared. Finally, I sent the crankshaft away for repair, and got the machine going again.

Joy's sister Susan surprised us one day by announcing that she was going with Brian Winter, from my school days. This was the one with whom I'd had a shoving match when he came to the school when we were about 9 years old. I voiced to Muriel my reservations about him, but it was not our problem. After a few months, when Muriel, Susan, and I were in our kitchen, with him in the living room, she announced that she was going to marry him. I said words to the effect that she must be crazy. She burst into tears and ran to him and told him what I'd said. Not a very good start for brothers-in-law. They got married a month or so later.

One day a little girl about 8 years old was in the shop and was frozen with the cold. I knew her as she lived only about 30 yards away around the corner. She said she was locked out and nobody was home. She asked me if I could get her into the house, so I said, "Let's go and take a look". She took me to the back door, which was a conservatory door, (a glass-enclosed lean-to), and the door was locked, but the key was in the lock on the inside. It was an old-fashioned lock which took a key on each side, and you could see if the key was in it. There was a gap under the door, so I was able to push the key out gently so that it dropped on the floor, and then I was able to slide the key out under the door with a pencil. She got into the house and I thought I'd done her or her parents a favor. I knew what it was like to be locked out when it is getting cold and dark.

A day or two later, her mother let me know that they were not pleased that I was able to open the door. It wasn't my fault, but they just felt I had invaded their territory.

Almost immediately following that, the little girl came down with Polio, or what we called Infantile Paralysis, and she was shipped off to the Bath Isolation Hospital. This hospital was at the top of Brassknocker Hill overlooking the Limpley Stoke Valley on the way to the Admiralty where I used to work. Within 10 days I was there also with Polio.

We had been at the shop for 10 months and the Polio epidemic had everybody scared. I always supposed that I must have caught it from the little girl. She was in the next glass-enclosed room to me, and she was in a coma for days. My infection didn't get paralytic, but I had excruciating backache. In the meantime, my employer called the hospital to enquire about my prognosis and was told that I might be there for years, so they gave Muriel notice to leave the accommodation. So here we were, me possibly disabled for life or worse, no job, no home, one baby, and Muriel pregnant, but other than that we were OK.

The polio epidemic had everybody terribly scared. Nobody would come near Muriel for fear of catching the Polio. She was only able to come to see me in the hospital because her tough little Auntie Celia would look after Christopher by taking him to the park. Muriel was not allowed to go to work until I was pronounced OK, but her pay continued.

I had been in hospital for almost a week when the little girl in the next room suddenly came to, and got out of bed, swaying like a drunken sailor. I rang for a nurse who came and got her into bed. Within a short time, she recognized me. Then I was moved out to make room for the really bad patients. I was taken to the next building, where there was a central nurse's station and office, with a large ward on each side.

As I was being wheeled in I saw the right-hand ward was full of children or young people with all sorts of harnesses holding up limbs etc. What struck me when I saw this collection of tragedies, was the laughter and chatter coming from these unfortunate ones. They were having a grand old time in spite of their adversity. I was wheeled to the left-ward, which appeared to be filled with iron lungs, (no people), which looked like big coffins on wheels. There were dozens and dozens of them plus lots of other big pieces of medical equipment. I was swung around and into a little ante-room attached to the center part of the building. In it was one bed, with a French window looking out onto the Limpley Stoke Valley. Also, there was a tiny window high up where the nurses could look through from their office. However, it was so high that only the very tallest could use it unless they stood on a chair. I hardly saw a soul all day long except for meal deliveries. My backache had gone, and I was beginning to feel better, but still seemed weak. Muriel came to see me in my new room and was overjoyed with some good news for once. The nice young couple who had moved into her mother's house in the flat we vacated was now moving out, and we could move back in, but this had to be accomplished while I was still in the hospital. Brian Winter, Joy's sister Susan's husband was the only one who would help Muriel move even though he was terrified of catching polio. Everybody else in the family was too scared to help.

This hospital room that I occupied became a nightmare at night. I was constantly disturbed by feelings of movement around me when there was nobody there. I woke up once with a start. There was something like a hand clap right in front of my face, and I saw hands withdrawing from right before my eyes. I have never had another experience like it. I made up my mind I was getting out, but the first thing to do was to get to walk again. The only advantage of this lonely room was that I could do what I liked without being seen, and I went to work. The first thing was to sit up without feeling giddy, and then get my legs over the edge of the bed. This I accomplished by the next day. By the third day, I made it to the bathroom in the corner of the room and walked around a bit. I told Muriel I would be coming out the next day and to bring my clothes with her. Muriel protested and was very worried. She talked to a nurse in charge who said it was impossible as I might have a relapse and they would not take me back etc. (They always say that).

On the third day, I was walking at will, and a doctor and two nurses came to see me. I informed them that I was not staying in the room another night and they said they were full up with the epidemic, so I had no choice. I told them I would go home then, and they told me that I couldn't go home until I could walk. I said, "Fine, I could walk", and they laughed until I got out of bed and walked around.

Muriel arrived with my clothes, and to dire warnings, we left and went home to our old flat. I didn't feel too good for the rest of the day, but by the next day, with a good night's sleep with no ghostly visits, I was feeling like I was getting back to normal. That afternoon I rode my motorcycle back to the hospital and delivered a box of chocolates to the nurses. I lost a lot of weight in those two weeks, and we look back at photographs of that time and can't believe how sick and skinny I looked then. However, in a way, it was one of those unfortunate times which turns out to be for the best.

Within a few weeks, I was almost back to normal although very thin. My next task was to find a job. My sister Brenda sent us money, which helped us no end. Muriel had no running about delivering Christopher on her way to work. She just had to take him down the stairs to her mother, and that was good. It made her day much shorter. Christopher was now walking, and more trouble as he was into everything, but he had admiring aunts who helped out. He was a lovely little boy.

By this time I was no longer high jumping in a serious way. I could still win without really trying.

I saw an advert in the newspaper for two vacancies at the Thames Rubber Co., about 12 miles from Bath. They manufactured all sorts of tires, (tyres in England), and all sorts of industrial rubber goods. I was interviewed by a personnel manager named Walt Taylor, who decided I was best suited for the higher-paying job of the two, which was working as assistant to the export executive, Eric Bull. But first Eric Bull had to interview me. He came to Walt Taylor's office to take me back to his office, and as we were going up the stairs, with him in the lead, he threw me a question, "How much are 120 tenpences?" Poor man, he didn't know that at school I had always been way out in front of all the other kids in all mental arithmetic tests. Before he finished speaking I gave him his answer, "ten pounds". He told me later that my immediate answer got me the job. However, it was a week before I got the formal appointment. I started with more money than I'd received at the shop. Things were turning around.

Within a few months of all this, David was born. Muriel had tasted the luxury at the Forbes Frazer Hospital, and wanted a repeat, so that is where we went on Sunday, 22nd December 1957 at 8.30 am. David must have been eager because he was born at 9.05 am, just 35 minutes later. He weighed in a 7lbs 10 oz. This time Joy was in there for 10 days.

I will never forget how unusually depressed I was as Joy was in the hospital over Christmas. My family was in Canada and America, and Christopher, at 18 months, and I, were alone. Muriel's mother later in the day, did ask us to join them for Christmas dinner which we gratefully accepted. She had 8 younger children at home and didn't need more problems.

I have often wondered about the depression that hit me at that time. I have never had a problem with depression, and the only reason I can think of was that my unhappiness was increased by the fact that little Christopher wanted his mother so badly. We made a very unhappy pair. In England, at that time children were not allowed in hospitals, just one of those silly rules which don't make a lot of sense. He didn't see his mother at all while she was away. Visiting times at the hospital were, an hour in the morning and afternoon, and in the evening you could stay a bit longer. Muriel got a bit upset if I didn't go all three times if it was humanly possible. Muriel's family had Christopher for me. Now I had the motorbike which made it easier.

At last, we brought David home. He was lighter than Christopher had been but somehow seemed heavier and bigger. He was completely different from Christopher, who had a small button nose. David had a real nose. The most immediate noticeable difference was David had a voracious appetite. He would swig down everything offered and cry for more. Muriel had given up work when she was eight months pregnant with David so she was able to stay home with the boys. We were saving like crazy and had cut out many expenditures. I could not jump higher than 5'6" due to being a bit weak from lack of food, but it paid off.

David was seven months old and Christopher was about 2 years and we moved into our own house at 7 the Vineyards, Bath. The house had 3 floors and a semi-basement. We used the basement, and the next floor up. The floor above that was already rented to an elderly, though active lady named Miss Andrews. The top floor was empty, and we advertised it and had 19 people apply for it. We interviewed all of them and a youngish German lady named Crystal seemed to be the best so she moved in. She had this older gentleman friend who visited her several times a week, but they were no trouble, and things went well.

One morning, soon after we moved in, Muriel had bathed David ready to go out and she had put him temporarily in the pram or perambulator, or baby carriage, depending on where you live, whilst she went to get ready. When she returned she nearly died of fright. Christopher, just over two, had grabbed the zinc and castor oil cream (like Desitin) and plastered it all over David's head and face. He looked like a ghost and Muriel could not think what had happened.

Another escapade of Christopher's around this time involved him trying to be helpful. Muriel had been washing the paintwork on the stairs using scouring powder. "Vim" in England, "Comet" in the USA.

Muriel had everything in the downstairs hallway, ready to put away, but she had to leave the area for a moment. When she returned, she found every stair had a liberal sprinkling of scouring powder. It took her ages to vacuum up the mess.

Over the first Christmas Auntie Dolly and Uncle Les, Auntie May and Uncle Fred and, son John came to stay. Auntie Dolly and Les lived in Winsley, near where I used to live on Winsley Hill, Limpley Stoke. Auntie May and Fred lived in Erith near where I was born in the London area. We were very poor but we had a great time. I shall always remember that it started to snow heavily on Christmas Eve and we had a beautiful white Christmas.

Muriel and I had bought two enameled slow-combustion stoves for burning coal, and we were as warm as toast in that house. One stove was going 24 hours a day. We found that if we bought the cheapest coal, which was large lumps and coal dust, it would stay burning all night, and the house was always cozy. With one large lump of coal, it sometimes burned from 10.00 pm until 9.00 am the next day. Regardless, it lasted mostly all night making the house very comfortable. The children would get out of bed in the morning, and run, with their clothes, to the room in which this stove burned.

I ran into Bill Lord, the person from whom I bought a motorcycle for 7 pounds when I was 15. He told me that Johnny Symes, my father's old friend, had been ill, and also had just got married. He gave me his address, and a few days later we got on the motorbike and went to see him. He was surprised and very happy with our visit. He asked me where we were living, and I told him 7 The Vineyards. He got sort of shocked look on his face. He said, "Do you remember my story about the hands around my throat in the night?" I answered in the affirmative. "That was at number 4 The Vineyards", he said.

While we are on this subject, I should relate more about our house.

When we were in our first winter, we found that in the basement where we were living, a draft came from the door at the front, and whistled along the central hallway to the back door. In order to slow this down, I put an extra door halfway down this hallway. It was hinged just at the doorway to the living room that we used. We obviously always tried to keep this door closed, but it would always be found open. We would close it again and within minutes it would be standing open. Now this door did not naturally swing open, it would naturally stand wherever it was left, and with the door latch in the closed position, there should have been no possibility of the door opening on its own. In desperation, I put a rubber band between the door and door-jamb, but this never did make any difference!

One evening, Muriel and I were sitting quietly in our living room, with only the slight noise of passing traffic, when a rattle of the old and loose door handle caused us both to look up quickly, just in time to see the door knob turning. We froze. We thought that the two boys were asleep upstairs, and Miss Andrews was the only other person in the house, and she never came into the basement. The door swung open towards us and stopped at a right angle to the closed position. We waited for a second, but nobody appeared. I called out, "Christopher", no answer. I got up and made a detour to the fireplace where I picked up a long and heavy poker, and took a wide swing to see around the door without getting too close. It was dark in the hallway outside, and I could see nothing or nobody. I worked my way towards the door and lunged to the light switch for the hallway, but there was nobody there. The two children were sleeping soundly upstairs. It never happened again, thank goodness.

At work, at the Thames Rubber Company, Eric Bull, the Export Executive, was easy to get along with, and seemed to appreciate my work. He was responsible for exporting tires and other rubber goods overseas. The company had some overseas depots and dealers. For those who aren't familiar with international commerce, the export documentation requirements are different for every country. Also, there are all sorts of penalties including prison and financial penalties etc. for errors. It is a very difficult business and full of pot-holes. The actual paperwork was done by Ron Merril who also worked for Eric Bull, and it was my job to assist him later in the day, as the documentation was time sensitive. Merchandise was being shipped out from the Stores and Despatch, (English spelling), and the paperwork had to be mailed out to the shipping agent the same day. Ron was one of the world's strangest people. He was about 5'5", slim build, and a heavy smoker as was Eric Bull. Ron had married, at the age of 33, a lady whom he described as "plump". Later he showed me a photograph. "Plump" was extremely polite. She was short and was wearing a long dress, almost to her ankles, with a tight belt, making her look like a sack of potatoes tied in the middle. They had a one-year-old daughter.

Ron was renowned for his absent-mindedness. He would slip so deeply into his work that all else would be beyond his sight and hearing. Later in the afternoon, we would start to run back and forth, to invoicing getting the necessary paperwork, and one particular occasion we were both going up the stairs to our office, and he opened the door and pulled it shut in my face, and went on talking to me. I could hear through the door. Another time I had the top drawer of a filing cabinet open about 9", and was looking through the very front file, when suddenly the drawer was jerked open into my chest, a hand went into the back, and a sheet of scrap paper was pulled out, and the drawer slammed. I said, "Ron, what are you doing?" Ron said, "Oh, I'm sorry, I didn't see you." I'm not exactly hard to see from 2 feet away. This was typical of Ron. He didn't have a bad bone in his body, but he was almost dangerous with his absentmindedness.

I used to go to lunch with him at the company canteen and that was a real experience. Some of the girls from accounting would always sit at the next table just for the entertainment. They actually told me this. I was able to amuse Muriel most nights with Ron's latest escapades. I only wish I could remember more of them, but I will relate those that I can remember.

Ron and his wife used to divide up the cash in his pay-packet, with him getting money for his lunches and cigarettes, etc. and she got the rest for housekeeping. If either had money left, it went back into the pot, so both of them spent all of their share before that happened, a really stupid arrangement as they were working against each other.

Ron would often run low on cash before payday, and he would buy something inexpensive for lunch. The food was subsidized by the company and was excellent value. You could get the best meal for about 2 shillings, (24 pence), but you could buy soup or crackers, butter and cheese for four pence, and a steak and kidney pie for ten pence. The particular day I remember was the time he bought a steak and kidney pie on one plate, and a bowl of soup in another. The pie came sliding around on a regular dinner plate. The soup came in an English soup plate, which is like any other soup bowl except it has a flat rim around it about 1 ½" wide.

Ron sat down with these two plates, and studied the situation. He had brought a soup-spoon and a knife and fork with him. You could almost hear the wheels spinning. The light went on. A decision had been reached. He took the pie between thumb and forefinger, and dropped it in the soup bowl. Of course the extra volume caused the soup to flow copiously over the edge of the plate onto the table. Ron let go a loud "oh". Surprise, surprise. The girls from accounting tittered behind their hands. Ron composed himself very quickly but was now faced with another problem; his pie and the rest of his soup in the same plate. Should he use a spoon or a fork? I don't remember exactly what he did except he carried on in his normal way, lost in his own world.

Another of Ron's favorite tricks was to buy crackers, butter, and cheese, which he did probably 3 times a week. Now these English crackers were 2 1/2" square and completely brittle and crumbled easily.

Ron always held his knife in his right hand, with his index finger applying pressure halfway down the back edge of the blade of his knife. Consequently, he would get gravy or butter or anything he was eating on his index finger. (It should be noted that butter is a bit harder in England due to the lower temperatures). When it came to spreading butter on crackers, he would hold the crackers between the thumb and index finger of his left hand and spread butter getting a goodly proportion on his finger. Now here comes the good part which happened every time without fail when he ate cheese and biscuits. He would apply excessive pressure with the buttering and every time, the cracker would crack down the middle, and butter and crumbs would go everywhere to more titter from the audience. Also, he would get butter nicely smeared at the base of his thumb and palm of his hand. He did this at least once every time he had cheese and crackers. It was incredible that Ron, a reasonably intelligent person in most things, had such blind spots and never did learn. He seemed oblivious to the way that other people ate and did things.

One other amusing occurrence happened sometime later when the exporting increased. We had an additional man, Stan Black. He was from Yorkshire and was a slow, quiet, methodical man that nothing seemed to surprise. He was completely unflappable, in fact, he appeared to be half asleep, except he was good at the job.

By this time, I had been promoted to the position of assistant superintendent of stores and dispatch, at the other end of the factory. I still went to lunch with Ron, Stan, and my replacement working for Eric Bull, a young man named Bob Golding. Anyway, one day we all four sat down with our food, and Ron was sitting across the table from Stan. Ron reached for the salt and sprinkled it liberally over his plate. Then, to the surprise of the rest of us, he leaned over and liberally sprinkled Stan's plate. Stan's head went up with a jerk, which caught Ron's attention and woke him up. "Oh, sorry Stan," said Ron. "That's OK Ron", said Stan, and we continued as if nothing had happened. I was trying to not laugh, but the usual gallery of accounting girls was exploding on the next table.

Whilst we are talking about funny things, I had an experience that was very dangerous and frightening at the time but makes me smile now because of my reaction to it.

I'm not sure if I explained that our house at 7, The Vineyards was on a steep slope toward the road. The front door was level with the rear garden, but one floor above the road. However, there was a 12-foot wide sidewalk built upon arches, one level up from the road, on to which our front door opened. I kept my motorcycle in the center one of the 3 arches in front of our basement which supported the sidewalk. It was very convenient as I had immediate access to the road with the motorcycle. However, the center of the arch was only about 5'9" high, and I had to bend over and stay in the middle.

One day during a period of gasoline rationing, I needed to know how much gas was in the tank on my motorcycle, and the archway was very, very dark. I couldn't find a flashlight in spite of looking everywhere. I considered the use of a candle, but immediately dismissed it as a bit risky, but then decided that if I held the candle high, almost touching the ceiling, there would be a little risk as it would be 2 feet from the tank. How wrong can you be?

I raised the candle sputtering against the high point of the arch as I carefully unscrewed the cap, ready to peer into the tank. Immediately there was a huge blue flash, and a 12" flame erupted from the tank. The cap was in my left hand only inches away, and instinctively I smacked the cap back on, and luckily it went right into place. I seriously believe I broke all known world records for leaping away to safety behind the back wall of the archway. I waited for the expected BOOM. None came, but I was frozen in position for a minute or so before moving from comparative safety.

Why did all this happen? My explanation is that some gasoline was always evaporating through the bleed hole in the cap, and accumulating in a cloud at the high point of the arch. With no movement of air we had a nice reservoir of flammable gas, and holding the candle high was the worst thing I could do. Luckily there was no oxygen in the tank, which saved a huge explosion. I felt I had a very fortunate escape, but can't help smiling about it now.

Chapter 13 - Muriel Goes Back To Work

In order to accumulate some money, Muriel found an evening job, working as a waitress 4 nights a week, at a medium to low-class restaurant down by the railway station. Their specialty was in the area of sausage, mash and baked beans, or mixed grill of lamb chop, small piece of steak, liver, bacon, sausage, mushrooms, and fried tomatoes. This place would stay open until all hours, at least until 2.00 am. Then the owner, Mr Roberts would send all the workers home in a taxi. I would often wake up to the sound of car doors slamming, and Muriel would arrive and get right into bed. Mostly she was cold and had this habit of placing the flat of her feet on my calves. That really woke me up.

Because my arrival time for coming home from work was so unreliable, Muriel arranged to have her younger sister Pamela come to babysit, and when I arrived, I would take her home. She liked coming to our house, and she would sometimes stay for dinner.

I grew vegetables in the back garden, and I had this patch of garden where I planted spinach. At the end of the first season, it went to seed, and the next spring it grew again in a wide patch without being re-planted. I would cut it with garden shears, and clean it in the clothes washing machine, (rinse cycle) and then in bags, for final cleaning when we used it. We ate a lot of spinach in the summer.

One evening Pamela was there for dinner, and she declined to eat spinach. I prevailed upon her to try some with butter and pepper. She loved it and ate a pile of it, then confessed that she'd never tasted it before.

Mr. Roberts, the owner of the restaurant, was a drunk. He would come into the place after drinking all evening, and bully the staff. However, this didn't work with Muriel and she would tell him off. He had a wooden chair leg which he would carry around the restaurant brandishing it. The customers were not the highest class of people, and if he didn't like the look of somebody, he would give them a bad time. Somehow they always came back as it was the only place open.

When Muriel had only been there a week or so, he announced that he would not pay them as was due that night. The old staff said that he was in one of his moods, and they would not see the money tonight. Muriel stood up to him and told him he had no choice and he'd better pay up. He argued, but finally gave in and left instructions to pay everybody. Later, he took Muriel aside and gave her a flat raise of 10 shillings a week, but said to not tell anybody else. From that time on he slipped the extra money to Joy on the sly, not putting it through the books so that nobody else knew.

Muriel used to tell me of this nice youngish man who paid lots of attention to her. He told her his name was Jack Peters, and he worked at the Thames Rubber Co. I recognized the name as one of the men who worked for me. He always gave her very large tips and made it obvious that he admired her. She did not say that I worked at the same place as I was not too excited to broadcast that my wife worked at this sleazy place as a waitress. I was now a member of the upper staff.

One night, one of Muriel's customers ran out without paying, and Muriel followed him outside and came back to yell, "Call the police". With that, she ran up the road after him and in spite of him running also, she caught him about 200 yards from the restaurant. He was a bit drunk, and he went down on the ground and Muriel sat on him. A regular customer had heard Muriel yell and followed the chase. He came puffing up and helped Muriel hold the criminal. The police arrived immediately. The police station was 200 yards away. He was hauled off in handcuffs. Mr. Roberts gave Muriel one pound reward and later told her that the criminal was in the Navy, and AWOL.

Apparently, the local newspaper picked up the story and it was in the headlines the next day, "Mother of two detains runaway customer". They made it sound dramatic, giving her full name and adding in the first few lines that she was married to Brian Walters, Somerset County High Jump Champion. This completely identified me with Jack Peters. Suddenly, Jack Peters stopped going to the restaurant and acted very awkwardly towards me for a time.

Another time Muriel was questioned by the police about whether she remembered anybody spending lots of small coins. She did remember somebody paying for a meal with small coins, and so she went to the police station to look at mug-shots. She found him but was surprised because the man she identified had seemed so nice to her. He was arrested for breaking into church collection boxes.

She had to go to court, and give evidence, and he yelled out that he would get her, etc. He went to jail as a habitual offender.

Chapter 14 - Life Gets Better

Every year, for many years, we took the children to Swanage, a seaside town on the south coast of England. We would go for one week in June and another week in September. We picked on Swanage because I read that they had more sunshine than any other place in England. For year after year, we had the best weather, and people started asking us when we were going away so that they could pick the same weeks.

The first time we went, Mr. Roberts volunteered his wife to drive us and come and pick us up for the return journey, which was very nice. Mrs. Roberts was a nice classy lady and a good driver. Mr. Roberts came with us the first time, stayed on a few hours, and rented a sailboat and a skipper so that he and I could go mackerel fishing.

The clouds were scudding along at hilltop height and a stiff wind was blowing. Swanage is in a semi-circular bay, and the waves were coming into the bay like big old rollers maybe as high as 6 feet. I believe that Mr. Roberts was trying to scare me as he kept grabbing the tiller and running parallel to the waves, and the skipper was wrestling with him at times to change course. At times the boat was swinging from side to side almost 180 degrees. It was a wonder that the boat didn't turn over. We caught 9 mackerel which the skipper kept, and we got off the boat after 3 hours of bouncing around. I felt a little bit seasick, but was not going to let Mr. Roberts know that.

We usually rented an apartment, not always the same place, and sat on the beach most days, whilst the children played in the sand and the water. We both remember so clearly a picture of David at about 12 months, with a big scab on his upper lip, in a diaper, and jiffy pants (the name given to water-proof pants over diapers), wearing only a blue cardigan to keep the wind out. He was covered with wet sand, having a whale of a time with his brother Chris. David had fallen and really banged up his upper lip just before we'd left for the holiday.

One morning early on one of our vacations, we were horrified to see that the baby, (not sure which one) had found a place where the wallpaper must have had an edge not quite glued down. He had pulled off a triangular patch about 12" by 9". And even worse, it was then torn into the tiniest pieces, none more than an inch square. The pattern was all tiny flowers. We went out and bought a bottle of office glue, and I spent most of the day re-doing a repair job like a jigsaw puzzle. It was harder because of the tiny pattern. Before we left, we felt obliged to tell the owner, who said, "You should have told us, we have rolls of that paper in the basement".

It was probably on the trip in the next September when David was about 22 months old that we drove to the hill overlooking the bay for a last goodbye when we were on our way home. There were lots of large horse chestnut trees, and what we called conkers (horse chestnuts) on the ground. Anyway, we proceeded on our way home but stopped for lunch at a small restaurant in Shaftsbury. As you know some English people who think they are special or are trying to make you think it, are a bit snooty, or to use a cockney expression, "toffee-nosed", or "stuck up". Shaftsbury is a bit "posh", and I think all the local snobs were in that restaurant that day.

David's behavior was completely out of character for him. When his food came he would not eat. He wouldn't even pick up his spoon when normally he'd scoff down his and anybody else's food if they weren't watching.

I struggled with him to get him to pick up his spoon, but he wouldn't even open his hand. I finally tried to pry his fingers open, but he snatched his hand away, and with a flick of his arm, a conker flew through the air across the room, bouncing from one table to another to the startled looks of the occupants. There was a deathly hush. Then everybody looked at us. We were mortified. However, David's food was gone in a trice. He had clutched that Conker in his little hand for a couple of hours since leaving Swanage.

On a later trip, we took Pamela with us to Swanage. We had now got an inflatable raft, with two floats, and a frame with a seat. Pamela wanted to have a go, so off she went. The wind was blowing off the land, and suddenly we realized that she was being blown out, and was paddling the wrong way, pushing the paddles instead of pulling. I ran and got a rented peddle boat, and caught up to her, but the wind was too strong, and we made no headway. The raft was the problem, it was catching the wind. Finally, a young man who was renting out the boats grabbed a rowing boat and came out fast, and assisted us, and we got the raft and Pamela back OK.

It was about this time that Muriel's brother John came back after his stint in the Southern Rhodesian Police. He moved back into his parents' home, but before long he clashed with his father. The outcome was that he asked if we could find him a room, which we did and he lived with us for a time. He applied to Thames Rubber Company and started work in the sales department.

Christopher and David enjoyed the walled back garden. The house was about 200 years old, built on the grounds of a convent, on the vineyard in particular, hence the address. There were two houses to the right, then an old church. The neighbor to the left had a small Bath stone building at the end of his garden, and it was said that there was an underground passage that went all the way to Bath Abbey, about ¼ mile away. Apparently, it was full of rubble, and not useable currently.

Our house had some walls which were 2 feet thick and will be standing in another 200 years.

David and Christopher were up in their bedroom one day, playing, and there was a knock on the front door. When Muriel answered it, she was greeted by a person holding out a "D" size battery. Apparently, it had flown out of the window and just missed her walking past. Muriel apologized and went up the stairs to check things out. She found a dressing gown hanging over the window. (The windows were the old slide-up and-down type, with very large glass panes, about 2 1/2 feet square). She went to remove the dressing gown and was greeted by shouts to the effect that they were playing and they wanted it dark. Muriel removed it anyway to loud protests and found a battery size hole in the middle of the glass.

We had a near catastrophe. Christopher and David were in the living room, and Muriel was in the kitchen. We had this old reliable "Valor" paraffin (liquid) heater, like everybody used as a cheap way of heating a room quickly. It was in the room in which the two children were playing. Muriel just finished hanging out a load of laundry on the clothesline, and she went to check on the children. She got to the door, and the children were on the other side, trying to get out. The glass panels in the door were black, and the room was solid black smoke. Just then the doorbell rang. Muriel pushed the children into the kitchen and answered the door. A passer-by was there to say that there was smoke coming out of the window. Just then the fire department arrived. Apparently, the stove had malfunctioned in some way and poured out smoke through incomplete burning of the fuel. The children had black faces, and clothes, and there was soot everywhere in the room. We had only just finished painting and hanging new wallpaper in that room.

Before my promotion, I had worked in an office with about 10 people. Eric Bull shared another, smaller office with his boss, Harry Williams, who was manager of distribution, domestic, and export. He also was responsible for the Stores and Despatch (English spelling) department where all production was stored and shipped out by lorry (trucks)

There were four men in the office who worked directly for Harry Williams. They handled domestic distribution, and they sat with four desks pushed together. They played around all the time, telling loud jokes, and generally causing a fuss. When the vacancy occurred for an assistant superintendent of stores, we had to endure days of loud discussion about which of them would get the job. To everybody's surprise, including mine, Harry Williams selected me. Harry's words to me were, "How could I send one of those clowns to do a job like that?" It is an exercise in memory for me to remember the names of these 4 clowns, and that is what they were. Harry was not stupid. There was Fred Ford, average height and build with white hair and a very ruddy face. He was the senior one there and very occasionally would say, "Come on boys, let's get the work done". Next, was Jim Fowler, short, a little bit tubby, but the nicest one, then Tim Sanderson, the biggest, but fat with it, and finally Neil Goddard, again, very average in all ways.

I got a large increase in pay with the new job, and things really began to pick up for us. David was now 1-year-old and Christopher was 2 ½. David would go out in the back garden and play with Chris, and they had a grand time.

True to form, David was always hungry, and one day Muriel caught him munching on a fat garden snail. He was doing his bit to keep the garden pests down. Another time, in the house, she found him with pieces of something black around his mouth. It appeared that he had tried eating a piece of coal. We never did find out if he liked it.

Miss Andrews had left us by this time, but not before she called the RSPC, the Royal Society for Prevention of Cruelty to Children. One day an inspector showed up at the door and advised Muriel that "somebody" had reported that we were extremely cruel to our children. Apparently, she had seen one of us spank one of the boys, and she thought it was cruel. He was invited in to see the boys, and he looked them over and asked to see where they slept and appeared satisfied. When I came home from work to be told this I saw red. By this time we had bought a small car, and off I went to see this inspector and dragged him to our house in his shirt sleeves so that he could see them in the bathtub, and see that they were not bruised or hurt in any way. Actually, I really went to see if I could confirm our suspicions about Miss Andrews's involvement. He would not say for sure, but he didn't argue too much when I let him know we didn't appreciate having a meddling old lady spy living in our house. The outcome and confirmation came when Miss Andrews behaved very strangely and avoided us, and soon moved out to a flat 2 houses away where there was a family of about 4 or 5 kids. They were a noisy lot, with the mother continually screaming at the kids. Eventually, she called the RSPC to that household and then left there. That was the last we saw of her.

When Miss Andrews left we took over the rooms she occupied. As I said before, the very top floor was occupied by a youngish German lady named Crystal. Finally, she left and a Miss Massey took over the top floor. She was a timid little lady with a lisp. She had spent her life as a companion to rich old ladies, and the last one had died and left her as much furniture as she could use for her lifetime, then it reverted to a niece. She had one room packed to the ceiling to the point where you could not even get inside the room beyond the area of the door.

Miss Massey had not had much of a life, and as is normal for somebody of this type, she was very kind and considerate. Every time she went out, she tapped on our door and said to Muriel in her lispy way "any methage Mithis", or any message Missis. Muriel lived in fear of the times she would invite her up for a cup of tea. Her cups were filthy and stained. Sometimes she would bring a cup of strong tepid tea down for Muriel, and we didn't want to hurt her feelings so we thanked her very much, and it went into the kitchen sink. Muriel would scrub the cup, hoping that she would get the cleaned cup the next time she was invited upstairs.

Sometimes in the evening when Muriel was not working, we asked Miss Massey to keep her eye on the 2 children when they were in bed asleep, and we'd go for a walk. She loved to do this. She had never been married, and she really enjoyed our children. We always went down Milsom Street, and sometimes we would buy some chips (French fries). We always returned the same way. Milsom Street as you learned earlier is a street of large and expensive shops, and they were all lit up at night, although closed. Most of these shops had display windows, and to enter the store you had to walk as much as 25 feet between display windows to reach the entrance. One night, we were walking up the slight rise of Milsom Street, on the way home. I had packets of chips one in each pocket of this large coat I was wearing. I was eating from one and Muriel was putting her hand in the pocket nearest her and helping herself to hers. There were only about 10 people in the whole street, and as we passed Lawleys, a glass and china shop, I saw a tiny lady way inside the display windows, looking in the door toward the inside of the brightly lit shop. I suddenly realized it was Miss Thomas, the teacher with the ruler.

I pushed Muriel forward out of the line of sight and crept between the display windows until I was a few inches from Miss Thomas' back. She had no idea I was there. At her 5'2", I filled any escape route. Finally, I spoke. "Remember me Miss Thomas?" She whipped around at midchest height, and her head snapped back to look up at me. "I was 9 then, now I am an adult," I said in an unfriendly tone. "Do you remember rapping my knuckles with the edge of a ruler when I was 9?" She stuttered a bit and said that she did not. I was still standing close and said, "You were completely unfair, and made no attempt to find out what happened. That sort of thing could be very dangerous for you, you never know whose knuckles you might be rapping unfairly". I stood there, not moving for many long seconds more, then walked slowly away. I felt good about that encounter. Maybe several scared 9-year-olds were saved from a traumatic and unfair experience. It is unfortunate, especially in the schools for younger children, that the teachers in England at that time, were largely women and unmarried. They seemed to exist solely to vent their sadistic personalities to the kids. Of course, there were many good woman teachers, but funnily, they seemed to be all the married ones.

In my new position at Thames Rubber Co., I was responsible for supervising 90 store men with 3 foremen and ordering all the transport for outgoing products. My boss, the superintendent was Mr. George Henderson. He was 60 years old when I started there.

It immediately became clear that my size was an advantage in dealing with lorry (truck) drivers. The vehicles were supplied by British Road Services, a hold-over from the nationalization following the end of the war. The other big supplier was Spiers Transport, with the smallest, Pearces Transport. These drivers all belonged to strong unions and carried on like they were God. Mr. Henderson was a lovely little man at about 5'2", but was regarded as a joke when dealing with the drivers. He had started in that department when he was 15 and spent his whole working life working his way up.

The Lorries would come into the front end of the factory loaded with incoming supplies, and when empty, come to us for re-loading. Unfortunately, the front end would take their time unloading, and with 20 to 25 Lorries a day going out, we would be rushing like crazy as mostly we would get them later in the day. Many times I was the only one in the place assisting the drivers loading at 7.00 pm.

The Thames Rubber Company employed 3000 people and was in a small town near Bath which had a population of about 8000 people. Special buses would bring workers in from all over the Bath area and western Wiltshire County. Wiltshire had always been predominantly a farming county with very few towns.

About halfway to work, I passed through Atworth, a small village of no more than 200 people, just a bump in the road. It was notable for one feature. There were several disabled people who appeared to be mentally defective. There was one older one that you had to watch out for. He rode a large 3-wheeled bicycle. The speed limit for cars was 30 mph, which helped, but you never quite knew what he was going to do. There were two more that leaned over their front garden gates and watched the cars. They would be there at all times of the day. I put this sad situation down to the fact that Atworth being so far from other places, led to in-breeding in the past. This probably was the case as later you will hear of more on this subject.

Due to the limited area population, almost anybody could be employed at the company, and it was said that the Stores and Despatch employees were the rejects from other departments. If they were warm they were in. The foremen with whom I had to deal to get things done, had just been there the longest and were not necessarily the smartest. The senior one, Zachary Taylor, who had started work there the same year as Mr. Henderson, was normally a quiet pleasant chap, but he could not handle the stress, and he would become quarrelsome and argumentative. He was directly responsible for the loading deck and getting the Lorries out according to the list I gave him every evening for the next day. He did not have the strength of character or confidence to deal with the 90 men who had the power of a union behind them. Also, I heard that he was expecting to get the job that I had. This did not make it too pleasant as he also seemed to resent taking orders from a 23-year-old. We had many a loud discussion on the loading dock. After about a year, his hair started coming out in clumps. He would show up in the morning with a bald patch at the side of his head, maybe half an inch wide, with shiny pink skin showing. This got worse, to the point where the bald patches became predominant, and the widely separated clumps of hair were the exception. We all felt sorry for him, but he was the one that would work himself into a tizzy all the time. The job was just too much for him.

The next one in age and seniority was Derek Armstrong who was in charge of the miscellaneous rubber goods on the top floor. There was an invisible person if I ever knew one. He was never there when you wanted him. I never did really work out exactly how he passed his time.

The last and most junior and the best foreman was Neil Green. He was in charge of the second floor where auto tires and motorcycle tires were stored. There was a spiral chute from there to the loading dock, and Neil always had the merchandise ready on time and in the right order. Neil's son Ted also worked for the department, at some menial job moving stock around or something. Neil Green's side-kick and chief tire pusher was none other than Jack Peters, Muriel's admirer from the restaurant. I don't think he realized that I knew about him, but he was a little awkward with me for a short time until he got used to the idea that his boss's boss, either did not know or did not care about him.

One day Neil Green's son, Ted did not show up for work, and this went on for a few weeks. Eventually, a story filtered through that he had gone a bit funny and was in a sort of trance. He was in hospital, and from there he was moved to a hospital in Bristol, the other side of Bath from the factory. Often, when the Lorries were late, Bill would stay behind and help load. Then he would drive himself all the way to Bristol, passing my house in Bath. He would do this maybe 3 times a week, which was very handy. I would travel to work on the works bus, and then scrounge a ride home with him, saving me driving my car or catching a regular bus which got me home after 7.00 pm.

During one of these trips home, he told me about this hospital. Apparently, it was full of people with physical abnormalities, such as tails, two heads, large heads, and baby bodies, etc., etc. Further discussion brought out the fact that Neil Green and his wife were both born in Atworth. This, I felt lent credence to my thoughts about Atworth. Neil's son was in that hospital for good.

Ted had a wife and two children. It was a real sad situation. I admired Neil for visiting 3 times a week, driving at least a 65-mile round trip. I paid Neil for giving me a lift, and he seemed to enjoy the company.

There was another funny person in the stores and despatch. His name was Geoffrey Steele. He was the man who handled small package shipments and had a cubbyhole of an office in the corner of the loading dock. From his office he could see out into the road, and when he saw a young lady walking by he had this series of sayings that he would trot out. For instance: “She’s so beautiful I could drink her bathwater”, or “I could kiss her bottom when she’s passing water”. He was a local person, and like so many people in the area he had a defect in a semi-paralyzed left arm. He could use it for many things, but it still was not completely normal.

Chapter 15 - The Family Grows

We got news that my eldest sister Christine had just had a baby boy, John William, and there was a good chance they would be coming to England for a visit. Some months later they arrived and my mother and younger sister, Rosemary, and my sister Brenda and her husband Frank, came at the same time.

Frank and Brenda bought us a new television set. We did not have one before as they were too expensive. They also gave us a cuckoo clock, which hangs on our wall to this day. It is still in working order, but needs cleaning. They also took Christopher and David out to a toy-shop and said they could have anything they wanted. Unfortunately, they were too young and did not pick worthwhile items.

David was 2 years old and Christopher was 3 ½, and Joy was pregnant, and very excited about it. Joy's sister Susan had just had a daughter, Julie, and I was an uncle again. Muriel was still working at the Dorchester Restaurant, Tuesday and Thursday evenings, 7.00 pm until 2.00 am, and Saturday and Sunday 4.00 pm until 2.00 am. Of course, I looked after the children. It was not much of a life but necessary to achieve what we wanted.

Nicholas Robin Walters was born at 11.30 am on the Monday 8th of August, 1960. He weighed 7lbs 2ozs. The lightest so far. I spent the next 10 days running between home, the Forbes Frazer Hospital, and Muriel's mother's house. All I seemed to do was get the kids up, take them to Grandmother's, go to the hospital, pick up the kids and give them lunch, take them back to Grandmother's, go to the hospital, pick up the kids, feed them, pick up one of Muriel's sisters to baby-sit, put them to bed, go to the hospital, take baby-sitter home, and go to bed. When Muriel got home the boys told her that they loved my cooking. When she asked why, they said it was because they had lots of canned baked beans.

Nicholas was a very pretty baby, with petite features, and blond hair, and Muriel was very happy. We bought a new pram (baby carriage) which Muriel would put outside the front door for Nicholas to get the little bit of sun, and then at the back with his brothers, as the sun moved around.

Muriel went back to work at the restaurant after Nicholas was born, but gave it up after a few months. She just felt she could not face it any more.

It was September 1960 and Christopher was 4-years-old. He started his first day of school. He didn't cry, and took it in his stride although he was a bit apprehensive as would be expected. Muriel took David along, and he wanted to stay also, and cried all the way home. He wanted to stay with Christopher. The next day, Christopher was a bit reluctant, but forged ahead and accepted it. After the first week he settled down.

David moped for weeks without his big brother, although Christopher generally used him as a punching bag. One day David disappeared in the middle of the afternoon, and he returned home with Christopher. Apparently, he had gone to the school on his own to find Christopher.

When Christopher started his second year, his little brother David went with him, starting school at 3 years and 9 months. The first day, he rushed in but found that he was not with his brother. Everything changed and he fought to go to the school for ages. It is interesting to note that the 2 little boys of approximately 5 ½ and 4 were perfectly safe walking a mile to and from school. They had 3 small roads to cross but no main roads.

A parcel of clothes arrived from my sister Brenda. There were little overcoats, and long trousers for Christopher and David, plus many other useful items. Brenda's gift parcels were a great help to us, and the children enjoyed the beautiful clothes she sent. (Of course, they were handed down to the younger boys. Later on, she also sent clothes for daughter Helen, our baby, who was the best-dressed little girl you ever saw).

When the weather became colder, the boys were sent to school in their long trousers. You never saw young boys in long trousers at that time, and the school told Muriel they could not wear them to school because "it was not done". Muriel's answer was to the effect that it was about time that it was done etc. A compromise was reached where the boys would change into short pants when they reached school. They never did get chapped knees like all the other boys.

It was the 12th of December, 1961. Nicholas was 15-months-old. The office phone in the stores and despatch rang, it was for me. It was one of the company switchboard operators saying that she wasn't sure but she thought she'd taken a call from an operator in Ohio, who said they would be putting a call through shortly for me. This was in the days when very few people had telephones at home, and you certainly did not get or make calls to and from America just like that. You had to wait until an operator made the connection and when it was made they called you back. There was nothing like the direct dialing as there is today.

I told the company operator that I had sisters and parents in America so we all sat back and waited. Shortly, the phone rang again, and an American voice asked if it was me. Frank McCloskey, Brenda's husband was on the line asking us to come to Florida for Christmas at their expense. I told him that we could not as Aunts and Uncles, May and Fred and Dolly and Les were coming to our house for Christmas as usual. Frank's answer was "Bring them too". Then I said that we didn't have time to get passports and visas. He asked us to try, and that was how we left it. I phoned May and Fred, they had a phone, and they jumped at the chance. I drove 15 miles to see Dolly and Les. They declined on the spot and asked us what we thought they were going to do for Christmas if we went as if we had some definite responsibility to be there for them. We were not about to get too excited about letting them down after this statement.

We went to work, and got passports going, then arranged to go to Cardiff, Wales, the nearest American consulate for visas, and we were ready with all paperwork in 8 days. (In those days you had to get visas to enter America. It is a shame that this is not the case now). We went to the London area to stay with May and Fred on the 21st December, and went to London Airport on the evening of the 22nd December.

We boarded the plane in the late evening. Muriel gave the children some mild knockout medicine given to her by the doctor. And they settled down and went to sleep. The plane was a Bristol Britannia, one of the first turbo-props. As we started up the runway around midnight, we could see that there was heavy rain, which apparently was hitting the ground and freezing. We were really moving along, and suddenly the engine roar died and the brakes went on, and we came almost to a stop, and slowly turned back and stopped at the gate we had just left. We had electrical trouble, and everybody had to get off. We protested that our kids were asleep and should not be disturbed. We were allowed to stay on, and we watched as mechanics took the floor upright by us on the other side of the plane. It was about 12.30 am. After a couple of hours, everybody got back on the plane, and we heard that they were treated royally, with food and drinks. As the plane started off again, the children woke up and fidgeted for the rest of the 12 ½ hour flight to Bermuda. Originally, we should have stopped in Newfoundland but due to the delay, we bypassed it. Nicholas at 15 months crawled around over Muriel and me the whole time. We could now understand why people wring kids' necks.

Finally, we arrived in Bermuda with a warm wind and a bright sun. We were allowed off the plane for an hour and we walked down to the ocean. There we found white sand and the clearest water we'd ever seen. We took off again and landed in Nassau, Bahamas in a heavy rainstorm. We were almost down at wave-top height and the plane was rocking and swinging about in the powerful wind. Then there was land underneath us. We must have touched down in the first 20 feet of land. The palm trees were blowing almost doubled over in the wind. I think that the runaway must have been built out into the ocean as there was water and waves close up to the runway on both sides.

We left Nassau, on the last leg of that plane. The next stop was Miami and then we had to catch another plane to Orlando.

In recent months at that time, one type of airplane (aeroplane in England) had been crashing all over the place. It was the Lockheed Electra, turbo-prop. The American authorities were working on solving the problem which had afflicted one plane after the other. I was hoping and praying that we would not have to go on one of those, but I kept this to myself.

We arrived in Miami at around 5.00 pm. We boarded the Bristol Britannia 14 hours before! It was very hot with a stiff breeze. I remember that I saw my first tumbleweed blowing across the airport.

We were now on the other plane. It was ¾ empty, and we were taxiing around. The airport was filled with the same plane that we were on. They were all over the place, but there was no way of knowing what they were. We taxied down one leg of the runaway, and engines on one side roared, and we swung around to the main runway, and then all 4 engines opened up. As we swung around, in the cabin window on the far side to us, I saw the front of an identical plane and as we moved forward the window moved along the length of the other plane, and on the tail were the words "Lockheed Electra". I knew we were all going to die, but I kept it to myself.

By the time we got to Orlando, it was almost dark. In that latitude, the sun drops quickly. Frank and Brenda, and Sylvia and Charles were there to meet us. There was Muriel, me and the 3 children, and May, Fred and son John. I remember the tinted windshield in the Cadillac in which we rode, a beautiful blue at the top. When you rarely see the sun in England you don't need tinted windshields, and I'd never seen one before.

We arrived at Brenda's, to be told that my parents, who now lived in California, were staying with Daphne, who lived a couple of miles away. Apparently, they knew nothing about our visit. Brenda had invited everybody that evening, and Daphne was to blow a couple of blasts on the car horn when they came around the corner. Brenda was to phone a neighbor who would leave her phone off the hook so that Brenda could use her phone extensions to pretend to be talking with me in England when my mother arrived. We were all sitting by the pool with me on a phone extension, with only the in-pool light on.

I heard the clip-clop of heels on the kitchen floor as I heard Brenda say, "Hello Mother, I'm talking to Brian, come and say hello to him". Then my mother said to me, "What a shame you are not here, everybody else is here". Then she said, "Maybe you can come next year" etc. etc. Finally, she said that she had to go and meet some of Frank's relatives who were out by the pool, and she shouldn't spend too much of Brenda's money on the phone, so she said goodbye.

The glass door slid open, and in the semi-darkness, I saw my mother and Brenda and Frank come out and walk toward us. I stood up and in an instant, my mother must have recognized my silhouette, as her knees buckled a bit, but the others caught her. As you would expect, she was shocked. I had just gotten over telling her on the phone that I couldn't possibly go to America next Christmas with three little kids, and here we were.

Frank was a very generous man who got great enjoyment out of doing things for other people, and it wasn't until much later that I got a chance to get to know him, but by then it was too late. (Read on).

The next day, the normally warm and sunny Florida was in the grip of a rare cold snap. Frank had heated the pool to 90 deg. F. for us, and when we woke up to our first Florida morning, the pool had a fog hovering over it, and the surrounding orange trees had icicles.

We were amused by a strange picture when we were out that day. We saw a man who had on a woolly knit hat, a heavy jacket, a scarf wrapped around his neck, big gloves, and . . . . . shorts and sandals with no socks, and funniest of all, earmuffs!

While we were there, Frank took us bass fishing. He drove us to, I believe, the St Johns River, which runs into lakes every so often. He tried to start his boat motor and it wouldn't go so we fished from the bank while he bought another motor. We went off with a guide finally, in a rented boat. These waterways are used as highways in that area and there were lots of skinny boats whizzing up and down at a minimum of 15 mph. Anyway, we spent the day fishing but had no luck.

On another day we went to the circus winter quarters in Deland. The elephants were training, and when they had finished they made a bee line for us at a good pace. We were sitting in Brenda's car watching and didn't know what was going on, but suddenly realized that we were stopped in front of the water tanks. We soon moved.

Something that intrigued us was that when we thanked somebody, say a waitress, they always replied with, "You're welcome". We had never heard this before, but now we are in the same habit without even thinking about it.

We went to Sea World, and to a dog racing track owned by a friend of Frank's. We were in the owner's box, and picking dogs for bets and Frank was paying. We did this in every race, and with a bunch of us doing it, and only 5 dogs in a race, it is amazing to think that we didn't pick one winner.

It remained cold for the whole time we were there except for the last day. The sun was shining every day, but for Florida it was chilly. And then it was time to leave. When we got to Miami, we were told that the plane back to England was delayed one day. We protested and finally, they put us all into a hotel. At the airport, there was one thing that sticks in my mind. Fred had put a bottle of bourbon whiskey in one of his bags, and he must have put it down with a bump as the bottle broke and seeped out on the floor. A black man was brought to mop it up, and Fred told him that he'd broken this bottle of "scotch". The man said, "That isn't scotch, that's bourbon". I remember thinking that he must be quite an expert to know the difference.

When we got back to England, it was dark, freezing, and late. We waited outside the airport terminal while Fred went to get his car, and when he arrived, we couldn't believe how small it looked compared to the American cars. We stayed with them overnight and left early the next day for Bath. We arrived home at about 4.00 pm, and I phoned work and told Mr. Henderson that I'd be in the next day.

We went to bed early, and the next thing we knew it was 12.30 pm the next day. All of us including the children had slept right through to midday and past. I phoned Mr. Henderson, told him what had happened, and said I'd be in the next day for sure, and we did exactly the same thing, all slept until midday.

On the third day, I made it to work on time. Our internal clocks really had got confused.

While we were in America, we had been involved in some discussion about us emigrating also. We had seen a different way of life, which was attractive, and the weather was so much better. We came to the conclusion that we should proceed with it.

We wrote to the American Embassy in London and requested the forms, and duly filled them out. We had to have a physical examination, and we were given the name of a doctor in Bath who could do this for us. We had the physicals and X-rays for which we had to pay, but before we sent the forms back we had second thoughts. We were doing fine in England and there was no really compelling reason to throw it away and take the risk of starting over. The idea died, and life proceeded in England.

Chapter 16 - Life Continues

Just before leaving for the Christmas trip to America, we realized Muriel was pregnant again. Nicholas was 2 on the 8th of August 1962 and Peter was born 4 days later on the 12th of August. He was 8lbs 4ozs, the heaviest of all. He had lots of jet-black hair on his head, and some on his back, but this rubbed off very quickly. He was a very nervous child, crying if he could not see you. Muriel would have him close at night to hold his hand or he would wake up and cry.

By this time Muriel's sister Susan had given birth to daughter number 2, Sarah.

All the time we had lived at that house I was working on some project or other. I pulled down a couple of walls of the downstairs bathroom and rebuilt it larger. I remember that I had to extend some water pipes. Now at that time, most water pipes were made of lead, and joins were made by butt joining, and with a blow-torch, joining them up with a big bump of solder, wiped into position with a piece of leather smeared with a wax-type of flux. The first joint took me 4 hours. The second one took 10 minutes. It took a while to get the hang of it.

Another job had to be done to conform to the local city council's requirements. The house was part of a historic street which meant that it had to conform to certain standards, and work was needed to the parapet, 3-storeys up. We were not about to pay somebody to do this, so we bought an extending ladder. On closer examination, a whole block of Bath stone was needed, weight about 150lbs, plus a decorative capstone, about 70lbs. This all seemed quite straightforward, and the necessary stone was ordered. It arrived, and then the real work started. I had to remove the decayed Bath stone which was porous and comparatively easy to handle as it was going down with the help of gravity, being lowered with a rope. However, the new stone was a different matter. It was a solid new piece and going against gravity.

The construction of the roof and the decorative upper wall did not lend itself to a pulley, so after giving the problem lots of consideration, I decided that the only way was to make a sort of toboggan, which fitted over the ladder. It had a ledge at the bottom on which the stone rested. The stone was tied on. The plan was to loop a rope over the top rung, and hang down the underside of the ladder. I had to inch my way up the ladder, very conscious that the combined weight of me and the stone may be more than the ladder could hold. After moving up to each rung, I rested the stone on my knees and pulled the rope tight, and secured it before moving to the next rung.

It took 45 minutes to reach the top, and the worst part was still to come if you don't count the fact that in the middle of the ladder, it bent and swayed alarmingly. Now I had to get the stone from the ladder, and lift it onto the top of the wall through the gap left by the removed stone.

I think it took me several hours to recover after the stone was in position. I would never attempt anything like that again.

A couple of times over the years, when I answered the doorbell, I would see through the frosted glass, the outline of a person who was dressed in very colorful clothing. Before I opened the door I knew it was my mother paying us surprise visits from California.

When my parents first left England, they went to Winnipeg, Canada. Because it was so cold there they moved to Calgary, near my sister Christine. It was a bit warmer but still cold, so they eventually went to Florida, near Brenda. But that was too hot, and with too many large bugs. Finally, they moved to Santa Monica, California, by the sea, at the recommendation of an old uncle of my mother's. He lived in Pasadena, up against the San Gabriel Mountains. It is about 25 miles inland from Santa Monica, on the east side of Los Angeles. It is the smog capital of the area.

My youngest sister, Rosemary had lived at and visited many famous places and landmarks in North America, and probably didn't realize how lucky she was.

One day when Peter was about 6 months old, he was in the pram in the backyard, and Nicholas was playing in the same area. Muriel went to check on them and to her horror she saw a gaping cut on Peter's neck. It was at least ¼" deep and about 1" long. It was not bleeding.

It seems that Nicholas, at the age of 2 ½ had found a rusty old garden knife and decided to try it out on his brother.

Muriel rushed both children to the local Hospital, about 4 miles away, and got a tetanus shot and stitches for Peter.

Peter was about 9 months old, and the Bath Co-op Fete (carnival) was approaching. Miss Massey, our tenant suggested to Muriel that she enter him in the baby show. He won his class (age), and was also pronounced the best baby in the show. He won a small silver cup, and 10 shillings, equal now to about $20. His photograph was in the local newspaper the next day.

When Peter was 15 months old, on 10th November 1963, we had Helen who weighed in at 6lbs 15ozs. The boys were tickled to death to have a sister at last. She was a very good baby especially noticeable after the difficulty of Peter.

When the Co-op Fete came around again Muriel entered Helen, at the age of 6 months. She won her class and got the customary 10 shillings. The newspaper had a write up and mentioned that her brother was champion of the previous year's show.

By this time we had applied again to emigrate to America. It had been talked about, and we'd been for it, then against it, and it was time to either do it or forget it. Muriel announced that I should make the decision, and I finally decided to go.

I painted the house where it needed it and fixed things up to sell it, and put it in the hands of a real estate company, Louis Powell, but within a week or so our next door neighbor had found a buyer, and we paid off Louis Powell and went ahead with the sale, which included the furniture. The factory manager at the Thames Rubber Co. called me to his office and for two hours promised me the earth to stay, which I turned down. We were committed, but I often wondered where we would be now if we had stayed. I know that we would have made great progress as I would not have suffered the interruption to my personal growth that starting again in a strange country caused. I was highly regarded at the Thames Rubber Co., and the youngest assistant superintendent in the whole company.

Chapter 17 - The Move Is Near

The last couple of months were hectic. We packed up some large crates of things we needed to take, and I got British Road Services to carry them to Liverpool Docks for virtually nothing. The shipping agent that the company used was Immediate Transportation Services, and my contact was Tony Sawyer. I remember it was so cheap, that the whole thing from our door in England to Long Beach, California, cost less than the cost of getting the crates from Long Beach to Santa Monica, 20 miles.

I left work a week before our departure. Mr. Henderson, my boss got a bit emotional, telling me that I had been like a son to him. We spent the last few days doing all the loose ends that needed doing, staying with Muriel's parents as the house and all furniture and possessions were either sold or on the way to America.

Muriel's family came to the airport with us in a rented bus. About 15 people in all. We had said goodbye to Muriel's family and were in line, about 10 feet from going through the passport check when somebody grabbed my arm. It was Mr. and Mrs. Henderson. They had driven the 100 miles just to see us off, and only just got to us in time. In another minute they would have missed us.

We exchanged Christmas cards for many years and called on Mr. Henderson every time we visited England. He lived to his nineties, re-marrying when his first wife died. His daughter and husband came to San Diego on a tour, and we met them and had dinner together. However, since then we have lost touch.

I visited the Thames Rubber Company in 1974 (10 years after leaving), and found that Eric Bull and Harry Williams had died, along with several others with whom I was in daily contact. The only one left that I wished to see was an old (young in age) friend, but he was about to leave the company as business was not too good. I was left with a feeling of sadness and depression about the situation of a vibrant growing company with vital people, and it seemed it was all gone.

We met this friend once again in England, some years later. We arranged that he would visit us on his way on a trip to Australia that was planned. However, we heard no more from him, which continues what I feel as the aura of sadness around that company. It is clear that we made the right move.

Chapter 18 - We're On Our Way

We were on a TWA Boeing 707 from London to New York, and some hours into the flight, Helen, who was 11-months-old, was due for a bottle. We had asked several of the stewardesses to put hot water into the bottle, which already had the necessary other ingredients. Each one had said that they'd be right back, but 40 minutes had gone by and no one came back. They were busy selling drinks to the adults. We were new at this traveling game and didn't want to make a fuss, and I'm sure it showed, and they took advantage of it. Helen was hungry and crying, and I was getting madder by the second. Finally, I took the bottle and went to the little kitchen area. One of the stewardesses was there and I asked her where the hot water was. She said, "I'll do it and bring it to you". I advised her that we'd been waiting for almost an hour and I would wait no longer. I put my hands under her elbows and lifted her to one side. She seemed somewhat shocked as she silently watched me fill the bottle.

One of the first things I did on arrival was write to TWA, but I never did get any response.

Upon arrival in New York, we had to go through the immigration process which took several hours, much longer than expected, and we missed our connecting flight to California. We caught the next plane, and I remember seeing Pikes Peak to the west, the highest mountain in Colorado, silhouetted against the darkening sky when the sun had nearly gone down.

We were nearing the end of our journey with 5 little kids, and we were all very tired, and the kids were grumpy. Christopher was the eldest at 8 years of age.

Finally, we descended into Los Angeles airport at around 10.00 pm. We had been traveling since about 7.00 am GMT, a total of 23 hours, and it wasn't over yet.

My parents, my sister Rosemary (now 18), Sylvia and Charles, and a host of their friends were there to meet us. They had been to the airport to meet the earlier plane we'd missed and returned for this one. Santa Monica, our future home, was about 10 miles away.

We were greeted like heroes and escorted to my parent's house in Santa Monica by a fleet of huge American cars, and the party continued.

Everybody admired the children. My family had never seen Helen and Peter and made a big fuss of them. All we wanted to do was sleep, and my parents had rented the house next door for us, and had got some beds and sheets, etc. We soon excused ourselves and got into bed.

In retrospect, the children were incredibly well-behaved in spite of the hours spent traveling.

The next day we were up early based on our English inner clock. My father had one car, a Chevrolet Biscayne, with a 350 brake horsepower engine and automatic transmission. My mother didn't drive, but Rosemary did. Rosemary drove him to work and returned with the car and we had the car to ourselves as long as we picked him up at 5.00 pm. Rosemary showed us around Santa Monica that day, but we took it easy. I went with Rosemary to pick up our father, and I said to him that I should try driving, and he repeated something which both my parents had repeated several times, "Never, never drive on the freeway". Then he said that I couldn't possibly drive on the other side of the road until I got used to it, which would be weeks. In the house, I showed him my international license, stuck inside my English driving license, and he warned me again about the dangers of driving in America.

I apparently put my license down somewhere, because the next day Rosemary encouraged me to try driving, but I couldn't find my license. We turned my mother's house upside down looking for it to no avail. About mid-morning Rosemary said let's go down and you can take a driving test and get your California license. I couldn't believe that you could do it like that. In England, you had to wait three months for a driving test. She had a book on the highway rules, and she helped me go through it, and before lunch, off we went.

First, there was the written test, a multiple-choice test. Most of the answers were so obvious, that you couldn't miss them. Some required definite knowledge, and as pre-arranged, Rosemary stood at right angles to me. I held my pencil against each answer on the few questions I didn't know until Rosemary gave me a sign for the correct answer.

I got 98% and 10 minutes after arriving I was in the car with the examiner. I told him I had a British license, but had lost it. He said to drive around the block. In the last stretch, he asked me to back into a space and park, which I did in one reverse movement. He said, "You're fine", and gave me my temporary permit. He walked back smoking, but I had to get Rosemary. In half an hour we were home.

That evening, Rosemary said, "Why don't you get Dad on your own?" Seemed like a grand idea, so off I went. He saw me coming and he was working himself up into a tizzy long before the car stopped. "You'll get arrested". "You'll get us killed", "You'll go to jail", etc. etc., all the way home. He was telling me all the bad things that could happen to somebody driving without a license. Did you notice that, "Driving without a license?" I had a British license, and had not told him it was lost?? The significance of this became known months later.

When we arrived home, we were sitting in the car and I pulled out my permit. He took it, looked at it, and walked up and down outside for a few minutes, reading it. He came in and gave it to me without a word.

6 months later, my mother told me she was changing the liner in my father's sock drawer, and to her surprise, what did she find? My English driving license. He had taken it and hidden it.

Some days later, Kay and Reuben (friends of my mother) and Rosemary, and our little family drove to Santa Barbara. We went to the mission, and on the tour, the guide took us to the very oldest room. He announced in a dramatic voice, "This room is . . . . . . 205 years old". I couldn't help saying in a stage whisper, "That's 5 years younger than the house we just left in England". The room echoed and it came out a bit louder than intended, and everybody looked.

Muriel and I took Chris and David to the local school to enroll them. We sat in the principal's office, and when he came to David, who was 6, he said, "We'll start him in the first grade". We protested saying he's been at school for more than 2 years already and can read very well. He had nothing with which to test him and I suggested he give David his newspaper. This he did and got a surprise when David read it fine. He immediately said, "I'll put him in second grade".

Almost right away, we were encouraged to go to the local Christian Church with my parents and Rosemary. They were well known, and we became mini-celebrities because of the number and our well-behaved children. It was a small church, probably not more than 150 members.

Within a week or so Rosemary, who was having singing lessons, was pressuring me to go to choir practice with her. She is an alto with a very strong voice.

Finally, I succumbed and went along one Thursday evening. I met Dr. Don Richardson, the choir director, a wonderful, quiet, kindly man with whom we still have contact. There were about 20 choir members, and I was placed in the bass section. I was given music, and felt like a fish out of water, trying to make sense out of these lines and dots. Luckily, I have a good memory for tunes, and I had spent years listening to my father sing the bass part to every song, to the point that I had a natural feel for the bass parts without the music. I gradually got to the point where I could use the sheet music as a guide to my memory, and then to the point of knowing the jumps between notes.

The next step was, Rosemary was asked to arrange a duet with me, "Jesus Lover Of My Soul". I nearly died when Don brought this up, but Rosemary thought it was OK, so with trepidation I practiced it with her, and then the big day arrived. I understood then about knee knocking. Mine did not knock as I expected, side to side. They knocked as they passed, wobbling back and forth.

The organ started the introduction, and I now understand what guillotine victims went through. There was no turning back, and the noise continued to the point where I had to sing or run.

It was easier after the first few notes, and we finished it with relief on my part. A few months afterward, a serious Don Richardson approached me and said, "I think you're ready for a solo", eeek. The eeek was mine.

Lois Getman was the organist and she encouraged me no end. I practiced with her, and she convinced me I could do a great job, and I stood up straight in spite of knocking knees and sang "The Holy City". Rosemary said I knocked them dead. I had lots of compliments, and it got easier after that. However, there is always a certain amount of apprehension when you stand up to sing, alone, in front of hundreds of people.

Gradually, we got together the bits and pieces of furniture we needed. We had been sleeping in our house, but mostly living in my parents' house during the day. We gradually became independent. We bought a second-hand fridge and a gas stove from Vim, a short fat Dutchman acquaintance of my parents. He used to take a truck ahead of the garbage trucks in Beverley Hills and Hollywood and pick up anything which might be worth something, and sell it. This is where our stuff came from. We were shocked at the way Americans threw away useful items because they were tired of it, or didn't like the color, etc.

We soon bought a very old Ford Station Wagon, and we were now completely independent.

Next, I had to find a job. My parents knew another Dutchman name, Nick. He had a little handyman/construction business, unlicensed, and probably a bit cheaper. He had all sorts of jobs lined up, and he agreed to employ me at $2.50 an hour. The first day, I was put on laying floor tiles in a garage. He took me there, leaving my car back at the other job, set it up and left, saying he'd be back in a while. He came back about 2.00 pm, and was very surprised to see I had finished much earlier, but had no way of contacting him. He stayed then, and we were joined by this other fellow named John, and proceeded to build cupboards in the garage, and a redwood container for several garbage cans outside. He had a table saw and asked if I felt I could operate it. After a few instructions, he worked on the cupboards with John, and I made the garbage container. It came out very well, and both Nick and I were pleasantly surprised

I noticed that in a corner of the first cupboard, he had a bottle of wine from which he kept sipping.

I worked for Nick under the condition that I would be looking for work more in my line, and leave him when I was ready, but I must say that I enjoyed what I was doing, so didn't look too hard. Also, we were able to save money in those first few months.

The next job after the garage was putting in a bathroom heater and modifying the bathroom, and a few other jobs. Nick discovered that I had a rudimentary knowledge of electricity, and wiring, and was excited by that. I found myself crawling under this house looking for a live wire to fix a dead outlet. I found one with a flash which took a chunk out of my screwdriver.

I was not at all familiar with the construction methods, only seeing bricks and mortar in England, and so when Nick asked me to run a wire to the ceiling heater, I carefully cut a thin slot in the wallboard, taking about 15 minutes. He came along and with a large hammer, and smashed a whole section out in 15 seconds, replaced the wallboard and plastered it.

The next job was to build a lean-to-covered patio on the back of a house, and we made a very attractive job of it, then we moved on to the beach in Malibu.

I had pretty well landed a job as plant manager at Collins Engineering in Culver City. I was waiting to hear the final details, which took about 10 days.

This Malibu job was the best. This house was on the beach, built on stilts. (Telegraph poles buried in the sand). The owner had realized that if he built another floor under the house, he would still be 10 feet above the sand (and waves). We bolted 4" x 12" beams to the poles and built the floor. We had nearly finished the floor when it was time to stop for the day.

The next day, I arrived at the site, and John rolled up a minute later. We waited for Nick, but he didn't show up. He had the table saw which we needed to finish the floor. Nick put it in the back of his van every night as he was leaving.

It was about 9 am when his wife arrived. She appeared very distressed. She told us Nick was dead. He was driving home along the coast highway the previous night, when he'd swerved for some reason and hit a power pole. The table saw had flown to the front of the van and killed him. What she didn't say was that he was probably under the influence as he always was by the time he went home. John and I went home. Our money was delivered to us at the funeral a few days later.

Nick was very nice to me and I thoroughly enjoyed the three months working with him and John, but we were on a long journey, and this was just the first step. The experience I gained working for him was invaluable to me at a later date.

About 3 weeks after we arrived in California, a family arrived in the house on the other side of my mother's. They were from communist Poland, and couldn't speak a word of English. We heard they had escaped under the barbed wire. There were two small boys and a mother and father. The children soon started playing together with ours, and language didn't appear to bother them. Eventually, Muriel and the other mother whose name was Anna, would wave, and gradually got more familiar. The father, whose name was Jergy, now changed to George eventually learned a bit of English with Joy teaching him from children's story books.

Anna had relatives in Santa Monica, and we got to know them, and some of my mother's friends sort of adopted us, and in no time we were surrounded by people we knew. As time went on we became firm friends and spent lots of time together.

Chapter 19 - It's All About Work

I started work at Collins Engineering and felt that it was not a terribly good move, but it was a start. I was responsible for the plant, unlocking the place, and locking up and supervising activities. Joe Collins, the president, was short and fat and quite old. He was polite and pleasant to me, but not to anybody else. (Don't know why, but I have a suspicion that some American people are a little in awe of the English for some reason). The company sold hydraulic pipe fittings for aircraft and the rocket industry. They were very expensive and high-tech.

The conditions were not too good, and we had a very high turnover. There was a union, which appeared to be ineffective. This was borne out one day when I had a visitor come to see me. Now I was used to dealing with an English union representative, Ted Aldridge, who came almost every day to see Mr. Henderson and me with some minor complaint, usually about me as I had contact with the workers. He was so petty and he whined and complained about everything. That was the English unions, and thank God that Maggie Thatcher got rid of most of them. They held England back for many years.

My visitor introduced himself as the union representative. He was well-dressed and appeared to be reasonably intelligent, and even a bit sharp. After the usual pleasantries he got up and closed my office door. He said, "Brian, there isn't anything we can't sort out easily between us. All we need to do is come up with a story to shut these idiots up". Boy o boy, what a different sort of union. I liked this.

I had been there a week or so when one of the salespeople, a 20-year-old, paid me a visit, and he commenced telling me all the things I should do and how to do them. I'd seen him around, but. I didn't know who he was, so I just listened. I was always conscious of being in a new country and in a new company. He was such a cocky little twerp that I felt it necessary to find out who he was. It turned out that he had started with the company a couple of days before I did, and was the most junior salesman. He came back again and this time I told him he had 10 seconds to get out and back to his office. Three days later he was fired for entering fictitious orders, and getting all sorts of merchandise shipped to unsuspecting customers. He had to know that he would be found out. A real example of the criminal mind.

Because of the high turnover, I had weekly meetings with Mrs. Crystal at the California Department of Employment. She would keep an eye open for replacements for me, knowing the history of the company. One day she asked me what I thought about the company, and I said, "Not much". She asked me what I wanted to do, and she suggested I take an aptitude test, which her department ran. I showed up for a test and went through the motions, and was told afterward that I would be called in for an interpretation interview on the results. Sometime later Mrs. Crystal called me and told me that there was no point coming for the interpretation because there were no weaknesses in the test results. She said that I could do anything I wanted to do. She also said that she would keep her eyes open for an opening with a decent company, with some sort of a future.

Within 10 days I went for an interview with the largest capacitor manufacturer in the world at that time. Out of the 6 people interviewed, I got the job.

I worked in the Western Regional office, as one of the three inside salespeople. There were 10 traveling sales engineers, 5 secretaries, 2 teletype operators, and the sales office administrator, my immediate boss. The western regional manager worked out of this office and had a secretary, plus there was a personnel manager. Also at the same facility, there was a manufacturing division making electronic filters, and interference-free shielded rooms. The headquarters and main factory were in Massachusetts. There were a total of 25 factories spread around the country.

At work, I was a bit of an attraction at first, being newly arrived from England. One of the teletype operators, an older lady named Sarah would way-lay me at every opportunity and question me about everything. I was a bit tired of her constant questions and started giving her all sorts of rubbishy answers, the first one that came into my head. She asked me what Joy was like and I told her she was a bit stout, around 300lbs. She swallowed all of it.

A month later, the company had a party, and wives were invited. We had a job finding the place and were late. We walked in the door, and a deathly hush fell over the room. Every eye, of about 50 people, was on us, and the silence was deafening. It seemed ages but was probably 3 seconds before the murmuring re-started. What we didn't know, and I didn't remember was the story about Muriel weighing 300lbs. Later in the evening, the secretary to the Western Regional Manager, told Muriel what Sarah had told everybody. The secretary apologized for the incident. Now it became a joke. Following that we joined the bowling team and had a lot of fun on a social level. Muriel got the trophy for the most improved player. She started so badly that she had plenty of room for improvement.

Muriel became good friends with the Western Regional Manager's wife. They were compatible. We are still in touch with them, and also my old secretary, Eva, to this day, 35 years later.

Shortly after joining this company, I was sent back to the head office in Massachusetts. It was a small town built around the factory. The Los Angeles office had two contacts at the head office who looked after the west coast customers, and I was to replace one of them for two weeks. He was going on vacation. He asked me to stay at his house and feed his dog etc., and drive his car to and from work. This I did, and I bought my own food and cut the grass, and generally took care of the place. His mother-in-law lived along the road and checked in with me regularly. I heard later that they were very impressed with the clean condition in which I left the house and garden.

I must digress for a moment. Muriel had tried her hand at a couple of driving lessons in England, but she had refused to drive in the US, although we had a second car sitting there waiting for her to drive it. I took her out to practice driving a couple of times, but we finished yelling. One time, about 2 miles from home, she advised me that she was not going to drive anymore and got out of the car. I let her walk home, although I stayed in the vicinity to watch her. We made no progress on this. She still avowed that she didn't need a car and preferred walking with Helen, a baby, and Peter and Nick, toddlers. Of course, we all knew the real truth.

When I was returning from Massachusetts, I felt it in my bones that our friend, Fran, would have forced the issue regarding Muriel's driving. Fran had 4 children and had tried to encourage Muriel to drive and often said she would teach her.

Sure enough, Muriel showed up at the airport with the children. She had just passed her test. However, she wanted me to drive home. She said that driving into the airport scared her to death. Within a couple of months, one of the cars needed service, and Muriel had to go without a car for a day. She expressed a great deal of dissatisfaction with this. Of course, I reminded her that only a few months ago she argued that she didn't need a car. She certainly had changed her tune.

About 4 or 5 months after we arrived in California, we had both got a bit homesick, and I wrote a letter to the personnel at the Thames Rubber Co. in England, suggesting that I was interested in returning. A month or more later I got a reply, from Reggie Room the corporate personnel manager, who said that if I cared to return and go and see him, he thought they could do something for me. This was a bit lukewarm, and by that time we were in the process of buying a house, our homesickness was driven away by the thought of the miserable English weather.

The house was really a duplex, (2 houses joined together, semi-detached in England, except that one house was behind the other, echelon style). We bought this so we could get some income to help with the mortgage payment. We lived in the house at the back, with a large yard with thick springy grass. The kids could wrestle and bounce around with no damage. Although it was small, they really enjoyed that house, and the kids around. This was where our life in California began as we were fast becoming used to our new surroundings and customs. We rented the other house to my parents.

Next door was another duplex, both houses occupied by English people. The house nearest the road was occupied by Edith and Jack Hallett, from Yorkshire. The house level with us was at first occupied by Jimmy and Pat Bird, then later by Violet Barton, all English. We still talk to Edith by phone. She is about 102 years old today.

We had a standing joke. Several times Muriel had some food scraps, and she would yell, "I'm going to throw this out for the birds". I would say, "Keep your voice down, we don't want to insult the Birds". These neighbors joined in the group of friends which now consisted of Anna and George, their German and Polish relatives, and some of my mother's friends. All from Europe. Many times we would have 30 people at our house which was really far too many for that small house, but we had lots of fun. We would have wild parties with Heinz (from Germany), playing his guitar, Reuben, (from Wales), playing the piano, and Jack (from Yorkshire), with all sorts of percussion instruments, including bongo drums, sticks to bang together, and a wooden fish-shaped thing like a comb, which had to be scraped in rhythm. Everybody else sang. At times we spent more on liquor than on food, but we have great memories of those early days in California.

Every Christmas Eve for many years, we had a party starting after we returned from the evening church service. A few party guests would also go to the church with us beforehand.

These parties became a tradition, and they would last into the early morning hours, and often we would have to complete the wrapping of the children's presents before going to bed.

It was still dark outside when the children would get up and look at their gifts under the Christmas Tree, and we'd have to drag ourselves out of bed with only a few hours of sleep. My father who lived right next door, (see below), would get up and be Santa Claus, and hand out the gifts. It would take us until mid-morning to complete the job. Muriel would really go overboard with over a hundred packages for each child. I repeat, hundreds of packages each.

My mother had this thing for ballroom dancing and wanted to go to a local club for old people nearly every night. My father didn't have the same interest, and would only go once or twice a week, so she would go with an old couple they knew. My father was 70, and still working as he was quite fit and active.

This dancing was a continuous source of friction and it finally came to a head when my mother was a bit late coming home one night. Finally, she arrived around 10.30 pm, in the car with the old couple, and he went out to the sidewalk. He was in his slippers, and as the car door opened he reached down to help her, and he slipped on the wet grass, and pulled Mother out of the car and on top of him in her homemade dance dress. She immediately went and packed a case and she and Rosemary went to live with my sister Sylvia. My father's attitude was that he was alone most evenings so what was different?

In the past, my father always got my mother to go back to him, but this time he did not bother. He stated to me, that he was alone most evenings, and he might as well be on his own for good. She decided she would show him, and served him with divorce papers. He tore them up in front of me. Suddenly they found themselves divorced, and I know that it sounds silly, but I believe that they were both surprised at what happened.

We had been in the house a year or so and it was getting a bit small. The boys were growing fast and needed more room. We decided to add on to the house. First I built a lean-to patio, 20' x 10'. It had a roof of corrugated orange-colored fiberglass. Then I put bug screens all around, with a screen door, and it was like an additional room. We used to eat most meals out there except in the really cold weather.

The next thing was to add rooms to the house.

I went to the building department and picked up some pamphlets on the codes for floor, ceiling, and roof supports etc., and started my plans. Somebody advised me to put in a few obvious errors and they would not be too picky about the rest. Apparently, they always need to find something to change.

The plans went in for checking, and in a day or so they came back with my obvious errors changed in red. I had put in every detail so that they could check everything and then I knew that I couldn't go wrong.

A few nights later, I got Chris and David lined up to start helping me with the foundations. We had a lot of dirt to dig out. Our backyard sloped a bit to one side and so we were able to spread this dirt and level it up. It was a great improvement. George our Polish neighbor from our first house, came along to help. George had been working as a painter for a black man named Mr. White. This was a job that Muriel had got for him when they first arrived. We were all amused that a black man was named "White", but it worked out well as George was a hard worker, and did enough work for both of them. Mr. White began leaving all the painting to George, only showing up occasionally.

The main foundation hole was finished, except George and I had to dig the footing channel 12" wide, by 6" deep, with vertical walls. Suddenly, I realized that George was coming along behind me chopping the inside edge at a 45 degree angle, instead of going in the opposite direction, doing the same as me. I evidently didn't make it clear what was needed. It took about 2 hours and extra wide footing to fix it.

The foundation form passed the inspection and I called for Ready-mix concrete.

The truck arrived, and I was very nervous. Here I was, not really knowing what to expect, and with a couple of cubic yards of concrete. Concrete can be a real commitment. You can't change your mind, and if you do it wrong, you're stuck with it. Luckily the driver was experienced and he helped me enormously all the way, and we had a good foundation. I wrote a letter to the company telling them of his help. The next day the owner showed up with a photographer to take pictures and a statement from Muriel.

The building was completed within three months, and we now had and extra bedroom, an extra new bathroom, a large additional living room, and a new front door area. It made a huge difference in our lives.

Shortly after the completion, we had several of Muriel's relatives come for a visit, and one of them remarked that she kept getting lost in the house, even though it was not that big.

My employer was having a hard time replacing the company switchboard operator who was in the hospital. Several temporary employees from an agency had been tried, without success. Finally, after the last one had quit in the middle of the day, I suggested that Muriel might be able to handle it as she had worked on the long-distance manual exchange in England. She was asked to come and look it over, which she did. She started work immediately, working part-time. A secretary filled in at other times.

However, the company's policy did not allow family members to work at the same company facility, so they had to be somewhat creative about paying Muriel. The problem was solved by the company buying us a pair of chandeliers and some other items that Muriel wanted. Soon the regular switchboard operator returned after her operation. Eventually, it led to Muriel being offered the position of secretary for a subsidiary company that happened to be operating out of the same building. Muriel continued working for about a year or so, until the time we were contemplating a move to San Diego.

During our time in the house in Santa Monica, there were several significant family events. The first occurred in 1966. We decided to make our first phone call to England, which was terribly expensive. We were on the phone for about 5 minutes, but there were more tears than talking, but it was important because it was the first voice contact for two years, and brought England a bit closer. 2 years later, in 1968 Joy's mother, her sister Susan, and Auntie Celia arrived for a month visit. We took them to Sequoia National Park, Disneyland, Tijuana (Mexico), Sea World, Knotts Berry Farm, Busch Gardens, and the Bonanza set at Universal Studios.

In order to get 10 of us to Sequoia National Park for a few days, I made a camper shell which I built to mount on a car. I took the trunk (boot) lid off, and stood the back end inside, with the rest of it resting on the roof of the car. The other car pulled a small trailer, 5' x 7', which had sides that opened out with bunks inside making beds for 4 kids. Muriel and I had a mattress on the floor, with a small bunk across the front for Helen. Actually, Muriel and I and the kids used the camper on this trip, as the older relatives could not climb up above the roof of the car in the camper.

On the way, Muriel was driving the car with the camper, and the car in front of her dropped a folding chair in the road, and Muriel could not avoid it and ran over it with a large bump, and the ceiling liner came down. We stopped the cars to catch our breath, and I went over to talk to Muriel. Her mother pointed to the ceiling. She had said nothing about it to Muriel. I immediately saw what had happened and gave it a bang, and it popped back into place. Apparently, they thought the camper had come down through the car roof.

We had a great time in Sequoia. At one point we had a few drinks, and the girls got a bit emotional, and Muriel was hugged by her mother for about a half hour. She was on her knees beside her mother's chair and couldn't move, and got really stiff. The trailer was bumped in the night by a bear, and I was stung by a hornet when my foot went through a rotten log into a nest. This visit of Muriel's family was typical of a dozen made over the years, mostly 2 or 3 people at a time and every year. We went to the same attractions year after year (which is where they wanted to go) to the point that the kids begged to not have to go.

By this time Christopher and David had evening paper routes. They made about $30 a month. They were saving money, and they decided they would like to go to England for a trip now that they could afford it. The relatives in England were happy to accommodate them, so the trip was booked. Muriel and the two younger boys, Nick and Peter, arranged to do the paper routes in their absence. A week or so before they left for England, I wrote a letter for them to put in with the newspapers. The letter said that they had saved up the money for a trip to England and their mother and younger brothers would be doing the route, and to call our phone number if there was a problem.

They had a wonderful response in the form of over $100 each in tips to spend on their vacation. Christopher was 14 and David was 12, and they had a wonderful time. I remember them coming off the plane when they returned. They had lost their American accent, and had rosy cheeks with white skin, not the tanned color with which they left. In the meantime, Muriel and the two younger boys did the paper routes, and Muriel and I collected the money. I collected on David's route, and a couple of people were always bad payers. Apparently, one guy had not paid David for 6 months and, of course, David was being charged for the paper. This fellow would not answer the door to David.

When I realized the situation, I nearly knocked the door down to the point that he peeped out of the window, allowing me the opportunity to tell him what I thought of him. He would not answer the door, and so I stopped the paper. David was upset with this until I explained that if he didn't get paid he didn't have a customer.

One lady yelled at me twice to come back later. On the second visit, I told her, "Pay me now or the paper stops". She paid. Most people were very nice and asked how the boys were doing in England.

Son David had always made a bee-line for any piano, even when he was only 2 years old. Now he wanted to have lessons. Our friend Fran (from church), taught him for about 6 months, then said he was beyond the level she could teach. Muriel and I had both had lessons when we were young, but not with quality teachers, and we learned nothing. This time we enquired about the best teacher in the area and we were given the name of Elizabeth Withrow.

We visited her and found that she looked exactly like Horowitz, the famous pianist, and her hands were very large, just like his also.

She made David play the piano with coins on the back of his hands. After this, she agreed to take him.

He continued with her until we moved to San Diego. (When we were moving, we asked her to recommend a good teacher in San Diego. She gave us the name Onalee Jones).

I became well-known to the company's big aerospace customers. I was easily identified as "that English Guy". I gradually accumulated the big customers, and within 18 months, I was the new Sales Administrator, supervising the operation and the day-to-day activities. I worked for this company for the next 5 or 6 years until a new company came to town. They asked all the big customers who was the best capacitor man in Los Angeles County. They were given my name by everybody. This company called me and offered a large increase over my current salary, and I changed jobs.

On the strength of the increased income, we bought a new full-size station wagon in which we could seat 4 across the front bench seat with a squeeze.

The new company was a distributor of capacitors, not a manufacturer like the last company. I hated it almost from the beginning. It was 25 miles away, in the north end of the San Fernando Valley where day-time summer temperatures can reach 110 degrees F. I let it be known at the old company that I was not happy, and three months later, the old Western Regional Manager called and said, "Name your price to come back". I was back there in 5 days. Being so keen to get back, I underpriced myself, although I was still getting a great salary, 50% more than when I left.

It took 2 months to get the system back on track, but eventually, everything got straightened out. The employee below me when I left, had been promoted, but he had not been able to do the job and was released. I had to fire the extra employee, hired in at the bottom when I left. Lots of customers were complaining that we had ignored their requests for quotations, and I found a 6" stack of them, hidden in the new guy's desk. That took care of the staff problems.

I regularly had to travel around the South West to the Western region branch offices. The regional offices had quite a turnover, and new staff needed training. Rather than flying, I drove and took Muriel and the children. We had some nice trips, seeing sights along the way. The new station wagon was wonderful for traveling with children. With the back seat down and a covering of foam rubber, they had room to play or sleep, whatever took their fancy. We used it eventually to sleep in and on it. I built a foldout sleeping compartment that strapped to the roof. It folded down to about 6" high, but opened up to about 3 feet high, enough to crawl into and lay down. At a traveling height of about 6", it was not noticeable. It took Muriel and me about 20 seconds to raise it up for sleeping, and it stood up to any sort of wind with no problem.

Chapter 20 - San Diego, Here We Come

Two years later I started getting regular job offers from a company that was a competitor, but I refused them. After about another year, the competitor announced they were moving to San Diego. This was attractive as we had been thinking of getting out of the Los Angeles area, and I agreed to work for them.

I started work for the new company, Brady Corporation, manufacturers of high-frequency electronic interference filters and ceramic capacitors. They were in Inglewood, about 12 miles from home, and about 2 months from moving to San Diego. Their General Manager was the same man who originally hired me at the old company when I had arrived from England. I had moved into his position when he left for this new company.

I soon found out why they wanted me to work for them. The sales department was in chaos. For the first month, I worked every night until 8.30 pm or 9.00 pm with my secretary going through piles of paperwork, and finally, we got caught up. The unfortunate thing about it was that all my work started paying off, and with a few weeks to go before the move, we had record-breaking sales which could not be filled before the move, and start-up at the new location would delay delivery even more. This was not necessarily a bad problem, but it kept me hopping for the next 4 or 5 months.

Before the move we went to San Diego several times on Saturdays, looking for somewhere to live, and finally found a 4-bedroom house which fitted our needs. The move took place. We paid rent for a month as the sale could not be completed in time.

Muriel was hired by this new company to handle payroll and personnel matters and went to work for the last three days in Inglewood to learn the ropes so that she could handle it in San Diego.

The company was paying removal costs, and the day came for us to get everything packed. Four men showed up with mountains of paper and cardboard cartons. It took them all day to pack and load the truck. We had an empty house by 6.00 pm except for the stuff we wanted to move in our cars, plus sleeping bags. It was our intent to go to the new house and sleep there as the truck was going to arrive at 8.00 am the next day.

We had decided to not sell the Santa Monica house but to rent it out in two apartments. We had found one tenant for the house we had occupied, and my father stayed on alone in the other house.

Before we left for the drive to San Diego, all the neighbors and friends came to our empty house with drinks and a cake, and we had a party. At 10.30 pm, we got into our two cars, me in the station wagon, and Muriel in the Ford Galaxy, and left for San Diego. We arrived after midnight and went to the real estate agents house to pick up the keys. We got her out of bed and got the keys and went to our new house.

When we arrived, we saw lights on in the house. We went in, to find lots of furniture there. Our stuff was arriving in a few hours! We locked up and went back to the real estate agent. She got dressed and returned to the house with us. She said we should move in there anyway. Finally, we bedded down in the house in our sleeping bags, and she left. We put a note on the door to the effect that we were in the house.

Early the next day, a Saturday, I had to go to the new office as the company trucks were arriving at 8.00 am also. There were only about 6 people that transferred to San Diego with the company, and every hand was needed. I got a call from Muriel to say that the previous owners were getting divorced, and the wife had not told the husband of the closing date of the sale, and he had shown up at about 9.00 am. The removal people refused to unload the truck while the other furniture was there and said they would come back later. The previous owner came back for his stuff with a truck at about 10.00 am, and he was gone by lunchtime, but asked if he could leave a few very heavy items which was OK. The truck with our belongings, all 5 ½ tons, showed up at 4.00 pm. They were drunk but got it unloaded anyway. They said they had been to Tijuana in Mexico. I got home at about 6.00 pm and had to start getting beds assembled with the help of the boys.

Although we were in a housing development on the edge of North San Diego, just a mile away, on the way to the new office, a coyote walked across the road in front of me. It was a wide-open space then. Today it is in the middle of a small metropolis.

The next day, Sunday, I went to the office again as there was still work to be done. We were interviewing and hiring on Monday. Muriel was now employed full-time, and was an important part of the hiring, so she had her plate full. The kids had to fend for themselves to a great extent for the first few weeks.

In no time we got the company going, but we had this huge backlog of orders to fill. The manufacture of ceramic filters and capacitors is an art, and there are so many variables. I spent much of the day smoothing down impatient customers who couldn't wait. I would not want to go through this period again, but we were out of the Los Angeles area, and away from the crowds.

Just down the road about 300 yards from the house was this wild canyon, which was wonderful for all the kids. Across the road from our house was a family with seven children, mostly boys, of ages similar to ours. All our children were happy with the move once they settled in.

After a few months, in addition to having the sales responsibility, I was now also responsible for material and production control, packaging, shipping and receiving, and purchasing. I rarely got out of the office before 7.00 pm, and I also was in on Saturdays.

One of the first things we wanted to do was to try to contact Onalee Jones so that David could resume his piano lessons. If you remember, this was the name given to us by David's piano teacher in Santa Monica. We found the phone number and made the call, but no answer. We called two or three times a day for a week, then every few days when we would think of it, but there was never an answer.

It must have been more than a month after we had given up calling when we were sitting down to eat lunch one Saturday when I heard a voice in my head clearly say to me, "Onalee Jones just came in". I was shaken as I had not given the name any thought for a week or so. I repeated the words to Muriel, then said, "I'm going to phone him". I went to the phone and dialed the number. It was answered by this gruff voice that advised me, "This is Onalee Jones". It was a woman. I told her that we'd been calling for weeks. She said that she'd been ill and had been away, and had just arrived home a minute before my call. This was the sort of thing which gives goosebumps.

She agreed to see David when we mentioned Elizabeth Withrow's recommendation. As a result, she did have David as a pupil. We had originally bought the cheapest piano we could find in case David was not too serious. Within a few months, Onalee said David needed a better piano. We questioned David as to his level of seriousness. He said he was very serious, so we went out with him and Onalee and we all four chose a black 6-foot Knabe grand piano. It had the best tone in the store. We finally gave this piano to David after he was married some years and had a house large enough to accommodate it. He bought his own upright piano when he first got married and we are storing it for him. He plays it every time he comes to see us.

We were going to a church of the same denomination as the church in Santa Monica. However it was so small, our 7 made a total of 37 on the first Sunday we attended. The minister, Ned Roberts, was a semi-retired missionary. His wife's name was Jewel, and she had a lung problem. She used an oxygen tank.

During the time we were going to that church, I installed artificial stained glass (plastic) in the main east window above the altar. I made a manger scene for Christmas. We were able to buy a complete set of Nativity figures, shepherds, animals, etc., for the ridiculous sum of $18 for the lot. The figures were plastic and more than 2 feet high, and realistically painted with light fixtures inside. The stable we made was plywood and hinged to fold up for storage. The boys and I put the whole thing on a flat roof at the church for the first Christmas, and it was shown on local TV. We have never understood why we were able to buy what was a set of figures and animals worth several hundred dollars for only $18. Divine intervention maybe?

Our children, especially Christopher and David, were very active in the youth group at the church. One weekend there was a camping trip to the Cuyamaca National Park, about 30 miles east of San Diego. We were chaperones and sponsors, and took all our kids. We climbed to the top of Cuyamaca Peak. I carried a young kid on my shoulders all the way up, as he couldn't keep up. Muriel did all the cooking for the group which included 20 people and only one other adult couple.

The church was normally only half-filled with chairs, with the rest of them stacked at the back. One Sunday, I saw some people come to the door and look for some empty seats. They left when they could not see any. After that, when I was lining up with the rest of the choir, to start the service, I used to tell our boys to put out more chairs if there were no spares left.

The minister spoke to me a bit later and asked me to stop it, as he didn't want too many people in the church. We decided to help his problem by going to another Church and left to go to Torrey Pines Christian Church. This church is in an upscale area and was financially supporting the old church. On our last Sunday there, Jewel, the minister's wife said to us as we were leaving, "You should go to Torrey Pines, they're your type of people". This was said in a very sarcastic manner. So much for devout Christians.

We went to Torrey Pines Church from that time on for 27 years.

Chapter 21 - Spirits and Mysteries

It was about 6 months after we left Santa Monica that my father announced he was getting married. She was a member of his church, and by coincidence had the same name as my mother, "Lilian". Her last name had been "Justice".

A few months later, my mother, who had now gone to live in Florida, announced that she was getting married also to a man named Arthur Edgar Jelliman. My father's name was Arthur Edward Walters, so we had 2 Arthurs. My mother's new initials were L.J., and my father's new wife was L.J before changing to L.W. which had originally been my mother's initials. Strange coincidences.

My father moved to Mission Viejo with his new wife, halfway between San Diego and Santa Monica.

Son David was making good progress at the piano and would sit for hours playing, and sometimes he just let his fingers wander over the keys creating all types of melodies. I set up a tape recorder on which he would record the tunes that came out.

One day he wanted us to listen to one of his recorded musical passage about 1 minute long. It was in a class that seemed way beyond David's capability. We listened to David play it many times.

Sometime later, David came tearing out into the kitchen yelling that somebody had messed with his special recording, and sure enough, right in the middle of his special piece of music was a gap of maybe 5 seconds.

We held a family inquiry, but could not explain the gap. I really believe that nobody had touched the tape recorder.

It was a couple of days later that David again came into the kitchen to say that he had turned up the volume on the tape recorder and could hear this croaky voice speaking in the gap in his music. We listened and sure enough, this croaky voice was very indistinct but seemed to be speaking almost in rhyme.

Our first reaction was that it was saying "I am in heaven, I am 57". We could not make sense of this and in time we forgot about it. More about this later.

At work, Muriel shared an office with Agnes, (2 doors down from my office), who was the company accountant. She was about 48, a bit on the heavy side, unmarried, with coke bottle glasses. She was good fun, and popular and Muriel got on well with her. Agnes shared a house with her female friend Fred (I suppose, short for Fredericka). During the time that they worked together, Muriel's and Agnes' discussions turned to the subject of ghosts and ghost stories.

We have not mentioned before that both Muriel and I have an interest in this subject, and have read many books which include those on spiritualism, and the afterlife.

Now Agnes and Fred were complete skeptics, but in time Agnes became interested and curious and finally went to a spiritualist meeting.

In no time Agnes became a believer and eventually became a healer, and the prime skeptic, Fred, was now having doubts. She reported strange happenings at the meetings which she attended with Agnes.

Some months later, Agnes proposed to Muriel that she bring her teacher to our house one evening, and Muriel leaped at the opportunity. A date was set up.

One of the most prominent spiritualists who ever lived was Arthur Ford, who was at his greatest in the early 1900s. His spirit guide was known as Fletcher. Arthur Ford was assisted in his shows by a lady medium, famous in her own right, named Ida Hill. We have read many books about them. Arthur Ford was said to be an alcoholic, and it was Ida Hill's husband's job to make sure he was ready to perform.

The time came for Agnes and her teacher to arrive at our house. The doorbell rang and we went to the door to meet Agnes, and we were introduced to her teacher, Mrs. Ida Hill. Surprise, surprise.

Ida was obviously very old, but active in spite of being heavily built. She greeted us but at the same time she was talking quietly toward her left shoulder saying things like, "Go away now, I'll talk to you in a minute".

Our youngest son, Peter always shared a bedroom with Nicholas, and was always a nervous child. He always complained of, "People walking around in his bedroom at night", and he slept with an eighteen-inch long machete under his pillow.

As a child he would often come running out of his bedroom, scared, saying that things and people were coming out of the closet, and we always treated it like it was nonsense. This situation with Peter was worse at this house, even though he was now 8 or 9 years old.

After the usual pleasantries with Agnes and Ida, we suggested that Ida walk around the house and give us some idea of what she felt. She said that we were a strong family unit and that we were a good example for uneducated spirits. Muriel asked did she mean evil spirits, to which she answered, "There are no evil spirits, just uneducated ones".

In the walk around the house, all was plain sailing until she reached a certain spot in the passage between the bedrooms. Ida clutched her chest with a gasp, and said, "Somebody was shot here". Next, she came to the doorway of Peter and Nick's room and said, "Oh, there are uneducated forces in here". Then we told her about Peter and his fears, and she said that he obviously had psychic powers, which attracted spirits to him, and that his fears were real. She recommended that we leave a Bible open to Psalm 94, and Peter would not be bothered again. This we did without giving the reason, and we didn't hear any more complaints from Peter . . . . . . Until some months later. He came out of his room one morning complaining that "they" were back. We hurried into his room and found the bible had slipped down the back of the chest of drawers on which we had placed it.

When we told Peter the reason for the Bible, he made a frame to hold the book open and in place.

Later on, we asked a next-door neighbor if there had been any violent deaths in the house, and they confirmed that some years ago, a person was shot in the passageway in the exact spot in which Ida Hill had experienced chest pain.

Whilst Ida was there she met all the children and told us some startling facts. She said that Christopher, our eldest son was a Red Indian in his last life, and was killed by a snakebite. She couldn't know that Chris was terrified of snakes. Then she told us that David, our 2nd son (whom she hadn't met at the time as he was out) was being coached at the piano by Beethoven who was in the house as she spoke. This was some startling information as Beethoven was David's idol and he had many books about him, and lots of his music, although none of this was in view.

Suddenly, at the mention of Beethoven, a bell rang in my mind. I found David's tape and played the "gap" at full volume. I said, "What is that?" She answered, "That is Beethoven saying, I am Beethoven, I am 57".

I asked, "What is the 57 for?" She said, "I don't know, but often they try to give proof that it is them". I found David's music encyclopedia and found Beethoven. He died at the age of 57. I got cold shivers up my back again. We still have this tape today. The only question in my mind is the fact that mediums, palm readers, etc. seem to inexplicably know all sorts of strange facts which they shouldn't know, but when we ask questions, they mostly don't know the answers. If Mrs. Hill was talking to spirits and was told that Beethoven was in the house, how come she couldn't ask the spirits the significance of Beethoven's message of "I am 57". However, I still think there is so much that is not explained, and there definitely is something mysterious here.

Ida said that Nicholas was a French soldier killed in battle in his last life. She couldn't know that he can mimic perfectly with a French accent.

About Peter, she said he was oriental in his last life. She couldn't know that in Santa Monica when Peter was young, the backyard was always full of his oriental friends.

About Muriel, she said she was the favorite lady in waiting for Queen Victoria. Muriel had been told this by another lady in England who was flippantly described as a witch, and who was a friend of Muriel's Aunt Celia.

Ida said that I walked with Jesus in Biblical times. We don't remember what she said about Helen. The whole evening was filled with so many facts, some only known to us, that we were convinced, and could not explain it away.

David arrived home halfway through the evening along with a young lady who was in the church youth group to which our boys belonged. She was much older, and we weren't sure we liked the situation.

Ida saw David come into the room, but the young lady sat on the step into the room, behind Ida, and was not in Ida's field of vision, and would not have been heard as the carpet was thick and muffled all footsteps.

The young lady piped up, "Can you tell me about Steve?" Ida grabbed her chest. She said, "Steve is very sorry. He shot himself. This is not the first time he's killed himself and he's in real trouble". I knew the story. Steve was the young lady's boyfriend until he shot himself about a year earlier. The rest of the evening was filled with mysterious statements and messages which were strange enough to make us very uncomfortable.

Chapter 22 - Moves At Work And At Home

It was about 6 or 7 months after moving to San Diego that we heard that our company, The Potter Company was being bought by a large competitor. All sorts of their people arrived, and we did an inventory of the material in the stock room. The final details of the sale were not finalized very quickly, and we did a complete inventory of all raw materials every week on a Saturday, for about 6 weeks, until the final papers were signed.

Muriel was made Personnel Manager by the new company, a large elevation in status for her.

The people from the new company were a bunch of chumps. They arrived thinking they were the bees-knees and that everything in the old company was no good, and they replaced all the ceramic formulations (recipes) with their formulations. When we tried to make filters with new ceramic capacitors, we would sometimes have a 75% failure rate, and then we would have to go out and buy all new capacitor cases, seals and cores, and go through the process again and again which caused havoc with the costs and delivery times. Sometimes we would have 4 or 5 shots to complete a little order. I spent hours looking around the stockroom for the old type capacitors to fill orders. Also, we had 5 General Managers in the first year, each one knowing less than the one before. The load fell on me as I was running everything except production.

After a while the new company decided to separate sales and operations divisions in line with the rest of the company. I was doing both. They now decided that I should do only one, and I chose Sales.

A so-called expert was employed to run Material and Production control etc., and I went through the process of handing over to him, but he was not too interested. He was a retired Naval Officer, and really felt that he knew it all. I told him to give me a shout if he needed help. He never did call on me.

In about 2 ½ months, production came to a complete stop with no material to work with. This new guy's car was parked outside my office window, and at 4.00 pm on a Friday, I saw him loading his stuff in his car. I groaned inwardly knowing what was coming. I didn't have long to wait. The General manager asked me to go to his office and he told me I would have to take back Operations, and that they would get a new person for Sales, but in the interim I'd have to do both again.

I got so fed up with the problems caused by the quality of the ceramic products that I bought replacements from another large competing company, and we had our best months ever for shipments out the door. Then the president of the company paid us a visit, and found out about it. He stuck his head in my door and told me to stop it, and our shipments went to hell again. Using the competitors' capacitors, we had about a 98% yield of filters. With our own capacitors, we were lucky to get 50% yield.

It was November 1973, and Muriel said, “Why don’t we go to England next year?” My first reaction was about the money. We added up how much, and when we would accumulate enough money. We worked out a very detailed budget of what we could spend and what we would be able to save etc., and stuck to it and to our surprise, we were on target for the first 3 months, so we went ahead with the plan and booked 7 tickets.

It was incredible how close we were able to stay to the money forecast. Some weeks we were within $3 of our target. On the day of departure we had exactly the money we had forecast 9 months earlier.

3 weeks before the planned departure date in August, we bought new shoes for all the boys. On the day we were to leave, Peter’s feet had grown so much in the three weeks that he couldn’t get his new shoes on, so he had to wear old ones. He was the youngest boy so there was no hope of passing them on.

Our trip included a stop in Bangor, Maine, the home of New England clam chowder. I can see a picture of Nick sitting in the airport restaurant at a table, tucking into a bowl with a big grin on his face. We believe he had two bowls.

When we arrived in England, we hired a Volkswagen mini-bus, and whizzed around all over the place. When we weren’t traveling on trips, the 4 boys went off into the City (Bath), with Uncle Paul, (Muriel’s youngest brother, between our sons David and Nick in age).

This was our first trip to England for 10 years. Mr. Henderson, my old boss had lost his wife, and was remarried. The stores and dispatch at the Thames Rubber Company had been moved out of the factory as they‘d had a fire in the old building. My old boss, Harry Williams had died. My Auntie Dolly had died also, and her husband Uncle Les lived alone with the same dog, Bruno. We went to see him, and this old Labrador came waddling along the sidewalk towards us, and we didn’t know if it was Bruno, but he sniffed us, and immediately wagged his tail. He knew us after 10 years.

One day we were visiting old neighbors in the Vineyards, when we heard some awfully noisy children coming along the road, too far away to recognize anybody. When this rowdy bunch got closer, you guessed it, it was our boys and Uncle Paul. They were drinking milk from pint milk bottles, and they were eating cockles they had bought from a fish-monger.

Muriel’s sister Jane re-scheduled her wedding to take place while we were there in England. An enjoyable celebration was had by all. All too soon it was time to return to California.

When we arrived back home, there was a banner across the front of the house saying “Welcome Home”, from the neighbors. The battery in the station wagon had gone dead, but that wasn’t too bad, it was 6 years old.

The neighbors who organized the welcome home were the James family. This is the family that lived close and had 7 children, all living in a 3 bedroom house. All the children mixed with our children.

Father was ex-military, and worked for General Dynamics, and when military business slowed he was laid off. He was off work for some months and they were in dire straits. We took them bags of food, but Mrs. James, who was a very staunch catholic, insisted on buying things for us almost to the value of the food we bought. This was most annoying so we got smart and delivered bags of groceries by our David creeping up to the door in the dark, ringing the bell, and running away. This solved the problem. We denied it was us and this seemed to provide enough doubt to allow them to feel OK. They were wonderful people and we were happy to help.

Mr. and Mrs. James met when she was a nurse and Mr. James was a patient in a military hospital. A romance blossomed but marriage was impossible because she was a Catholic and he was not. They eventually solved that problem by Mr. James becoming a Catholic by mail order.

If you wanted to have a sensible conversation with Mr. James it would have to be before 7.00 pm. After that, he was out of it. He drank one beer after another for most of the evening. He just sat in a chair with his eyes half closed. Mrs. James drank only ice water. We often wondered how they had 7 children. She must have been a determined woman.

The children were quite well-behaved and obedient. They had never been out of San Diego County. Our children used to beg us not to take them places as they had been all over the south west of the U.S.

Back after our trip to England, there was a pile-up of work, but the company was transferring somebody from the sales office at the North Carolina factory where he'd been for 18 years. We should have wondered about the reason he was being moved after so long. Was he being moved away to get rid of a problem? It turned out to be this. Some customers eventually refused to talk to him and kept calling me and asking me to handle their business, which I couldn't do as I was now in the sales division.

The house we were living in had 4 bedrooms, and 2 adjoining living rooms, a large kitchen, big enough in which to eat, but no dining room, all on one floor. In addition, the 2 car garage had been partly turned into a very nice room, 22' x 20'. It was paneled in a dark wood, with a nice ceiling with exposed antiqued beams. It had a red/orange shag carpet, which was bright but somehow fitted the room very nicely. But there were two problems with the room. The main one was that you had to go through the kitchen and utility room to reach it, and the other one was that all around the base of the walls was a tiny red brick wall 3 bricks high, meant to cover up the foundation which is always exposed about 6" in garages.

I got the bricks out and stained the foundation with wood stain and it looked like a battered old wood baseboard which matched the room perfectly.

If you walked out of the front door in a straight line for about 12', you would walk into one of the outside walls of the "garage", now room. I built an outside wall, filling in the 12 feet which included a new front door, at the right angle to the original front door, and knocked a doorway into the "garage", or new room, which allowed access to our lovely room. It made a tremendous difference to the house.

As I said earlier, over my last year at work, we had five General Managers, each one knowing less than the last. Our lack of good production was due entirely to the poor ceramic components going into filters, ruining the final product, but the company had a blind spot being under the impression that their ceramic was good. They put the blame on Production and Material control, and one day, a consultant from a nationally recognized efficiency company, showed up, and engaged by the corporate office to straighten out our "problem". The real problem was that they were trying to solve the wrong problem.

This consultant spent hours with me, then started showing me his solutions. One by one he agreed his solutions wouldn't work, and on the fourth day he was replaced by another "expert". In less than a week, he gave up, and a few days later the man in charge of the Anaheim office showed up. The first thing he wanted to see was the procedures that I had written for Production, Material Control, and Purchasing. He spent most of a day reading them, and remarked that he could not find fault with them, but, "Let's take a closer look".

He was there for 6 weeks and took up hours of my time, and had only 1 suggestion to improve the system. That was, instead of stacking work orders in date order for the scheduled or estimated date they would be released to production, he recommended that they be kept in Pendaflex hanging files! In other words, instead of stacking them vertically, stack them horizontally. The company owed them $22,000 for that gem.

We went along with that suggestion, but of course, it made absolutely no difference. A few weeks after our expert departed he called me asking for copies of my procedures as they would not pay without written procedures from the efficiency outfit. Guess whose procedures were submitted for payment.

The day that the 5th General Manager, a new hire, called us together to announce his taking over the running of the company, I quit. I'd had enough. I was in a bad state of stress and I'd had enough of those clowns. They eventually hired 3 people to do my work, and in 9 months they dropped the whole ceramic filter product line. They just didn't have my capacitor knowledge to keep it going. Plus the new guy in sales was a disaster, and helped put them out of business and he was finally removed. They moved into a completely new product line, the design and manufacture of micro-circuit materials. In my opinion, the only thing which kept the filter product line going was my capacitor knowledge in substituting all sorts of different types of capacitors in the filters we were making. It is significant that the 5th General Manager called me a couple of times asking me to go back to work for them. Maybe a few people did recognize my contribution. In the meantime, Muriel continued as Personnel Manager.

As you would expect, in her dealings with people and their problems, she had many funny and interesting experiences to relate to.

One interviewee made it quite obvious that he was quite happy to remain unemployed, and in the middle of the interview, he laid his head on Muriel's desk and closed his eyes, paying no attention to Muriel. She soon showed him to the door.

Another applicant for employment sat in Muriel's office talking to her when she suddenly realized that she could see a glowing aura surrounding his head. She was shaken by this and brought it to the attention of the applicant. He calmly told her that it had been seen by many people. He was not in the least surprised.

While we were in the house in San Diego, we had a couple of visits from Muriel's relatives, but the frequency slowed somewhat. Every visitor was taken at least to the San Francisco area, Yosemite National Park or Sequoia, and Las Vegas and Grand Canyon, plus Sea World, Disneyland, and Tijuana, Mexico. We have been to these places so many times now that we have no real interest in going to any of them anymore.

Christopher was 18 and graduated from high school at this house, and started going to Mira Costa College. David was 16, Nicholas 13, Peter 11, and Helen 10. One day I was painting on a ladder by the front door and Helen came home crying saying some boy had hit her. I told her to go and see her mother. Within seconds, 4 brothers rushed out of the door nearly knocking me off the ladder, to go after that luckless boy.

On the work front, I went to Management Recruiters, a head-hunter in Anaheim, and they sent me to a company called Stephans Applied Engineering, which needed a product marketing manager. I was offered the job, but they were 82 miles away. It was a good opportunity and we decided Muriel would give up her personnel manager job, and we would move to the area. I drove to work there for two months, and we went on Saturdays, to look at houses. We didn't like anything there, so decided we would move north from San Diego as far as we could with Joy still able to travel to her current job.

It was meant to be. One Saturday, we drove as far north as was reasonable for Joy to drive to work and arrived in Carlsbad and got off the freeway. There was an "open house" sign right by the freeway off-ramp. It was about 3.00 pm. We followed the signs to 4400 Highland Drive, Carlsbad.

We were so impressed by this house and both fell in love with it. We walked around and around. Muriel loved the view of the ocean at the front. I was most impressed by the view of the canyon and lagoon at the back, although we both agreed there was no way we could afford to buy it. We were at the house for a long time, and gradually it felt more and more like home to us. Before we thought what we were doing, we had filled out an offer form with a ridiculously low price, predicated on selling our San Diego house, and the duplex in Santa Monica. We left and drove straight home, wondering what we had done.

We hadn't been home long when the phone rang. It was the real estate agent saying that the owner would like us to raise our offer. We offered a bit more, and they took it, but we added a condition that we bring the children immediately for their approval.

The children were extremely upset at the thought of leaving their friends and the place they enjoyed. They moaned and groaned all the way to Carlsbad, and then we turned into the driveway of the new house to dead silence. I stopped the engine and the silence continued. We saw the owners, and they took us into the house, and the kids were smiling. All traces of their previous misery disappeared.

Chapter 23 - Life In Carlsbad

The offer on the new house in Carlsbad went into a 90 day escrow, contingent on us selling the Santa Monica and San Diego houses. We immediately contacted a neighbor in Santa Monica, who was in real estate, also the father of one of the boys' friends, and the place sold in 9 days for more than twice what we paid for it, although it was less than the market price. We were glad to see it go. The San Diego house took a little longer, and I had to do some things to it to meet the buyer's mortgage requirements, but we sold that eventually. On the 15th of May 1976, we moved into 4400 Highland Drive, Carlsbad.

In the meantime, during the 90 days escrow, I left Stewart Connector Co. I was there for 61 days. The headhunter that had found me the job, got paid by Stewart Co. on the 60th day. I will relate my complicated work history until retirement, then come back chronologically for everything else.

The main reason for leaving Stewart Connectors was the distance; 83 miles from the present house in San Diego, but 55 miles from the new house. But there was another reason. The VP and general manager, his name was Ed, was a bit crazy. He would shout abuse at people, especially those who did not stand up to him. He would appear to get into a rage over the silliest thing and used the worst language. However, after about 2 weeks, at weekly product meetings, he started using me as an example of somebody who did the job right, which was a bit embarrassing as I was so new. Then I found out that in about a month, was the annual sales meeting at a local hotel, with all the bigwigs and sales personnel present, about 80 people. All 10 product marketing managers had to make a presentation about their product line. This included making a booklet about it with photos and diagrams. Ed said that as I was new, he would help me with mine when he got time.

Time was passing, and no help, although he said don't worry, he would get to it. I was impatient and decided to start on my own. It was a completely new product and so I created an index of all the things that I wanted to know, which anybody else would need to know in order to sell it. Once I got the index, it fell into place. I wrote the rest. I told Ed the VP what I was doing, and he was quite pleased and said he would go through it and clean it up and make it right. I finished it and at more than 3/8" thick, it was typed for him to see.

He went off and was reading it for hours, and then returned. He found fault only with one descriptive word which was used all the way through, and said if I changed that it would be excellent. The mistake was that I described the action of the connectors as "insulation piercing", and he wanted it changed to "insulation displacing". In 30 minutes, the change was done. Then Ed asked if he could use my index as he was helping another Product Marketing Manager. Of course, I had no problem with that, I was just amazed and relieved it was done.

The sales meeting started. Apparently, they always voted to see whose presentation (booklet) was the best and gave the most assistance to the sales department. The same product marketing manager always won, and he did so again, but I was voted 2nd best. I was congratulated more than the winner as everybody knew I'd only been in the company 6 weeks.

A short time later, I got a phone call from a James Fisher, who was a VP of a company in Vista, just 9 miles from our new house. He was looking for a person to employ who could run the sales administration for him. I had been recommended to him by their Quality Control Manager with whom I had worked at 2 previous companies. With the close proximity to the new house, it seemed too good to miss, and so I went to see James that evening.

I felt more like I was interviewing James rather than the other way around. He spent most of the time trying to convince me to take the job, which I did before I left that evening.

The next day, the 61st day at Stamford, I was waiting for a good opportunity to drop the bad news on Ed, the VP, when I happened to pass him in the engineering department. I was carrying the first plastic molding for a new product in my line, and for the first time he spoke to me in a very rude manner saying something which was completely unnecessary, "Where the f… are you going with that?" Here was my chance. I said, "Ed, I want to see you in your office right now". I was angry at his tone. He stopped, turned around, and meekly followed me to his office. I closed the door and said, "Sit down". He sat. I said, "Ed I'm leaving". He looked at me for a moment as it sank in, and you'll never guess what he did. He burst into tears and sobbed with his head nearly down on his desk.

When he recovered somewhat he asked me why, and I felt it was a chance to do something for the people he commonly abused. I told him his behavior was very bad and any decent person would not put up with it. Over the rest of the day, I was called to the Contr. office who spent ½ an hour trying to get me to change my mind, then later, the sales director did the same thing. He added, "I wondered how long that big Englishman would put up with Ed".

After much effort to persuade me to change my mind, I left a week later.

In the meantime, Muriel continued progressing in her personnel experience and had more amazing stories to tell. One day, there was a fire alarm, and in no time the whole building was destroyed.

Almost immediately a new facility was leased, about another 20 miles further for Muriel to travel.

They all went through the expected trauma of starting up again and making do until everything could be brought up to speed.

There was a complaint from one of the employees that there was no refrigerator in which they could keep their lunchtime food. This lady was from the Philippines and a recognized malcontent. Muriel asked her to be patient saying that back home they didn't all have refrigerators, just like in England, so it should not be too much of a hardship. The lady filed a discrimination report based on Muriel's comments and caused all sorts of trouble for her, but eventually, it died.

Very soon a proper facility was leased a bit closer for Muriel in a place called Scripps Ranch, northeast of San Diego.

Within a year, they sold out to Mathey Smith, a British-owned company. Very soon, the company laid off about 2/3 of the employees and consequently, Muriel's job was greatly reduced. She was asked to take on some accounting, but she refused and resigned.

After leaving Stewart Connector Co., I started at the new company, Secure Connections Corporation, working for James Fisher. I always felt it was a strange name for a company, but it did describe what they did. Temporarily, I had to travel 27 miles from our San Diego house in our full-size station wagon. (27 miles seemed nothing after the 83 miles to Stewart Connectors). We still had about 6 weeks to go with the escrow on the new house, and I took the opportunity to transport loads of packed boxes to the new house on the way to the new job. The current owners gave us permission to put it in the 2-car garage as they were not using it. By the time we moved in, there was only a small pathway through the garage. The rest was filled to more than 6 feet in height. We made the main move with two loads in an 18-foot-long rented truck, which we accomplished on a Saturday.

In the interim, I had several further calls from Stewart Connectors begging me to return, but I always turned them down as the distance was too far. I didn't mention the distance as that would have let Ed off the hook. I often wonder how far I would have progressed if I'd stayed on there. Ed seemed to think I was the bees-knees, but I'm sure I would have had a constant war with him if I had stayed.

I soon settled into the routine at Secure Connections. James Fisher was so easy to work for. Unfortunately, he tended to be bullied by some people because he was a nice man, so easygoing and quiet.

Within the first week or so, I remember one run-in with John Hayward, the Operations Manager, who was a cocky little know-all and one who was completely lacking in any humor. He was telling James all about how an order should be written up. This is an area where I've had lots of experience, and couldn't help getting involved, and put him straight in no uncertain manner. He slunk away and James laughed his head off. From that moment I routinely teased John at every opportunity, to the point that he was nervous about even talking to me. For example, I used to grow vegetables in the garden and one day I had an excess of turnips. One of the engineers at the company really loved turnips and I brought some to work for him. During lunchtime, I had a call from General Electric, our largest customer, who wanted information that had to come from John Hayward. "Ha ha", I thought, "I'll get a rise out of him". I walked to his office with this huge turnip in my hand, held by the tip of the leaves. The root was dragging on the floor.

I stood in John's doorway with the turnip in one hand and asked him the GE question with a very straight face. He looked at me and at the turnip several times with a slightly surprised but cautious look on his face. I awaited a question from him as to, "What the hell I was doing with a turnip in my hand?", but it didn't come. I was prepared to answer saying something like, "Everybody should carry a spare turnip as you never know when you will need one".

He gave me the answer for GE, looked me up and down a couple more times and went back to what he was doing. I believe he realized I was just waiting for him to say something and he was not going to give me a chance to "zing" him anymore. John and I continued to have mild differences and there was always a little unspoken tension between us, and he seemed generally cautious in his dealings with me. He stayed away, which was good as he had previously tended to bully my boss James.

The company was running along nicely, and we had a huge order come in for electronics for a Massachusetts bus Co. It involved development of a new product. Within 10 days we received an order for the same item from Sacramento Bus Co. and charged development money again for the same product. The two orders equaled the whole of the previous year's total incoming orders. Unfortunately, this gave the president of the company a feeling of invincibility and this was the start of some very serious problems. However, in the interim, the company accumulated quite a healthy bank balance.

Shortly, on the strength of the newfound wealth, we heard that we were acquiring another company in San Diego, with 400 employees, and they were all being moved to our facility. This was the president's way of putting the large profit earned, to good use. But this was not to be. Another plant was leased on the other side of the parking lot, and the move started to take place.

The main product of the acquired company was linear amplifiers for CB radio. James Fisher was adamantly against this acquisition as he was aware of a move by the Federal Communications Commission to outlaw linear amplifiers.

James Fisher was a founder of the company and a large shareholder, and also a member of the board, and could not be fired. Because of his opposition, the president took away all of James' responsibilities and people. I now worked for the president, and he looked at my resume and discovered that I had experience in production and material control. I was now given the additional job of straightening out production control on the linear amplifier line and then doing the same for material control.

At the same time, the president of the company being acquired had this pet product which he'd been unable to produce, and this also caught the imagination of our company president, and so we started this project also. The concept was good but the costs were out of line. It was a special alarm, meant for the consumer market, an area in which our company had no knowledge or experience.

Now we added some space next door for the additional alarm product line, and all the necessary packaging and promotional material was designed and purchased in massive amounts. Parts contracts were entered into for the next umpteen years. It was at the time of the influx of thousands of Vietnamese people into the US, and about 200 were hired. Production went into top gear, and then there were almost 100,000 alarms stacking up. TV advertising was running in selected areas. Suddenly came the realization that the money was nearly gone, and the advertising was not being paid for. The ads. were pulled, and the merchandise sent to some of the drugstore chains was being returned unsold.

It now became obvious that the acquisition, and the failure of the alarm product, had put the company in serious financial condition. The production control was a disaster. I took a complete inventory of sub-assemblies being made for the amplifier line and found we were making thousands of them. Unfortunately, most of them could not be used as other sub-assemblies necessary for a complete shippable item, were not in production, and the material could not be bought due to lack of money. For instance, for a product needing 6 sub-assemblies maybe only 2 or 3 of the 6 were being made. This meant that money was being spent on manufacturing items that could not be shipped. Half of the work-in-process had to be left on the shelf, and new work orders were created for the sub-assemblies needed to make complete items. When I told the president this he went ballistic as he was desperate to get complete products out of the door before the FCC closed the door.

Finally, a telegram arrived from the FCC giving us 30 days' notice to stop the manufacture of all linear amplifiers. Production went into high gear for 29 days.

Within a week or two the board of directors threw the president out and made James the president. John Hayward came down with cancer of the lymph system and was gone. It was at this point that I was appointed General Manager, the day after that the company declared Bankruptcy.

This was one time in my life that I would not like to go through again. The bank had a representative (meet the mailman) every day to collect all checks coming in against their secured loans. We had no money or assets, except what we could ship after bankruptcy. We were able to get money wired to us by GE for products shipped to them after the bankruptcy. The money arrived at our new bank in the middle of the afternoon of the day that the first post-bankruptcy payroll was due. (GE needed us as much as we needed them). Many of the key employees had bailed out, and we owed money to all the suppliers and they were angry. I was chased around the boardroom table by the irate and tearful wife of a small company owner that we couldn't pay (under the laws of bankruptcy).

I sent letters out to all suppliers promising them that we would do business only with them, based on past pricing if they would continue to work with us. Strangely, they all agreed, and for the next 20 years I continued this, at two companies at which I worked.

Within 3 months, we were doing better. It was December and James suggested that we come up with an incentive for the workers for a Christmas bonus. I made a pact with the production employees to the effect that for every $1000 in product shipped above the previous months shipments, the company would contribute $20 to a fund to be distributed to them based on the number of hours each employee worked.

We were down to about 15 production workers now, and for Christmas 1978, they received an average of $150 each from the incentive agreement. They were very happy bearing in mind that a couple of months earlier they thought they would lose their jobs. This record month did wonders for the company's cash position and for the employee morale. Within 14 months we were discharged from bankruptcy and had paid off a fortune to lawyers and secured loans from the bank.

At this point, a company which had been loosely allied with us sent a notification to all our shareholders saying they would pay them 10 cents per share immediately, and 25 cents per share in one year if they signed over their voting rights. The shares had been selling at about $1.75 before the bankruptcy. To our surprise, they got a majority, and I got a visit from the president of the other company along with his attorney and they told me they had control of a majority of shares, and I should hand over the keys to the plant as they were taking over.

I invited them to use the door saying, "Get me a court order". They went to court, and through a technicality they got control.

All personnel were kept on, and the new president spent mornings at the other company and afternoons with us. He left me alone and seemed to be very cautious in dealing with me. He was very impressed with the progress we had made and did not want to rock the boat.

It was about 2 years later that the company president advised me that he wanted to combine the two companies under one roof, and I could no longer be the manager of the company as the two companies would be combined. My salary would be the same and I would concentrate on sales, which I had always done even when I was the general manager. The move took place.

I could not believe what I saw in the production area at the new place. Every production worker had his own little area with partitions and shelves around them. They had potted plants and photographs, and it was deadly quiet, with very little activity. I have never seen a production area like it. Their production costs were way out of line. They were lucky they were in a niche industry with hardly any competition.

This was the place in which our products were to be made. It lasted about 1 year before GE advised me that they could not continue with us as they were not getting the service from us anymore, and that they would be making their own equivalent products in the future.

Secure Connections had not designed a new product for a couple of years as is necessary to compete in their industry, and was reduced to about 1/3 of its previous size. All the work to keep the company alive was wasted, and I could see the way things were going. I got out and retired, so

I thought. A footnote, the other parent company eventually failed due to their high costs, and they continued with the Secure Connections products only, but the costs were higher under their management, and after a few years, it faded to nothing and disappeared in spite of an influx of money from outside investors.

I had been retired about 7 months at the age of 53 when I received a call from the original president of Secure Connections who had been fired. He was an electronic engineer and had designed 5 good electronic products. He proposed that we get a company going. I was a bit leery and looked into the products quite thoroughly. They passed the test. There were some companies interested in buying the products. I proposed that I work 4 hours per day for 1 month, to see how we progressed. It went well, and I started full-time on the understanding that we would eventually build a low cost mobile data terminal. I would not get paid in cash at first, but receive shares at later date, based on a fixed pre-arranged price each. The objective was to build the company to the point we could sell it and re-retire.

Starting a company from scratch is a complicated undertaking. Component, sub-assembly, and top assembly part numbering system, drawings, parts lists, and specifications are the first things needed before any manufacturing can take place. Then, sources for purchasing needed to be established, and then sales literature and product photographs. I left the accounting and engineering to the president who made up the production and test procedures. This was just the beginning before getting into internal forms and procedures, and terms and conditions of sale etc., and personnel management. It goes on and on. Every month there is a need for more and more forms and procedures. The president and I each made our own "wish list" of features and specifications for the new mobile data terminal, and then put them together. It looked like a great product at a very attractive price. (We realized later that Secure Connections Corp. was now offering a similar product that didn't do half of what our terminal did, but cost twice as much. We sold thousands of terminals, and Secure Connections Corp. eventually went out of business.)

We added people and grew and became profitable. I eventually got on the payroll. We hired my son Nick to do the purchasing and run production, and the mobile data terminal became an excellent product. It was far cheaper than any of the other competitors and had many times the capability.

We found a niche for it in the Ready-Mix concrete market, and sales took off. We sold a few terminals to other markets such as Taxi, Garbage trucks, small police forces, Ambulances, etc. etc. This product became our main source of revenue, and our efforts in the other products ceased.

After a couple of years, we were approached by a group representing some small-time investors, and an agreement was reached to sell the company. I re-retired while the negotiations were in progress due to the fact that success was again affecting the judgment of the president, and I quit, much to his anger. The next day he fired Nick out of spite, and within 3 days Nick was re-employed by another company. Over the next 3 months, the president hired 8 people to replace the work done by Nick and myself. The group acquiring the company finally saw the danger, and approached me to return to the company with the intent of firing the president, and again I went back to work now as the complete boss.

I couldn't believe what I found. In the 7 months I'd been gone, the payroll had exactly tripled from the day I left. The inventory had increased 6 times, and we owed more than was owed us. It took me 4 months to slim the company down to a point we could manage the payroll. I hired Nick back, and he was able to return some of the inventory to the suppliers and cancel some of the long-term contracts for enormous quantities of components that we could never use. It was an incredible situation.

However, the most incredible factor was that in my absence the ex-president had hired John Howard, now recovered from cancer, to do nothing but write procedures for the company. He had reams of procedures written, all designed for bigger companies with many products, and people to do nothing but keep track of the movement of products and inventory.

Small companies have different problems than larger companies, and if you try to run a small company like a big company then you have twice the problems. This is what the pair of them were doing, creating unnecessary work and problems, and it was costing a lot. I got John Howard out of there, toute suite and simplified everything back to where it was.

It is interesting to note that over the next 11 years I never used any of the procedures written by John Howard. Another interesting note, the fact that some of the procedures he wrote were copied word for word from procedures I'd written years ago which I used at Secure Connections. He must have got hold of them and kept copies.

Chapter 24 - Wisdoms

I stayed at that company for 11 years, retiring for the last time, in October 1999. Now that I've finished my work history, we must go back many years to 1976 for the rest of the story, when we first moved into 4400 Highland Drive, Carlsbad. But first I want to relate some other thoughts as follows.

After I got my own laptop computer, some time in about 1996, in a bit of spare time at work, I was able to pick up some of the mysteries of computers. It was especially convenient as I had several software engineers and other computer experts working for me and I was able to pick their brains as needed.

I have always tried to make sense of the things which happen day to day, and I've endeavored to take note if there is anything to be learned, at which point I've filed these lessons away in my head for later use. This was my chance to put these lessons into print for our children and grandchildren etc. I believe that if we don't learn from experiences, we make little progress, which can lead to the need for going through the same things, possibly painful, many times. I don't profess to live exactly by the following, but they have helped me at times. Some parts may have been mentioned earlier in this narrative.

With the tools and the time, I decided to write down what I called, "my wisdoms".

The first one I learned when I was about the age of 11 or 12 years old. It came about from doing, or not doing homework at the proper time. I call it "Eat your cabbage first". Here it is followed by the rest of the "wisdoms":

Eat The Cabbage First

How many times, when you were young, did you have a good meal put before you, and you were very hungry, and there was cabbage!!! You hated cabbage, and the whole meal was ruined for you because your mind was full of you having to eventually eat cabbage!!! Solution, eat it first, then enjoy the rest of the meal. When I had lots of homework, I had a choice of doing my homework first or going out to play and doing it last or not at all. If I went off to play first, the black cloud of homework hung over me. Doing homework first gave me such a joy of freedom and play was more enjoyable. However, the actual fact was that I often went out to play and stayed out late and was faced with trying to do a third-rate effort early the next morning before school prayers or in other classes. Some other examples come to mind. The lesson is, Do first whatever you have to do. Think about the:

* People who habitually pay bills late and have to pay interest or worse.

* People who don't bother to lock their cars, and have to walk because their cars are stolen or damaged.

* Leave their income tax returns until the last day etc.

Design Problems Out – Have a Plan

I always try to think of what can go wrong, and have a plan. Too many people suddenly have obvious problems blow up in their faces and all they have is surprise. Also, so many everyday common occurrences are a surprise and we put up with them year after year. A cold damp winter always seemed a surprise in England. The houses were apparently built for continuous summer when it is normally cold and miserable for more than half the year. Open fires, the norm when I was young, roasted you at the front (if you could get near it) and you froze at the back. All the warmed air was being sucked up the chimney along with the draft coming into the room from every window and door.

A frightening story on this subject happened and a plan saved the day. We had just arrived in the USA, and we had bought a really old station wagon. We had 11 people in the car and had to travel down Malibu Canyon. We approached the very steepest bendy part, which happened to have a sheer drop on the "up" side of the road. There was a cliff wall on our side. At the top of this dangerous part, I said to myself, "Drive into the cliff at the first sign that the brakes are not holding". I felt it was better to do this than to lose control and go off the outer edge. We were halfway down, with the brakes full on, and suddenly, the car was gaining speed. Immediately, I turned into the cliff, and ploughed into a pile of soft earth. We all got jolted, but there was not a scratch on us or on the car. Without a plan, we could have had a serious accident.

Design Problems Out – Again

Are you doing all the things a prudent person would do to keep life's problems down to the ones which you cannot avoid? Are you covered by insurance? Do you drive defensively so that you stand a better chance in accidents both for injury and being responsible for the damage? Do you lock your doors, car, and house? Do you know how to turn off your gas, electricity, and water? Are you careful with household chemicals, and always read the handling instructions? Do you always think ahead for the safety of family members, especially children? Do you pay your bills on time, and respect all laws? Do you drink and eat too much? Do you go without sleep? The list goes on and on.

Opinions Are Deceiving

Knowledge is power. Having some idea of why people behave the way they do can be of great assistance. Also, it can help you know yourself. Your own attitudes and opinions can be the result of assuming opinions expressed by parents or teachers etc. or based on many other influences. Human opinions, in my opinion, are rarely based wholly on facts and figures. I find, that, to a great extent, opinions come first, then, later, when needed, come the facts to support those opinions. Often, when you challenge somebody's opinion with facts, you find yourself faced with no facts, just opinions. Sounds like a parent telling a child to do something, "Because I say so". The only problem with not having facts supporting opinions is that you could be wrong. However, as long as you are open to changing your mind when faced with a preponderance of facts, then everything is OK. There is nothing more pathetic than somebody who is adamant about something in the face of facts supporting an opposite view. I remember a good example of having a point of view for an invalid reason.

When I was 18, somebody with whom I worked, was retiring and we collected to give him a small gift. He chose to have an electric razor. I didn't have an electric razor, and spent days producing reasons why an electric razor was a poor choice. I couldn't change his mind. Two years later, I was leaving and was asked what I would like. I chose an electric razor. My opinion deceived me. Beware of your reasons for your opinions.

Solve The Problem Not The Symptoms

In working for almost 45 years in many companies in England and America, I have observed very similar human traits. For example, every staff meeting I ever was required to attend had the same tendencies. Hours were spent on things other than the real problems or the real subject up for discussion. The basic problem is that people tend to put their efforts into the most obvious things, which are often the symptoms and not the real problem.

There is a common phenomenon at staff meetings. Within a very short time, the discussion wanders off the subject and turns to loosely connected or irrelevant items, usually between two or three people while the rest sit and observe. What is wrong with this? Could it be that the person in charge has not got a clear idea of the real subject at hand? Maybe this is an exaggeration, but it happens very often. I made sure that my own staff meetings stuck to the point. Also, I've left many a meeting where I was not in charge, in which we decided what needed doing with no arrangement for somebody to take the necessary action, and no timetable.

The most commonly used phrases at my meetings were "That's irrelevant" and "That is something you can solve between the two of you outside of this meeting". My meetings usually lasted 10 minutes or less, with a job list with names and deadlines.

Start With The Simple

I wish I had a dollar for every time that there was a problem that I observed where the simple solution fixed it when a complicated one didn't. Several times I have witnessed situations, for example, where some electronic device didn't work in spite of everything that was tried until somebody asked, "Is it switched on?"

This particular thing happened to me. I believe it was my son Nick who at the age of about 6, arrived home with the components of a large stereo, which he found in somebody's garbage. (We lived in Santa Monica at the time and our children knew the alleys like their hands). The equipment he found needed at least 3 trips as he was so small, and finally he had a turntable, a heavy amplifier, and the part with the controls. We were very poor in those days and I remember 6-year-old Nick saying, "Can you use this, can you make it work Dad?" I told him that I'd have to see if I could connect it up and make it work. I proceeded to plug it together on the patio table just outside of the kitchen window and ran an electrical extension and turned it on. Nothing. Nick and I were very disappointed. I turned the volume up to the maximum, but still nothing.

Muriel was in the kitchen watching out of the window, and I told her it was no good. She commented that it might sound better if we had it connected to a speaker. I found a speaker and used toothpicks to jam the wires into the speaker connector. Suddenly, the heavens opened with a deafening sound. Remember, I had everything turned up to maximum.

Cut Your Nose, Spite Your Face. Regret At Leisure

How many times have we acted in haste or out of bravado or anger and done things which felt good for a fleeting moment, but for which we've paid a high price later? As I related earlier, when I was about 5-years-old, I was given a Bakelite mug. It was pink with yellow ducks all around it. Bakelite was the first plastic that I remember seeing, but it was apparently more brittle than I realized. Compared to glass or china/earthenware, it was very durable. I clearly remember that I was in the room where we kept the pump organ, where the French windows had been blown out by a nearby bomb. I was talking to my Auntie Winnie and she was admiring my mug, and I accidentally dropped it. Auntie Winnie said, "Be careful or you'll break it". My answer was, "No, it won't break, look", and I slammed it against the floor with all my might, where it shattered into a hundred pieces. It was a large price for me to pay for a second's triumph. I loved that mug, and have never forgotten that lesson. The moral of this story is to try to keep future payments to a minimum by practicing self-control.

The Grass Is Always Greener

Let us take job changes as an example. The old job and the people and the boss seem to all be pains in the neck. You get dumped with all the extra jobs while Smart Aleck know-all stands around talking and impressing the boss. You wish there was another company where everything would be wonderful and you'd be happy as a lark. A new opportunity comes along and you grab it and now everything is going to be great. All the people you meet are wonderful, (or maybe just on their best behavior). You settle in and . . . . gradually you realize that the job, the people, and the boss are all the same as the old job. For some years this confused me until I realized that they are all people, and therefore they all behave the same way. If I wanted changes, then they would have to be with me. I got smart and adopted the best of the tactics and attitudes, and my life became much easier with less stress

Don't Solve Problems You Don't Have

Have you ever met people who spend time worrying in terms of, "What if XYZ goes wrong"? They are spending time and energy on the wrong thing. They should stop moaning and concentrate on action which mitigates damage if XYZ does go wrong. If you are or can become the type of person who looks ahead, designs problems out of your life, and takes care of your responsibility, you have done all you can. The chances are that XYZ will not happen anyway. Apply your energy to things where something useful can be accomplished.

"Killing the Messenger" Is Alive And Well

We all have been amused at the misfortune of the poor messenger who was executed for bringing bad news to the king. I guess that the illogical behavior of the king adds to our amusement. However, it wasn't a bit funny to the messenger. I bet he didn't die laughing. . . . . . . Guess what, in spite of us thinking the king was crazy, we still do this today in this age of enlightenment.

We have this strange romantic idea that it's only a really good friend that will tell you what everybody else knows, and what you should know, but everybody is reluctant to tell you. However, in my experience, these really good friends are treated almost the same as the messenger of old. If the execution was legal, that would fill the bill. If no real harm is done keep quiet, but if a third person is at risk of harm, something should be said but only by a close relative.

Expect resentment. Why this resentment? Why do human beings do the crazy things they do?

Here's an example. It came to the notice of somebody I know that the teenage son of his friend was routinely, daily, stealing from his employer, and taking the merchandise to school and selling it. In order to save this young man from the risk of capture, the friend called the father and told him what was going on. The father did nothing to stop the stealing and refused to speak to his informant for eighteen months.

Who Likes Who

Why does one person like or dislike another? I don't believe it is such a mystery. Basically, there are two reasons for dislike. One is the fact that some people are just plain mean and obnoxious, including the unwashed, the lazy, the overly officious, and those who are difficult for the sake of being difficult. The other reason is far more complicated and includes jealousy, resentment, or fear. Very often, these attitudes spring from the same source, and are from a feeling of inferiority. This is probably due, maybe, to the fact that the other person is a strong outgoing person who can cope with the world, and you feel they may inadvertently make you look inferior or give you the reason for embarrassment. The problem is not theirs, but yours. Relax, accept people for what they are, and don't blame them if you feel they are better than you. Here's a suggestion, think of a person that you dislike and try to honestly nail down your reasons. You may get some surprises. The next wisdom is connected.

Everybody Loves Me – Maybe

Did you ever like somebody who dislikes you? No, you don't, and you're not likely to for a very good reason. You like people who are nice to you, and they are nice to you because they like you. Conversely, dislike for a person shows in your dealings with them, and so they treat you the same, with mutual dislike. Mathematically, this means that if you want to get along, you have to appear to like people. Obviously, complete honesty is more important than being popular, but then you will not be liked by everybody. Complete honesty can lose some points for you. Real friends appreciate you for the good and the bad.

You Like Doing The Things At Which You Excel

You will never find a person who hates to do something at which they excel. Conversely, people hate to do things which they find hard to do. So, what is the moral of this? What can you do with this gem of wisdom? Not much except it helps you understand yourself and others. Or maybe it will help you get things done. Convince those around you that they are the best at the task, and you are more likely to get them to do it for you.

Who Creates Our Monsters?

To a large extent, we are responsible for some of those people around us who are rude and inconsiderate. This can also apply to normally good people who unwittingly cause us annoyance. (This does not include the mean, nasty people, for whom there is no hope).

If we, in our day-to-day relationships, take minor abuses without protest, we do two things. One, we can gradually build resentment, and two, we are guilty of encouraging the perpetrator to escalate the abusive behavior by implying that you are too weak to stand up for yourself in the pecking order.

I knew a lady who would never complain when minor abuses occurred until they built up to a major problem. Then, she would explode, causing a major confrontation and alienating everybody around her. The correct way would be to politely draw attention to the abuse immediately when it occurs, and you stand a good chance of keeping a friend and discouraging the development of a monster around you.

The last word on this is that I disagree with the parable about turning the other cheek if somebody slaps you. This only encourages cheek slippers. A swift punch in the nose is the appropriate response in my opinion. That would tend to discourage cheek slappers and reduces a problem for everybody around them.

Should We Argue?

Should we stand up for our point of view when some would say "let it go"? This is somewhat related to the above subject. "Letting it go" on a regular basis (if you are right) does little more than encouraging the other person to risk getting further and further from reality or the truth, plus you are now on the way to creating a know-all or even a monster. If you sincerely believe you have the facts, repeat, the facts, then have at it, but keep it nice. If your opponent has a preponderance of facts, then "fess up" immediately. You don't lose by this; you earn points. You lose "face" and arguments only by trying to stick to your guns in spite of overwhelming and indisputable facts to the contrary.

Is There A Lesson Here?

I mentioned this one before. Tony Tandy was 9-years-old and small for his age. He was the class wimp and mostly ignored. He was pushed around by everybody. During one summer vacation, a new family moved in next door to Tony's house. They had a son named Michael Collins, at about the same age as Tony, and naturally, they got to be acquainted. Apparently, they got into a fight, and Tony won.

We were back to school, and Michael Collins joined the same class as Tony and I. Michael Collins turned out to be a loud mouth bully type of "rough" kid who was prone to using bad language and threatening behavior. In no time he had all the smaller and average size boys intimidated, except one, Tony. So, we had a strange situation where Michael Collins was scared of Tony but nobody else was, and almost everybody else was scared of Michael.

My conclusion is that bluster and bullying can unreasonably take in a large part of the population, and intimidate them. See the following subject which is connected.

Power For The Taking

Have you heard the old saying "power is to those who take it". In my opinion, this is a very important lesson to learn, not necessarily for personal use but to understand what makes people tick, and why we respond to others the way we do. Have you ever noticed that when somebody yells, "OK let's go", for example, everybody gets up and follows? I have wondered about this and come to the conclusion that in the absence of orders or decisions expressed in an authoritative manner, leadership is up for grabs to the first person who takes control. I also believe that there are an awful lot of sheep in the population, just waiting to be told what to do.

When I was growing up in England anybody with any appearance of authority was able to issue orders and people complied without question. During a visit to England, I was passing through one of the buildings in the Tower of London and came out of a door at the top of some steps which led down to the main courtyard. It made an excellent picture. I got out of the camera and took aim. A loud-voiced Beefeater yelled in my ear saying, "You can't do that here". I said in an equally loud, "Who says I can't", and took the picture. He didn't say a word. I don't think he had ever been defied before. We both took power in that instance, and I came across stronger than the Beefeater.

Cocky Eats Humble Pie

There is nothing as pathetic as a cocky, bossy person who has to eat humble pie. This puts him 10 paces behind a humble person who normally expresses himself in a cautious manner. The cocky, bossy person has great trouble accepting another's point of view, being absolutely certain of his position to the point of being unable to accept any alternative. He always makes pronouncements. The humble person speaks in terms of "I believe it is so", instead of, "I am right without question". Solution, always adopt an attitude of "I believe I'm right" and you will face less frustration and stress, and it is easier to back off when proved wrong.

Money Cannot Buy Discipline

I have been reading with horror over the last 25 years, the amounts of money poured into schools and still, the standards are nearly the lowest in the world. We appear to be suffering from an illness started by Dr. Spock, and in spite of him admitting he was wrong, we perpetuate the situation. We have confused being good parents with giving our children everything they want and allowing them virtually complete freedom to do almost anything. The problem with the school system is not lack of money but lack of discipline. Going to school, paying attention, doing what you are told, having respect, doing homework, and doing chores on time are all work type items, not play, and therefore they do not come naturally to young people. They naturally play, but they do not take naturally to work, and this is where discipline comes in. To train children to be the way they should be is plain hard work, and more than most parents of today are prepared to or even capable of doing. Unfortunately, today's parents were brought up in, what I call the Spock manner and haven't had the exposure and benefit of real discipline. Added to that they have taken away the ultimate weapon or threat that schools had, i.e. pain, and as a result, schools are a war zone run largely by thugs. Isn't it a shame that otherwise lovely children are allowed to run wild, become obnoxious, and are disliked for the shortcomings in parental control? The children eventually get blamed.

The final result is that it holds the good children back, and costs a fortune with poor return on our taxes.

When I was a child I was in classes as large as 45 or 50 children, and we learned. We didn't dare do otherwise. We respected people and property. There have been cases where parents of children who misbehaved in public being prosecuted for spanking their children. They should be given medals for doing their bit to make good adults. I'm afraid that America has gone mad in this regard, and the country will suffer eventually.

Are You Getting Enough Sleep To Work Smart?

A famous baseball manager made a wise statement saying that fatigue makes cowards of us all. My interpretation of this says that if we are tired, (not getting enough sleep), we do everything with a lack of enthusiasm. We become less creative and go through the motions, doing the minimum. We weaken our ability to work smart and probably have to work harder to make up. I'm sure that everybody has experienced a day when you just don't feel like starting a project and put it off, and the other days when you can't wait to dive in. The difference could be the lack of energy, which could come from lack of sleep.

Make a list

Have you ever felt overwhelmed by all the things you have piling up for you to do? Try making a list and I guarantee that it isn't as big a list as you expect, and also, you will finish sooner.

You Can't Tickle Yourself

Oh yes you can, but it is a complete waste of time. There is no response, so how is it that somebody else can do the exact same thing to you and get a response? Doesn't make sense, does it? Here's something to try. Get somebody to tickle you when you are expecting it, and make yourself NOT respond. You can do it. The tickler will give up immediately. It will be the same to them as tickling yourself, with a complete lack of response.

Poor Little Rich Kid

Seems a contradiction, right? Maybe not. As you read earlier, when I was young, in the Second World War, I lived a few miles southeast of London, right under the pathway to central London for the German bombers. We lived for months in our own hole in the ground, an Anderson air raid shelter. I have 5 sisters and parents and the shelter was jammed. There was no electricity, no heat, and sometimes the water supply and the gas mains were damaged. On top of this, there were no cars (no gas), and very little food. This teaches you to be careful with resources, and you learn to appreciate special treats. You also have lower-than-average expectations and you enjoy simple things more than others who didn't have the benefit of your background.

I have always loved canned apricots, and during the dark days of WWII, there were few canned apricots to be had. Occasionally, you could get a can, but you gave up a lot of your staple food allotment (food points) to get them. I even dreamed about canned apricots, and bananas, which were not seen in the stores for the whole 6 years of war. If my mother splurged and bought a can of apricots, I cut my share into tiny pieces and ate them slowly, one little piece at a time. Too soon they were gone, but I made my share last for the maximum time. Even today, a .75-cent can of apricots can make my day, and I have been known to eat a whole can by myself. I am very lucky. I can be happy for .75 cents when today, people need a new car or a boat or some such expensive item to be as happy. What is this to do with rich kids? Well, nobody can get a new car or a new boat every day, and if they did, it would soon grow boring, so they are driven to look for new thrills and experiment with drink, drugs, and other dangerous and reckless things. They kill or maim themselves and sometimes, innocent people, and end up in therapy and clinics. They are generally less fortunate than normal people. See how lucky you are if you are poor.

Increase Your Efficiency, Take A Vacation

My desk was never tidy as a rule. I seemed to have so many things going on at one time. However, when I knew I would be going on vacation, I seemed to be able to finalize nearly everything and have a nearly clean desk. Somehow, knowing I'd be gone I was able to become more efficient and put most things to bed.

At other times, if I seemed to be getting too much piling up, I would play a trick on myself, and pretend I was going on vacation. It was amazing. The work got cleared up in no time.

Better Late Than Never?

Why do we instinctively brake to avoid hitting a pedestrian when driving? It is to save killing somebody because we instinctively know that is bad. Not because of laws, but because it is instinctive, and already programmed into us.

When somebody dies, their time on earth is used up, and we are sad. This all brings up the question. If we regard our time and the time of others on this earth as so important, how come we take it so lightly when we arrive late for appointments, and social dates, and various arrangements to which we've agreed to meet? If we use logic, a person who takes all of the rest of somebody's life is called a murderer, and he can forfeit his life. If somebody wastes an hour of somebody else's life, is he a partial murderer? Should he be punished?

What Value For Doing It Right

An ex-domestic employee of an acquaintance, asked to be taken back to work for just two days a week. She begged to not have deductions taken from her pay. This was reluctantly agreed to. She lasted three weeks and phoned to say she could not continue, and promptly filed for unemployment. This could have been nasty for our acquaintance. Another situation arose when an employee in a live-in position at a facility requiring finger-printing, wanted her boyfriend to also live in, with the statement that "he wouldn't hardly ever be there". Corners were cut and he was not fingerprinted. Later, there was a dispute with this employee, and the employee used the fingerprinting situation in filing a complaint against the employer.

A professional employee of mine was crawling under his desk to retrieve something when he banged the back of his head. Three days later he was suffering considerable pain and reported it to me. I pressured him to go to our Workers Comp. Doctor, but he refused. A report was written up to the effect that he'd refused treatment. Days later, he was in lots of pain, and he went to the emergency room. Later he was being hounded for payment by the hospital, and came to the company for help. If the maximum pressure had been applied for him to go to the Workers Comp. Doctor in the first place, a problem would have been avoided. The moral is that following the rules exactly is necessary for designing problems out of your life, the subject of earlier writing.

Chapter 25 - The Carlsbad house.

Some of the things we did when we first moved into the house in Carlsbad, were to plant some fruit trees and try to get some decent grass growing in the back garden. Half of it was bare dirt, with a few sparse blades. It was largely sub-soil where the lot had been bull-dozed flat.

At the other end of the garden a few patches of native grass were spreading from the canyon, so I dug up dozens of patches and transplanted them all over the bare area, and now we have all the grass we need.

Our lot is about .85 of an acre. The back garden is about 40 feet deep, and flat, from the house to the edge of the canyon which slopes down to the valley at about 35 degrees. It is possible, but not easy, to walk up and down the slope if desired.

65% of the lot is at the front which slopes gently to the road. The road is about 70 yards away from the house.

We bought a roto-tiller and planted an area at the front with vegetables. The stuff grew really fast and we had too much produce for us, but the gophers helped a bit by eating some of it. We poured a lot of water on the ground otherwise the leaves would wilt. We caught many gophers. I would stand still for a moment and watch, and many times I would see foliage moving, and I would attack with my spade, and sometimes get them. Also, if I put a hosepipe in the hole, sometimes they would come up spluttering and were banged on the head with anything handy.

My son David took it upon himself to set traps, and he would catch perhaps 6 per week, and the dog would catch them occasionally. Also, we always had a cat or two around and they would catch them, but they still kept coming.

Occasionally, I would skid on something in the grass and find it was a rotted gopher body or part of a body. We had one cat that would leave half eaten gophers on the mat by the back door. There were always stray cats around our area, and Muriel would feed them as they helped keep the mice and squirrels down.

I remember one cat which was a domestic cat gone wild. It showed up one day for food, with 3 tiny kittens in tow. It was happy to eat the food but would spit and squeal at you if you tried to go near. Anyway, over the period of a few weeks, I got to the point where I could get a hand within about 12 inches while it was eating, and it would spit at me then eat for a bit then spit again. This would go on for 5 minutes till the food was gone.

We watched the kittens grow up to ¾ size, but gradually, the mother disappeared followed by most of the kittens until one day I saw the last kitten streak across the grass into the hedge at the south side of the back garden. I was in the kitchen and went to the window to look out to see a large coyote walking across the backyard. I think these cats became meals for the coyotes.

We got some sad news. My sister Brenda's husband, Frank, had lung cancer.

In time he deteriorated somewhat, and she needed some assistance. I went to Florida three weekends running, leaving Los Angeles late on Friday evening, and arriving Orlando in the early morning. Then I went to bed for a few hours and was woken up by the gardener with his lawn mower early every Saturday morning.

On one of the visits I spent a whole afternoon talking with Frank in the hospital. Brenda said this was remarkable as he seemed to be beyond talking much to anybody. The truth is that I had never talked to Frank for more than a few words at any time previously. Sadly, somebody who I now see as a great and generous man, died and I only got to know him better for a very short time. There was one thing left that I could do for him and I was able to do that sometime later when I sang a solo at his funeral.

Nicholas had always wanted a dog, and we'd said, "No". We felt we had enough problems without adding a dog.

One day he told us about this wonderful Brittany Spaniel that was available. He promised faithfully that it would be no trouble, in fact, he said that they hardly ever barked, and were very friendly etc. etc. He said that he would look after it and it would stay outside and we'd hardly know it was here. He was right, it was a lovely dog and no trouble or noise. However, within 3 or 4 weeks Nick left home! Daughter Helen looked after the dog thereafter.

The dog had pups after we'd had it for about a year, and we had to take them to an adoption organization. I still regret that we did not keep one we named Rocky. He seemed to be a dog in a million with enormous personality and energy.

Eventually, the dog started roaming and one day we had a call from the Highway Patrol. The dog had been killed on the freeway. Helen was distraught. Nick returned home a month or so after this but didn't seem too concerned.

My son David was keeping company with a young lady named Susan. He was working part-time at a supermarket and going to college. This young lady had been married before and had two small sons.

David had been a volunteer at hospitals and clinics since he was about 13. He went to the local hospital near our house when we first came to the San Diego area. It was always our understanding that he wanted to eventually work in the medical field, and also he studied, at a local college, the subjects he needed to enter medical school. He was volunteering one evening a week at a free clinic in San Diego and was well thought of. He had been introduced to this by a doctor friend of ours from our church choir. David's job at the clinic was to interview each patient, getting all personal, and illness details. We heard later that he was nearly always right when determining the illness or complaint.

It is probably easy to understand that we were somewhat disappointed when we got to hear that he was talking about giving up school and working full-time at the supermarket with a view to getting married. He had also given up the free clinic, and we received a call from the director of the clinic, who told us that David had great potential, and should pursue a medical career. We used to pick our doctor friend up and drive him to and from choir practice, and he actually cried in our car about the situation.

We made our feelings known to both David and Susan to no avail. We offered to help them financially if he would continue his medical career but with no success. David went to work at the supermarket full-time. They soon arranged a quiet wedding in the San Francisco area, without us.

My other son Christopher was working part-time at another supermarket, and going to college. However, he was not too enthusiastic, and he gave up college after a couple of years.

I believe that the problem was that both Chris and Dave were earning what to them was a good wage, and they couldn't foresee a time when it would not be enough. Christopher became a full-time employee and is there to this day. Recently he received a gold watch for the 25th anniversary of his employment.

Shortly after David's marriage, Christopher announced that he was getting married to Mary. They had been going together for some time. The open-air wedding ceremony and reception were held in the gardens of Darlington House in La Jolla. The wedding was performed by the lady minister of Chris and Mary's church.

This church was run by what I would politely call a "progressive" minister. We understood at the time that she said that "if it felt good it must be OK". She arrived for the wedding about 1 hour late, and a goodly amount of wine had been consumed in the interim

Chris and Mary left this church eventually, and later we heard that the lady minister had absconded with the church's money, and an actor from a popular TV show, but we have no proof of this. At the time of writing, we've heard she is back and has started another church in San Diego. Christians must be some of the most gullible people.

Nick, my third son, was going with our church minister's eldest daughter, Laurie, and had introduced his brother Peter to her younger sister, Luanne.

The association didn't last long with Nick and Laurie, and Nick began seeing Karen, who worked at the same company as Nick. Within a short time, Nick and Karen decided to get married and had the ceremony at our church, with the reception at a club in La Jolla. Everything went well.

A year after David and Susan were married, their son, Daniel was born. To this day, they had a total of 3 sons, two from previous marriage. Scott was the eldest, and several years older than Shane, who was about 2 years old when the marriage took place.

Shane was an adorable little boy, and once I had him for the day. He had a slight speech impediment and was a bit hard to understand when he was about 2-years-old.

I remember a funny incident. We were standing at the edge of the canyon at the back of the house, holding hands, (I used to get back ache-holding his hand as he was so small), when he looked up at me and said, "Grandpa, are there *nakes* down there'? I must have been having a dense day as I had no idea what he was trying to say, and I told him so. He repeated his question several times, and I still couldn't get it. He stamped his foot and got really frustrated until he finally said, "Are there *rattlenakes* down there?"

It wasn't long before Peter and Luanne announced they were getting married. It took place at our church, officiated by Luanne's father. The reception was held at the church hall, and the whole congregation was invited.

Chris and Mary had been married about 2 years when they presented us with our second grandchild, Lauren.

A few months after this, they decided they didn't like the condo they'd bought so they moved in with us temporarily, and put the condo on the market.

I clearly remember that every evening I would sit and hold baby Lauren. She was a very happy and smiling baby and she seemed to enjoy our nightly cuddling sessions.

Peter and Luanne presented us with a third grandchild, Michael.

A few months later, on a Thursday morning, Muriel was talking to her friend Trish, when she was interrupted by an emergency call. It was daughter-in-law Susan, calling from the emergency room at the local hospital. Daniel, at about 2 years of age, had come down with encephalitis and was in convulsions. We rushed over there to see him. He was bouncing about on the bed. They couldn't stop the convulsions in spite of maximum doses of Pheno-barbital or Dilantin. Can't quite remember which. They called for an ambulance to take Daniel to Children's hospital in San Diego, and this huge vehicle arrived complete with a doctor and two nurses. It was like a mobile operating theater.

We followed them to Children's Hospital with the last words from the emergency room still ringing in our heads. "He may not survive the journey". He did, and by the next Sunday, he came out of the coma and stood up in the crib, and asked for "salty chips". Susan had stayed at the hospital all the time, and ran to get some potato chips from the cafeteria.

We called that evening to David's house, to find out how Daniel was doing, and we were shocked to hear that they had brought him home!

Daniel seemed to be doing OK.

David and Susan had been in the Sierras for 2 weeks, just before this happened. There were lots of mosquitoes about, and there were suggestions at the time that they could be carrying encephalitis. Apparently, this was the case.

It was the next Thursday and the phone rang. It was Trish again, enquiring about the emergency interruption of her call a week before. Muriel was telling her the story when a phone operator interrupted them again with an emergency call. It was Susan again. Daniel had just been brought back to the hospital in convulsions again. We went through a repeat of the week before, rushing to Children's Hospital, knowing Daniel might not survive the trip. In a few days, he was OK again, but on drugs at least for a long time.

Before all this happened, Daniel had been able to ride a two-wheel bicycle at two years of age, but he was put back considerably. His whole development seemed to go on hold for many months. However, today at 21 years of age, he is well over 6 feet tall and doing well.

It was 3 months later, and Peter, Luanne, and their son, Michael were living with us, between house moves, and it was a Saturday morning. Peter had gone out early and was sailing with a friend. Baby Michael was about 8 months old and had seemed unwell the night before.

At about 9 am that morning, Luanne told us that Michael seemed worse, and we went to see him. He was curled up in his crib, with his eyes closed and moaning gently. Muriel and I were both shocked, and we both felt the same thing, that he was very ill. Muriel and Luanne left immediately for the pediatricians' office, and she took one look at Michael and told them to go immediately to Children's Hospital. She diagnosed meningitis.

Here we went again within a 3-month period, a second grandson who was not expected to live. Michael did survive except he lost his hearing in one ear, and had a 10% loss in the other. Michael is very bright and has been able to compensate.

We hoped that this sort of thing would not continue, and luckily it didn't.

Brenda's husband Frank had been dead for some years, and now Brenda was getting married again to Dennis, an ex-policeman from the Chicago area, now living in Florida.

We were invited to the wedding and of course, we went.

The reception was held at a very classy and probably expensive hotel. I was able to meet the bridegroom's father for the first time, and he was blind drunk. The bridegroom called on me for assistance to seat his father who was a very small man.

The bridal party was seated on a 10" high platform across the front of the room. I can see it now. We placed Father on the left end of the platform. We had to virtually lift him onto the platform, and we jammed him in tightly against the table so that he couldn't move, so we thought. The 4-tier wedding cake was on a small card table about 3ft from Father's end of the platform.

Standing in a row next to the cake were 4 waitresses in their frilly aprons and caps. The rest of the wedding guests were seated at tables 4 or 6 per table. They all appeared to be well off.

Everybody was seated and the speeches were underway. Suddenly, Father was on his feet and standing on the edge of the platform facing away from the edge. He swayed and everybody held their breath, and ever so slowly he back-peddled with his arms, trying to keep his balance.

It seemed an eternity that he hung in the air, defying gravity. There was not a sound as he floated backward, with his flailing arms and shoulders hitting the cake, which flew in all directions landing around the feet of the waitresses. The embarrassed silence was deafening. My sister, the bride had her head in her hands, but nobody else moved for what seemed an eternity. I broke the silence with a loud, "Wow, that must have taken lots of rehearsal", which broke the spell and everybody laughed. Luckily, Father was not hurt, and the waitresses were able to put together the larger parts of the cake to make enough.

My daughter Helen announced that she was getting married to Kirk, a friend of my son Christopher's. Kirk was of Dutch heritage, and had worked with Chris for some time, but was now awaiting his posting to Sacramento, to the California Highway Patrol Academy. This was what he wanted to do, and he had been accepted. His father was a captain in the Highway Patrol.

Helen had made a reservation with our Church, Torrey Pines Christian Church, for the ceremony and the reception. Eddie, our neighbor to the north, was very artistic and had a talent for wedding receptions, so he was engaged for that.

It was about 3 months before the wedding date that Eddie called the church to find out about the reception hall and was told it was not available. Somebody had fouled up, and not made a record of the booking.

Helen called all around to find there was no place available and so we were forced to hold the reception in our back garden. I raced to build a stone wall at one end, and I built 3 large planters.

Kirk graduated and the wedding took place about one month later. We went to Sacramento for the graduation and met Kirk's parents.

We rented a large marquee for the wedding reception. It covered 1/3 of our backyard grass area, and Eddie rented 300 potted plants, and 20 potted trees. It all looked very nice and worked out very well, probably better than if it had been at the church. (The church would not allow alcohol).

By this time, Peter and Luanne had a daughter Keri, a sister for Michael. But here again, there was a problem.

It was New Year's Eve, and we took Peter, Luanne, Chris, Mary, and possibly David and Susan, (can't quite remember) to a local hotel for the celebration. I clearly remember Luanne was dancing up a storm at about 8 months pregnant.

In the early morning hours, at home, Luanne went into premature labor, and Keri was born at the local hospital. She was immediately transferred to the Children's Hospital in San Diego. Her heart was not completely formed.

She was there for 10 days and incurred $48,000 in hospital charges which were not covered by their insurance. A note of caution. Normally, group insurance covers the birth, but a child is not included on a parents' insurance for 30 days. Therefore, a newborn baby is not covered unless special insurance is purchased for the 30 days. Peter had to sell his house to pay for it. They moved back in with us for some months to allow them to get a new start.

Nick and Karen had a son Robin, and Chris and Mary had a sister for Lauren and named her Chelsea. Peter and Luanne had their third child, David.

Robin was born through a Cesarean operation.

There was just one other panic in the family. When Peter's son David was about 3-years-old, he had his tonsils out. A couple of days later, he was in bed one evening when they heard him making a gurgling noise. His operation had opened up and he was hemorrhaging.

When Helen and Kirk had been married about 15 months they had a son Andrew and 2 years later, a son, Matthew. Peter and Luanne's son David, was born 10 days before Andrew was born,

I was in the room just seconds after Andrew was born, and I think I was the first person on whom he focused.

At the point he was born, Muriel asked Helen if I could come into the room and she OK'd it, and I saw Andrew carried to the little "warmer" bed/container. I stood at the foot of it and noticed that he was almost touching the top and the bottom.

I believe he was 24" long and 9 ½ lbs., just a big baby.

I was the only one standing by him, and he finally got his eyes straight and focused on me. I moved from side to side and his eyes followed me. From that time on he did appear to attach himself to me.

I remember that when he was about 6 months old, Kirk's mother picked him up, and he cried and held his arms out to me to take him. She was very upset about this.

Chapter 26 - Hard Work Changing the House

We have made many changes to the house over the years, but those changes will be related in due course.

When we came to this house it was on one floor, with 85% of an acre lot, and about 70 yards from the road. It is on a hill, about 300 feet above sea level with a front view overlooking the ocean and a lagoon. The blacktop driveway is in the shape of a “9” with a 30 ft wide level area along most of the front of the house. The total area of the house was 3700 square feet, with 4 bedrooms and 3 bathrooms. We had a large living room and den and a dining room that seemed small in comparison to other rooms. We also had a 22ft square games room with a bar, and a breakfast room, plus a tractor garage which also doubled as a utility room. It was a big house by most standards.

At the front, the ocean is about 1/2 mile away, with the lagoon coming right up to the base of our hill to within 150 yards of our house. From the main living room through the 16-foot view window we can just see the waves on the beach.

At the back of the house is a flat area for about 40 feet out, where our boundary ends. Beyond that, is a sudden slope of about 35 degrees into a canyon with normal wild vegetation. At the bottom of the canyon is a road and houses. From the back garden, we can see more of the lagoon which continues from the front, around the south side of our hill and extends up the canyon behind us. In the distance, we can see 7 layers of hills culminating in mountains which are snow-covered in winter. This house is in a really beautiful spot with almost 360 degrees views. Our own trees, of which we have about 12, are the only impediments to a complete view.

We soon completed the move-in, helped by the fact that we had more room. We didn’t have any more moaning about having to leave friends etc. in San Diego. We continued to attend the same church, and singing in the choir although it was 26 miles away. The children liked their schools, and everything seemed good.

Although the dining room was adequate for us, it was a bit small if we had guests, so we decided to extend it.

It looked out onto a covered patio, and by moving the outside wall out, we could double the size of the room. This is what we did, and in a month we had our larger dining room. Muriel was thrilled to bits with it.

The next Christmas we noted that the living room, which was 17 feet by 23 feet, was crowded with all the children sprawled about. We had nearly the same situation as the dining room, with a partially covered patio outside. You guessed it, we moved the wall out within a month and extended the room to 24 feet by 23 feet. Muriel was thrilled to bits with it. Now I’m a bit worried. Muriel is beginning to feel that I do these jobs easily.

Although I haven't said much about Muriel's family coming to see us, we'd had visits from them nearly every year since 1968, and it was now in the late 70s. They came in two's and three's and usually stayed 3 to 4 weeks.

We arranged trips to all of the same famous tourist spots year after year with different relatives, to the point that we were unable to face the trips again. We wrote to every relative in about 1977, to the effect that we would do one last trip, and that they should all come at one time. We had a travel trailer and a motor home and could accommodate 12 people.

The following year we had 9 visitors and arranged a trip. With Muriel, Helen, and me, it made a maximum of 12. The boys were old enough to stay on their own and didn't want to go with us anyway.

We traveled up the California coast to Solvang, which is a replica of a Danish village. We camped the first night on a small cliff right by the beach. The next day we went on to San Francisco, and stayed overnight on the famous "Fisherman's Wharf", right in the middle of the town. Then southeast, on to Yosemite National Park, and passed through, climbing to 9,945 feet to Tioga Pass, and then back down 5000 feet to the east gate. This road is the last one anybody should go with a motorhome pulling a trailer, as it is extremely steep, with a sheer drop on one side of the road. Muriel's younger brother, Paul, drove our station wagon, which would hold all of us for side trips. This would save us dragging the trailer with the motorhome at about 6 miles per gallon of gasoline.

Now we turned south towards Bishop, a mountain town. However, we had a problem with the clutch of the station wagon. We needed a throw-out bearing replaced. I finally found somebody in Bishop who could do the job, and so we all got into the motorhome, dropped the trailer at the side of the road, and went south to a point where we could view Mount Whitney, the highest mountain in the continental US.

We were gone for about 2 ½ hours, and when we came back for the trailer, the road was being re-surfaced. They were within about 50 yards of the trailer.

We hooked up and covered a couple of miles north to Bishop, and the station wagon was fixed, and now we had to climb east over another mountain range.

The road we had to take (to avoid another 200 miles) was about 12 feet wide, almost vertical, and not suitable at all for motorhomes, especially one pulling a trailer. We were advised to not take this road. It was built in a "wash". Apparently, when it rains, water gushes down in a torrent. Luckily it was dry. My main concern was that the steepness would cause the trailer hitch to pull out or break, and the trailer would go backward down the hill.

The steepest bit was near the top when I had to put the motorhome into the lowest of the 5 gears. The top speed for this gear was about 5 mph, but it saved us that day.

Muriel's brother, Paul had overtaken us in the station wagon and had to wait for us at the top. Once we got past this hill, we had a pretty straight run into Las Vegas about 170 miles away. I should add that we were in temperatures around 95 deg. which would get much higher as we approached Las Vegas, which is usually around 110 degrees in the summer.

After a day or so in Las Vegas, we went to the Hoover (or Boulder) Dam, which is on the way to the Grand Canyon, about 250 miles east. After the dam, we drove partway, and stopped at a campsite about 150 miles from the Grand Canyon.

The next day, early, all of us piled into the station wagon and went east through Flagstaff then south to the Oak Creek Canyon, Sedona, Cottonwood, and Jerome, an old copper mining town clinging to the side of a mountain. Jerome is now a quaint tourist attraction, but everything is gradually creeping down the hill. Sidewalks and buildings are cracking and showing signs of movement.

From Jerome, we retraced our steps to Cottonwood then turned east and then north to the Indian cliff dwellings, and from there, back north to Flagstaff and then continuing north again about 70 miles, to the south rim of the Grand Canyon.

I clearly remember we stopped on the way out of the Grand Canyon Park in the dark. We bought hamburgers as we had not had dinner. We drove and ate at the same time, arriving back at the trailer at about 11.00 pm.

The next day we made for Lake Havasu, right in the middle of the desert, where we stayed for a couple of days. We were going generally in a south-westerly direction, pointed almost directly toward home, but 300 miles away. The temperature was in the 90's, but we enjoyed it. We drove back from Havasu in one day, completing a trip of 3,000 miles in two weeks.

This trip was very typical of the trips we did nearly every year, but we usually only had 2 or 3 visitors. The problem was that we always used up our vacation time and didn't see anything new.

Muriel's younger brother, Paul had decided, a few years before that he wanted to live in the USA and applied for an immigration visa. He was 18 years old.

Paul had not heard from the Immigration Department after a year or so, and he decided to pay us an extended visit.

While Paul was with us I suggested that he go to the San Diego Immigration office and apply. Within 2 months he had his visa, and I got him a job in the accounting office of Secure Connections Corp.

Muriel decided we should have a pond, so we made two ponds. One about 20 feet by 7 feet, and the other about 8 feet in diameter and about 20" higher with a water-fall between them. Paul helped me with the building.

We bought expensive fish to populate the ponds but they didn't last long and were replaced with goldfish and tiny native fish, a bit like guppies.

When Paul had been with us for about a year, hc announced on a Wednesday that he was returning to England on Friday!

It is interesting to note that about 18 years later, we received notification from the Immigration Department, that Paul's original application had been approved.

As you already know, my father had remarried and lived in Mission Viejo, about 50 miles north of Carlsbad, with his second wife Lilian. He loved coming to see us, which he did, about every three weeks.

During one of our times of excessive vegetables, I asked him if he would like some turnips, and he was very enthusiastic about getting some. I asked him how many he wanted, and he told me that about 5 would be enough.

What I didn't tell him was that they were huge and had reached this giant size in about 60 days, and weren't at all tough. I went down the garden with a brown supermarket bag and pulled the biggest 5 I could find.

I held the bag out to him saying, "Is this enough?" He took the bag from me and it hit the floor. They were so much heavier than he expected. He said, "I only wanted 5". I told him he only had 5. We weighed them and found their weight was 22lbs. It was one like this that I carried into John Hayward's office as related earlier.

Muriel wanted to make sure we planted plenty of beets. The first year, I planted what I thought would be enough, and we had so many that I was bringing them to the house in a wheelbarrow. We had large jars around the house with beets pickling in vinegar. It took us months to use them all up, but they were very good.

One day I was working in the front garden on my vegetable patch and there was a car parked across the road with 2 people who appeared to be admiring the view, except that the man was also watching me. I stared back. Suddenly, he got out of the car and crossed the road and walked up the drive toward me. My first thought was that he didn't like me staring back, and I walked over to him. He said, "My name is Art Craft". The name was somehow familiar, and then I remembered. That name was written all over the plans for the house. He told me that he had been a building contractor and had built the house for himself, but his business had moved north and he had sold the house. He explained that he grew vegetables like I did, and he was glad we liked the house and view etc. As he was leaving, he said, "By the way, you have 2-floor foundations, good for a second floor if you ever want to build up".

I thought that was an interesting but irrelevant piece of information, and nonchalantly related it to Muriel. Immediately I recognized my mistake, even before she said, "Let's build a second floor".

Here we were with children leaving home and in this large house and talking about doubling the size of it.

Of course, I took absolutely no serious notice of Muriel's talk about building a second floor. It was a huge project and could not be done by me anyway, so it was at least 3months before we started taking the roof off. I had decided to start in the middle of the house, get the new roof on that, and then move south to the next two sections. (We were not going to build on the northern section at this time). We started, the boys and I, on the 4th of June 1982. By 26th December 1982, we had the structure built and the roof on and the stucco finished. It was now watertight. For the next year, I worked on the inside walls and ceilings, putting up paneling and doors, putting in a fireplace, and all the other little details that take so much time.

We were in the middle of construction when Muriel's brother John, wife Mary, and their 4 children arrived from England. We had been working with them on their immigration for 12 years.

Things were a bit cramped with so many people in the house but we managed. Also, it was more hands to help with the construction and there was the hope that with the extra help, we could complete it and make good use of the extra room.

However, they got their own house before completion and moved out.

As usual, when my father came to visit, he would climb the ladder to inspect our progress on the new upstairs before going into the back garden to play soccer with the boys. He was 82 and still very active.

It was my birthday, 23rd May 1982, and he was playing soccer with the boys. After a while, he came back in saying how tired he felt. Within a week he had been to the doctor who phoned me to say he had liver cancer.

Within 3 weeks, he was in a coma and was expected to die within 3 weeks of that. Every evening, I would work on the house, building for a couple of hours when getting home from work. Then Muriel and I would drive to Mission Viejo to see him. I fed him apple juice with an-eye dropper as I'm sure they didn't bother much at the nursing home. I would sleep all the way home with Muriel driving.

It was way past the time they said he would die when we got a shock. As we entered his room, he was laying on his side facing the door looking at us. He gave us a weak smile, and I was able to communicate with him by him answering "yes" by blinking his eyes and "no" by moving his tongue. We had a long conversation that night. It was the last. He lapsed back into the coma and lasted until 25th September 1982. He lived twice as long as they expected. They said he was so strong that his heart and lungs would not give up.

The new building on the house was almost finished; it must have been autumn of the same year when Muriel came home to say that there were large cuts in the staff at her company, and she was informed that she would have to do accounting work part-time along with her personnel work. As reported earlier, she declined and resigned the same day.

Muriel spent a little time looking for a new job, but personnel positions were hard to find, so she was especially intrigued by a suggestion from a neighbor.

Eddie, a neighbor living on the other side of the empty lot on our north side, had a business where he looked after elderly people in his home.

If your house could meet, or be adapted to meet certain requirements, you could apply for a state license for "residential care", for up to 6 elderly people. The requirements were quite stringent, and inspections were frequent without prior notice, and citations were given for the slightest thing.

Eddie encouraged Muriel to start doing this, offering a lady to start her off, and 89-year-old Alice was moved into our house.

The second-floor addition covering about 2/3 of the downstairs, was partly finished, but we were able to use a couple of upstairs bedrooms. I was constantly working, gradually finishing all the rooms.

The upstairs consisted of a living room, 4 bedrooms, and 3 bathrooms. We had 4 balconies, 2 in the front and 2 at the rear of the house. All bedrooms had access to balconies, the largest 2 of which were also accessible from the living room as well. The living room is 30' by 26', with balconies and great views, front and back.

By this time, we had several old ladies, and Muriel was running all day long looking after them. She had a cleaning lady who came two days a week, and we had relief people for Thursday evening (for choir practice), and Sunday morning to allow us to go to church.

The boys had mostly left home by this time, and we had room to have live-in help, but Muriel would not have "live-in" workers in the house.

I finally said that if Muriel would not have strangers in the house, (she apparently didn't count the old ladies), then I would build a separate apartment for us and then she could not claim that a "live-in person" was in our house. She still would not consider having live-in people to help her, and "live-out" people turned out to be very unreliable.

However, about a year after finishing the original second-floor addition, I overheard Muriel telling somebody that she was going to have live-in help and that I was going to build a separate upstairs apartment for us!! As is normal, the husband is the last to know.

Although there was only 1/3 of the length of the building still to cover with a second floor, it was the deepest part, 24 feet wide by 42 feet deep. I started the plans which included balconies front and back, a second set of stairs, a larger bedroom and bathroom for Muriel and me, a large dining room with a wet bar, and a second smallish kitchen.

The work took about a year without any extraordinary happenings. The only memorable item was getting the roof trusses in position. These trusses, 52 feet long, including a 5ft overhang at each end, were made from 2 x 4's and very bendy. Also, they were extremely heavy and awkward to handle.

We had the wall frames up, and now we were ready for the trusses. At the mid-point, they were 5 feet high, and would easily pass between the studs of the front wall. We put them up one at a time by getting one end (with the peak down) propped up on the front edge of the second floor, with 2 sons up there to pull/slide them in. There were 2 sons and me on the ground to push and lift. Eventually, we got each truss on the new second floor, with many feet still sticking out through the front wall. Then we all got on the upper floor, lifted one end of each truss up onto the back wall, and pushed it out until the front end of the truss could be lifted up and pulled back to rest on the front wall. They hung between the walls with points down. The most dangerous part remained, namely swinging each one up until the peak was at the top.

If anything went wrong with this last part before it was nailed into position, the truss peak would swing down and kill somebody if it hit them.

We achieved this last stage by the use of a long, notched 2 x 4, with everybody standing back. I was on the top of the previous trusses with a hammer and nails and a 2 x 4 brace.

We only had one truss which got away from us, and swung down. It took about 20 pendulum swings before we could get near it, but everybody had jumped well clear.

Everything in this new section of the house was finished except the upstairs kitchen at the time of Helen's wedding, mentioned earlier. Son Peter was making the kitchen cabinets, and the basic plumbing was in. We bought a new refrigerator a few days before the wedding, and temporarily put it in the back garden to store wedding food etc.

Muriel had 4 bedrooms downstairs assigned for housing up to 6 elderly ladies, for which she had a license. (She would not take men. She did have one decrepit old man on a temporary basis, and all the 80-year-old ladies panicked and placed chairs up against their doors).

With just 4 rooms, it meant that there were 2 ladies in two rooms, and this caused problems as they would have disagreements, and in one instance, a fight. One lady hit the other with a pillow, then followed it up by throwing water over her. This caused us to think about adding a couple of rooms at the front south side.

I was back to drawing plans, etc. The plans were for two bedrooms, three half-bathrooms, and a central shower, all on the ground floor. This would allowed every lady to have her own room and bathroom, or half-bathroom. With this addition, the ground floor would have 6 bedrooms plus a large room for a live-in person, a living room, a dining room, a breakfast room, a storage room, a utility room, a kitchen, 2 full bathrooms, 5 half-bathrooms, a separate shower, and a large entrance hall, with a covered parking area adjacent to the front door so that Muriel could get in and out of a car under cover.

Upstairs, we have 5 bedrooms, 4 full bathrooms, a large living room of 30 x 26 ft., a kitchen, a very large dining room, 2 inside sets of stairs, 5 balconies, and an outside staircase that leads down to the pool, added late 1997.

In the pool area, we have a pool house with solar panels on the roof. In the pool house is a bar, 2 refrigerators and a TV plus changing space, with an attached portable toilet cubicle.

Finally, Muriel engaged staff that lived in. The first was a friend from our early days in California. This incredible story follows.

Many years ago, one of Muriel's cousins, named Helen, had come from New Zealand to the USA with a friend named Anne, who also knew the family in New Zealand. They were in Florida when Muriel's cousin became ill with some kidney problem.

Apparently, the real nature of the problem was not recognized and she died. Anne stayed on in USA and eventually married an American, and lived in the Los Angeles area.

Shortly after we arrived in America, Muriel's other cousin, Gifford, from New Zealand, brother of the dead cousin, was coming to California. Anne and her husband were going to the airport to meet him, and we went along also and met Anne and her husband for the first time.

Anne and her husband were very nice and later invited us all to their house for dinner a couple of times, and we got to know them. After years of trying, she eventually got pregnant and had this very pretty baby boy. Unfortunately, she spoiled the child to a ridiculous degree and I remember telling her that he would give her problems later if she didn't expose him to some discipline.

Some years later, a strange thing happened. We dropped in at their house in Los Angeles one day, and after several rings at the door, the husband finally came saying he had flu, and that Anne didn't live there anymore, and he was obviously sick and in pajamas. He sounded really bad. We did not pursue it, and left, very confused.

We heard nothing more for some years until one day she arrived at our house to pay us a visit on her day off. She was Catholic and was housekeeping for a houseful of priests.

She told us that when she was still living with her husband, she had taken her son to church after many years away from it and she wanted a confession. She was told that it was impossible because she was living in sin as her husband had been divorced before he met her, and the Catholic Church doesn't recognize marriages of any divorcees.

Following that, she moved into a different part of the house, away from her husband.

This went on for quite a while, and the husband finally got tired of the situation and divorced her.

Anne took the housekeeper job at the local home for priests, which provided a home and income for her and her son. However, Anne was not too happy at this job, so Muriel suggested that if she ever wanted a change, she could work for us with the old ladies, and that was the last we saw of her for a couple of years.

One night we were awoken by the sound of a car outside the house, and Muriel leaped out of bed. It was about 2 am, and here was Anne arriving in a nightgown that was ripped, across one shoulder and down the front leaving her somewhat exposed, scratched, and bleeding.

Apparently, her now teenage son was a drug addict and habitually beat her up for money to buy drugs.

On this particular evening, she had locked herself into her bedroom after a confrontation and had climbed out of her downstairs bedroom window and run for her life.

Muriel put her to bed. The next day they agreed she would work for us, and I arranged for a truck to go to pick up her belongings. She was terrified of her son, but he gave me no trouble.

As is my usual practice, I try to finish each story even though it may take us years ahead. If we were relating this story in purely chronological order, it would be more like a diary, and full of disjointed facts, therefore I will complete the story of Anne and then return in time.

Anne worked for us for about 18 months, and in that time we found that she was an excellent cook, but had a drinking problem. What we didn't immediately learn was that she also suffered from delusions.

In no time, Stewart, Anne's son was living at a local residential hotel and doing odd jobs for them. He would appear at our house occasionally, and harangue Anne, obviously for money.

He spoke to me once telling me that we were taking advantage of her. I didn't know what he was talking about until much later when he repeated this, and I said I thought she was well paid, naming her salary. He was astounded, indicating to me that she had told him she was paid much less, I suppose, as a way of avoiding giving him money.

She had two days off per week and on at least one of these days she arrived home around 10 pm in an inebriated state, and she seemed quarrelsome and angry.

I remember that Muriel and I were in the downstairs kitchen one night and she staggered between us, scowling. I made a comment about her condition and she yelled, "Bug off Brian". It struck us as quite funny. Following this, she told me about her friend Jonathan who was a tough guy and a marine, and he was going to come and beat me up. Jonathan was said to be very wealthy and extremely smart, and completely superior in all characteristics, and they were going to be married at some point in the future. Remember this Jonathan as there is more to come.

One late evening, I was upstairs, and I heard strange crying and moaning. I crept partway down the back stairs in the dark to listen, but the moaning had stopped. I returned back upstairs, but then it started again. I quietly came back down the stairs, and the moaning continued.

The door to the bathroom at the bottom of the stairs was open, and the noise seemed to be coming from there. There were no lights on. This bathroom was next to Anne's room and was primarily used by her. It is an inside bathroom, (no windows), and dark unless the light is on.

In the gloom I could just make out the silhouette of Anne, sitting on the toilet and moaning away. I don't think she saw me as she happily continued moaning and crying.

There was another similar situation late at night. Anne's room was directly beneath our bedroom, and we were awoken by yells and loud crying. It was a woman's voice so Muriel got up and went down the back stairs again and this time Anne was in her room with the door shut, and Muriel could pick out words to the effect that "Bimbos are after my son" and she was saying bad things about the Pope and about a famous movie star's wife.

This movie star, comedian and wife, and the Pope were a large part of Anne's delusional state. Apparently, according to Anne, this star made large donations to the Catholic Church, and his wife occasionally visited the place of Anne's employment at the home of the priests. The story goes on with woeful facts about the wife and the Pope trying to steal her son away from her. From what I knew, it would have been an excellent move if they had succeeded.

The drinking began to be a problem. She was under the influence of alcohol on the job and Muriel had to fire her giving her one months' notice. At the end of the month she had made absolutely no provision, and we took her to a hotel, and gave her $200.

Little did we know that there was much more to come.

About one month later, we received a phone call from Anne to the effect that she was sorry and would like to come back, and she promised that she would not drink etc. After a long discussion we agreed to take her back.

Everything went well for a time, but it was obvious she was drinking on her days off, which was not really our problem. However, it did cause everyone a problem finally.

At 2.00 am, we were jerked awake with a call from the local hospital. "Anne was ready for release after a driving accident". She was on her way home after spending an evening drinking, and was followed by 2 concerned citizens as she exhibited obvious signs of being incapably drunk. She had missed the bend along our road and plowed into a low wall and turned her car over, just 300 yards from our house.

The car was totaled, and she was banged up a bit, but with nothing permanent. The roof of her car was opened as if by a can-opener so that she could be retrieved. The next day I took her to the car junk yard for her to get her belongings. The car was a mess.

Some days later she had to go to court, and I drove her there and sat in court for an hour or so, but I had to leave and go to work.

She was ordered to appear later for trial. However, she refused to go and her court appointed lawyer called and called, to no avail. She just ignored the whole thing, and to our horror, she got away with it as she was never arrested or contacted by authorities in any way. Makes you think, doesn't it?

Now she had no car. One night, very late, we received a phone call from her to the effect that she had missed the last bus and was at the Oceanside Harbor. I really had no alternative but to go and fetch her. I finally found her, sitting in the dark about 30 yards from the road, looking out to sea.

She came over to the car and threw herself at me trying to kiss me and thanking me for coming for her. She reeked of booze. Apparently, she was in a good mood for once, after drinking.

It appeared that she was reverting to her old ways, with drinking and delusional conversation, and we were concerned that she was a possible danger to the old ladies, and herself.

One evening the phone rang and Muriel answered the phone, and a voice asked if this was a lunatic asylum. It was the "Jonathan" that Anne had said was going to beat me up if I gave her a bad time, and marry her.

After a bit of conversation, it appeared that Jonathan was a boat salesman in Anaheim, who was over 70 years of age, married, and he'd been pestered for years with phone calls and visits to his office from Anne. He told us he'd tried to get her to leave him alone, including calling the police, and nothing had worked. He said that he'd originally met her on a park bench years before.

Now that she had no car, she was calling his office asking him to pick her up from the Greyhound Bus Depot.

We were asked to talk to her and try to get some sense of the situation. We did this, and she agreed to stop, but apparently, nothing changed.

We eventually reached the point where we had to do something about Anne, and Muriel gave her a months' notice. We offered to pay her fare to New Zealand where she had a sister, but she didn't want that.

A few days later, she showed up with a new Cadillac!! Shortly after, we received a phone call requesting employment verification which of course elicited the information that she was serving a months' notice of termination.

Within a day we received a call from the Cadillac dealer asking why we reported her lack of employment prospects with us. Shortly after that, we got a threatening call from some bigshot at the Cadillac dealer saying that we could not tell the facts we'd reported. He was invited to jump in the lake.

The Cadillac was re-possessed.

The time came for Anne to leave, and on the last day, she showed up with a 34-foot motorhome. It was so large she could not get it around the driveway. I had to drive it for her, and then I helped her load her boxes, and after I drove it out to the road, she left.

A week or so later, we got a call from a car rental company, asking for Anne, but then asking her whereabouts. We had no information. Apparently, she had rented a convertible car also. A day or so later Jonathan called to say she was parked all day, outside his office so that he could not come and go without being accosted.

We got another call from the car rental company and we told them Jonathan's office address. Apparently, the car was filled with her boxes, but they took the car back anyway.

Now we were being pestered by the motorhome rental company, and finally, we gave them the approximate area in which we thought Anne might be. They went to all campsites in the area and found the motorhome, and took the vehicle back.

A week later, Jonathan called to say that Anne was still waiting outside of his office every day. She was obviously living on the streets as she was dirty and unkempt, and she was stealing food from the local cafeteria, but they were turning a blind eye to it out of pity.

Jonathon called the police and the welfare agencies who said they could do nothing unless she broke the law.

Following all of this, we felt something had to be done, and so we called Dick, Anne's ex-husband. He said he would try and find her. Apparently, he did, and he sent her back to New Zealand.

Now started the contacts from a credit card company. She had run up $4000 in credit card debt. We are still getting occasion letters from collection agencies. And, surprisingly we have even got offers for new credit cards for Anne.

We heard from Joy's cousin Giff, that after her return to New Zealand, Anne was living with a man who both he and Anne had known many years ago, and Giff was put in the awkward position of avoiding him in order to avoid Anne. Then we heard a couple of years ago, that she was back in Los Angeles. What a sad story. Later we heard that she had died.

Now back a few years to the time that Anne first came to us. We suddenly realized that we were a bit freer, and could travel a bit, so we booked a trip to Bath, England, and there we would join a bus tour to 7 European countries.

We met the bus in Bristol, 10 miles from Bath, and traveled to Dover to join up with several bus loads from other parts. Then we boarded a ferry to Ostend, Belgium.

We arrived in Ostend at about 6.00 pm and boarded a bus for sightseeing in Belgium.

That country is very small and completely flat, and we were able to see the highlights and drive into Germany by 9.30 pm, where we checked into a hotel. Our next stop and night stay-over was in Munich, where we spent the evening in a huge beer hall. There we watched a show with yodeling and various forms of music.

The next day we drove across Germany. We went on a 3-hour Rhine cruise, then on, stopping for a variety of attractions, including the City of Rothenburg, which is a walled medieval city still in a state of perfect preservation. Rothenburg is a wonderfully scenic city with beautiful Bavarian-type buildings, and well worth a visit.

There was one memorable thing that happened in Rothenburg.

Just off the main square, there is a tower which gives a panoramic view of the surrounding countryside. It can be climbed by 600 steps, which leads to a small top floor with a walk-around balcony. There was a lady on this top floor, selling postcards and other small touristy items.

We went out onto the balcony and the view was spectacular. I was filming with a video camera, and moving around to get views from all sides, except that on one side the camera went crazy, with the picture dancing across the viewer. I was absolutely stunned. The cameras appeared to fail just halfway through our trip. I moved around further and the camera suddenly righted itself. I went back and forth and found the camera went crazy just in one spot.

Years later, when cell phones became popular in the US, I realized that the tower, being the highest spot for many miles, most likely was a micro-wave relay point. The lady who spent her days selling to tourists was probably getting a healthy dose of radiation every day. I wonder if she is healthy today.

After leaving Rothenburg, the tour guide brought up the subject of The Romantic Road and Oberammergau. The spelling may be wrong, but it is the place where they have a religious Easter Pageant to commemorate the fact that they survived the plague in medieval times. Apparently, they made a pact with God that if they survived they would put on this pageant every 10 years, and they still do to this day.

The tour guide told us that The Romantic Road etc. was not on the itinerary, but for an extra $25 per head, the driver and the tour guide would sneak it in for us. Of course, this was just a swindle for the benefit of the driver and the tour guide, but we wanted to do it anyway, and so we did.

We visited the castle of Prince Ludwig which was very scenic, and full of history, then we went on to Oberammergau. The bus stopped at a parking area on the outskirts, right across the road from a restaurant. Muriel and I carried our own dried apple, nuts, trail mix, crackers, etc. as we usually do, and off we went into the town for an hour and a half. Everybody else went into the restaurant and came back out and got on the bus without seeing the town.

It was a delightful little town. All the buildings were Bavarian type, all brightly painted with pictures, and decorated with carved woodwork.

Then, we entered Austria and stayed overnight at Innsbruck, the site of the Winter Olympics some years ago.

Of all the places we had been and have been, Innsbruck remains clear in my mind as one of the most beautiful mountain areas that I've ever seen. It is surrounded by the most spectacular snow-capped peaks.

Innsbruck is memorable for 2 other things. There was a public toilet in the bus parking area, and as usual, as soon as the bus arrived, there was a rush for it. What a disappointment. The toilets were cubicles, some communal, with holes in the middle of the floor surrounded by a concave concrete surface, which sloped toward the hole. Many of the cubicles were under 1" of "liquid", and seemed most unhygienic.

The other memorable thing was that we were given a couple of hours to walk around what was a very pretty city, and we sort of got lost. We knew where we had to get to but there were no roads through to get back to the bus. We were worried but finally found a way through, and just made it with seconds to spare.

Our next stop was the outskirts of Venice where we stayed for 2 nights.

The hotel was very nice, surrounded by gardens.

Early the next day we all boarded the bus to drive toward Venice, which was about 20 miles away. Then we boarded a water bus, the only way into the center of the city.

I was amazed at the speed of the watercraft. There were 70 feet long water buses, water taxis, and private boats all whizzing up and down. How they avoided each other was a mystery, but there is no other way of getting around.

The water buses stopped every so often and people pushed and shoved their way on and off. Most of the bus stops were floating platforms, with tiny walkways connecting with solid ground.

The tour included a trip through the canals on a gondola, and our group needed about 6 of them. The group was to be accompanied by a singer, and a piano accordionist. As luck would have it they were on our boat, and we had the serenading all the way around the small canals and the Grand Canal, etc.

It came to lunchtime and lunch was part of the trip.

We were ushered into a restaurant and pushed and shoved toward a table by the rudest waiter I have ever met, which was typical of the treatment we experienced in Venice.

We were now making our way back to the bus and hotel, but we had to go by water bus, which meant lining up at the nearest bus-stop platform.

The bus came but there was only room for half of our group, so we stood aside and let the natives get on. By the time the next bus came, a dozen or so Venetians had pushed their way to the front, and we only just made it with the group on this second bus.

While in Venice, our group was scheduled to pick up another passenger, and we had met him in St Marks Square. He seemed a very strange character. He accompanied our group back to the hotel.

The next morning we were supposed to be at breakfast early, and we arrived at the entrance to the dining room to find it locked. We were told that somebody had broken in and trashed it. Apparently, there had been some trouble with our new passenger, and it was thought that he might be responsible, but he could not be found.

Finally, they cleaned up the mess and we got in for breakfast, but without our extra passenger.

We were waiting on the bus while the driver searched the grounds and the hotel, but he was nowhere to be found.

Finally, very late, we left to go to Switzerland. We were about 5 miles from the hotel, and who did we see walking ahead? It was our missing passenger, which gave credence to suspicions that he was responsible for the problem with the dining room. He had run away.

He got on the bus, and on we went. We stopped in Lucerne in Switzerland, and we went around the lake in a nice big boat with Bavarian-type music, and then we walked the town which was largely built along the lakeside. Our hotel was away from the lake, in a slightly lower-class business area. We had arrived early in the evening and had time to explore the town.

Our mysterious extra passenger had disappeared again. It seems that he had gone out and had not come back in time to join the group for the evening meal and entertainment. That evening we were taken to a restaurant/beer hall and we had a thoroughly enjoyable time. I admired the beer glasses and one lady from our bus suggested that I take one. They were too large for me to hide on my person, so she said, "Give it to me".

This lady was about 350lbs in weight. A very large lady who ran her own business in Florida. She supplied ladies who would come and do house cleaning in the nude!

She went off with a glass and came back a few minutes later with no sign of it.

The show went on and we were entertained with yodeling, flugelhorns, accordion players, and those huge 12-foot Alpine horns which were used to communicate in the mountains.

On the bus on the way back to the hotel, she produced the glass, and it was warm. It is in use to this day. Of course, it was thoroughly washed.

The next day we learned that our extra passenger had got lost and couldn't find his way back to the hotel. He had gone out upon arrival and didn't bother to find out the name of the hotel, so could not get back. Apparently, the police called all the hotels before finding our Cosmos tour group.

The next day we left for Paris. On the way we all gradually realized that our extra passenger, who spoke to no one, had an obvious dislike of water as he stank like a polecat. Then we found out that he was leaving us in Paris, and there were no regrets about this from the rest of us. He sure fitted in amongst the population of Paris.

We were 15 miles from Paris and we could clearly see the Eiffel Tower.

Due to the amount of ground we covered in the one week tour, we did not have much time in any place, but we were driven extensively around Paris, only stopping at a view point 100 yards from the Eiffel Tower, which was very spectacular.

We stayed overnight in Paris, and the next day we drove to Calais for the return ferry ride.

In 7 days we had covered in excess of 4000 kilometers through 7 countries. It was really an excellent overview and very reasonably priced.

Shortly after arriving back in Bath, we had to return to California. I had 8 hours of video tapes and at the end of the trip, several people asked for copies of my tapes, so I offered copies to everybody at cost, and 11 people requested them.

I edited the tapes to about 4 hours, 2 tapes, and the cost with shipping etc. was $23. I received all the money from everybody, and then I received a copy of a tape made by another passenger, but it was not very good, but a nice thought.

Chapter 27 - Some Of Our Travels

In the meantime Muriel had hired several ladies, one after the other, to assist her with the care of the elderly. The helpers were mostly marginal and didn't last long. There were the ones who swore they didn't smoke but we found them smoking. There was the one who turned out to be a drug addict. There was the one who was from Hungary and would only whisper in the house "so that the FBI would not hear her". If you wanted to speak to her in a normal manner she would run outside before talking normally.

There was another one that I fetched from a house in south San Diego. The house was in a disgusting state with cockroaches crawling everywhere. I had to wait a few moments for her and didn't even want to breathe there.

She was gone from us in a couple of weeks, but the cockroaches lingered on at our house. It took months for us to clear them out.

Finally, Terry arrived. She was skinny and not too bright, but just bright enough to get by. And just getting by, was the main characteristic of her performance. But at least she was dependable enough to do the minimum that was necessary.

During Terry's reign, we were able to book another trip, and we picked a tour of Greece and booked the cruise of the Greek Islands.

We flew out of London to Athens and were taken by bus to a hotel. Muriel's sister Susan came with us.

Over the next few days, we were taken all around Athens, and to the Parthenon, etc. Then on to Delphi, (home of the Oracle in Biblical and pre-Biblical times). Muriel and her sister climbed up the mountain to the ruins where the Oracle operated.

The tiny town of Dephi is high in the mountains and we stayed overnight in a hotel with a veranda attached to our room which looked over a view of the Bay of Corinth. Corinth was at least 40 miles away below us but could be clearly seen. Cargo vessels going in and out of Corinth looked like toys. We could see higher snow-covered mountains to our right. We walked around Delphi from 8.00 to 10.00 pm on a warm evening. All the stores were open and people were very friendly and helpful. We had an enjoyable evening chatting with the natives.

Next, we went to Corinth and crossed the bridge over the Corinth Canal which had been cut through rock to a depth of at least 300 feet, starting in Biblical times. Then, we were due to board a cruise boat for 4 days cruise to 3 or 4 Greek Islands, but the tour guide got us together for a meeting.

She had some good and some bad news. First, the bad news was that there was no room on the 4-day cruise. Groans!! Then, the good news, we could go on a 7-day cruise at no extra charge. It also included more islands and bus tours on land.

Guess what we chose.

The islands we visited were Crete, Rhodes, Patmos, Mykonos, and Santorini. On the way around the Aegean Sea, we visited Istanbul and Kusadasi in Turkey.

In Istanbul, we saw the Blue Mosque and several other Mosques. As you know, one part of Turkey is in Europe, and across the Bosphorus is the other part, which is in Asia. The two parts are joined by a huge bridge which we crossed by a bus. Included in the bus trip was a certificate saying that we had been in Asia.

Also, in Istanbul, we visited a huge bazaar and were entertained later at a dinner show which was mostly different belly dancing groups.

After Istanbul, we sailed overnight to Kusadasi, from where we boarded buses to Ephesus, the historic seaport which figures largely in the Bible.

Today, Ephesus is miles from the sea, when in Biblical times, it was a busy seaport. The historic part of the city covers at least 20 acres, and you can still see the columns on each side of the main street that led to the docks. The condition of the buildings is remarkable, with the library being the most outstanding.

Amongst other things, we saw what was a communal toilet, which consisted of a circular stone ledge or seat, about 20 ft. in diameter, with a circumferential 4" wide slot running along the middle of the seat. If you looked into the slot, you could see, about 15 ft. below, a gushing stream of water. This was designed to immediately carry away all waste products.

We were told that it was an important meeting place for both sexes.

We sat in the arena where Paul preached to the Ephesians. The acoustics from the speaker's stone (which we stood on), were excellent, so we can understand how voices were carried without electronic assistance.

Upon our return to Kusadasi, we had time to walk around the town. It was a delightful place, the exact opposite of Istanbul. Everybody was happy and friendly.

Muriel and her sister wandered in and out of the stores, and had cups of apple tea, and gossiped with the store-keepers while I sat outside and waited. I bought a very nice leather jacket there which would have cost far more in the USA. Muriel's mother's maiden name was "Osman", a very important name in Turkey. They mentioned this to the shopkeepers and were treated like royalty.

We saw some children going home from school. They were in their school uniforms, just like little English children.

They seemed so cute that we tried to photograph them but they would not stop, so I held out some money. The shopkeepers who were sitting outside their shops encouraged them to allow the photographs, and then the children weren't so scared, in fact, they were very polite and grateful.

Of the Greek Islands, two of them still burn brightly in our memories. On Mykonos, the beaches were spectacular, with small fishing boats, framed with rows of Greek windmills, with sails made from white cloth. There were large white pelicans which would try to bite if you got too near. Their beaks made a "hollow log" clacking sound when they tried to bite.

The Island of Santorini was completely different. The boat anchored in an almost enclosed circular bay, probably 8 miles in diameter. It is said that it is the caldera of a huge volcano, which exploded eons ago. There is also a school of thought that this was the site of Atlantis until it exploded.

It is obvious that the bay is all that is left of a volcano, borne out by the fact that the edge of the land all the way around the bay is a vertical cliff a couple of thousand feet high.

From the boat, Santorini looked like a toy mid-eastern village with lots of cube-like houses clinging to the top of the cliff, extending downwards for 50 ft. or so. All buildings were painted white, and blinding in the bright sun.

We were taken ashore in rickety local boats, loaded so heavily that there was only standing room. Then onto tiny old buses to climb the steep winding road cut into the side of the cliff.

The town (village) was exquisite, with narrow alleyways going between typical Mediterranean houses with stores on the ground floor. The alleys ran mostly parallel to the cliff edge. There was no way that motor vehicles could use these alleyways as they were too narrow and there were steps every few yards.

It was most noticeable that everything was clean, and freshly painted a gleaming white. This truly was a wonderful experience.

From the village, we left by a regular size bus and went inland around the island and to an archaeological "dig" which was still in the process of being uncovered. (How did they get those big buses ashore from big boats when our cruise boat couldn't get close)?

This dig of about one acre, was roofed over with galvanized metal on a metal frame. It was the remains of an old town and is thought to be a most important find. In fact, there was a program on TV recently about the importance of it.

We returned to Santorini, to board cable cars down to the beach, and onto the rickety fishing boats, which ferried us back to the cruise ship.

When we arrived at Patmos, again we boarded rickety local fishing boats and made it to shore. There we boarded buses for a trip around the island. The bus groaned up the large hill overlooking the bay and we could watch our temporary home (the ship) grow smaller and smaller below us.

At the very top were a monastery and church buildings. We had to walk the last 200 yards as the roadway had ended and the pathway was extremely steep with steps every few yards.

The buildings were extensively decorated with statues and paintings, with ancient icons with antique gold and silver religious items of every description. After the time spent in the monastery complex, we retraced our steps back down to a very special spot on the side of the hill with a panoramic view over the bay. There were steps leading to a cave and from the cave mouth and we could again see our ship like a tiny toy.

We were told that this was the cave in which John the Divine had written the book of Revelations.

Every time you turn around in this part of the world there are historical places and attractions that are famous. It gives me a weird feeling to think that some of the mysterious places I first heard about in church as a small boy, now exist in our extensive library of vacation videotapes. It is hard to believe that I have actually been there. These places exist in such numbers that you cannot take them all in. For example, we just casually drove past the Pillars of Hercules, either on the island of Crete or Rhodes, (can't remember which), without even slowing down.

Now, that we have started talking about our travels, we might as well complete them to date. It was a year later, in 1995, that we went on another Cosmos trip, a cruise out of Nice, France.

We flew to New York and changed planes for a direct over-night flight to Nice. In Nice, we were transported from the airport to the boat by bus, a distance of about 12 miles, but because we were too early to board the ship, we detoured in a westerly direction, passing through many famous resorts like Cannes and Antibes.

The cruise ship was small with only about 450 passengers.

Our first stop, on the second day, was at a French port called Sete.

There was a bus tour available and for the one and only time in our travel career, we decided to miss it, as it seemed to have very little appeal. And we chose wisely. Passengers who went said they saw swampy grass and some wild horses only.

We walked into the town of Sete, and it was very picturesque. We found out it was called the Venice of France as it was crisscrossed by canals.

There were small colorful boats and fishermen all along the streets at the edges of the canals. There were some very interesting buildings, and everything was very colorful. We were happy that we saw the town. The bus trippers did not see much of the town.

The next day we stopped at Barcelona, Spain, and joined a bus tour of the city with a trip to the Montserrat Monastery.

This monastery is built in the Montserrat Mountains, which rises to about 5000ft out of what is otherwise a low-lying plain. This tiny mountain range is only about 5 miles by 1 mile but very jagged.

The Abbey attached to the monastery, created in the 11th century, houses a unique item in the form of the Black Madonna. The only known black one. Also, at regular intervals, you can hear the famous Montserrat boys' choir, named Escolania. Also, we were lucky to hear a visiting Japanese children's choir.

On the way back to Barcelona and the ship, we stopped at the Olympic Village, and the Spanish Village (a restored old Spanish village) for a late lunch. There was a small calamity at the village restaurant.

It was in the open air, and big steel trays, about 4 feet in diameter, were brought out, bearing all sorts of cooked seafood. Some waiters carried them around, swinging them about, showing everybody how clever they were, when they got too enthusiastic, and half the seafood went on the ground from one tray. I expect the next lot of customers got the cleaned-up, pre-cooked seafood.

The next day we went ashore in Minorca, a beautiful island.

We arrived at dawn. The approach to the harbor took about 1½ hours gliding along with hills on each side, covered with colorful houses, and many small boats at anchor. The sun was low, just rising, which gave everything an unusual tint.

We did a bus tour of the island, which included lunch at one of the famous restaurants overlooking one of the most popular beaches and a private boat harbor. A highlight was a trip to the highest point of the island, which is otherwise quite flat, from where you can see the whole island spread out before you.

On we went, sailing overnight to the island of Sardinia. We went on a bus trip around the island finishing up in Alghero, the capital, where we went sightseeing in the local shops and market areas. It was quite quaint and interesting and the people were pleasant and polite.

That night, as we were leaving Sardinia, the weather, which had been sunshine every day up until now, took a bad turn and we were advised that there was a stormy night ahead. We were on the west side of Sardinia and had to travel east to Italy. To avoid the worst of the storm the ship would go around the south of Sardinia, rather than go the shorter northerly route where the storm was thought to be the worst.

The storm hit with a vengeance, and this was a small boat, but it seemed more like a cork, pitching and rolling.

By dinner time, half of the passengers must have been ill as the dining room was half empty. All gangways had vomit bags spread out every few feet, but Muriel and I were OK.

Walking about was a slow process as you had to hold on to a rail to stay upright. Many times, when crossing a space, people would be grabbing onto each other to keep from falling around.

We went to the theater as usual after dinner, to see if there was a show, and it appeared that there was, so we sat down. The show started, and everything was fine for a time, but soon, it was announced that the show would have to stop.

When we finally went to bed, which was a small 2'6" bed each, at right angles to each other, we had to lay on our backs and hang on to the bed frame on each side.

We eventually got to sleep, and the next day we awoke to a fine day. We were docked in Livorno, Italy.

From Livorno, we went by bus to the historic city of Florence, or Firenza as the Italians spell it. (I can't think why we don't call it the same name).

On the way there we could see the Leaning Tower of Pisa and never did find out why this was bypassed.

For those who don't know, Florence is famous for its gold jewelry. We should have stayed away.

Of course, Florence is also famous for many other things. Our first stop in Florence was on a hill overlooking the city. We could see the river, the bridge, the Ponte Vecchio, which has been lined with jewelry stores since the late 1500s, and the churches, especially the one with the famous red dome, which shows up brightly.

Then we went down into the center of town and visited the Duomo, Santa Maria del Fiore Cathedral, the main square, and then we were free to wander around.

Suddenly, we found ourselves on the Ponte Vecchio, surrounded by jewelry stores, and we were going upstairs to a secured second floor where they opened and re-locked the door when you entered.

There was a room with maybe a dozen customers and behind a counter were about 5 young ladies.

Muriel asked to see gold necklaces and she was shown a skinny little thing about ¼" wide. She asked me if I liked it and I told her it was too skinny, so the next one was fatter, but still too skinny for my liking.

We worked our way up until there was one that wasn't too skinny and suddenly, through a haze, I got the impression that my approval of the size of this necklace, had been interpreted as this was the one to buy!!!!

I was feeling so weak that I could not utter the words that I needed to say such as "We can't afford it", and we found ourselves outside with Joy dragging with the weight of this gold thing around her neck. I couldn't get back into the store to say it all was a mistake as we were locked out.

We made our way back to the square to meet up with the rest of our group, and a couple of ladies came running up to Muriel saying, "You got it then???" I had this distinct feeling that I had missed something or had been left out of a loop. Apparently, I was the last to know.

By the way, there are supposedly only 3 bridges in the world which have stores on them, and they are, the one in Venice, the one in Florence, and the one in Bath, Pulteney Bridge. We have been over all of them.

Overnight we cruised to our last port of call, Portofino in the northwest corner of Italy.

We arrived early in the morning and it was just getting light as we appeared on deck. We were not ready for the view that greeted us. It was breathtaking. We were anchored just off a tiny semi-circular bay, 150 yards across, which was surrounded by tall buildings reminiscent of Bavaria, all bright and colorful, with small, brightly painted boats pulled up on the beach.

On each side of the bay, were cliffs with Mediterranean villas dotted from the beach to halfway up. To the right or south in the distance, was what seemed to be a larger town. We were taken by tender to a small landing stage and we boarded a small motor cruiser for a trip up the coast.

We traveled north about ¼ mile off the coast, which consisted of high cliffs. The sea was very choppy. We nosed in toward land, and round a bend was a small inlet, less than 50 yards wide, surrounded by sheer cliffs. As we got closer we could see a sandy beach and a little landing platform. Also, taking up most of the flat area was a large church. Dotted around, perched on little flat spots around the base of the cliff were a handful of small houses. This was a fishing village, which was only accessible by sea. There was no way out by land except by climbing the vertical cliff.

We went into the church for a look and found it very ornate. We were amazed that there was such a church in so tiny and remote a place. There could not have been more than 25 people in the whole place. So much for the Catholic Church.

On board the little cruiser again for 15 minutes, running parallel to the cliffs, still going north, and we came to what appeared to be a large dent in the coastline, and what looked like a sizeable town, even though it was backed by a not too steep cliff 100 yards from the water.

As we approached, we could see that there was a quay, and a sea wall, and in order to land, we had to approach toward the quay and take a sharp right around the sea wall. There was hardly any room to pass between the dozens of other moored boats within the shelter of the sea wall, and there was a considerable swell, but we made it.

Within a few yards of the point at which we landed, was a Catholic church, and there was a service going on, and we went into the door. Again we were astounded by the ornate decorations and statuary, and glittering gold ornaments. I would guess this town has about 3000 population.

Upon closer inspection, there was a road that snaked up the side of the cliff, joining what seemed to be a busy road along the top of the cliff. The quay and the area around it were exactly what you would expect. There was all sorts of boating equipment, potted plants and flowers, and tiny shops.

Off to one side, there was a narrow passageway which was a pedestrian tunnel that led to more tiny shops, and it had started to rain, and so we took shelter in this covered area. It was warm, however, the rain soon stopped so we were able to continue investigating.

We came to the bottom of the winding road out and there were more tourist shops. We walked part way along, and at the side of the road, just past a spot where a building straddled the road, there were several 10 or 12 feet diameter steel discs, leaning against a high wall. We enquired about their use. We were told that they were used at the town's annual festival. They were covered with seafood and fires were lit underneath, and they fed the whole town. These discs were similar to the 4 ft. diameter steel trays we had seen in Barcelona. We bought ice creams and sat and watched a photographer taking photos of an Italian wedding, which took place on the sea wall in an open paved area just above the waves.

It was time to leave, and we boarded a bus which groaned up the winding road to the top of the cliff and turned south along the coast road. It was beautiful scenery.

We came to the end of the bus trip at the town we saw in the distance, south of Portofino. We spent some time there before getting on a ferry back to the cruise ship.

The next day we were due to dock in Nice, back where we started, but before that, I want to relate an interesting story about the evening shows on the ship.

As it was such a small ship, the scope of the shows was somewhat limited and consisted of an activities director, who was really a comedian, two young ladies, and two young men. These four young people were dancers and singers.

The comedian was Lenny Windsor. He had been a script writer for Benny Hill and had lots of Benny's characteristics. He was rude to his audience, made fun of people and seemed to get away with it, and had people laughing to boot.

For some reason, he immediately picked me out of the audience to help him in various ways. He gave me 2 identical ties and asked me to wear one to the next evening's show. The plan was for him to call me onto the stage and cut the tie off with scissors, I would put the pieces in my pocket. Later, he would call me back and I was to hand him the other good tie, and he would wave a wand and magically display what appeared to be the mended tie. It worked to plan.

On another night he asked me to pretend to be a policeman and he asked the audience if there were any other police in the audience. He was quite small and did he have in mind some skit to bully some big policemen??? Anyway, there was a sheriff who was about 6'7" tall. I don't remember what happened, but there was some good-natured clowning.

Then there was the talent show. I went to the meeting and entered my name to sing "The Hippopotamus Song". At the meeting was a young lady who said she wanted to sing but was a bit scared to sing on her own, so I offered to sing with her if we could find a suitable duet. She loved that idea and we got copies of a duet from Phantom of the Opera.

The show was days away but the lady kept phoning me to meet her all over the ship in deserted places so that we could practice. There was a problem, however, she couldn't sing.

The big night came and I was on first with the Hippopotamus song and some old gent whistler followed, and then it was time for the duet.

I was so worried about the woman's capability and had my mind on it that I started to sing an octave too high. I only knew that it seemed higher than it should be. Before it was time for the lady to come in, I stopped the accompanist with a loud protestation that he was playing it too high. The audience tittered. The accompanist started again a few notes lower. I started to sing but it was still too high. We repeated the process and the music started again a few notes lower but still high, and now we got as far as the lady starting to sing. Within a few notes from her, Lenny Windsor came rushing out yelling at her, "You can't sing, get off the stage". The audience was roaring with laughter.

I had my harmonica in my pocket, and Lenny Windsor and the lady were having a big argument at the rear of the stage, and the microphone was free with no show going on. I started to play "Ruby" on the harmonica. Lenny whipped around and started yelling insults at me now to get off the stage, which I ignored. About the time I finished "Ruby", the lady picked up the trumpet in the musician's area and was blowing it loudly. Lenny was going crazy, yelling at us and waving his arms in mock fury. The audience was rolling in the aisles.

Finally, things calmed down, and Lenny got us off the stage. Now he came to the microphone and started to announce the next contestant, and was fumbling through his pockets.

He yelled at me, "Come and play something else. I've lost my list". I went back up on the stage and played "Moon River". Before I finished it, he was yelling again. He had found his list. Note: A fellow passenger later asked, "How long did you practice that skit"?

Prior to the show, I had arranged a little conversation with Lenny. It was just a month after our 40th wedding anniversary. He was to ask me how long we've been married etc., and I was to answer in terms of not having made up my mind to keep Muriel yet as I hated to rush into things. Then by pre-arrangement, I was going to sing, "Once Upon a Time".

We had our arranged conversation on the stage, and the audience laughed and laughed. It went down very well. Then I sang the song. Little did I know the effect the song would have. By the time I'd finished singing, many of the women in the audience, and Muriel, had tears and mascara streaming down their faces. I particularly remember that the lady sitting behind Muriel had a real mess. She must have been particularly heavy with the mascara.

Lenny came and presented a bottle of wine to Joy, the talent show winner's prize, saying, "You should have this as he's upset you".

The song and dance group came and asked if they could use "Once Upon A Time", and borrowed my music to copy.

At every show, Lenny referred to the fact that for the next 2 weeks the boat had been booked by a club of "gays", and that he was a bit nervous about it. Hardly a night went by when this subject didn't come up.

Also, he kept on the whole week about a magnificent award that would go to the person who contributed the most to the shows. At the last show, Lenny made this marvelous presentation speech and presented me with. . . .A Regency Cruise Line key ring.

We were leaving the ship in Nice, and at the top of the gangplank, Lenny stood saying goodbye to everybody. When he saw me he feigned relief and spoke in the same vein, but I shocked him speechless by saying something which just came into my mind, "See you next week", with the gay club???

It was about 6 weeks before we left for this trip to Nice, that Muriel remembered that she'd promised her mother that she'd take her to Nice, one day. So we arranged to fly to England for 4 days after the cruise, and then bring Muriel's mother and her sister Susan back to Nice for 3 days. This we did, and we rented a car and drove them along the south of France to the east, Monte Carlo, and Monaco, to the west as far as the road would go. Joy's mother and sister were booked to go back on Sunday and we took them to the airport early after having the buffet breakfast at the hotel.

We couldn't get on a plane for USA until the Monday as the Sunday's flight was full, so we went back to the hotel and discovered that the buffet was still open. We decided we would get another breakfast and save money on later meals.

We were busy eating away when I noticed an obvious situation at the next table where two men were sitting and talking in low confidential tones.

They appeared to be very friendly, Of course, they were going on the cruise boat, so I struck up a conversation with them, asking the obvious, "Were they Americans". Of course, they were. I'd heard their speech. Then I said, "I'll bet you're going on the Regency cruise ship". They were surprised and wondered how I guessed.

Taxis from the hotel to the dock cost $40 for a trip just down the road and around the corner. Quite exorbitant, and I told them about it and they were shocked. We had the rental car, and we had nothing better to do so we offered to take them on a drive as far as time allowed and they jumped at the plan. We offered just to be nice, and they were very appreciative.

It was about 10.30 am, and off we went. We drove them to Monte Carlo and Monaco, and this time we went on a different road and saw lots that we hadn't seen before.

We arrived back at the ship at 2.30 pm and drove right up to the tables where the crew were booking people in.

Right there was the song and dance group at one of the tables and they yelled out, "Hello, what are you doing here"? Then, I spotted Lenny at the top of the gangway. He was busy talking.

I ran over and got the OK from the guard to just run up to see Lenny. He was busy talking and didn't see me coming until he turned as I arrived. "I told you I'd be back", I said. Lenny nearly fainted.

This Mediterranean cruise was the best one we've done. The scenery was the most spectacular and the small boat was the most enjoyable.

The next day we flew home.

We saw a good price advertised for a cruise along the Alaskan Inside Passage, and we went for it. We flew from Los Angeles to Anchorage and then did a 200-mile bus trip to Seward, a tiny place out in the boonies with just a couple of shacks around a sort of fjord, and there was the cruise ship looking most out of place among a few canoes in this wild area.

It looked strange. This huge boat tied up at a small dock and towered above everything around it. There were no real buildings, just trees and grass, and the small concrete landing stage. We boarded through a ground-level doorway and found our way to our cabin which was surprisingly large.

The cabin was up the front end, about where the boat begins to narrow, and this was the reason for the large size. Because of the slightly less width, we had equivalent to 2 cabins length.

For those who are not familiar with the geography of the area, there is a line of large islands running parallel to the Alaskan mainland, from just north of Vancouver, Canada, to the Anchorage area. Hence, the name "Inside Passage". The cruise ships sail between Seward and Vancouver.

It was a routine cruise, with all the usual things. I had made up my mind that I was not going to get involved in any talent shows and other show involvement, as it is too stressful, so I was able to relax.

On the way south we saw the College Fjord and the Columbia Glacier.

The first stop was Valdez, in the Prince William Sound in which the tanker of the same name went aground and spilled all that crude oil. Valdez appeared to be a town of about 3000 people, surrounded by snow-covered mountains, and very beautiful. The town is quite new, having been moved from the old site which is now almost underwater.

We were told the reason for the flooding, but I cannot remember what we were told.

We did a tour of the town, which took at least 5 minutes. I had lost my comb and got the bus to stop at the drugstore while I bought another. Then we went up the mountains to see the local glacier. It was quite small, only about 50 feet across at the bottom end which was just about 50 yards from the road, but the mountain scenery on the way was wonderful and the best part of that bus tour.

After Valdez, we sailed into a bay, which was blocked at the far end by a glacier (Hubbard Glacier). It was about ½ mile wide and at least 150 or 200 feet high. The ship sailed to within about 100 yards and turned sideways onto it.

It was freezing cold. This cruise was the last one for the season and the weather was deteriorating. We watched huge walls of ice peel off and crash into the water, and become mini icebergs.

The bay was filled with these ice floes, and upon closer inspection, we could see that many were covered with seals.

The next stop was Skagway. A little historic town with old pioneer buildings, and a few stores with touristy things.

The ship was traveling in a generally south-easterly direction so that the land was on our left, and the islands were on our right. The coastline was all snow-covered mountains for the whole trip.

Our next stop was Juneau. This was a larger and busier town with quite a large population. We boarded a bus and went to see the Mendenhall Glacier. We had to walk about a quarter of a mile from the bus to the viewpoint. It was a medium size glacier with a backdrop of high mountains, and very picturesque. The next stop was a salmon hatchery with a small museum about Alaskan fish and animals.

At the hatchery, we saw the adult salmon coming in from the fjord, and pushing to get into the tanks at the hatchery where they were born. The fish were about 3 feet long and fat looking.

Along the road on the bank of the fjord were several fishermen, and they all had a couple of huge salmon lying on the bank beside them.

Our last stop was Ketchikan, where the weather was a bit warmer and the sun was shining. Of course, it was the southernmost stop except for Vancouver.

We docked against a wooden pier, with a space of about 70 feet wide alongside the ship. On the far side of this space was a line of tourist-type shops, which continued around a corner into the street.

We were booked on a small boat for a cruise of the harbor which was a long channel about ½ a mile wide. We went off to the left and saw all sizes of ships and boats, and something which is common all over Alaska, seaplanes or float planes. Apparently, when the water freezes over, the floats are replaced with skids.

Up until this point we had only had glimpses of the bald eagles. Whilst on the harbor cruise, we saw several on the far side of the channel, which was undeveloped.

When we went to the right in the harbor we saw some historic buildings, namely the brothel, and further down, a collection of Indian totem poles.

After we finished the harbor cruise we looked at a few jewelry stores for the best deal in a tanzanite ring for Muriel. We walked up and down comparing sizes and designs but didn't really settle on anything. We were told in one store that our ship was the last for the year and that all the stores would be closing for the winter when our ship left in an hour or so.

The 3 men in one of the stores were Asian Indians and we started to talk about dealing for one particularly large 9-carat tanzanite ring with a circle of diamonds. We were a bit surprised because they immediately offered a 50% reduction. We dickered and said we had to go as the ship would be leaving soon. They were actually in the process of closing up as we talked. Finally, without much argument, they offered the ring at about 1/3 of their starting price, and Muriel boarded the ship with one extra piece of jewelry.

That night, on the way to Vancouver, the ship was advised that we were going to run into a storm which would be felt at its worst when we were sailing in the open sea between the shelters of two islands.

Over a matter of a few minutes, the motion of the ship changed from choppy to violent motion, and for 3 hours we were bounced around until we got into the shelter again between the mainland and the next island. The extreme motion of the ship stopped as quickly as it started.

Overall we were a bit disappointed with what we saw. We had been told it was stupendous, but by somebody who had not traveled too much, so maybe this is the price you pay for seeing lots of the world's wonders.

Soon the cruise was over, and we were met in Vancouver by my sister Christine and her husband Bill. We had a nice lunch with them, then back to the airport to complete our journey home to San Diego.

Our next trip was a Cosmos tour of Italy and Sicily. We went to England first to see Muriel's family, and then met the tour and flew to Rome with the rest of the group.

In Rome the next day, we were driven around, then up into the mountains. We had lunch at a restaurant where we were serenaded by a group of 3 men playing guitars and a piano accordion. One of them had an excellent tenor voice, and really blossomed after I gave him a tip. I was filming him singing and he sang directly to the camera. He sang Ave Maria, and the rest of them stopped after playing one verse, but he motioned for them to continue. This was his big moment and he sang three verses.

After lunch, we went to a town called Tivoli, 30 miles east of Rome, on the top of a mountain. We visited a large house, Villa D'Este, with 5 acres of gardens on the side of the mountain overlooking the Rome area. This is said to be in the words of the travel experts, "Undeniably the most famous water park of Europe". It was very impressive.

The next day we went to Sorrento and stayed overnight after a day of sightseeing. Then we drove to the base of Vesuvius and climbed it up a steep footpath. It was quite a small mountain and at the top, we looked over the crater which was about 100 yards in diameter. There was smoke and steam coming out of a couple of cracks in the side, but there was nothing startling there, but then, years ago, it had erupted and completely covered Pompeii and Herculaneum with ash, and they were miles from the volcano. Then we went to Pompeii and spent several hours walking around in the reclaimed city.

The next day we drove around Naples and we were sitting in front of the bus and there was Italian opera music playing. In a lull in the music, I teased the tour guide about the fact that he should sing to us as he was Italian. To my surprise, he burst into song and did a very passable job.

The next stop was an overnight stay on the island of Capri, a beautiful island just off the coast of Sorrento. The hotel was the best of the whole trip, and was right in the middle of the shopping area, much to the delight of the ladies of the group. Capri was made famous in England by an old-time British song, sung by a popular singer in the Second World War. Her name was

Gracie Fields, and she retired to live by the beach on Capri. We could see her house from the hill above.

We were all looking at the view, and I took the opportunity to tidy up my camera bag and had it all spread out on a picnic table. Suddenly it started to rain with big raindrops, and we all ran for the bus. Only later did I remember that I had left my walking stick (cane) on the table. Following our stay in Capri, we returned again to the Sorrento Hotel. That afternoon, we went for a walk in the town, as we had done a couple of times before.

We found this nice little open-air place to have coffee and pastries etc. and we stopped there several times. On this particular day we also had to buy a walking stick (cane), and we found a very stout one for $15. Then we looked for gold bracelets for Muriel and we found a nice one that was made by the shop owner. We bought it. Although Muriel thought it was very nice, it was not exactly what I wanted for her, so I kept looking.

At some point in the trip, and we can't pinpoint it now, we did a bus trip to what they called a typical "hill town".

There was no road to it so we walked up a wide pedestrian walkway with 4" steps every few feet. On each side were small houses with people sitting in the sun. At the top of the hill, we came to a square, where there were stores all around, with a huge underground toilet taking up most of the paving on one side of the square. One other item was immediately obvious. Once again, there was an enormous cathedral. It always struck me as strange how the tiniest of community's had their big old church, way out of proportion to the population and the local ability to build or support it.

We were shown around the church which again was incredibly ornate with many statues etc. It was a hot day and when we came out into the square, most of us made a bee-line for a shop with tables and umbrellas outside, and obviously a source of cold drinks.

There were probably 10 of us that went into the store to buy cold beers. The first few people got a bottle of beer and a glass. We were a bit behind and got a glass of beer only. The glasses only held 2/3 of a bottle and so we realized we'd been cheated. I said to Muriel, "I'm going to tear somebody's head off". Muriel was against making a fuss and talked me into accepting it, but I was mad. We drank our beer, and the empty glasses (with a nice crest on them) were sitting on the tables as we sat and talked. I thought, "I'm going to get even and steal the glass", and I told the others at the table. I opened my shirt and slid the glass inside. Shortly, we got up to leave, and, there wasn't a glass to be seen on the tables, and everybody was smiling. The store lost several glasses that day.

A highlight of the whole trip was a bus ride along the Amalfi Coast, said to be one of the great beauty spots on earth. It was very nice, similar to the coastline just south of the San Francisco area, except that it had buildings clinging to the cliffs. Again, we have seen so much that apparently, it takes a great deal to impress us.

The next day we were off to Sicily. We drove to almost the most southerly part of Italy, arriving at the ferry at about 2.30 pm. We could see Sicily across the water, and now we, (still on the bus) were loaded on the ferry, a huge boat, and we were off.

It was only a 15 minute trip and we were soon on our way to our hotel for the night in Taormina. For once we lucked out. The coast road in Taormina was right next to the beach, and what a lovely beach. A little cove with rocks and sand and palm trees, and a brilliant blue ocean. Our hotel was across the road and we were on the 4th floor at the front, with a small veranda. As we investigated the view, we saw that several from our group also were checking out their balconies. In no time, we had a party going on our balcony with several bottles of drink which we had bought along the way.

Unfortunately, during the night the old lady in the next room, one of the party, became ill and had to go to hospital, and the tour went on without her and her husband. Apparently, the Cosmos tour company arranged for them to do the rest of the trip in a private car as soon as she was able. We told them we would send them copies of our photographs, and this we did, but it took us 2 years before we got around to it. We have talked to them several times on the phone since. They live in Leeds, England.

Taormina was an extremely attractive little resort.

That evening we went to dinner with a show to follow, and we had an excellent time.

The next day we went to see Mount Etna, which is an occasionally active volcano. It is over 11,000 feet high compared to Vesuvius at less than 5000 feet. It sits on a comparatively level plain, which makes it seem higher.

We could see Etna from maybe 100 or more miles away. It filled the horizon for most of the morning. The bus drove halfway up until it got too steep, then we transferred to strange small buses that were perched way up on big wheels and tractor tires. These vehicles took us up to about 500 feet from the summit, from where there was a considerable amount of smoke issuing.

To go further up, you had to go with a guide, and Muriel wanted to do this while I sat in the little store in the warm.

About 15 people went off for the walk to the top, and I saw them winding up the slope until they disappeared over the ridge. They were out of sight for at least 2 minutes when there was an explosion, and the ground shook. A big cloud of smoke gushed from the top of the mountain. Within a few seconds, we saw heads showing above the ridge, and the party tumbled into sight and rushed headlong down toward us at the store.

We resumed our bus ride continuing westward toward Palermo, and again Etna took hours to recede from view. We stayed overnight in Palermo, with the warning to not leave the hotel as

Palermo was too dangerous. However, we went out for a walk in the town. The next day, we boarded a large ocean-going ferry for an overnight trip back to Naples.

The conditions on the ferry were very primitive. The toilets were disgustingly dirty and messy, and the sleeping accommodations called for 4 to a cabin. We opted for sharing with an English couple who seemed wholesome. They were from Devon and named Allen and Margaret. We still correspond with them to this day.

At the docks in Naples, we somehow managed to get off the ferry a long time before the rest of our group, and we sat on a bollard awaiting them. Muriel had on her fat gold necklace, (bought in Florence on a previous trip), and there was a man, the only other person within 100 feet, standing and watching us. He came over to us and said in English, "Put that necklace away, you're not safe".

As we sat there, we were watching some mysterious goings-on. It was a massive area of open space with cars and buses in the distance. Suddenly something must have triggered activity, as a small car, full of people careened off at top speed, and several other cars screamed off after it. It looked like it was a police chase.

From Naples, we returned to the hotel that we'd stayed at before in Sorrento and had a party on the roof with some of the other people from the tour.

The next day we toured Rome and visited the Colosseum, then on to The Vatican. Although the architecture was awesome, I was most impressed by the paintings on the ceilings and walls. However, it should be seen, to be appreciated as it defies description in a way that conveys any sort of impression of its grandeur.

The next day we returned to England and then home to San Diego.

Our next trip was a cruise out of Miami, to Cartagena, Columbia, and through the Panama Canal, stopping in Costa Rica, and at Acapulco, and Manzanilla in Mexico. Halfway through the Panama Canal, we experienced a most spectacular thunderstorm with teeming rain. We should have stopped at Porta Vallarta, but one of the ship's 3 engines failed, and we had a reduced speed and so we ran out of time. However, we had $100 each in compensation.

This trip started with a flight from Los Angeles, and after arriving in Miami, we were taken to a hotel on the outskirts. It was a very expensive-looking place, and this was reflected in the cost of the meals. We had a nice dinner but when the bill came the waiter had added a 17% tip. I gave them a bad time about that and complained to the manager, and he muttered something about, "Are they still doing that", and made some excuse to quickly leave the area. However, we found a small bakery/café a few yards away and ate all of our meals there for the rest of our time in that hotel.

There was a very unfortunate occurrence that first evening as we were walking around the hotel, trying to find the restaurant. We were walking in bright sunshine and saw a door into the restaurant, and entered. It was very dark, and just inside the door were 3 steps down. Joy was in front, and couldn't see the steps and went flying, knocking over a sign in the process. Everybody looked up, including the waiters, but nobody came to help. Luckily she was unhurt. There was some illumination of the steps, a strip of tiny lights, but in the inside corner of each step, not on the edge, and not seen from an approach from the top. This was another thing I complained about to the manager.

We booked our next adventure. On the day appointed we flew from Los Angeles to Tahiti, a long trip to the other side of the equator. We were met at the airport, and transported for two nights, to a very nice hotel right on the beach, with a large swimming pool, and tropical gardens with palm trees all around. However, the hotel was some distance from the town.

Our room overlooked all this, and in the distance, we could see the mountains of the next island, Morea. Quite quickly we learned that it was very expensive like all French places. A hamburger in the restaurant was $15. Dinner was about $35 each.

Soon after arriving, we got into conversation with a young couple who had been there for almost a week, and they told us that they bought food at a store along the road about a mile, and didn't use the restaurant, so Muriel walked there and bought French bread, cheese, tins of pate, wine, fruit and several other items, and we ate quite well for a reasonable price.

Being a French island, there were the usual things we associate with the French. The hotel staff were quite rude, and at the swimming pool, the women went topless.

We did a bus tour of the perimeter of the island and it was a mixture of beautiful beaches, fancy resorts, and squalor in places. It had quite a large population.

It was time to get on the ship, and overnight we sailed to the next Island, Morea, just 15 miles away. We anchored in a bay with rocks sticking out of the water nearer the shore, then went ashore by tender to a small concrete landing stage. At the dock, we had to run the gauntlet of a line of stalls selling tourist items and individuals with all sorts of wares. We toured the island in a bus that, unknown to us, was a cut above buses we would see on other islands.

Morea was really beautiful, with mountains covered with tropical vegetation, and palm trees lining the beaches. The beaches were typical of the idea that everybody has of tropical island beaches, with no people, only waving palms, white sand, gentle waves, and blue skies. There were few people, but occasionally there was a clearing, with a few sheep, and an occasional cow. The guide told us that "South Pacific", was filmed in Morea.

We drove around the island, and up a narrow winding road to a high point, then to the only thing that passed for a town, one hotel, a couple of stores, and a few houses. We all went into the hotel to use the toilet and paid a visit to the gift store.

Our next stop was Bora Bora. The countryside was similar to Morea but less mountainous, but the tour bus was really an experience. It was built on a long flatbed truck out of 2x4's and ½" plywood. It had a roof but a wooden rail only for the sides. The seats were so small with minimal knee room that we overlapped into the central aisle. And it was the ultimate in a bumpy ride over very poor roads.

At one stop, I remember seeing some very large ants scurrying around. Other than that I don't remember anything outstanding about Bora Bora.

The next island was Christmas Island, 3 days sail away in the middle of the Pacific. We crossed the equator on the way and had a celebration with the crew putting on a show with dressing-up, paint and wigs, and general clowning around.

Christmas Island, not to be confused with the larger Christmas Island in the Indian Ocean, is an atoll, and at its highest point, it is about 5 feet above the sea level. It is surrounded by a coral reef on which the waves break, leaving a calm sea at the island beaches.

We went ashore by tender to land at a small pier, with just room for one tender at a time. The pier was built in the Second World War by the American Navy. There was a small rusty wrecked boat off to one side of the pier.

There was a clear sandy area by the pier, about 40 yards square, with some tables spread out under a tarpaulin. The tables had island handi-craft items for sale, except for one table, which was the post office. Yes, you could buy postcards and stamps and leave them for the weekly mail boat. We have the postcards we sent to our children to prove it.

The island had no stores, no hotel, no electricity, very little water, and no toilets. The only buildings were grass huts all around the bay, interspersed with coconut palms. The population appeared to be considerably less than a hundred people, and they were all at the dock. There was a group doing their dances, and then there were some children doing their little dances also. We spent 30 minutes looking along the beach for sea shells, with some of the children trying to sell shells which they had obviously found previously. This was one place where I would not want to be stuck. The smallest tidal wave would wash the place away.

Now we were bound for the Hawaiian Islands which were 2 days sail away.

We visited Hawaii, Oahu, Kauai, and Kona. On one of the islands, can't remember which, but we think it might be Oahu, we bought Muriel an amethyst pendant. On another island, we bought matching amethyst earrings.

We did bus tours on 3 of the islands, but they are mostly a blur now as they all seemed similar, except, we did visit the extinct volcano (Diamond Head).

We left the ship at Honolulu, and moved into a hotel at Waikiki for two days, just across a quiet street from the beach. We could cross the road, and use the beach of a hotel. They had chairs, a bar, and music, all on the beach, and we had a good time. The weather was perfect, but too soon we had to catch a plane home.

It was April of 2000, and we were off to England again. After a few days, we left for an arranged trip to Cyprus and a cruise to Israel and Egypt. We went with Muriel's sister Susan and Susan's friend, Inge.

We flew into Limassol, the capital of the Greek (southern) part of Cyprus. For those who don't know, the island of Cyprus is partitioned into two separate parts, under Greek and Turkish influence. Cyprus was a British possession and a major military outpost for British interests in the Mediterranean until after the Second World War.

I remember when I was young, following the time when British possessions were being given independence, there was a Greek priest named Archbishop Makarios who was a real trouble-maker, and started it all. There were all sorts of fighting between the Greek and Turkish Cypriots. I have a vague recollection that finally the British government stepped in and arranged the partition between the two factions.

We were warned to not venture across the border as we would be arrested. It would not be difficult to cross into the Turkish part as the streets ran into each other in Limassol, with no barriers. We went to the top of the Woolworth building, right on the border, and could see extensively into the Turkish part, and it was run down, with empty buildings and neglected streets. We could even see trees growing through some buildings.

On arrival in Cyprus, we were taken to a lovely hotel on the beach, on a tour bus. The guide took reservations for bus tours around the island for the next two days.

The next morning we were told that there was no room for us on the bus, so we would have to follow the tour bus in a taxi, which is what we did. The bus was so slow, and the people took so long to get off and on the bus that we decided to go on ahead as we had the itinerary, and the driver knew the attractions. We saw much more than the bus did that day.

During the day, we discussed with the driver the next days' itinerary, and he could do it cheaper, so we cancelled the next days' booking and had the taxi driver come back.

Would you believe it, we arranged for the taxi to meet us at the next hotel up the road so that the guide would not see him pick us up, and as he drove in, so did the tour guide.

Anyway, we had a marvelous day, and at one point, leaving the sunny, warm lowland to go up into the mountains and play in the snow! We saw some enchanting villages, with some very interesting little souvenir stalls. We saw much more of the island than did the bus passengers and finished up the day having the driver join us for dinner. He was born in London and spoke with a Cockney accent.

The next day we went to the docks to join our cruise boat to Israel. It was not a top-notch ship, and the accommodation was cramped and sleazy. However, the food was reasonably good. We had to bear in mind that it was a cheap trip. Muriel will always remember that the toilet was in the same cubicle as the shower, and the shower drain was in the middle of the floor. However, the shower water was slow to run away, and as the boat rocked, the slow-draining water slopped from end to end, making our feet wet when we used the toilet. But this was a small annoyance. Susan, who suffers from claustrophobia, had to keep her cabin door open to stay calm, so these are just some of the things which make trips memorable.

We arrived at Haifa, Israel, and I was surprised at the size of the docks, and the apparent volume of traffic through the docks. There were large freighters and hundreds of trucks.

We boarded the tour bus early, and drove miles and miles until we reached Bethlehem, and we stopped at a diamond jewelry store. This is one aspect of tours that annoys me. Apparently, tour guides are paid by business owners to stop at their stores, because we have been taken to carpet stores in Turkey, to a souvenir store in the middle of Munich, to leather and fur shops in the middle of the Italian Alps, and linen stores in the middle of the mountains in Cyprus. These places were out of the way and of little interest to tourists.

We went on to a large church in Bethlehem which, we were told, if my memory serves me right, encompassed the very spot where Jesus was born. (Some years later, this was the church in which hundreds of Palestinian militants were holed up, defying the Israeli army for several weeks).

We went on to Jerusalem and retraced the route of the cross, The Via De La Rosa, and went to the wailing wall, then on to the Garden of Gethsemane.

Our Jewish guide for this part of the trip told us that the original ground level of Biblical times was 100 feet below the present-day level, so you don't know quite what to believe when they tell you, "This is the spot etc."

The Garden of Gethsemane was the one place where we both felt something special. The Mount of Olives was above us. The olive trees of the garden were gnarled and ancient, some were there in the time of Jesus. This was the one place with "presence", and left a lasting feeling with us.

It is interesting to note that the Via De La Rosa, the Wailing Wall, and the Garden of Gethsemane are all within easy walking distance, and the Mount of Olives is really only a 700-foot-high hill on the side of which is the Garden of Gethsemane.

I remember that down the road from Gethsemane, there was a camel sitting at the side of the road, and the smell from it was overwhelming from 50 feet away. Another thing I remember was that on the bus, there was a speech by the little Jewish tour guide to the effect that we should all buy diamonds while in Israel, to help Israel. Seemed rather a strange speech in the circumstances. Now we were going back to the ship for we were due in Egypt the next day.

It was the next day, and we were now docked at Alexandria, Egypt.

The bus pulled up alongside the ship, and we were off to see Cairo and the Pyramids etc. However, not so fast. We had to wait for an armed police guard, and there it was, a tiny pick-up truck with 5 heavily armed guards sitting in the back. Then we noticed there was another similar truck behind the bus, and off we went, in convoy. We were now out in the countryside. There was more agriculture than I expected, with plenty of water, probably from the Nile, and then we crossed the Nile on this huge bridge over a river that must have been a ½ mile wide.

Cairo was a sprawling area, with mile after mile of 3 and 4-storey concrete buildings on each side of our raised highway. We were told they were apartments.

Suddenly we could see Pyramids in the distance. Soon we were there, and getting out of the bus. There were a few armed guards and a lot of peddlers walking around pestering the tourists. Also, there were camels and riders posing for photographs. The armed guards were occasionally shooing some over-aggressive peddlers away, but we saw one lady running from a peddler who was chasing her, and Muriel screamed for me to rescue her, and I hurried toward them, and he saw me coming and backed off.

We were told to not try to photograph the camels as the owners expected to be paid. So what did Susan go and do? She thought she could sneak a photograph and get away with it, but alas she was caught and we saw her running and being chased by a camel and rider. It looked really funny. Muriel screamed at me again to go and rescue her and as I hurried towards her, the camel rider appeared to give up. We don't know if Susan paid him or not.

The Pyramids were about what I expected, but the stones that were used were much larger than I'd anticipated, and much rougher. Also, instead of the Pyramids being out in the desert, they were on the edge of the town with buildings within about 150 yards.

After the Pyramids, we went to see the Sphynx. I found it smaller than expected. Then we went to the Cairo Museum and saw all the mummies and statues and all that old stuff that sends people into orbit but bores me to tears.

We headed back to the ship, destined for Cyprus again. We had two more days at the same hotel in Cyprus before flying back to England. We had one arranged dinner at a restaurant in the town. It was a typical Cypriot meal, and very interesting.

It was the middle of June and we were going to Florida in time for my mother's 97th birthday, but we were making a detour to spend a few days staying with Ruth in New Berne in North Carolina. Ruth and her friend Alice were our table partners on the trip through the Panama Canal and were living in New York at the time. However, Ruth retired and bought a lovely house in New Berne. She had invited us to stay for a few days.

We flew to Atlanta and we were scheduled to catch a hedge hopper plane to Raleigh where we had a rented car awaiting us. The hedge-hopper was at the next gate to the one at which we arrived, but they had no luggage exchange agreement, so we had to run 300 yards to an airport train, travel through 5 stops, walk 300 yards, get the bags, and return the way we came. We had 55 minutes to do this and arrived back at the hedge-hopper plane as they were closing the doors. We just made it. After that, we had 200 miles to drive, and it was about 9.30 pm. Also, there weren't any freeways, just good regular roads.

We found Ruth's house, in the middle of a golf course, and she was still up at 1.00 am, looking out of the window. Actually, we had to drive in a loop around part of the golf course, and she could see the car headlights from miles away. She knew it was us as there were no cars around in the area at all at that time of night. It is a country area with very few people.

The area was very flat, and green. Ruth's house was new, and at the end of her garden was a small lake with a line of trees on the far side.

We bought a small wooden table/chest for Ruth as a gift. She told us it was something she wanted. I assembled it for her. It took me 2 hours and it was a really tough job. As the house was new Ruth had little furniture, so she was very pleased with the chest.

We had a good time with Ruth and played scrabble which Ruth enjoyed but normally didn't have anybody with which to play. We went out on the nearby ocean sailing around some of the nearby islands and she thoroughly enjoyed our visit as did we.

Then it was time to start our trip to Florida. We really moved along and made it to Savannah, Georgia at about 3.30 pm. We had not stopped for lunch, so went to the Denny's right next door to the hotel, where we had a bowl of soup and a salad, with the plan to return for an early dinner. Then we drove off to see Savannah, but drove around and couldn't see anything of any great interest, so drove back and went to Denny's.

We were waiting to be seated when an old lady grabbed my arm. She cackled a bit as she said, "It's no good waiting here, you'll never get any food". The restaurant was quite empty. It was early for dinner and we didn't know what she was talking about.

We were seated and after about 10 minutes we had only seen one waiter hovering around. We were approached by the same lady that we had seen on our earlier visit. She was the manager. She told us that we would have a long wait as the cook and a waiter had got into a knife fight. They had both been taken to hospital, and some other staff were sick, so they were extremely short-handed.

We explained that we were staying next door and had the whole evening available. The food was poor with things missing from the advertised meals, but we didn't mind, in fact, we had a good laugh about it.

The next day we drove the rest of the way to Altamonte Springs, which is about 10 miles north of Orlando, central Florida. My mother was in a nursing home and my sister Daphne also lives in the area. We stopped for lunch in Daytona Beach and drove around a bit for Muriel to sight-see. I've been there several times.

On the way, a few miles north of Altamonte Springs, we ran into a very serious thunderstorm with rain and hail that caused all traffic to come to a complete stop on the freeway. It was the heaviest downpour that I've ever experienced.

My mother was in fine shape for a 97-year-old. Her memory of current things is not too good but she remembers perfectly, the things that happened years ago. Daphne had a party at her house for Mother, and several old friends attended.

It was pre-arranged that we would travel south after the party, and visit with my sister Brenda, who lives in Palm Beach Shores. Then we went on south to the Florida Keys and stayed overnight at Key West. We went back to Altamonte Springs to see my mother before our return trip to California.

It was early August, and it was about now that we learned that 12 of Muriel's relatives were planning to come from England, to stay for 3 weeks at Christmas. We owned three cars at that time, one of which was getting old but still running well, but car sales were on. We decided to take advantage of the cheap prices available on the internet, and we bought a Chevrolet Impala for a very good price. It was delivered the day before we left on the following trip. Now we had enough cars to go around.

It was still August, and we went to England for Muriel's niece, Karen's, wedding. Karen is the eldest daughter of Muriel's sister Pamela and her husband Norman.

All the family members were there, and it was a lovely wedding. The next day we went on a tour of Ireland, flying out of Bristol, near Bath. We took Muriel's sister Susan with us.

One thing we remember was the tight security at the airports, especially going into Ireland. We were photographed and our baggage was x-rayed. This was soon after the Catholic and Protestant troubles.

We arrived at Dublin airport and were met by a bus, and driver/tour guide named David. The tour was by a company called Wallace Arnold. Susan and Muriel got to sit in the front seat and I got to sit behind them.

A thing that struck me after a couple of hours was the regularity of the Guinness signs. It seems to me they were placed every 20 feet or so in the towns.

Some of the highlights were the visit to the castle which houses the Blarney Stone, also the nearby quaint little village. Close by was a large lake on which we spent several hours on a large passenger boat. I believe the lake was in Killarney. Following that we rented a horse and buggy with the driver, and toured the wild country park nearby. We visited the Cliffs Of Maher, some sheer cliffs rising hundreds of feet out of the Atlantic. On the way there we passed a medieval castle, partly in ruins. The Ring of Kerry was one of the best and most scenic parts, in the southwest corner. We saw beautiful bays, coastline, green fields, and cottages etc.

One of the saddest parts of the trip was Londonderry. There were houses with pictures painted on them, depicting scenes from the "troubles" as they call it. They were scenes depicting heroic and sad events in the fighting between Catholics, Protestants, Irish Republican Army, and the peacekeeping British army.

Another sad item was a statue of a little boy banging on the door of an orphanage. This was commemorating the Irish famine when the potato harvest failed, and thousands died of hunger. It was said that orphanages had to turn away orphaned children as there would not have been enough food to save the ones already inside.

Generally, I was not impressed by Ireland, it was OK, but no different from England. Since they joined the European Common Market, European money has poured in, and it seems that the country has been modernized. We expected to see peasants, and some primitive housing, but we saw none of that. What we did notice was that the place is full of Public Houses, which are full of people drinking draft Guinness.

We had a couple of days in the Killarney area and found some interesting stores in the town. We also found a short street with 47 Pubs, all in a row. At night they all played loud music, with people spilling out into the street.

We were due to arrive back in Bristol at about 7.15 pm Saturday night. I was worried that the Hertz office might not be open, so I went into the Hertz office in Killarney, and they assured me that it would be. I had also asked this at the time of booking in the US and was assured they'd be open.

Our trip was soon over, and we landed in Bristol, got our baggage, and walked to the Hertz office to find it closed. We were 19 miles from Bath where we had to go. In the same area were 4 other car rental companies, all open, but without any available cars.

I was able to reach the Hertz counter, and use their phone and spent an hour phoning every Hertz main office for which I could find a phone number but nobody could or would help. Eventually, somehow I got connected to an office in Ireland and for once somebody was able to make a decision. I was told to get a taxi and I gave them Susan's phone number (where we were staying) so that they could contact me regarding a pick-up of a car. They were to pay for all expenses.

The next day, I received a phone call to say that if I went back to the Hertz office in Bristol Airport, there would be somebody to give me a car. I got Susan's daughter, Julie, to drive me there, and got the car.

I wrote a letter of complaint to the European head office and got no reply in several weeks, so wrote one to the US head office. Eventually, I got the expenses paid by both offices and each one sent me a voucher for use in future Hertz rentals.

It worked out OK, but I think in the future we will use Budget.

It was October and our biggest trip was almost upon us. On the 15th of the month, we caught a plane for Auckland, New Zealand, and after flying all night we landed in Auckland, up near the top of the north island. We transferred to a smaller plane to fly south heading for the bottom end of the south island.

As we took off from Auckland we could see the bays, inlets, and islands off the coast, then we were heading for Christchurch, which is on the east coast of the south island. We waited there while passengers got off, and new ones got on, and we were off to what I feel was the best part of the trip. The next stop was the southernmost town of any size in New Zealand, Queenstown, where we had a small motor home booked. On the way, we flew parallel to the incredibly beautiful mountains that stretch north and south for 300 miles, on the western half of the south island. The highest mountain is Mount Cook. I believe it is about 13,000 feet high, but the whole range is extremely high and snow-covered. This accounts for the dozens of rivers that rush toward the sea.

We approached the Queenstown airport with snow-covered mountains (The Remarkables) towering above the plane on each side and landed in an area that seemed just like Switzerland. It was cold, about 40 degrees, with a partly cloudy sky.

The southern end of New Zealand is frightening near Antarctica, and we were here at the end of their winter, or equivalent to our April. Apparently, they had received the heaviest snowfall of the winter the day before. There was no snow in the town, but halfway up the surrounding mountains, it was glistening white.

We went into the Queenstown airport building which was no more than 60 feet by 40 feet, just big enough for rental car counters and a couple of small stores. I found the "Maui" motor-home rental counter, and Muriel went into the jewelry/gift shop. I went looking for her when the rental paperwork was being completed and found her with a beautiful fire opal pendant.

The New Zealand dollar cost us 42 US cents, so everything was quite cheap for us, and this was the rationalization she used, so we bought a fire opal pendant.

The motor home was described as small, and small it was, but it was cheap and adequate. It cost us about $30 per day and did about 25 miles to the gallon. Gasoline was quite expensive but with the favorable exchange rate, it was better, but still higher than the USA. In New Zealand, they drive on the left side of the road, the same as in England, and with this and the strange vehicle and in a strange city, it took me a little while to adjust.

The first thing we did was to find a supermarket to stock up on food. From the parking lot, which was in a wide open area, we could see all around, and the scenery was spectacular.

The rental people gave us a map to find a campsite for the night, and we drove around and found it close by the side of the large lake bordering Queenstown. We settled in for the night after filling the water tank. We slept very well even though our internal clocks were all out of whack.

The next morning we checked out of the campsite and went to the local cable car station that took us to the top of a mountain that was towering over the center of Queenstown. We were the first of the day and enjoyed the view all to ourselves. We went to the cafeteria for some hot chocolate as we were feeling the cold at the altitude, and they were not ready yet, so we sat and warmed up looking at the view until they were ready.

The view from the verandah was of snow-covered mountains, with the lake winding around the valleys. We cannot understand why this area is not much better known for its scenery.

We left Queenstown mid-morning to make our way in a northwesterly direction. This would take us to the road that runs on the west side of the mountains, close to the west coast.

It was amazing. We saw 2 or 3 cars per hour, and the scenery was spectacular, with mountains, rivers, and lakes, plus an occasional glimpse of the ocean. But, there were very few signs of habitation. Where there was grass, it was the strongest, brightest green we'd ever seen, and, it grows on vertical banks.

The vegetation was very different. There were very few trees and shrubs that we recognized, and the birds were all new to us. And guess what, the sun traveled the opposite way. We were in the southern hemisphere.

Campsites abounded, even though there weren't any people around. Apparently, we'd picked a good time to go. However as we worked our way north, we saw more and more people, and then we started to pass through small towns.

The first town was Franz Josef, which bears the name of the nearby glacier, which we went to see. Apparently, it is very famous, but we couldn't believe it. It was only about 70 feet wide, very small by the standards of glaciers we saw in Alaska. However, an enormous amount of water gushed from it causing a very turbulent river thundering along at probably 20 miles per hour.

We were approaching a wide bridge, and I saw a car ahead come to a stop on the far side of the bridge. I slowed down, and as we got to the bridge, we glanced around, and to the right, from where the water was coming, was a wide valley with the most magnificent view of Mount Cook, filling the horizon from left to right. We were no more than 5 miles from it. The mountain was completely white with no bare rock showing, it was a most imposing sight.

A short time later we came around a bend, dropping into a valley and there it was again from a different angle, only it was a bit further away this time. We could see a large part of the associated range.

Some other sights we saw on the way were the Pancake Rocks, a strange rock formation by the ocean where the cliffs looked like they were made from pancakes piled up in neat stacks. We also stopped at a historic village with old shops and other buildings which were preserved, with an old steam train taking visitors for rides into the dense undergrowth. On this train trip, we saw what we all took to be a kiwi, but it was some other flightless bird which is very similar in appearance. Apparently, kiwis only move around at night.

Gradually the mountains petered out, and we were at the northwest corner of the south island. It was a medium size town by the ocean, by a large circular bay, and it was Sunday morning. We passed a small church, then decided we would go back and see if there was a service soon. One was starting almost immediately. They made us very welcome, and we had a nice chat with everybody with a cup of strong tea afterward. We were making for Nelson to stay overnight, then we were due in Picton, about 30 miles from Nelson, to catch the ferry to the north island, landing in Wellington, the capital city.

In Nelson, we found what seemed to be a nice campsite on the edge of town, but in the late afternoon, dozens of people and motorbikes were in close proximity, revving their engines and whizzing up and down. However, they moved out in the evening. The next morning we left for Picton where we were booked on an afternoon ferry to the north island.

In order to be on time, and not knowing the roads and the ferry area, we arrived 2 hours early and took the chance to drive around the bay, which was surrounded by hills. It was beautiful, and from the hilltop we watched the ferries coming and going below us.

It was time to get on the ferry, and we got in line. We drove onto the boat, and the vehicle was chained down to the deck. It was about a one-hour trip on the ferry, and we were being met by Giff, Muriel's cousin, when we reached Wellington.

The trip was nice with the scenery when we were coming out of Picton, and then it was time to get back into the motor home and drive off the ferry.

We had to watch out for Giff, and there he was waiting on a little island in the main road. We stopped, holding up traffic, and he jumped in saying he couldn't find parking close in, so we drove to his car and then followed him to his house.

The motor home just fitted into his parking area in front of his garage, and we removed our luggage and stayed in the house for two days. It was nice to have a bit more room.

While we were in Wellington, Giff and his wife Pip, took us around showing us the sights. It is in a beautiful area, and like Auckland, surrounded by ocean, with bays and islands and channels. We went to the top of a hill in the center of a promontory sticking out into the ocean, and we could see all around, including the ferries coming and going.

At the very highest part was a huge tower with a windmill and generator on the top. The wind was steady and constant, an excellent place for a wind generator.

(Special note. I have played a harmonica since I was 12 years old. Some months before this trip, a friend's wife called me to say that their children had ruined their father's harmonica, and she wanted me to tell her what sort of replacement instrument to buy as his birthday was approaching. I gave her the information, and then, because she seemed in doubt, I suggested that I go and buy it and take it to her, which is what happened. It cost $196.

When I got home with it, Joy asked me why I didn't get one for myself, but I felt that the price was too high. She seemed disappointed).

In Wellington, being very conscious of the favorable exchange rate, I had a brilliant thought. I called a music store and asked if they had the harmonica that I wanted. They said, "No, but we can get one". I pointed out that I was leaving the next day and couldn't wait, but they told me they could get it by that afternoon. The price was $170, and I asked, "Is that New Zealand $'s"? They told me it was. The real price to me was $70 US. I said I would like one.

The salesman advised me that he could also get me the professional harmonica for $400 if I preferred it. I didn't even know there was such a thing, and declined. I told Muriel the story, and she insisted I get the professional model, so I called back, and then the salesman told me he had given me a wrong price, the basic model was $140 not $170. The cost to me was US$59. I told him I would like the professional model. The cost to me was equivalent to $168 US. I picked it up that afternoon.

It is a beautiful instrument with a very mellow sound. I often wondered why my harmonicas always sounded a bit tinny compared to the professional sound, and now I know.

It soon came time to leave Wellington, and we drove north. We had 4 days to drive the approximate 300 miles to Auckland where we were going to stay with Muriel's cousin Anne and husband Howard. We drove fast, and the roads were quite good with no scenery, and little traffic. After about 200 miles we came to Lake Taupo, where Giff and Pip have a lakeside house. It was about midday, and we stopped and had lunch and a good look at the large lake. Then we found that there was a river running out of it through a narrow gorge, and we went to see that. It was incredibly wild, even a bit scary with the speed and the volume of water moving along it. You could hear the thunder of the water from a hundred yards away.

It was getting late in the afternoon, and we were looking for a campsite, and we saw a sign, and followed the directions along a river bank to where the road ended. No campsite. We returned to the main road and asked for directions, and we were sent off in another direction. After about 10 miles we gave up on that and returned to the main road again and continued northwards.

Now it was getting dark, and we were almost in Auckland, and still no campsite.

The road was now a freeway. We came to the off-ramp for Anne's house and we took it for want of some alternative. We were lost and it seemed we were in the Indian quarter as everybody was wearing a turban or a white scarf over the head.

We stopped at a gas station and convenience store to see if they knew the way, and after the manager and several customers had put their two cents in, and a call to Anne, we had some idea of which way to go. However, we were amazed that Anne and Howard really didn't know their way around their own area.

Anne had this large wild dog that would go for strangers. Joy is terrified of dogs, but they didn't seem too concerned about it. They let it come into the house and Howard held on to it when we were around which was not too comforting because he started drinking in the morning and was a bit far gone by lunchtime.

Anne did her best to make us welcome and comfortable. They had a spare bedroom with a queen size bed, which was extremely nice.

On our first full day, we went off in the motor home for sightseeing around the area. Howard stayed at home, and Anne directed us. Again we were amazed at the little knowledge she had of the way around the area. Apparently, they never went anywhere. They just stayed home every day, except Anne went to work one day a week, otherwise, they were both retired.

On the second day, all 4 of us in the motor-home, went to visit Anne's youngest son who had just bought a house and was about to start work on fixing it up. He was very pleasant and obviously a hard worker.

We decided we would buy fish and chips for lunch that day, and we found a fish and chip shop run by some Chinese people. There was a bit of confusion in the store and Howard started yelling at the man behind the counter, and caused quite a scene. He was quite unjustified and really showed himself for what he is, unfortunately.

That evening we (all four of us) arranged to meet both sons and the wife of the eldest son, for dinner. The eldest son and his wife were a delightful couple. We had a good time. Apparently, you can take your own drinks, wine, beer, etc. to certain restaurants in New Zealand, and the eldest son brought a wide choice.

On the appointed day, at the appointed hour, Muriel and I drove to the Maui motor-home facility near Auckland airport and turned in our home of the past 10 days. Then we caught the shuttle which carried us into downtown Auckland. At one minute to 10.00 am, we arrived at a large hotel, and at the counter, I asked for the Cosmos tour guide. As I spoke to one clerk, the tour guide was standing right beside me at the counter, asking another clerk if they had any information about us.

We were joining up with a 5 week Cosmos tour of the Orient and everybody else had just arrived in New Zealand from the US. We had been told to meet at 10.00 am, and we were right on time. God has always looked after us and our arrangements, no matter how complicated, they always seem to work out perfectly.

From Auckland, the tour went by bus to Rotorua, a town on the north island where there are geysers and other manifestations of volcanic activity.

The scenery in the north island is not too inspiring, with mile after mile of flat land with bright green grass, and some trees. There are millions of sheep and some cows, but we didn't see much evidence of growing grains, fruit, or vegetables, but it was their springtime, maybe too early.

When we reached Rotorua, there was an overwhelming smell of Sulphur. Our hotel was 200 yards from the small park with the most geyser activity, and we could see all the action as we were high up, looking down on the steaming pots, etc.

The next day we went to this park which is on Maori land and had a closer look. The river which ran through it was also steaming. The guides in the park were Maori.

Next, we visited a Maori village and saw their meeting house, all painted inside with stripes, wood carvings and other decorations. There were demonstrations of how they prepared their materials for grass skirts and other items they manufactured.

The next stop was a weird place where we were introduced to New Zealand's largest industry, sheep farming. They had examples of every breed of sheep, then they sheared a sheep for us, and we saw a bunch of baby sheep. All of this was followed by an introduction to a New Zealand cow, all taking place on a stage at the front of the building.

Members of the audience were invited to go on-stage and milk the cow, but in the middle of this the cow decided to get its own back by creating an emergency need for a bucket to be rushed to its back end.

That evening we were entertained by a group of Maoris doing their dancing and grunting and pulling faces as was their way of scaring the neighbors, years ago. Then we were fed dinner consisting of typical Maori food which wasn't bad.

The next day we got on a plane and flew to . . . . You'll never guess. . . . Well OK, you guessed, Queenstown again, right at the bottom of the south island. Nothing much had changed in the 10 days we'd been away. The weather was a bit warmer, and the snow on the mountains was slightly less, but otherwise, about the same.

However, this time we were in a hotel by the lake with a view of the "Remarkables" mountain range.

The first morning everybody except us, went to the cable car to the top of the mountain while we got to prowl around the town. It was a very nice place for tourists, with the type of stores that Muriel loves, with postcards, souvenirs and jewelry, etc. We had lunch in a rowdy sort of hamburger place, but the food was good.

After Queenstown, we went by bus in a southerly direction for 70 miles, then west for 70 miles, then north for 70 miles then west for another 50 miles. In a straight line from Queenstown, our destination was about 130 miles away, but there was no direct road, so we had to do the roundabout trip of 260 miles. Our destination was Milford Sound, supposedly one of the great beauty spots in New Zealand and, in fact, the whole world.

We boarded a boat, and were issued with a packed lunch, and a drink, and off we went down the fjord to the sea.

I was more fascinated by the airplanes that were flying sightseers along the south side of the fjord. They were taking off about every 10 minutes, and the engines were making a terrible noise like they were overloaded and barely making it. It took them ages to climb up to about 1000 feet to clear the cliffs which rose up out of the water on each side of the fjord.

We saw waterfalls, seals, and sheer cliffs, and there was an island with a sheer-sided mountain on it. However, the road trip over the last 15 miles to Milford Sound was through some of the most spectacular snow-covered mountains I have ever seen, and we have seen some spectacular mountains. The only other place which had mountains that were close in majesty was at a stop we made in Austria, some years before, but those mountains there were farther away from us. The mountains near Milford Sound towered over us and were almost sheer from the valley in which we traveled. We returned to Queenstown that night.

The next day, we all got on the bus and left for a bus trip in a north-easterly direction across the plain to Christchurch. This was opposite to the direction we had taken in the motor home, and was all new to us.

We got to Christchurch in the late afternoon, and checked in to a hotel, then went off to dinner at a restaurant at a wild animal park, which was where we had arranged to meet Giff's daughter (Muriel's cousin), Jane. We last saw Jane when she came to America with her parents when she was 10 years old. Now she is married with one small daughter. Jane showed up right on time, and we found her to be a delightful lady. She joined us for dinner and toured the park with us, and she saw a kiwi for the first time ever. How's that for somebody who has lived in New Zealand all their life?

After dinner and the tour of the park, sadly, we said goodbye to Jane and went back to the hotel, and the next morning we were off to the airport for a flight to Australia.

We landed in Melbourne after a 3½ hour flight of about 1700 miles. By now I had ascertained that the tour guide was the ultimate "female libber", and overripe for teasing. Of course, I didn't miss an opportunity like that.

Our hotel was in the center of town. Melbourne was an average large city with no really outstanding features other than a few large churches. We went to one of them on the first full day there. It was Sunday. We walked in and found a nice seat, then we began to be surrounded by sailors. Apparently, it was some Navy memorial service, and we were sitting in the wrong seat, but there were no signs or cordons so we stayed put. There really were no special sights to see except on the main street there were two 150 feet towers about 50 feet apart, with a bungee-type cable or rope between the tops of the towers. They had a set of three seats and a rope attached to the middle of the bungee, and they pulled the seats down until they were at street level. Then passengers were strapped into the seats, and then the seats were released and flew up in the air, and turned over and bounced around for a couple of minutes. What fun if you are brave enough to try it.

The next stop was the magnificent city of Sydney, and what a beautiful city it is. It is spread around a bay with many inlets and islands, with the famous Sydney harbor bridge, and the opera house.

Our hotel was very nice, The Novus Hotel, right on the water overlooking Darling Harbor, which is one of the small arms off the main part of the bay. We were on about the 5th floor and a few floors below our level was an overhead light mono-rail which toured our part of the bay, and ran into the center of the town.

Across the harbor were the large buildings of the city, and a huge tower, at least a thousand feet high, with a restaurant at the top which rotated very slowly. Anchored below was an old steamer (boat) which was also a restaurant. While in Sydney we ate at both places, the steamer and the tower.

In the bus, we toured the whole of the Sydney area, and the Sydney Harbor in a passenger boat. Sydney is an exciting and beautiful place to visit as Melbourne was boring. Sydney is probably the most exciting and picturesque large town we have ever visited, and well worth a visit for anybody who goes to Australia.

Wouldn't you know it, our video camera went wrong, and rather than miss a record of our trip, we bought a new camera in a local store. It was the European format but better than nothing. It cost us $50 to get the tapes turned into the American format when we arrived home. We eventually sold this camera to Joy's nephew for $200 as they use the same format in England.

Along one side of Darling Harbor was a shopping mall, and we spent lots of time there. Muriel spotted a very nice amber pendant, set in silver, also some fake topaz earrings, which matched a real 69-carat topaz pendant Joy had at home. We had looked for real matching earrings but had not found any to date. (Special note: We have since had some real matching topaz earrings made).

In the mall, there was a memorable sign outside a liquor store. It was an advert for a beer company. It proclaimed they had been "helping ugly people have sex for 20 years".

After 3 ½ days in Sydney, we had seen all the main highlights, although we could have spent more time there from choice. And now our group boarded another plane for Cairns, Australia, a 3-hour flight northwards to just below the most northerly point of the east coast of Australia.

Cairns is a relatively small town with no special features except one. The Great Barrier Reef is just offshore, and we were going by boat to one of the many islands that dot the reef. There was another memorable thing at Cairns, it was extremely hot and humid. As you know, the north coast of Australia isn't too far from Malaysia and other tropical areas, and it felt like it too. This was the first of weeks of hot humid weather in store for us on this trip.

It must have been 95 degrees and 95% humidity out on Green Island on the reef. Luckily there was a swimming pool and plenty of shade trees. We went out in a glass-bottom boat and saw some assorted little colored fish, but we were a bit disappointed. As we came back toward the island, the guide threw some food on the water, and dozens and dozens of large fish appeared turning the water to froth around the boat.

The next day we all got on an old steam train and it huffed and puffed its way, for 3 hours, climbing up and up into a small town in the mountains. We traveled through a rainforest at the lower elevation, then it cooled down as we gained elevation. On the way, we saw rivers, waterfalls, and cataracts, plus views back over Cairns and the coastline.

The town was quaint, but mostly of stores for tourists. I bought my Australian Bushman's hat there, of which I am very proud. We saw our first Australian Aborigine there.

The return journey was something out of the ordinary. We got on some cable cars, 4 people per car, and we were off across the countryside for about 30 miles in a straight line, all the way back to Cairns. The support towers were on the high points of the land, and at times we were swinging many hundreds of feet above the trees. We crossed a small lake and saw a dam, then we were over the rainforest.

At the midpoint, we had to get off and line up to catch the next stage. At the midpoint station, there was a close view-point overlooking a waterfall which we had seen from the train.

The last ½ mile in the cable car was downhill into the edge of Cairns.

We boarded a plane in Cairns, stopping at Darwin and then we flew the last leg of the flight to the island of Bali. It was even more stifling hot and humid there.

The hotel was really strange. The main building, restaurants, lobby, desk, etc. was under a roof with only a small amount of support wall, being mostly wide open to the elements. The restaurants were at the end away from the road and overlooked the beach on which there was an occasional near-naked lady bather.

The rooms for this hotel were across the street. A crossing guard was on duty 24 hours a day and seemed to have life and death control over the traffic which stopped for us with a wave of his hand. To get to the rooms we walked between gardens and ponds and along open corridors.

Our room was conventional and clean except for the fact that the bathroom had an opening into the bedroom on one side, which came with a drop-down raffia drape.

We traveled over the island by bus. It is mostly agricultural, and green, with many religious shrines. Most houses had their own tiny shrine, and large shrines were to be seen all over the place. We stopped at one large Buddhist shrine, which was very old and surrounded by many historic monuments. Then we visited another place which was a plantation of some sort, and the trees were full of fruit bats, and monkeys. The bus was met by dozens of young oriental-looking ladies who tried to attach themselves to us and escort us as we walked between their stalls selling local handicrafts. Our group was heading for an area where the monkeys were supposedly the most active. The girls would not be turned off and my knees were aching, so I returned to the bus. From the bus, I saw the very best monkey activity in the parking area.

On the way back, it was early evening, and some of the bus passengers saw several of the locals strip-washing in the rivers and streams as we passed, which is some indication of how backward the island is. It certainly was more squalid than one would believe from the stories, and films like South Pacific.

Our next stop was Singapore. It was very modern and clean and our hotel was in a skyscraper. We were on the 16th floor. From our hotel window, we could see a few very old buildings with obvious Chinese influence, but it was mostly newly built buildings. Also, all over, there was evidence of British influence.

We went on an excursion to an island by cable car, followed by a trip around the island in a train on an elevated track. On this island, there were all sorts of attractions and things of interest. The first and most obvious was a 60-foot tall statue of a lion, said to be the guardian of the island. Then we saw colorful dragon statues outside the entrance to the museum which was entirely devoted to the Second World War, and the occupation by Japan.

While we were on the island, we had a most intense rainstorm with thunder. I remember how the rain poured down as we passed the beach area filled with palm trees and palm-thatched little shelters on four poles. The rain was a welcome cool period, but soon it was gone.

Our time in Singapore was over and we were off on another airplane to Bangkok, Thailand. Again, we were high up in a skyscraper hotel in the middle of the city.

On the first day we went for a trip on a riverboat, one of those long ones with an outboard motor with a 6-foot propeller shaft. They whizzed around leaving big wakes in the gray-brown water. We stopped at a market, but I stayed on the boat. Joy bought me a straw hat, but it was too big. (We gave it to her brother, Paul).

Later in the day, we went to one of the many canals which crisscross Bangkok, and boarded a small boat, with a long propeller shaft. It was just like a movie, with old ladies in canoes offering all sorts of food and other merchandise.

We stopped at a waterside market and I bought some silk shirts and a straw hat that fitted, and then we went on in our speedy boat and returned to the bus. That boat trip was a real experience as we passed hundreds of water-side homes, where people were doing laundry and washing dishes and their bodies, all in the gray-brown water. I just didn't want to ask what happened to sewage.

That evening our group went off on the river to have a typical Thai dinner with Thai dancers etc. It was OK, but it is not really my thing.

The next day we went to a sort of park where there was a show of Thai dancing, wrestling, and kickboxing, plus some funny antics and clowning. It was quite good, and something different. At the same place, most of our group had an elephant ride of about 30 yards. We didn't bother as you were hardly on before you had to get off, and also we had elephant rides at the Bristol Zoo in England, when we were kids.

That evening we went to a famous street market in the center of Bangkok. It was in a narrow street and jammed. You could hardly move for people. I had my wallet in a deep front trouser pocket and kept my hand on it. There was every conceivable thing on sale, and the prices were quite good, so I bought a couple of items. When we had seen enough, we rented a two-seater peddle taxi and were taken through the back streets to the hotel.

Our last day in Thailand was spent on a trip around the countryside where we stopped at a typical Thai family home out in the country. The garden had many trees like breadfruit, mangoes, and coconuts. Chickens were in and out of the house, and there was a pet snake. It was eye-opening to see the way they lived.

Surprise, surprise, we were off to the airport again on the way to Hong Kong. Only one more airplane to go to get home.

Again, we were housed in a very nice hotel right in the middle of the city. The first excursion was a bus trip up one of the surrounding mountains from where we had a great view of the bays and inlets, and the buildings on every bit of space, including the steep sides of the foothills.

Hong Kong is an area that compresses millions and millions of people into a tiny space. There are blocks and blocks of apartments as we have seen nowhere else. They are at least 20 floors high and ½ a mile long, and there are rows and rows of them

That evening, we boarded a ship for a dinner cruise around the bay. The first thing that strikes you about Hong Kong is the number of tall buildings. The ones around the bay appeared to be commercial buildings, and every one of them was lit up with commercial signs. I think that every company in the world of any size had a huge logo and their name in lights on one of the buildings. It truly was a sight worth seeing.

The next day we were off to Canton, China. We started on a bus that drove around the bay close to the water, and we saw several large bridges and islands. We stopped, then we got on a passenger ferry boat for a couple of hours and, voila, we were in China proper. If you have heard that there are lots of people in China, you have not heard half of it.

We had to go through the passport examination, along with a sea of oriental people, then walk to a bus, about a quarter of a mile away on a quiet little street. There were skinny little police or army men all over the place at the dock, and around outside.

Then there was a holdup and we sat on the bus for 20 minutes. I believe one of our party was lost or had a passport problem, but eventually, we were off, and a little way into the journey we were joined by a young Chinese girl who was the government guide.

We drove along a good quality road with traffic lights and modern vehicles, for a couple of hours. The buildings were all modern with a few skyscrapers in between. The impression was that we were in a medium-sized American town that was growing fast. Building was going on everywhere with only a very occasional patch of obviously cultivated land with a ramshackle wooden reed thatched building in the center. This was probably a leftover from the real China.

As the guide spoke with an almost continuous commentary, we gathered, from reading between the lines that the area between Hong Kong and Canton, through which we were traveling, was a show area. Apparently, young people who had an education were paid a premium wage to go there to live and work in an effort to modernize and industrialize the area. From what we could see it was working.

We had one stop at a Chinese equivalent of a supermarket. There were little children outside, begging, and inside it had two floors with wide stone steps, and it smelled like an old-time butcher's shop. The ground floor was where they sold the packaged items and cans, but we couldn't recognize most of the merchandise. Upstairs was the place to visit though. There were live creatures like chickens, eels, fish etc., plus what was to me, all sorts of unsavory meat items. It was interesting but not enjoyable by any means.

By the time we arrived in Canton, it was lunchtime, and we left the bus and walked along a street that was closed to vehicular traffic and the reason was obvious. Apparently, it was some sort of holiday, and there were thousands and thousands of people milling about, with no room to walk without virtually pushing your way through. We stopped at a restaurant and went upstairs to a room set aside for us. We all sat at round tables, 10 people per table, with a large turn table in the middle. There were probably 10 dishes put on the central turn-table, and we all helped ourselves. It was very good food even though we didn't recognize everything.

When we left the restaurant, we had to walk another 1/4 mile back to the bus, and I believe there were more people than ever, now. It really was a sea of people. We stood head and shoulders above everybody.

The next stop was a museum, with lots of copies of Chinese artifacts for sale, plus some jewelry, then we went to a zoo where we were driven through to a spot by the panda enclosure. This zoo was different in that you could drive around and stop wherever you wanted.

I remember that the bus had to stop at one corner, and there were some people there with several tigers, just sitting there, apparently waiting for people to come and pay them for the right to photograph them. I filmed them from the bus and I got the feeling they weren't pleased.

For the return trip, we were taken to a railway station and got on a double-decker train. We sat upstairs and had snack service, just like on an airplane. The train traveled at 100 miles an hour, but now we got to see a little more of what I'd expected in the form of small agricultural plots, with gardens of vegetables and water in ditches, with scruffy little thatched dwellings in the middle of the plot.

It was dark as we came to the end of the train ride, which took us right into Hong Kong, and we were transported to our hotel. We had most of the next day to roam around in the city, and later in the day, we were transported to the airport for the 12-hour trip back to California. I slept for 8 hours on this flight. We were not sorry to be going home now. Muriel and I had been away 6 weeks, and we'd been on 15 different airplanes, with about 18 landings and takeoffs. We were met in Los Angeles by my son Christopher. It was good to be home.

Chapter 28 - Visitors Descend On Us And More Trips

We arrived home just before Thanksgiving, and on the 13th of December, we had 12 visitors coming from England. There was Muriel's mother (she was 89 years old), Muriel's brother Paul, his wife, and two children, plus Muriel's niece Julie, her husband, and 5 children, mostly full-grown teenagers.

We had just about 3 weeks to do some fast moving to decorate for Christmas, move beds, prepare the rooms, stock up with food, etc. etc.

We went up to Los Angeles airport to meet the 12 visitors. There were two groups arriving on different airlines. The one which was scheduled for the earliest arrival was late and there was a lot of running back and forth before we got them all together. We took two cars and we got them to the rental agencies where they were renting a van and a car to do some long-distance traveling for the first 5 days. They followed us home. Somehow we lost the van driven by Julie and her husband, and they had no idea where we lived, but they knew the address. They showed up about half an hour after we arrived. They got off the freeway just north of here and asked the way.

A day or so later, they all, (except Muriel's mother), went off in the direction of the Grand Canyon, and Arizona. They turned the rental vehicles in when they returned. After that, Muriel's brother, Paul used our Chevrolet Corsica, and Muriel's niece used our 8-passenger station wagon, or our Buick for longer trips.

On Christmas Day we had 37 guests for dinner. In order to seat everybody we bought 2 sheets of 5/8" by 8' by 4' plywood, placed them on two 6-foot folding tables, and used a regular dining table for the overflow. All of our children and grandchildren also were there, as it was a unique opportunity to see the visitors.

The three weeks went in no time, and so we had to get the visitors back to the Los Angeles airport. It took 3 cars. Son Christopher drove the Chevrolet Impala, Muriel drove the Buick, and I drove the Chevrolet Corsica. We had to deliver them to separate terminals. There were tearful goodbyes, and they were on their way back to England.

The house seemed empty for a few days, but we soon adjusted.

Our next bit of excitement was 3 weeks later, the arrival of Muriel's cousin Gerald and wife from England. They also came for 3 weeks. During that time we took them to Las Vegas, Hoover Dam, and many closer areas worth seeing. On their own they went to various attractions in and around San Diego, using the Coaster, the train that runs up and down the coast between San Diego and Los Angeles.

Almost at once following Gerald and Linda's departure, we went on a cruise with our son Christopher and his wife Mary. We got on the ship in Long Beach, just about 80 miles north of Carlsbad.

It was a Mexican Riviera Cruise, stopping at Cabo San Lucas, Mazatlan, Porta Vallarta and Acapulco. It was an excellent cruise, and we went on excursions at each stop and saw some wonderful beaches and resorts. Christopher and Mary thoroughly enjoyed it, as did Muriel and I.

Within less than a month, in March, another of Muriel's cousins, Tony and wife Pauline arrived from England. For the second time in three weeks, we did the Los Angeles run, then we went off to Las Vegas, Hoover Dam, and Grand Canyon. They had stopped to see us on the way back from New Zealand and Australia and only stayed about a week.

Again we had the house to ourselves once more.

It was only 2 months later, in April, that we had a surprise awaiting us. My sister Christine's only son John William, suddenly announced he was married, and that they were having a belated reception. We were requested to attend. It was in Vancouver, Canada.

We have been to Vancouver a total of 4 times, and we feel very much at home there, and we were happy to see that our hotel was close to the beach. Also, a few hundred yards away was the entrance to Stanley Park, a large and beautiful park that stretches for miles, with all sorts of vegetation. It was spring and all the flowers were in bloom.

We had a rental car and went to the park for a drive almost every day we were there, except for the day we went to Whistler, the ski area about 70 miles north. There was no snow, except in the mountains, but it was a beautiful drive.

The reception was a very nice affair. The bride looked great as did John William. My sisters Brenda and Daphne and Daphne's husband Burt were there also. Unfortunately, Brenda slipped on the sidewalk on the way out and hurt her leg. We went back to the hotel, but Christine and her husband Bill, took Brenda to the hospital to be checked out, and luckily she was OK.

Shortly after our return from Vancouver, we were booked to go to England and Holland for 3 weeks. It was only mid-May, and it felt like we had been on the go the whole year. For this trip, we were accompanied by daughter Helen, husband Kirk, and their two sons, Andrew, 11, and Matthew 9.

The boys had not been on an airplane before, and Matthew had expressed some nervousness in the preceding weeks. However, he seemed OK on the day, and they settled down immediately.

We had 2 rental cars, and Helen and Kirk followed us to Bath. We were staying with Muriel's sister Susan, and Helen was staying with Muriel's brother Paul. The timing of our trip was based on a need to be in Bath for Muriel's mother's birthday on 3rd June, but we were going to Holland first for a 5-day tour. Helen's husband's ancestry is Dutch, and none of us had ever been there, so we went on that tour shortly after arriving in England.

For the Holland tour, we met a bus in Bath and were transported to Dover, then to France by the channel tunnel. We stayed on the bus which was driven onto the train. In about 25 minutes we were in France and driving off in the bus.

The bus drove across France and then across Belgium, which didn't take long, then we were in Holland, and on to our hotel. We stayed in Rotterdam at the Novus Hotel, a skyscraper.

It should be noted that Andrew, the eldest son, thoroughly enjoyed the food. Breakfast was buffet style, and he had a great time filling his plate at every opportunity.

Helen's sons were really enjoying the trip. With airplanes, busses, and ferry rides, there was something different for them every day. Their behavior was incredibly good. I don't remember one problem with them during the whole trip. Also, it was gratifying to know that they enjoyed it so much.

Holland was just as I expected, very flat with lots of ditches of water and canals. Almost every field had its own water ditch, fed from a canal, or vice versa. At first, we didn't see many windmills, but then later we saw them everywhere. They say that they are falling into decay and gradually disappearing. However, we visited a resort-type farm, alongside a wide canal, with 5 windmills that had been moved there and restored, and in working order.

This farm was just like it had been taken from a children's storybook. The grass was very green and there were sheep and lambs, goats, and ducks with their baby ducks on the brook. There were dairy cows and chickens etc and sailboats on the canal. It was a really delightful place, especially for children. They catered for adults also with a restaurant and several gift shops. It was a lovely sunny day with a perfect temperature.

Next, we went to a dairy farm where they made all sorts of cheeses. We sat in on a little talk about cheese making and then they showed us how they made wooden clogs on a lathe-type machine. A partly made clog was given to Andrew as a souvenir. We were given samples of their wine, and at the end, the owner and his wife appeared in traditional Dutch costumes, and we all took photographs of each other standing beside them. As the only children in the group, they made a special fuss about Andrew and Matthew, especially when they learned their last name was a Dutch name, (Van Orsdel).

The next day we went to the Zuider Zee, a resort town. It was very picturesque and unfortunately filled with tourist gift stores. As you would expect, Muriel soon found a jewelry store and they had diamond earrings exactly like she wanted. The last full day in Holland was spent in Amsterdam. It is a very attractive and bustling city. We rented a horse and trap for an hour and were driven around seeing several canals and the red light district. Then we went on a canal cruise in a large passenger boat. It was a hot day. We could buy cold drinks on the boat, which we enjoyed very much.

Because it is so flat, everybody uses bicycles. In the towns, there are hundreds of bicyclists. One aspect of Amsterdam was the apparent disregard for the law by most of the population. We were warned by the tour guide that none of the thousands of bicyclists would stop for pedestrians, and she was right.

The young lady that gave us the running commentary on the canal cruise, told us a story of when she first came to Amsterdam. She had only been there for a very short time when her bicycle was stolen. She went to the police, and they said, "So what, go steal one from somebody else". In the 9 years she'd been in Amsterdam, she'd had 18 bicycles stolen. What she didn't say was how many replacement bicycles she had stolen.

While in Holland we thought we would stock up on Advocaat, made only in Holland. The best Advocaat is made by a company named, "Warnink". We looked everywhere for it without success and bought another brand. It was awful, so we gave up on it.

On the way home through France we stopped at a huge supermarket, the last one before we boarded the channel tunnel train. The bus driver loaded the space in the luggage compartment of the bus with beer. We looked around and guess what we found, Dutch Advocaat. We bought several bottles.

We were back in England and Helen and Kirk went off on trips such as a visit to Stratford Upon Avon, Shakespeare's birthplace etc. On the way back, they visited Warwick Castle which is in perfect repair, with a magnificent museum of weapons through the ages.

We visited Cheddar, the home of the original Cheddar cheese. We sat in a restaurant while Helen, Kirk, and the boys went into the caves. Then, one day, Muriel's sister Susan who is very knowledgeable about the sights in London, went with them and showed them around for a day.

We covered all places of interest in and around Bath, such as Stonehenge, Wells Cathedral, Westbury White Horse, The Roman Baths, etc. They squeezed a great deal into their 3 weeks and had a great and memorable time.

That was our last trip to date, and we are not sorry to be having a rest from traveling.

Chapter 29 - Our Elderly Ladies Etc.

I've already related some of the stories about the employees who worked at caring for the elderly ladies that Muriel had. Now I will relate some of the very sad and a few funny experiences with the elderly ladies.

The first lady to arrive was Alice. This was in approximately 1984. She was a Christian Scientist, and 89 years old. She had come from our neighbor. Eddie who has had a residential care facility in his home for many years.

It was a bit strange for Muriel to have the responsibility of an 89 year old, after caring for children, but in no time life settled into a routine.

The only thing of significance that I remember about Alice was the fact that one day she asked me to get her parents on the phone for her. Of course I replied that it wasn't possible. She persisted and then I told her we didn't have their phone number, but she still persisted saying that I should call "information". I decided to put the problem on her when I asked her where they lived, and she really didn't know, but insisted that "information" would know where they were.

Finally, I decided that honesty was the best policy, and took her to her bedroom to talk, and I pointed out that she was now 90, and her parents would be 120 years old. I also pointed out that at that age they would have to be dead, or completely incompetent.

We talked for 20 minutes and she finally said that she completely understood, and she thanked me for taking the time to explain the situation. Her next words floored me as we left her room. She said, "now, would you please call my parents for me". This was a lesson, that in dealing with the elderly, sometimes you cannot win.

Muriel had an almost daily occurrence with Alice. Alice used to stand looking out of the dining room window, and she would comment about the lines of people marching across the hill behind our house. Muriel would tell her that she could not see them. By this time we had several more ladies in our care, and one day, when Joy told Alice she must be seeing things, Alice called Nina, another of the ladies, and asked her if she could see the people marching over the hill. Nina confirmed that she could see them with no problem???

Nina was a source of some funny things. Her favorite trick was to accuse Muriel of stealing her stuff, for example, her silver-ware, her green cart, various books, china etc.

A really funny time was when Nina asked to see Muriel regarding something of a personal nature. Muriel accompanied Nina to her bedroom for this important discussion.

Now Nina was 96 with a twisted spine, which made walking a painfully slow. Her steps were about 3" long, and as she walked, her whole body went up on one foot and down on the other.

When Muriel got Nina to her room, the conversation started with "Muriel, I think I should give up riding my bicycle".

Muriel struggled to keep a straight face, and agreed that this would be wise. She immediately felt she should leave the room before she was asked where the bicycle was, and then be accused of stealing it.

Muriel was relating this story to Nina's daughter, Rosemary, when the daughter suddenly remembered a funny thing which had happened recently. Apparently, Nina had told the daughter that she could not open her oven door, which was confusing to Rosemary as the residents did not have ovens in their rooms. When Nina was asked "which oven", Nina pointed to her television set. Apparently she'd been trying for days to pull the front open.

I should report other weird and funny happenings that we remember, with these elderly residents. They are, not necessarily in chronological order.

There was Flossie who spent most of her days looking around all the bedrooms for her sister with whom she had lived. She was very mobile and fast. All her movements showed her to be in an agitated state. She was up nearly every night, disturbing everybody, and whizzing around.

We remember the night that Muriel had to get up because of the commotion, but now, Flossie, the cause of all the trouble, could not be found anywhere. Alice was standing at the door to her bedroom and swore she hadn't seen Flossie. All the ladies were up, and Muriel checked all over to no avail. It was a good 5 minutes later that Alice said "there's a strange woman asleep in my bed". Yep, it was the missing Flossie, the cause of everybody being awake, and fast asleep herself, in somebody else's bed.

Judy, a Christian Scientist, who suffered from some delusions, had what we thought was a fictitious man friend named Bill. She had been transferred from our neighbor's (Eddie) house. Apparently, Bill "was going to come and get her to marry her". She left notes all over the place advising Bill of the whereabouts of her room. She taped notes on her door, and on the front door, and she would write letters to him and ask us to mail them. Once Muriel came home from shopping and found her at the mailbox, leaving a note telling the mailman to not deliver any mail to Eddie's house as it was the house of the Devil. She was terrified to go near our main entrance hall closet as she thought there was a tunnel to Eddie the Devil's house. She was really mixed up, and quite pathetic.

Her son told us that there actually was a "Bill". Judy had met him at a Christian Science conference and taken a serious liking to him. He was married, but that had not got through to Judy, and she had spent many years pestering him.

During her stay with us, she wrote to the Mother Church in Boston, (Christian Science Headquarters), George Bush, and Saddam Hussein to name a few.

Judy was very prudish. She saw me in the garden without a shirt on one day, and she carried on alarmingly. That is why the following was a bit of a problem.

Muriel had requested another light be installed in the main passageway between the bedrooms. I was busily working on it, with nobody about, when I got the feeling I was being watched. I looked up and there was Betty, quietly standing there near the bedrooms occupied by her and Judy. She was stark naked. If Judy had seen her, there would have been a hysterical fit of huge proportions.

I quietly asked Betty to go back to her room and put some clothes on, and she said "OK" in a very childish voice, and disappeared into her room. 5 minutes later, she was back, and we repeated the operation, and again she returned to her bedroom. This time she stayed there. Betty was a schizophrenic and often behaved like a small child.

A lady named Dorothy Fish was a real handful. The potted plants in the main entrance hall kept dying, and Muriel replaced them with artificial flowers. Then, Muriel found that Dorothy had a propensity for using flower-pots in the hall, as a urinal, and apparently had been at it for some time. Muriel caught her red-handed. This lady also would get all the ladies undressing in the main living room, much to Muriel's horror. She tore up some of our books, and took all of the dishes etc out of the china cabinet, which created another job for me in putting a lock on the cabinet doors.

We had a nice quiet lady with early stages of Alzheimer's disease. She was well-behaved except when her hair had to be washed, at which time she would swear like a trooper. According to her son, who witnessed a hair washing, he didn't realize she knew such words.

Every morning, Margery would re-arrange the furniture before Muriel was up. One day all our family photos, in frames in the living room, disappeared. One year later when it was time to change the air filter for the fireplace blower, I found the photographs in the filter cavity.

Muriel looked after old ladies for approximately 16 years and finally gave it up on 31st March 2000. It was precipitated by the fact that her "live in" help was disappearing.

As related earlier, a lady named Terri was reasonably effective at the job, which allowed us to start some serious traveling. However, after about a year, she felt she couldn't continue, and so her daughter, Donna, took over the job. Donna lasted about a year, and then Terri wanted to come back. She lasted about 6 months, and Donna returned, and stayed 2 years.

Following this, Muriel engaged a Mexican lady named Louisa, who lasted 2 years. She finally decided to move back to Tijuana, Mexico. However she promised to stay while we went on our trip to Tahiti.

Because of the staffing problems, we had given the elderly ladies and their families a month notice that we were closing, which took us to the time we would be back from Tahiti. But, just 3 days before we were to leave, Louisa announced that she was leaving that day. Luckily, Donna was able to step in and do the job while we were away.

A few days after our return, we reclaimed our house for ourselves for the first time for many years, and really for the first time since we had built the upstairs. It felt very good.

Chapter 30 - The Sad State Of Our Old Church

Due to the state of the economy, and the depressed stock market, we have avoided unnecessary expenditures, since returning from the England/Holland trip in May and June of 2001.

In the meantime, we left the church at which we were members for 30 years. There was a difference of opinion between me and the choir director. She is a rude lady, and I got tired of taking abuse and gave her a very bad time with a succession of letters before we finally decided to leave the church for good. One thing that makes me chuckle is the fact that I made a T-shirt with "I survived ...." with the lady's name, and a picture of an ugly witch. I wore it to choir practice where she could see it. Unfortunately, when I brought the problem to the attention of the senior minister, he was not prepared to take any action to put a stop to her antics, and I was not prepared to take any more abuse. I cannot understand why other people in that choir, put up with her. Her husband, in trying to apologize to me at the end, said, "I have to live with it". I told him that she needed more spanking, but unfortunately, he is not the man to straighten her out. In no time, the choir dwindled from about 40 to 17. Since then, we have heard that she has been asked twice to resign and she refuses and nobody stands up to her now that I'm gone.

After checking out several churches and choirs, we settled on San Deguito Methodist Church, mainly because the choir sounded so good. Another bonus was the fact that we saved 3,500 miles travel per year, and 20 minutes each way in travel time. We have been invited back to the old church several times, to the over-65 group which meets every so often. Also, I was asked to sing at the wedding of the daughter of the old choir president.

It is interesting to record the fact that when I asked the choir director at the new church if he knew the old choir director, he didn't say yes or no. He just said, "She's an obnoxious woman", which sums it up in a few words. Since then 2 other ladies from the old choir have joined our new choir due to dissatisfaction with the old choir director.

In the six months, we have been at the new church, we have got to know many people and become part of the woodwork, and feel that we belong. We held a party at our house and invited several of our friends from the old choir, and some from the new choir. We had a very enjoyable time with a sing-along, with friend Bob on the clarinet, and me on the keyboard. This new choir has grown with 4 additional singers in the past month alone.

It is with sadness that we have to record that the old church has suffered a dramatic decline since we left. Prominent long-time members have left and some are threatening to leave because of dissatisfaction with the minister. I must admit that when he didn't suggest that he try to heal the rift between me and the choir director, it showed some lack of the normal response that you would expect from a man of the cloth. Our financial contribution to the church was not inconsequential, and in addition, we contributed in many other ways. 2 months after we left, I was asked to do the big poster for the annual picnic, which, of course, I did. (A year later came another request for a poster for the next annual picnic. I obliged and got it delivered, but they didn't have the decency to tell me they had received it let alone thank me. It took 7 hours to complete, and probably $25 in ink. Of course, they have had their last poster done by me).

With the loss of the more prominent members, who happen to be the largest contributors, the income for the old church has dropped way below the expenditures. They have a financial crisis, and we have heard that all employees have taken a salary cut. Also, there was a meeting of the board, and it was leaked that the minister was staying on. I don't believe it. In the circumstances, they only have one option, to give the guy notice to find himself another position before more people drift away.

We were at the old church recently, attending the funeral service for the original founding minister, when the current minister approached me. He virtually apologized for not intervening in the quarrel between the choir director and me. I feel that we may have been used as one example of people lost to that church through his ineptitude.

Chapter 31 - Flowers, Pests And Improvements

Some months have passed since I last wrote the story. It is late June 2002, and nothing has changed much. We have completed our first year at the new church, and our choir is taking its summer break, returning in the first week of August.

We hosted a pool party for the new choir last Sunday. We had 44 people attend.

Muriel's flower garden is in full bloom. This became her hobby about 4 or 5 months ago, and after a couple of hiccoughs, it is looking really good.

One problem was that when she bought flowering plants, the rabbits ate them to ground level within 24 hours. I borrowed a .177 gauge air rifle from my son Nick, but this was not too effective. I tried my .22 gauge rifle and that woke up the whole valley with a massive reverberation. (I'm sure you know it is illegal to discharge a firearm within city boundaries). Nick suggested that I buy a .22 gauge air rifle, which was much more effective. A few rabbits did get to run away.

Next, Nick suggested that I might try some low-load .22 ammunition which was said to be quiet, but with 3 times the weight of the bullet when compared to the air rifle. That worked, and if the rabbits did run, they invariably didn't get too far away before collapsing. Now we have no rabbits and lots of flowers.

The local San Diego fair is taking place and our grandson Robbie, who is 16 now, won first prizes for both entries in the art competition. Last year he won a first and a second. He is going to England and Ireland next Monday, with his art class and is planning to meet with Muriel's family when the tour goes to Bath.

We were at my son Nick's house for dinner. He showed us a rock garden he'd made with two ponds and a waterfall. Muriel liked it very much, so I have to make a similar rock garden with two ponds in our backyard. We have one like this in our front yard.

I am working on enclosing with glass, our large balcony in the rear of the house. This is where I do my painting and need to have a place with good light where I can paint in the winter. I currently have two painting students and another who is wanting to start. I don't get paid, in fact, it costs us as we supply the materials needed. There seems to be a great interest in learning to create oil paintings by some people who have never done it. They apparently don't know where to start.

Today, we returned from Santa Barbara where we went to see Dr. Don Richardson, our first choir director from our church in Santa Monica. He is 77 and still teaches one day a week at Santa Monica City College. We had a most enjoyable visit with him and his wife. He writes music and gave me an autographed copy of a piece which he wrote for a local theater production.

Below, are our possible plans for the next few months.

Very soon we felt we should visit our youngest son and family in Nashville, Tennessee, but this will have to get some thought before we actually go. Also, for an excellent price we have seen an advertisement for one of the two cruises left that we want to do. It goes from Dover, England to all the Scandinavian capitals, stopping off at a Russian, and Estonian Port.

At the end of April, Muriel's cousin Tony, wife Pauline and her sister Sybil are arriving for a visit from England. They've told us that they would like to visit Yosemite, Death Valley, Las Vegas, and Grand Canyon etc. Unfortunately, when you live in England, it is automatic to think of distances as they are in England, and not as they are in USA. They will be here for 10 days, which will mean that we have to get a move on as the trip will be 1847 miles. Soon, Muriel feels we should visit her mother in England who will be 92 next June 2003. We shall probably combine this with the Russian/Scandinavian trip which we have now booked.

This narrative is up to date as of early 2003. To continue with day-to-day happenings would make it like a diary which could not conclude yet, and is something I want to avoid. I think we are getting near to a good point to rest, bearing in mind that I can always add at a later date.

Chapter 32 - Travel And Nostalgia

It is a later date. It is April 2003, and the weather is getting warmer. Actually, today we have a powerful Santa Ana wind and it is extremely dry and around 80 degrees. For those who don't know, these winds are sometimes very strong, and we recently had some roof shingles blown off, and the cover over one of our chimneys landed in the front garden. Also, some fiberglass panels over the Jacuzzi were damaged. Today is the second high wind in three months. These two powerful winds are the worst we've ever had in the 27 years in which we've lived in this house.

You will remember that some months ago, I was working on enclosing our back patio. It is completed and it has turned out to be a very good addition. In the morning, the sun shines into the 12-foot wide floor-to-ceiling windows, and we open the doors to the living room. The temperature is usually 10 degrees warmer on the patio (now sunroom), and it warms the living room up to a very comfortable temperature. In the summer, we will leave the outer glass doors open, with the inner doors closed, and it will stay cool.

Before Christmas, I made two ponds in the back garden. We put water in them, and fixed up a pump for a waterfall, but then found that the water got too hot for fish, but great for mosquito larva. We need fish to keep the larva down. In the last week or so, I've built the frame for a cover, 7 feet off the ground, and will put a trellis on the top, with shade cloth over it to keep the sun off. This will be completed within the next week or so, as soon as I've repaired the wind damage.

Muriel went to see her mother in February, as I mentioned earlier, and she spent 11 days with the family there. She was a bit nervous about traveling as the war with Iraq was imminent, in fact, it appeared that it would start before she went, but she managed to get back before the start.

This war is in full swing now, with US troops on the outskirts of Baghdad. This war is a very unfortunate thing, but necessary to remove the latest "Hitler" who would be a greater problem if allowed to get any stronger, as was the case with Hitler.

Muriel has just received a letter from her sister, Christine, with some enclosures which she requested whilst she was in England. The first one is entitled "We Are Survivors". Muriel wants both items reproduced for posterity, so here is the first one:

We are survivors. For those born before 1940. . . .

We were born before television, penicillin, polio shots, frozen foods, contact lenses, videos, the pill, radar, credit cards, split atoms, laser beams, ball-point pens, and dish-washers, tumble driers, electric blankets, air conditioners, non-iron clothes, and before men walked on the moon.

People got married first, then lived together, (how quaint). We thought fast food was what you ate in Lent, a Big Mac was an oversized raincoat, and crumpets were eaten for tea. We existed before househusbands, computer dating, and sheltered accommodation. That was what we called a bus shelter.

We were Born before daycare centers, disposable diapers, group homes, and had never heard of FM radio, tape decks, artificial hearts, word processors, or young men wearing earrings or women wearing rings in their tongues or navels etc. For us, time-sharing was togetherness, a chip was fried potato or a small piece of wood, hardware was nuts and bolts, and software wasn't a word.

Before 1940, "Made in Japan" meant it was junk, and making out was how well you did in your school exams. The stud was used to attach your collar to your shirt, and going all the way was staying on the bus to the terminus. Smoking was fashionable, "grass" was mown, "coke" was kept in the coal shed, a "joint" was a piece of meat, and "pot" was something in which you cooked. "Rock" music was a lullaby, "Eldorado" was ice cream, and a "gay" person was the life and soul of a party, while AIDS were make-up, which helped you look good, or help someone in trouble.

We who were born before 1940 must be a smart bunch when you consider how we have adjusted to everything new, and it is no wonder there is a generation gap today.

Below are some poems which Muriel's mother used to repeat to her and her siblings. Two of them seem a bit questionable for children, but they are from the time when life was not sugar-coated for children as is done today: Again, Muriel wants these recorded whilst they are in memory.

The cat's party

A cat once to her kittens said, "Come listen prim to me, your Pa and I have both agreed to have some friends to tea, now hurry up and wash yourselves and put your whiskers straight, and you may go and ask the guests to come at half past eight. But tell them not to venture out if bad or stormy weather, but if its fine, upon the roof we all will meet together".

First Mrs. Black, and her children came, next Pet, the youngest guest, then Mrs. Tortoiseshell and her son, who looked their very best. A Persian cat, whose name was Tom, Miss Smut, and many more, came rushing on the tiles of number twenty-four.

The first thing on the program was a song by all the cats, the kittens in the chorus joined in various sharps and flats. But in the middle of the song poor Pet began to cry, and sad to say, the noise awoke a man who slept nearby. We need not say that he saw all, but threw some water out, enough to say ere he retired, there were no cats about.

Five Little Mice

Five little mice sat down to spin, Pussy passed by and she peeped in."What are you doing my little men"? "Weaving coats for gentlemen". "Shall I come in and wax your thread"? "No thank you Miss Pussy, you'll bite off our heads". "I love your whiskers and round black eyes, your house is the prettiest house I've seen". The mice were so pleased they opened the door, and Pussy soon laid them all dead on the floor.

Mini and Joe

My dears do you know how a long time ago, two poor little children named Mini and Joe, were stolen away on a fine summer's day and were lost in the wood, so I've heard people say. Now when it was night, so sad was their plight, the stars did not shine and the moon gave no light. The poor little children laid down and died. Now when they were dead, two robins so red, brought blackberry leaves and over them spread, and all day long they sang them this song, "Poor babes in the wood, poor babes in the wood".

My sister Christine has just come out of hospital after having a 7 1/2 hour operation on her back. She has been quite miserable with back pain for some years. My other sister Sylvia has just come out of hospital after having pneumonia, and I'm planning on having my knees replaced this summer, otherwise, everybody in the family seems healthy.

Chapter 33 - More Travel

The cruise and trip to Europe was over. My knees prevented me from completely participating, but I managed pretty well.

Almost right away we had snags arise. On the plane to London, we were told we would arrive an hour early, but this turned out to be wrong when we landed exactly on time, at 12.10 (noon). We had to get to the boat at Dover, about 85 miles, for the 4.00 pm sailing.

We had ordered from the cruise line, pick up from the airport, and transfer, so we looked around for a Norwegian Cruise Line representative. There was not one to be seen. Luckily, Muriel was adamant that we didn't have time to wait, so she marched over to the information booth to have a Norwegian representative paged. One appeared, saying that she had all the people she was supposed to pick up, and we weren't on the list. Luckily, the last bus had room and was just leaving.

We settled in on the bus with about 15 people, to the tune of 8 Italians close by who conversed at the top of their voices. They were incapable of talking in normal tones, and this continued until we were about 15 miles from Dover.

Suddenly we were overtaken by screaming sirens from police cars and ambulances. A few miles on, the whole freeway, (motorway), was brought to a stop, and all traffic was ordered off onto the single-lane country roads.

We moved at a snail's pace through traffic lights and the famous roundabouts. It was about 3.20 pm, and the boat was due to sail in 40 minutes. The driver's cell phone was ringing constantly, and he was reporting our progress.

Finally, we arrived at the boat, and we were hustled up the boarding ramp to deck 7. Just inside was the counter for checking in. Muriel and I were the last on the boat. As we arrived at the counter, we noted that the boat was already moving.

We found our cabin, and we were agreeably surprised. We normally don't pay for a cabin with a porthole, as we feel that we can always go on deck outside if there is anything worth seeing, so we were happy to see a spacious cabin with a large window with a lifeboat partly blocking the view. A bottle of wine was sitting on the table, sent to us by the travel agent, so things were beginning to look up. Then, we found that the cabin safe was not working, and was not attached to the wall.

Due to the fact that we had a big party to attend in England, we had brought quite a bit of jewelry, and really needed this safe. I phoned "housekeeping" who promised to send somebody right away. We waited and waited, but finally gave up.

The next day, I phoned "housekeeping" again, and within 2 hours, we had two men fix the problems.

We spent the whole 2nd and 3rd days at sea and traveling through the Kiel Canal, which cuts across the neck of a part of northern Germany which sticks up into the Baltic Sea, a few miles from Denmark. I can't think why the canal exists. It didn't seem to serve any industrial areas and doesn't appear to save enough sea travel to make it worthwhile.

The first port of call was Tallinn, Estonia. I'm still trying to think why this was a stop, as there was absolutely nothing of note to see there. We boarded a bus and went straight through the town which was a typical European town, to the site of the annual singing festival. It was a stage at the center of a natural grass bowl, which held an annual song festival. We spent ages there and looked over stalls selling a variety of tourist items.

The next stop was a few historic buildings, but I didn't leave the bus as they didn't seem too exciting. This was about the extent of Tallinn's tourist places of interest.

Our next stop was St. Petersburg, Russia, and what a difference. We saw the largest and most ornate palaces and royal residences that you can imagine. The insides were even more decorated than the outside, which were covered in golden statues and every type of adornment imaginable. As great as they were, I can't help thinking of the cost to the average Russian of the building of these magnificent edifices. Those Russian peasants were barely able to survive, whilst the Czars were spending such huge amounts on themselves. It leads you to think that the Czars' arrogant and selfish ways were responsible in a roundabout way for unleashing 50 years of communism on the world. At minimum, the Russian royal family only got what it deserved from the Russian Revolution.

We had booked 2 full days of excursions in St. Petersburg, but the first day included much more walking than they advertised, and I was walked out the first day. On the second day, I stayed on the boat and Muriel went on her own. She thoroughly enjoyed it. I was not too disappointed as buildings are not my thing.

After it, the next stop was Helsinki, Finland. It was a nice clean town, but there was not too much to see. This was also somewhat true of the next stop, Stockholm, Sweden. It is surrounded by water, with canals and lakes, and a little bit more picturesque than Helsinki.

Overnight, we sailed to Copenhagen, Denmark, and we got on the usual bus for a city tour. The first stop was a visit to the famous mermaid statue in the harbor. There were so many people lining up to stand by the mermaid for photos that you could hardly get a second for your own "people-free" photos. It makes me wonder about simple-minded people who do these sorts of things. What is so great about a photo of a fat, ugly American, posing beside a metal mermaid? I suppose the statue is famous, so just photograph it??? I know, I'm a cynic.

The last port of call was Oslo, Norway. The approach to Oslo was called a Fjord, but it was a journey between low-lying small islands. It was a very pretty trip, but we didn't see any of the mountains we expected.

Oslo was the best part of the trip. The bay in which we docked was beautiful, and, for once we had bright sunshine which probably helped. The bus tour was very interesting, guided by a Welshman. We drove to the top of the local mountain and admired the view over the whole area. We saw statues of the king at the Winter Olympics Park and admired the ski jump.

That evening we set sail for our 2 days sail back to Dover. On the way, it is interesting to note that we saw several North Sea oil rigs in the distance.

We docked in Dover and we were off the boat by 8.00 am, and got a taxi to Hertz, where we had a car reserved for 9.00 am. We arrived at Hertz around 8.20 am to be told that our car would not be ready until 9.00 am.

It was a tiny little place with about 10 cars, with one girl behind the desk and a man wandering around outside.

At about 8.35, the girl got the man to wash off a car and check the tires and engine, etc. Then we waited, not knowing if this was our car. At about 8.50, we were told that another lady had to take the car to fill it with gas, but she wasn't anywhere to be found. Finally, at 9.05 am we got the car, and left for Bath, to stay with Muriel's brother, Paul.

I had estimated that it was about 165 miles, but it turned out to be over 200. We did the journey in about 3 hours, then took another hour to drive across Bath.

Chapter 34 - Back To Aqua Sulis

We were greeted like royalty in Bath as usual. We had 8 days. The day after our arrival was a big day. We were going to meet up with dozens of ladies who had worked with Muriel at the telephone exchange, 53 years earlier. Muriel has always kept in touch with some of them, and this meeting was arranged through them.

We were surrounded by these old ladies, who mostly looked and seemed far older than Muriel. I recognized many of them and was amazed that they seemed to have aged so much. England must be hard on people. One of the ladies argued with Muriel telling her that, "She was not Muriel Newton" as she claimed.

We had lunch together and had a good time, and have since heard that there was so much discussion after we left. We've received a postcard saying that they are still talking about our visit.

The next day, we had a dinner date with an old school friend of mine that I hadn't seen for 53 years. He brought his wife and we met at 7.00 pm in a pub (public house). We gossiped and recalled old times until 11.00 pm, and had a wonderful time. Their life has been comparatively quiet compared to ours. They are retired and live in a small house, tending their garden etc. We invited them all to come and see us, but generally only a small percentage come. The cost of travel seems to be not so easily available in England, and a surprising number of people seem scared of flying.

Our time in England soon went. We ate every day in pubs and covered lots of miles including a visit to the south coast to visit Muriel's sister Dawn, who is an epileptic, and in an assisted living facility in Brixham Devon.

On our return to Los Angeles airport, we were met by our son Christopher, and we were very happy to be home. There were no calamities except a can of juice had exploded in the kitchen freezer. Then we discovered that lots of food in the freezer was bad. We believe that the fridge door had not been closed properly.

Chapter 35 - I Get To Be Mobile Again

Now came the nasty bit. I was due to have a knee replaced 12 days after our return. First I had to see the doctor for the pre-op exam. This went OK and I was set for the operation on 16th September 2003.

I had to arrive at the hospital at 6.00 am, and by 10.30 am I had a new knee. Apparently, I had lots of bone spurs and other problems to the point that the doctor said he couldn't believe that I could walk on it.

I was out of the hospital in 3 days. The knee gave me no pain, but I had a rapid pulse for which they couldn't account. I made excellent progress and got the flexibility needed very early on. The waiting for the healing and strengthening got a bit boring, but other than that, I didn't have too bad a time.

In the meantime, our driveway to the house has been bad. We had roots from the trees tearing it up in one place, and some patching over the hole dug for a new sewer line, 20 years ago, was breaking up. Finally, our son Nick had some time to fix it for us, and spent two weeks, patching and then re-surfacing. It looks great now. Now we are going to get more jobs done whilst Nick has the time.

Nick wasn't able to do too much for us, but then my other son Christopher's company employees went out on strike. He agreed to work for us whilst on strike. We expected to have him for 2 or 3 weeks until the strike died, but it was almost 4 months. We got a lot of catching up on the jobs around the place that had been neglected due to my knee problems.

I've restarted writing this in May of 2004. I had the second knee replaced in January, and I am almost completely mobile. I still get a little ache in the last knee if I walk and stand too much. The first knee done (7 months ago) is almost 100%.

I have not added to this story for many months as I lost a part of it from a floppy disk, and just could not bring myself to do a re-write. It seemed that half a dozen pages just disappeared and were blank. This morning, I finally got down to looking at it and comparing the floppy to a printed copy, and to my delight, I had only lost a paragraph or two. Where did those blank pages come from? Due to my spending most of the last 7 months with knee recovery, there has not been much activity to report. However, there was one unfortunate happening a month or so ago.

For last Christmas, our children bought us a lamp post which I installed in front of the house, with Christopher's help. It is beautifully decorated, with 3 arms and beveled glass lamps. It really looked good when lit up.

More recently. We decide that we should cut down a tall tree that was growing about 30 feet from the lamp, and I enlisted the aid of my son Nick to do the cutting. To make sure that it didn't fall the wrong way, we tied a rope halfway up the tree and attached it to the base of another tree further away from the lamp. Without going into too many details, the rope broke and the tree fell right on the lamp breaking it into many pieces. It was made of cast aluminum and shattered.

We went back to the (department) store, but they had no more and didn't know where they had got them. I found a faint manufacturer's name but could find no trace on the internet. In desperation, I thought I would buy some epoxy and try putting the pieces back together.

I spent weeks gluing the pieces together with the epoxy and then reinforcing the breaks with strips of aluminum tightly wrapped with a fishing line with a layer of epoxy over the top. I also made many brackets with which I bolted the heavier pieces together, again reinforced with epoxy. Today, it proudly stands back in its old position and you have to get within two feet to see the repairs. Luckily, the epoxy is the exact same color as the lamp post, but I do intend to paint the epoxy as protection from rain and sunlight.

Muriel is in England at the moment, so I have the time to catch up. She left me with a list of jobs to do, but yesterday I did more than I should have and made both knees sore. This is why I am sitting here catching up on this story.

Due to the fact that I am now walking better, with no pain for the first time in 20 years, we are going to make up for lost time. We have booked a cruise out of Osaka Japan, spending 24 days visiting the Pacific islands which the older ones among us will remember from the Second World War, such as Saipan, Midway, Okinawa, Guam, etc. I will say more about this after we have completed the trip.

Chapter 36 - A Very Bad Year For Us

My words in an earlier chapter were about the fact that I was walking OK after my knees were replaced and we were going to do more traveling, starting with a 24-day Pacific cruise out of Osaka Japan. This was not to be.

It is about 9 months since I wrote this, in spring 2004, and things were very good for us all at that time. However, on Muriel's 70th birthday on 11th of June 2004, we were working hard on plans for a birthday party the next day, (a Saturday). The phone rang at about 9.00 am. It was daughter Helen, and with some of the worst news we could ever imagine.

She is our only daughter and announced that she had rectal cancer, and it had spread to her liver!

The party went on; it was too late to cancel. Helen came along with about 50 guests. At 7.00 pm, the party was starting to break up, but my 3 sons, Chris, David, and Nick, (the only ones in the area), got everybody together in our downstairs living room, and each in turn prayed over Helen. It was one of those magic electric moments which stay with you forever. There was not a dry eye in the place. Guests were driving off with tears streaming down their faces.

It is not pleasant for us and not our wish to dwell on this horrible period but we feel that it has to be documented as it is fact. Also, it is not completely over at this time, although we hope for better things.

The first move was for Helen to start on 5/6 weeks of chemotherapy and radiation at the same time. She withstood it very well, but near the end, she was badly burned and could not sit, walk, or lie down without considerable pain. They found that the rectal tumor was reduced, and the liver spots were down to about 1/3rd of their original size. A few weeks later, in September, she was operated on for rectal tumor removal. Unfortunately, they could not save her rectum. The plan was for her to recover and then go into 6 months of chemotherapy. December was the expected start date for this chemotherapy. However, in November, Helen started having difficulty walking, with weakness on her right side.

This next body blow was a tumor in her brain, affecting the motor area. Now we had been under the impression that her brain had been scanned. To our shock and horror, we found out that this was not so, and unfortunately, Helen and her husband apparently were not knowledgeable or experienced enough to know that the brain is always one of the first places to which cancer migrates. We also hold the doctors responsible for this blatant oversight. However, the operation went well, taking only 1 ¾ hours. In a week, she was in rehabilitation, walking etc. soon afterward. Again, she had to wait for recovery before starting chemotherapy, expected to start in early January.

On 1st of January, she started having some difficulty walking again, and almost at once, she had a serious seizure, one of the risks of brain surgery. A scan of her brain revealed that her brain tumor had returned, and had grown to ¾ of the size of the first one in less than 2 months, but was just under the maximum size for treatment by gamma-ray radiation. This is done on an outpatient basis, and Helen underwent this. They warned us, that by the time the treatment was done, it was at the maximum for the "gamma-knife".

Over the next week, the paralysis returned to her right side, and she went back to the hospital on the Friday following the gamma knife. The following Monday, the brain surgeon's nurse practitioner announced that Helen was scheduled for surgery the following Friday, which shocked us all. We felt we were losing the battle. Helen was destroyed emotionally. In the meantime, she was receiving diuretics and drugs for reduction of swelling.

On the Tuesday following Black Monday, the brain surgeon announced that he may not need to do the surgery as her paralysis was receding! Apparently, the problem was the swelling, not the tumor, and we all began to get our hope back. The next day Helen could squeeze my hand and move the paralyzed leg and she progressed from there. Today, 3rd February, Helen is walking unaided and will be released from the hospital tomorrow. Apparently, the gamma-knife reduces the risk of the brain tumor returning to about 10%. A week ago, she was completely scanned, and no new cancers were found anywhere. However, she will be scanned very frequently in the near future. After all this, chemo-therapy, (due to start in a week), for the next 6 months seems comparatively easy. Unfortunately, we learned that chemo-therapy does not get to and affect brain tumors, so she will have to be closely watched.

Since writing the above, Helen had several seizures, and the paralysis came partly back, and we feared the worst. She saw the brain surgeon who said that the seizures had caused the deterioration of her right side control, and she should make an appointment next week for the start of the 6 months chemotherapy. This was just one more of the constant roller-coaster rides we have all been on for 7 months.

Muriel has stayed at Helen's house on two occasions over the last 6 months, for 7 and 10 days, taking care of her. She plans to go for another week or so, to see that she makes a quick recovery in order to start the chemotherapy as soon as possible.

Chapter 37 - Hopefully, Better Things Ahead.

Our life has been on hold since last June. In the meantime, Nick's son, Robbie went off to art school in Long Beach near Los Angeles and seems to be settling in nicely.

About 10 days before Christmas, in a lull in Helen's cancer activity, son Peter and his wife begged us to visit them in Tennessee for Christmas. In assessing everything that we wanted to take, we had no choice but to drive, which would also give us a car to use there. The trunk was filled to capacity, and the rear seat was also, up to the level of the windows.

We covered 850 miles on the first day, which became typical for a full day's driving. We stayed overnight in Albuquerque, New Mexico. We took the northern route on I-40 as it looked a little shorter. However, there were hundreds of huge trucks. The second day was a similar day. We covered close to 800 miles, staying at a small place 20 miles west of Fort Smith. On the third day we had about 500 miles to our destination, but near midday, just west of Memphis, with only 200 miles to go, we ran into a storm that started as rain, but soon turned to sleet, then into a full ice storm. In no time we had an inch of ice all over the car with icicles hanging from the mirrors, and blocks of ice for windshield wipers. We kept the windshield free by directing heat to the inside of the window. We saw many vehicles in ditches, but, luckily, no collisions. However, we did have one hold-up of about 40 minutes caused by "rubber-neckers" ogling a semi and trailer in a ditch in the center of the highway.

I called Peter to say that we possibly may not arrive that day, and he said, "Keep going as the weather warms up nearer to Nashville". Sure enough 2 hours later, on the east side of Memphis, the ice started to fly off the car. There was another problem though. Chunks of ice were also flying off the trucks. Luckily we avoided damage.

By the time we arrived at Peter's, at 4.15 pm on 22nd of December, the ice was gone. However, the next morning it was snowing lightly and we had a white Christmas. It got colder and the temperature dropped into the teens for a few days.

We left just after Christmas on the 28th. This time we took the southern route through Texas.

On the first day of travel, we covered about 800 miles and stopped at Fort Worth. The next day we drove 916 miles, stopping in Tucson Arizona. The last 100 miles of this part of the trip was in the dark, and through mountains. It poured with rain and was a bit foggy.

The next morning was clear and sunny with only about 400 miles to go, so off we went enjoying this beautiful day in the desert. This didn't last too long though. We went between some hills, and into thick fog for the next 100 miles. Traffic was extremely light, with only a few cars to the mile, and almost no trucks. Visibility was about 30 yards at first, but improved to about 80 yards, which allowed us to get back to our normal speed of around 80 miles per hour. (It is worth noting that Muriel drove for about 5 hours for the whole trip, and I had a job getting her to stay under 90 mph). Later on, in the high mountains, the weather turned rainy, but by the time we got to California, the weather turned sunny again. We stopped for brunch at a Denny's in Yuma, and we were the only people in the place who were speaking English.

We got home at 1.15 pm with 4,369 miles on the clock for the round trip. The car, a Chevrolet Impala, did a remarkable 29.07 miles to the gallon. This was more remarkable because of the heavy load we carried on the outward part of the trip and the speed we were traveling.

We enjoyed seeing the 3 grandchildren, Peter, and Luanne. Also, we saw a lot of Tennessee and the rest of the country. This was a pleasant trip, and I must admit that I look forward to doing more of this as soon as Helen's situation stabilizes.

We have had to remove another huge tree, leaving us with only 4 large trees. The one in question was becoming a problem as it was against the perimeter of the lot, and close to the corner of the front wing of our house. Huge branches were hanging down over the neighbor's parking area also. The neighbor has a similar tree. During a recent windstorm, a 15-inch diameter branch fell on her sister's car and crushed it. We did not want this to happen with our tree.

We had quotes for the job as high as $1200, and they would keep the wood. One day recently, I asked our gardener if he knew somebody who would cut it down, and he said that he would do it with his cousin for $500 and he would cut it up to log length for us and remove all waste. Of course, we didn't want to miss this, so we now have piles of wood, including stacks of 2 and 3 feet diameter "rounds" which we have to split for burning.

Chapter 38 - Better Things Still Ahead Hopefully

It is 9th March 2005 and we are in Helen's hospital room in Scripps Hospital La Jolla. I have just finished a complete report on Helen's illness to send to all friends and relatives, and I think I should include the whole report even though some of it will be a duplicate of a previous chapter. Muriel did go back to Helen's for a third time for about 10 days after she completed rehab. (Her 3rd hospital stay) for the paralysis caused by the swelling from the gamma knife episode. This 3rd stay at Helen's by Muriel, culminated in Helen going to the hospital for the 4th time with 4 days of continual bleeding from the nose. Of course, there was no way she could start chemotherapy. Here is that report.

Ref Daughter Helen. The following is a complete update written in her hospital room where we have about 10 to 12 hours a day (time) to do this. I feel it is important to record this here.

To all friends & relatives.

Wednesday 3/9/05 at Scripps Hospital, La Jolla.

As most of you know, on 11th June 2004, Muriel's 70th birthday, Helen phoned to say she had rectal cancer and some liver tumors. After 6 weeks of chemo and radiation, the rectum was surgically removed. After her recovery, she was due to start chemotherapy for the liver at about the end of November. Then she became paralyzed on the right side, and a brain tumor was found to be the cause. It was surgically removed. Within 5/6 weeks the paralysis returned. Another brain tumor. This time it was treated by gamma radiation. It caused brain swelling and the paralysis returned for the third time about a month ago. Shortly thereafter,

3 ½ weeks ago, she started continuous nose bleeds for 4 days and was eventually taken to "Emergency" where her blood platelets were found to be near zero. Normal is 150,000 and up. For several days, she was kept from a massive hemorrhage by an infusion of platelets. Helen has been in the hospital for 3 weeks today, the first 10 days in intensive care.

As of Saturday before last, her platelet level was brought up to 11,000 with plasma and platelet infusions. Over the following days, her platelet levels, in thousands went 19, 51, 65, 83, 71, 73, 89, 105, 114, 143, and today, 159. She has not had infusions for over a week and definitely has regained the ability to make her own platelets again. It is thought that two drugs were responsible for killing platelets, heparin, and kepra. These were stopped some time ago.

Last week, her problems were: She couldn't speak, she was paralyzed on the right side, her arm and leg were useless, and the second brain tumor was said to be dying from the gamma-ray radiation treatment, but still causing brain swelling, also she had some bleeding in her brain from the low platelet count adding to the pressure. She had pneumonia in the right lung, she had a blood fungus/ yeast infection in her blood for which they had no cure, and of course, the liver tumors which have been growing gaily since her last chemo in about October. Also, they said she would have to have brain surgery to try to regain her lost capabilities, which would delay chemo for another month. If the brain tumors had not occurred, she would have had chemo for her liver in early December.

Last Wednesday, the 2nd, she was seen by a brain specialist who took us into the corridor to advise us that Helen would never talk or walk again and that her condition was hopeless. Friday, the Oncologist in charge of her case told Helen's husband that her condition was terminal. And all we could do was to pray for a miracle.

There have been prayers by hundreds of people in the US, Canada, New Zealand, Australia, and England, for many months.

Saturday, Helen spoke a few words, Sunday she talked on the phone to her Grandmother in England for several minutes, and since then, she speaks softly, but virtually at will. Sunday, they found an antibiotic which kills the blood fungus, and treatment started immediately. Monday, she was able to slightly move fingers on her paralyzed hand, and her pneumonia was gone. They found the cause of the fungus problem. It was in the port into which the drips are connected.

The fact that she could now speak and move her fingers a bit, indicated that the brain swelling was reducing, making an immediate brain operation unnecessary. (After the gamma-ray radiations, they said that the tumor would take 4 to 7 weeks to start to disappear. It is about 7 weeks now).

Tuesday, (yesterday), with the platelets at 143, the Oncologist said, "I think we have our miracle," and Helen started chemotherapy in the afternoon! This was more than we could hope for, but still, only the beginning. There are many more months to go and the outcome is not certain by any means. However, she is at last moving in the right direction.

We believe that this story has a lesson for us all. All things are possible with prayers. Don't give up hope as God still has his power to work miracles. Another thing that has occurred is that there are lots of people who have moved closer to God over this illness, and it has brought our family even closer together than before. Helen's brothers have been a rock and a joy, and an inspiration to Helen, Muriel, and me. To God be the glory.

Brian & Muriel.

This is the current situation. She is getting chemotherapy and has almost finished with her first 48 hours treatment after which she will get some days rest from it, and then start again. Her speaking is coming easier and she is answering the phone and talking to all and sundry. She is eating well, and feeding herself, although we feel that she is slightly weaker after the chemo.

I have to be careful that this will not turn into a diary, a thing I wish to avoid.

Since the above, after being in hospital 4 and a bit weeks, Helen is home, still paralyzed, but stronger, and has regained a tiny bit of movement in her right fingers. However, the doctor is very pessimistic about her chances but we are not giving up. He feels that the chemotherapy will just give her a bit more time and comfort. We had a miracle in her getting over the problems of platelets, pneumonia, blood fungus, loss of speech etc., and we are looking for more.

Chapter 39 - The Cruelest Blow.

Within a very short time, Helen weakened further, and with desperate sadness, we came to grips with the fact that she would not be able to stand chemotherapy, and that we were losing the battle. On Wednesday 13th April, she was barely able to communicate, and Muriel felt the need to tell her it was OK to go if she wanted. The next day, Thursday 14the April, Muriel persuaded Kirk to tell Helen the same thing.

On Friday, the 15th of April, I visited again, (Muriel was staying there, but there was not enough room for me to stay), and Muriel begged me to tell Helen that it was OK to go. Helen seemed to be only semi-conscious. At 4.25 pm, I said, "Helen, you know we love you, and if you want to go, it is OK. You know we will take care of your boys as necessary." As I said this, she raised her eyebrows in acknowledgement, which was the only reaction or contact she had made all day. Muriel saw it also. Following this, I was alone with her, except for a Hospice nurse behind me, and suddenly her breathing rhythm changed. She didn't breathe for several seconds. I called everybody in, and she took another breath, and then after a gap, another, but that was the last. At 4.33 pm, about 7 minutes after I talked to her, she breathed her last. Our one and only, beautiful daughter was gone.

Chapter 40 - Life Must Go On.

On Wednesday, May 4th, we did the last thing for our daughter that we were able. As requested by Helen, a memorial service was held at Torrey Pines Christian Church, conducted by Dr. Clair Berry. There were approximately 200 people in attendance, and it was popularly described as a beautiful celebration of Helen's life.

Brother number 2, David, did a marvelous job, speaking about his sister in glowing terms for 20 minutes, followed in a similar fashion by Helen's friend Nicole. When Helen was growing up, she attended that church and Dr. Berry was her minister. He also married Kirk and Helen

My sisters came from Florida and Woodland Hills, her brother Peter came from Nashville, and Muriel's sister Susan came from England, knowing that Muriel needed her. Kirk's father came from Northern California, a neighbor's son who knew Helen as a 2-year-old came from Oregon, and there were at least 20 Highway Patrol Officers there. Our friends from both Torrey Pines Church (which we attended for 30 years) and our new church, were well represented.

Dr. Berry is recognized as a great orator, and many people asked if he was the minister at that church as they were interested in changing churches. (Dr. Berry retired about 6 years ago). He had visited Helen every few days, in the hospital and at home, even though Helen lived 70 miles away in Hemet. His help in calming Helen's fears was immeasurable and made us less anxious about her passing.

The Memorial Service Celebration invitation and card included the words that in lieu of flowers, Helen would want donations to an education fund for her boys. To date, there is close to $5,000 donated with some more small gifts to come. Sympathy cards received by us number approximately 130. In addition, we have received meals, phone calls, flowers, plants, books, and every known expression of love and support imaginable. We truly are blessed with so many wonderful friends.

Some weeks before her death, Helen had a conversation with David's wife Susan about the transition from this life to the next being similar to a caterpillar changing to a butterfly. She asked Susan to buy a butterfly and give it to Muriel after her death. This Susan did, and Muriel has this beautiful crystal butterfly, of which she is very proud.

We are all in pain, but things are getting better. We are seeing her boys occasionally. Kirk has asked for time, and of course, we have to give him space. From what we can see Kirk and the boys are getting along well enough in the circumstances.

As a footnote to this unfortunate past 12 months, 4 days after Helen died on Friday, I felt her presence very, very close to me. When I got up on Wednesday, she was gone. The difference was so profound, and left me in no doubt that she had been there close to me.

However, at that point, suddenly I started hearing her voice. It started with her clearly saying to me, “Dad I’m OK”. This happened for the first time about 4 days after she left us, and when we were really upset and crying. Over the next few days, it seemed that she got more and more impatient with us as we continued to be emotional, to the point that she was almost yelling things like “Dad, I’m fine,” or “Dad, tell Mum I’m OK”. About 5 days after she left, she impatiently again said “Dad, I’m OK”, which I repeated to Muriel, and in the middle of me telling her what she’d said Helen interrupted me saying “And take care of Mum”. More recently, she doesn’t seem to volunteer statements anymore. She only answers questions when I initiate the conversations.

Most days, early in the day I ask “Helen, are you there”? She answers, “Yes Dad”, and I ask, “How are you today”. She answers, “OK” in a tired way as if she is a bit weary of me asking the same thing all the time.

Some of the other significant questions and answers are below. Some of my questions and Helen’s answers may not make sense but I have reported them exactly as they occurred. I feel embarrassed about sharing this with everyone as it does seem a bit “way out”, but I can only report the facts as I see (hear) them, and I must say that I do get some small comfort from this.

Q. How are you Helen?

A. I’m fine, so are you. (So am I??)

Q. Who is there with you?

A. X, X, X, and your other son Christopher.

Q .What is it like there?

A. Oh, you’d love it, mountains, trees, lakes and flowers

She knows I love to paint these.

Q. I suppose you have got your rectum back.

A. Ha Ha Ha, it’s not like that here, you’ll will understand later

Q. Are you worried about your boys?

A. Not a bit, we are spirit people but in the flesh and I know you'll take care of them.

Q. What do we do for Kirk? (Husband)

A. Just give him time. (I asked Kirk same Q.

He said "give me time"), same words

Q. Why don't you talk to your mother?

A. I do but she can't hear me.

Q. Will Christine's (my sister) back get better

A. Not really. (It didn't)

Q. Am I really talking to you, how is it possible?

A It's a gift from God.

Q. I regret that I didn't hug you more.

A. I knew that you loved me.

Q. Can you see us?

A. No, but we can feel you near. We know you're there.

Q. Have you seen God?

A. Oh yes, he's everywhere.

Q What does my mother say?

A. She sends her love.

Q. Is there time where you are?

A. No, no time.

Q. Do you eat?

A. (With a smile in her voice) no, we don't eat.

Q. Are you happy that I can hear you?

A. Oh yes, it's great.

Q. Do you miss us?

A. Yes, but I miss the boys more.

Q. Anything I can say to Kirk,

A. Yes, tell him I love him.

Q. Do you wear clothes?

A. Well yes, but they are heavenly garments.

Q. How did you feel about the cremation?

A. It didn't make any impact. (Like it was not important)

Q. Were you there?

A. I was there with you.

Q. How did you like the memorial?

A. It was beautiful, you all did a lot of work.

Q. Did you realize how many loved you?

A. No.

Q. Are you talking to anybody else?

A. No

Q. We have to go to choir practice now.

A. OK Dad.

Q. Is it better there than here?

A. No question.

Q. Where should we take the boys on Monday?

A. Anywhere you'd like. They will be happy to be out.

Q. Do our conversations impede you?

A. No way

Q. Do you like talking to me?

A. Yea, it's fine.

Q. Will we ever see you here?

A. No, afraid not.

Q. Is there a time limit on us talking?

A. No, I thought you had to go to choir practice.

Q. Goodbye Helen. (By both of us)

A. Goodbye Dad, goodbye Mum.

Q. Later same evening, hi Helen

A. Did you have a good practice?

Q. What was dying like?

A. It was so easy. Just like Dr. Berry said.

Q. Was dying scary?

A. No, I was surrounded by people I knew.

Q. Did you see us all there before you left?

A. Yes, I was sad to see you all so upset though

Q. Have you seen Scott?

A. Yes he's here and doing well.

Q. I'm going to bed now.

A. Sleep well, talk to you tomorrow.

Q. You took that diamond away, didn't you?

A. That was good, wasn't it? (Read the diamond story later)

Q. What are the trees like?

A. They're all in blossom.

Q. Does the sun shine?

A. Yes, all the time.

Q. Do you sleep?

A. No.

Helen's youngest son Matthew, (13) asked me to ask Helen the 2 following questions

Q. Does she hear me when I say good night?

A. Yes.

Q .I see shadows, Moving out of the corner of my eye, Is that her?

A. Yes, (to me), but don't tell him, as it might scare him

Q. How is it you can appear to Matthew?

A. Don't know. A special dispensation, maybe, can happen occasionally.

I asked Matthew if it would scare him, if it was his mother. He said "no", so I told him what Helen said and he seemed very happy with the answers to both his questions. Then I asked him what exactly he was seeing. He said that he would catch occasional glimpses of a white filmy shape especially when on a computer. I understand that some people are clair-audient and some clairvoyant. My (Brian's) mother and one sister are clairvoyant. Maybe, Matthew is clairvoyant also

Q. Were you with us yesterday? (Fishing with the boys).

A. I was there in the wind. (It was a very windy day) (Proof maybe)

Q. Would you like to go to England?

A. I can go any time I want.

Q. Do you know when people are going to die?

A. Long term no, short term maybe.

Q. Will you be there when I (Muriel) die?"

A. Of course.

Q. Have you seen Auntie Celia?

A. Yes, she's here.

Q. Did she cause the sparklers on the mirror when she died

A. Yes.

Q. Which of your brothers worry you the most?

A. Peter and David a bit.

Q. Do you mind me writing this and talking about it?

A. It demonstrates the power of God.

Q. Are you completely recovered now?

A. Yes.

Q. Will your mother's eyes be OK? A small surgery was recommended.

A. Yes, she'll be fine.

Q. How do you talk to other people there?

A. Same way I talk to you.

Q. Is communication like that clear and understood?

A. Yes.

Q. I suppose I'd better go and do some of my jobs.

A. You'd better take an Aleve (Pain pill for my back)

Q. Should I fix the shower faucet now?

A. Yes, it won't take you long.

Q. How long

A. About 10 minutes. (Took 15 minutes including tool collection)

Q. What should I do next?

A. Go and do the tires. (On my list which she apparently knew about),

Q. Am I really talking to you Helen?

A. Yes, Dad.

Q. I can't believe it, can you?

A. It's wonderful.

Q. Is there such a thing as reincarnation?

A. No (I don't agree with this answer) Very recently, I asked Helen if she was in a new body. She said she was in the body of a teenage girl in Florida. I asked for a phone number and she volunteered 407 xxx xxxx? She knew her own phone number! I chose to not pursue this, as much as I would like to.

Q. Do you use the same name (Helen)?

A. Well yes (There was lots of hesitation). .

Q. Is dying like Sharon and John Tyler report

A. It varies (more hesitation)?

Sharon and John, are our friends, but are unknown to each other.

Both had near-death experiences. They were basically the same with minor differences.

Q. Am I losing you?

A. No, some questions hard to answer in a way you'd understand.

Q. Did Matthew say goodnight to you tonight?

A. Yes, he's a good boy.

Q. We helped a friend financially.

A. God will pay you back

Q. Helen, we were given back over 10 fold

A. I told you!!!

My son David's father-in-law Max, died.

Q. Is Max there?

A. Yes, but not doing too well but he'll be OK in a while.

Q. Will Matthew (her son) be able to hear you?

A. Maybe, please try with him when he's a bit older.

Q. Are you there Helen?

A. Yes Dad, I'll always be able to hear you.

Q. How is it possible for us to still talk?

A. God is allowing it.

Q. Is God really the way the bible portrays him?

A. He's a lot less formal, very forgiving and friendly.

Q. Are there animals there?

A. Yes, it's just the same here as there.

Q. We miss you.

A. I know, but time will fly.

Q. What does God look like?

A. He's a man.

Q. But tell me more.

A. Goodness and love shine out of him.

Q. Am I holding you back by talking to you?

A. No, I'm always with you.

Q. Are you with your mother also?

A. Yes.

Q. You have said that you are with the boys.

A. I'm with them also.

Q. Does it worry you that your mother misses you so much?

A. Yes, it is upsetting. I'm OK.

Q. You really don't give me real details.

A. It is so hard to explain in your terms.

Q. You have said there is no time there and past, present and future are one, then when you say you are with us all, this probably means we are all with you, as we would be in our future.

A. You are spot on Dad, you've got it

Q. I made a joke with Muriel when she was in underwear, and Helen said out of the blue

A. You're funny Dad.

Q. Mum wants to listen to the memorial tape.

A. She shouldn't if it upsets her.

Q. Is there anything else anybody wants to say?

A. Uncle Fred sends his love. (Wow, Uncle Fred, out of the blue, what a surprise. Haven't thought of him in years)

Q. Should we meet the boys from school one day?

A. Yes, they'd love it.

Q. Why did God take you from us?

A. Ask Him yourself.

Q. God, why did you take Helen from us?

A. She was mine before she was yours. I asked this whilst typing, without thinking what I was doing. A different voice answered? Scary.

Q. Helen, did I really talk to God?

A. He's easy to talk to.

Q. You seem to be getting fainter lately.

A. You are just too busy to talk.

Q. I talk to you more often than I used to when you were here.

A. You are right.

Q. What do you think of my changes to our bedroom?

A. It is a smart move.

Q. Can you see your mother now I'm concentrating?

A. Yes faintly.

Q. Is this the first time you've seen her thru me?

A. Yes.

Q. Can you see me?

A. No.

Q. Wha t do you think of the hurricanes?

A. They are horrendous.

Q. Do you know all that goes on here on earth?

A. Not really, just some information gets thru.

Q. We are going to meet the boys from school tomorrow.

A. Yes, I know.

Q. Do they like this or just tolerate it?

A. I'm sure they love it.

Q. What about Kirk?

A. Just go along with him.

Q. What do you think of the book "Conversations with God"?

A. Believe it.

Q. Is the writer in touch with God?

A. Yes, just like you were.

Q. I don't agree with some of it.

A. The bulk of it is true.

Q. I feel my life is changing because of it.

A. It should.

Q. Do you mean that my life is wrong?

A. No, but you could stand some changes.

Q. What should we do?

A. Give more and be tolerant.

Q. Can we afford it?

A. Of course, you can.

Q. Is it true that you get it back 7 or 10 fold?

A. You know it is.

Q. Am I talking to God or you, Helen?

A. God talks thru me.

Q. I feel that I don't get real serious answers from you

A. There are things you shouldn't know.

Q. In the book, God answers every question.

A. That is his prerogative, He is God.

Q. Is Sam there?

A. He's fine, he's a lovely man. I got impatient with Muriel over a small thing. Helen said. You got angry with her, she's doing her best.

Q. Can I hear you because we are all one as in the book?

A. Yes, you know this.

Q. Should we work on you seeing thru my eyes?

A. Yes, I'd like that.

Q. Will God mind if it works?

A. I wouldn't think so.

Q. Shall we ask God for that?

A. That would be great.

Q. God, please allow Helen to see thru my eyes.

A. You'll have to work at that. (Helen's voice)

Q. Helen, can you see your mother?

A. Wow, I can see her. (I was concentrating) Seemed rather quick answer though))

Q. Doesn't she look good?

A. She looks tired. Take your glasses off.

Q. Helen, what am I looking at now?

A. My picture. (She was right)

Q. I mostly seem to have a click or switch-like feeling in my mind, before I get your answer.

A. No answer.

Q. But our conversations seem so ordinary, I don't seem to get significant info.

A. Again, no answer???? I was typing this and watching TV at the same time, possibly not paying full attention. As an experiment, I asked Muriel if any thought comes into her head if she asks Helen a question. She said "no". As an experiment, I asked Joy a question in my mind, like I do with Helen, telling her first not to answer, so that I could see if an answer came into my head as it does with Helen. The question to Muriel was, would she like me to buy her a dress tomorrow. No answer came into my head. Immediately I asked Helen, "how about you". She immediately answered "don't be stupid".

Q. Are you there Helen?

A. I'm always here, I'm part of you

Q. We are going to buy Christmas restaurant gift certificates for Gaye and Michi (Helen's friends).

A. They'll be happy with that.

Q. Why couldn't I hear you just now?

A. You were not turned on.

Q. I'm going to close down now.

A. Talk to you tomorrow. Muriel said to me, "I do believe you're talking to Helen. Helen heard and said "hooray".

Q. Helen, Andrew (her son) is 6'4" now.

A. Wow, I can hardly believe it.

Q. You know that the boys are sick, and we have them here.

A. Yes, you are taking good care of them.

Q. You don't ever seem concerned about them.

A. They can't hurt. They're doing their thing.

Q. We are concerned about them, not having you with them.

A. In 2 years it will all change. (This was end of 2006)

Q. Muriel said, "Ask if she feels the same about us."

A. No, things are different. I am more equal to you, and not like your daughter. This upset Muriel very much. Later Helen said Explain more to Mum, "Relationships like daughter, father/son, etc. don't exist here".

Q. I'm concentrating on your mother, can you see her?

A. Not really, now faintly, keep trying. You've got a diversion, TV's on

Q. Do you feel the same way about your sons?

A. I don't have the same connection as when I was their mother.

Q. I find it hard to understand.

A. It doesn't mean I don't love them. That's all there is, love.

Q. Am I really talking to you?

A. Don't have doubts.

Q. I get very sad when I think about what you went thru.

A. It was OK. It passed

Q. Was there rejoicing when you returned to Heaven?

A. O yes, much rejoicing.

** Sharon and John, friends, both had similar near-death experiences.

Latterly, I mostly get into conversation with Helen when I start it, but with the exception of when we get emotional, as mentioned above. Now, at months after Helen's death, we don't get so emotional, and I rarely hear her speak unless I speak to her first. Most days, I ask if she is there. She always says "yes, I'm here Dad".

I have had thoughts that maybe I was answering my own questions except for the fact that the answers come immediately, just as if there is another brain involved, and some answers are so wise and different from the answers I would give. In my opinion, one of the conversations I find most convincing that Helen is talking to me is the time when Muriel and I were in tears on the freeway, and out of the blue, I heard her clearly say, in an impatient tone, "Dad, I'm OK". I repeated this to Muriel, but halfway through my statement, Helen added, "And take care of Mum". I find it hard to believe that it is coming from me when Helen's voice interrupted me in the middle of me making another statement. It is significant to report however, that conversation is happening less and less, although that is due to me not taking the time to talk. I still do get a response when I ask "Helen, are you there" "or how are you" Also, I'm running out of questions.

Upon finishing the last paragraph, this was when I mentally asked Helen, "Why do I believe I am talking to you and why can I hear you". (This is included in the questions above). I didn't expect an answer, but it came immediately and clearly, "It is a gift from God". I was left almost breathless and with the certain feeling that she meant that this was a special dispensation to Helen and me, on a one-time basis, and not a gift such as the ability to draw or sing or write poetry. I repeat, THIS ANSWER WAS CLEAR AND IMMEDIATE. I don't understand it and can assure you that I don't generally suffer with flights of fancy. I can only report what happened.

It is worthwhile to note that the Hospice booklet "Gone From My Sight", (written to give comfort in the death of loved ones), states that it is not uncommon for the bereaved to hear the voice of a departed family member. Maybe I am not crazy after all.

Before I conclude this chapter, there is a very strange occurrence I must relate. Helen and Muriel were extremely close and on the same wavelength about jewelry. Some years ago, Helen had recommended to Muriel, a particularly pretty ring that was for sale in Hemet, and we saw it and we bought it. Helen always said that if it was hers, (and this was expected one day), she would have it made into a pendant.

A couple of weeks back, Muriel decided that she would go ahead and have it made into a pendant in Helen's memory, and this would require a visit to a large jewelry company in Tustin, California. However, before we made the trip, we discovered on the day of Helen's memorial, that a small diamond was missing from a ring of mine, which normally had seven diamonds. We looked around and in the box. My son Peter looked at the ring and the box and on the floor, but it was gone. We agreed that we should also take this ring and get a replacement stone at the same time. We all clearly saw that the ring had an empty space.

On the way to the jeweler about 60 miles away, Muriel suddenly decided that she would keep her ring as a ring and not have it made into a pendant. She doesn't know why she changed her mind. I suggested that we get a pendant to match the ring if they had one suitable. Muriel didn't argue with this, and so when we arrived, I told the sales lady that I wanted to replace the lost stone in my ring. She looked at it, acknowledged the space, and went off to get an estimate for replacement. In the meantime, we found a beautiful, large, and very expensive pendant with which Muriel fell in love. It was the best piece of jewelry in the store, and would definitely have caught Helen's eye also.

Back with the sales lady and 5 minutes later, she said the new diamond would cost $387, and then asked with a puzzled look, "Where did you want this diamond placed?" I said, "In the empty space". She didn't answer, but held out the ring to me, and I took it from her and couldn't believe my eyes. There was a bright flash of a diamond in the empty space! I swear that the thing winked at me, far brighter than the other diamonds. I said, "O, they've already done it". I held it out to Muriel. The sales lady said, "No it hasn't been done yet". We had all seen the empty space, and we were all in shock. For the estimator to give us a price, he had to know the size so he must have seen the empty socket. Logic tells us that the diamond had just come back.

The sales lady immediately gave us a large discount on the pendant, (I think she was in shock, just like Muriel and I were), and Muriel became its new owner. I feel that Helen was with us in the store, and had some hand in the mysterious thing that happened, and even influenced the pendant transaction. I think our Helen chose the gift for Muriel of the new pendant that day.

There is no doubt that the ring did have a stone missing when we entered the store. The saleslady's name was. . . . . .Helen.

As I write, Muriel is reading a book loaned to her by a friend. It is meant to be comforting to those who have lost loved ones. The book is entitled "Grief, Climb Toward Understanding" by Phyllis Davies. It speaks of ADC, which is, apparently, a commonly accepted thing in some circles, but which is recently new to me. The letters stand for After Death Communication. I am more convinced than ever that I am actually in contact with our Helen, and she is the same person she was here with us. She talks the same way and is not changed one bit. This all comes as a complete surprise to me. I always felt that a person would change completely after death, but she seems exactly the same.

I can't seem to finish this chapter as additional things keep popping up. The above was written some time ago, but on my 70th birthday, we had our three sons who live locally, to dinner along with four friends. When we were all assembled, I felt that it was a good opportunity to relate the diamond story, which I did. Nobody could offer any possible explanation and were as mystified as Muriel and I.

We had a good dinner, and later, people began to leave. My son David and his wife Susan, stayed on, along with Muriel and me. David announced that we may have overlooked the most important part of the diamond story. He felt that it was significant that the smallest diamond was missing from a 7-diamond ring. He pointed out that our family of 7 had lost its smallest and youngest member in Helen! Jewelry was a great interest shared by Muriel and Helen, and he theorized that maybe the inexplicable way the diamond reappeared was her way of saying that she was still here, which is my certain feeling. I don't feel that she is separated from us as I've felt with previous deaths of family members. Are facts stranger than fiction in this case?

Our conversations will be ongoing, and any significant items will appear in future chapters. More recently, with me running out of questions, we tend to converse in idle chatter. Yes, this is right. I am amazed that we can just talk about the small things, which have little significance.

It is almost a month since I wrote the above story, and now I wish to record another strange happening. First I should say that Helen was most faithful in sending greeting cards out on time. She always sent birthdays, Mother's days, Father's days, and other cards, with lovely messages in her beautiful handwriting.

Anyway, Muriel's birthday was approaching and four days before, I made a card on the computer and placed it in an envelope, and put it in a drawer as I usually did. Two days before the birthday, we had accumulated about a dozen cards by mail, from Muriel's sisters, etc. and they were piled up on the pool table. Muriel was out, so this was an opportunity for me to place the card I'd made, in the stack. This I did, placing it in the middle of the stack.

On the birthday in the morning, Muriel and I sat down together and she started to open her cards. As she read each one she handed it to me to read. After a while, I had my hand out for the next one, and she said, “That is all of them”.

I said, “Where is the card from me”? Muriel answered that there wasn’t one from me. We looked around but could find no sign of it. I immediately printed a new copy within about two minutes. I had the card in memory on the computer.

There is no question that I made the card, and put it in a drawer, then later transferred it to the stack on the pool table. 10 days later, we have seen no sign of this card. We have absolutely no idea of what happened to it. We have searched the place to no avail. There was nobody else in the house who could have moved it. We have no explanation.

Muriel was very upset on this birthday as this was her first birthday in many years without a card from Helen.

I’m adding this late note in July 2006. I am about to print and distribute this section and want this item included in this chapter. About a month ago during a quiet afternoon, I was sitting in my recliner, half asleep, but still aware. Muriel was playing solitaire on her laptop, about 5 feet away. Helen’s boys were staying with us. I had a long sleeve loose sweater on and suddenly somebody ran a hand up my left arm from wrist to shoulder, which caused my sweater sleeve to roll up my arm. I jumped, wide awake, startled. I actually heard the rustling sound it made. I asked Muriel if one of the boys had passed behind my chair. She said that both were in their bedroom and nobody was anywhere near me. I told her what had happened, and she said that she actually heard the sound coming from my direction!!!!! My left sweater sleeve was partly pushed up. I asked Helen if that was her, and she answered yes. She said she did it to tell me that she was still here with me!!!! I asked if she could always do that. Her answer was, “I can sometimes”. The touch was not light, but heavy enough for Muriel and I to be certain that it really happened.

Chapter 41 - Life Is Going On

On 12th July 2005, my son Peter and wife Luanne divorced. This was the first in the family and a very sad occasion for us. Their 3 children took it badly as you would expect. Both parents were equally loved by all the children. On our trip back to Tennessee last Christmas, we hoped that our presence would help matters but it didn't change anything, unfortunately.

Now, almost 6 months later (29th November), they have split their assets, and Luanne's houses have now been sold, and just after Christmas, she is moving back to San Diego. Peter brought his girlfriend to see us in October, with the intention of possibly getting married, but this didn't happen.

Peter has been living in a large house in Franklin, Tennessee, and was planning to do some improvements in the basement and then rent the house out. I went back there for a week to help him at least get started. We completed putting the sheetrock in his basement ceilings, but since then, he has been very busy helping Luanne finalize things and attending to his real estate business.

In the meantime, their eldest son, Michael, aged 21, has moved here with us and is attending college and working part-time.

Peter's second son, David (16), can't wait to get back to California and intends to spend time with his older brother, which means that he will be here a lot. Their Daughter, Keri (18) is in college near Nashville.

Muriel's mother has asked us to try to make it to England for Christmas, and we were keen to do this. However, we were unable to go in 2004 because of Helen's illness. But this year we made definite plans to go, so in September (2005) we booked our flight for 13th December, returning on 11th January 2006. I always felt that this was too long, but went along with it.

Shortly thereafter, Peter decided he wanted to go along with us subject to his business situation. However, due to some unfortunate things happening in England, we were obliged to reconsider. The outcome was that we cancelled this trip, and paid $400 penalty. This makes a total of exactly $5000 paid in penalties for cancelled trips, since September 2004, when we cancelled a 24-day cruise ($4600) out of Osaka Japan. This was due to Helen's illness. We have decided that in future we will book trips at the last minute.

In the meantime, Muriel has had a variety of little things taken care of. Earlier this year she had a painful arthritic finger operated on, which took 3 months to heal. She has no pain now. Then she found that she had the beginnings of cataracts in both eyes. She wanted to get all these things done so that she was in good shape, and so had both eyes fixed. She can see very well and can read at times without any glasses at all.

We are keeping in touch with Helen's 2 sons. We go and meet them out of school every couple of weeks, and take them for ice cream, and then shopping, for any little thing they might want or need. They are gradually getting comfortable talking about their mother. Andrew will be 16 in about 2 weeks and has passed his written driving test, and will soon be going for his driving test. When he can drive, the boys will be much freer as they live so far out they cannot get away from the house without somebody to drive them. Andrew is approaching 6' 5"!!!! Matthew has started growing and I don't think he will be far behind in a year or so.

Their father, Kirk does the best he can but has had to work nights recently, and sadly, the boys don't see much of their father. A lot of responsibility falls on Andrew as the eldest, but he is a very good boy, and mature for his age. They have bought a nice boat and go fishing together when they are able. This little family makes us ache, and we feel so helpless because being so far away, we cannot do much to help out.

Chapter 42 - As of March 2006

We spent a nice Christmas Day 2005, at David's house. Most of the local family was there also. Unfortunately, Kirk could not join us as I believe he had to work. Helen's sons spent Christmas day with their neighbor.

I have always been disappointed with Christmas in America mostly due to the fact that it is over in about 24 hours. The Christmases from my youth, in wartime, and the following years of shortages, were full of self-made fun and activity. We didn't have the money or "things" that we have now, but we drew on family and our own resources and it was much more enjoyable. Not only that, the English Christmas includes Boxing Day, the day after Christmas day.

Following the cancellation of the Christmas trip to England, Muriel promised her mother that she would visit in February, but this was not to be as she had a minor health problem that needed to be checked out. After weeks of tests and other delays, she got the news a week ago, that everything was normal and there was nothing wrong.

Muriel is now planning to go to England soon, but a complication has arisen. She has found out about a river cruise on the Danube which visits Prague, Budapest, Vienna, and a few other places which Muriel wants to visit. She is trying to decide whether to go from England or do the two trips separately. Separately, of course would cost more.

In the meantime, we have joined two more choirs, so that we go for practice on Mondays, to The San Luis Rey Chorale, Tuesdays to the Mira Costa College Choir, and on Thursdays, to our church choir. The Mira Costa Choir sings two performances this coming weekend at our church. We did this as we feel we need to have more activity, and singing is enjoyable and good exercise. Also, we feel that we are getting better at reading music.

As you know, Grandson Robbie, son of Nick and Karen, is at the University of Long Beach, majoring in art. He is working as a part time-manager at Starbucks, an upstart coffee (only) place. Can't think how they can exist, but it is amazing how much of a hold caffeine has on some people. They charge exorbitant prices. Anyway, Robbie is on the Dean's list for excellent work. He is working very hard and has lost weight, but seems to be having a good time. He appears to be making the most of his opportunity.

Luanne, now Peter's ex-wife has moved from Tennessee, back to California, and is living in Poway, near her parents, and about 17 miles from us. As reported earlier, Michael is living with us, and occasionally his younger brother David comes for the weekend. I pay him for doing little jobs around the place. He likes the money and enjoys the visit.

Other news from the family includes the fact that Nick and Karen have bought a piece of land in the mountains about 450 miles north of here near Bishop, or on the way to Mammoth. He says they intend to build a house eventually. Apparently, there are lots of lakes around there and being a keen hunter/fisherman he will be in his private heaven. Actually, he will also be able to enjoy the snow. They have three feet of snow at this moment.

Over the last few months, we have had Helen's boys here a couple of times, and we have visited them about every 10 days or two weeks. When we go there, we meet them from school and first take them shopping at Walmart where we buy them some of the little things they need such as school supplies, small toys, chewing gum, bike tubes, etc. Then we take them to Denny's restaurant where they have Banana Splits or fruit-covered cheesecake. After that, we take them home to do their homework, and either take them out to dinner or bring food home with us depending on how much time we have. It takes most of the day as we leave home around 11.00 am and get back around 9.00 pm. They seem to enjoy our visits much more nowadays than they used to. Maybe we reminded them of their mother and they found it upsetting in the months past

Chapter 43 - Busy Times, June 2006.

Well, Muriel went to England in early April, returning on the 12th. She felt that her mother was not quite as robust as she used to be, but at 95, this is to be expected.

One week after Muriel's return, we left on the 19th for 3 days in Prague and then the Danube cruise. I have omitted any mention of the back problem I've developed. It is stenosis of the spine and arthritis which is putting pressure on the nerves. Anyway, I had a real problem with the walking whilst we were away, but didn't miss anything. I could have done without the pain, but with a few days' rest it got a bit less crippling. Since then I've had 2 cortisone shots. The first one didn't do much, but the second one has helped a little. Since then, I've had 4 acupuncture treatments, and I'm taking some herbal pills. It is much improved, but I don't know whether it is the cortisone, pills, or acupuncture.

Prague was very impressive if you like buildings. The Danube was in flood, and because of the high water, the boat couldn't get under some of the bridges, so at the end of the Prague visit, we were bussed a couple of hundred miles across the Czech Republic, into Germany to Deggendorf, which was the closest place that the boat could reach. The original plan was to meet the boat in Nurenburg, then the next day, sail to Regensburg. However, after we boarded in Deggendorf, the next day we were taken back by bus to Regensburg, and the day after that we were bussed back to Nurenburg.

I was struck by the number of slightly off-color patches on the walls of the buildings in all the towns. I told Muriel I thought they were patched bullet holes. (At about our third town the guide confirmed this). There sure was a lot of lead flying about.

Nurenburg was interesting. We visited this huge building which looked like it covered 20 or 30 acres. Then we went through an archway and discovered that it was a grand-looking outer shell only. Apparently, Hitler had insisted that it be built, and it should have a roof with no inside supporting columns, which was impossible because it was larger than 4 football stadiums. So today it stands as a shell only, with trucks and trailers stored inside. Next to this is a large lake, and beyond that, a parade ground where Hitler could salute the troops.

Regensburg was a very pretty little town with lots of history. Of course, all these towns are built on the banks of the Danube.

The boat was very nice, meant to hold about 130 passengers, but there were only 68 on board, which meant that there was plenty of room. Our cabin was roomy and comfortable. The food was very good, with lots of choices. Whilst Muriel was in England I set out to lose some weight and did get 8lbs off. However, when she'd been home 4 days, I put 4lbs back on. Of course, on the boat, I gained it all back.

After our trips to Nurenburg and Regensburg, we sailed for the next stop which was Passau, Germany. It was more the same, lots of beautiful buildings, castles, cathedrals, etc etc. We were in one of the cathedrals at a time when there was a recital by a young lady violinist and the organist.

The acoustics were fabulous, and the organ was the most ornate one we've ever seen. I gave a photo of the organ to our church organist and she was overjoyed. She had always wanted to see Passau's organ, but never got there to see it. Apparently, it is world-famous, at least among organists.

Our next stop was Melk, Germany. More of the same, in fact, I don't remember Melk at all. Next stop, Vienna. Here the buildings were even more grand. We went to a concert with a small orchestra, singers and dancers. Bored me to tears but Muriel enjoyed it immensely. Next stop was Budapest. More of the same.

We flew Air France via Paris. Paris airport was a mess. No signs, and everybody giving wrong directions. We thought we'd never find the correct gate. We'd flown there in a 777, which had good legroom. The return trip was in a 747, and we were jammed in without room to move. My back was really bad.

In the meantime, my son Peter's property in Tennessee has kept him there, and now his son Michael has returned, and the younger son, David, living with his mother in this area, has decided to return to Tennessee also.

One of my granddaughters, the daughter of my son Christopher, graduates high school in about a month. She left yesterday for Europe on a trip with a school group.

The weather is getting warmer, and today, Muriel and I made a start on cleaning the pool ready for summer. We are a bit later this year due to so many other things we have to do. No doubt the pool will be up and running soon at Muriel's favorite temperature of 94 degrees F.

Now, Mid-June the pool is up to 93 degrees, just the way we like it. All we need is the time to use it, but we have decided that we have to not get so involved so that we can do some things for ourselves. Next spring, we plan to go to England and show our son David and his wife Susan around. We would like to take our other son Nick and his wife Karen at the same time also, but they are not too keen at this point.

Now it is mid-July. Unfortunately, Muriel's sister Dawn died on Monday 26th June 2006. Muriel went back to England for the funeral, which was held on the 6th of July. Dawn spent a lifetime suffering from epilepsy, and was kept alive on drugs. It is a miracle that she lived as long. She was 65 years old.

Special Addendum

It is 16th November 2009. I have been reading a book called, "Hello from Heaven"; one of a number of books loaned to us by friends who also lost a daughter just around the same time that Helen left us. These books are mostly about grief and after-death contacts or communications. You have already read about, what I'm convinced, are my communications with Helen. Since reading these books, there is virtually no doubt left in my mind that I am talking to Helen because of the almost identical words, phrases and the same anxieties addressed and answered by hundreds of persons interviewed about their experiences.

The particular chapter which caused me to write this addendum is about factual accounts of many peoples' experiences with departed loved ones whilst sleeping. This chapter has made me realize that an experience I had after my father's death, was very much more significant than I had given it credit.

It was 22 years ago, approximately a year after my father died. I was asleep and had this dream which was much more vivid and detailed than normal dreams, and I was standing in Northumberland Passage in Bath, England. It was a perfect bright sunny day with a pleasantly warm gentle breeze blowing. Northumberland Passage is a wide pedestrian-only walkway with stores on each side. It is known for the flower baskets hanging every few yards, and on my visit, they were exceptionally beautiful.

I was now an adult, and standing outside the newsagent store where 65 years ago on Saturdays, I would wait for my father to come after his Saturday morning work. He would pick up a large bundle of comics for me, and magazines for my sisters. I was always happy to be there and to see my father coming toward me from the Guildhall end. (City offices).

In this dream, I was enjoying just being there, and it was so real that I knew that I really was there. Then I spotted my father coming toward me, looking at me, just as he did 65 years ago. He seemed very young and healthy with a big smile. Instead of stopping, he kept walking. He passed within 3 feet of me, and continued, looking back and smiling at me. I was unable to move. It felt as if I was standing in 2 feet of sticky mud, and couldn't move my feet. When he'd gone about 20 feet past, the whole scene disappeared. I have only had one other occurrence in which a "dream" was so real, but that is another story. I remember this experience as clearly today as I did in the morning after it happened.

Now there is a very interesting sequel. Muriel's Aunt Celia came for a 4-month visit in 1986. Shortly before her return to England, she had a couple of bouts of feeling unwell. When she got home, it was found that she had leukemia, and was put into hospital. A few weeks later at almost exactly 11.00 pm. Muriel and I were just getting into bed when Muriel gave a surprised little shriek. She said that the whole wall of the mirror (cupboard doors) was covered with sparkling flashing lights. Before I could turn around it had stopped. Muriel said, "I'll bet Auntie Celia died". About 20 minutes later, the phone rang. It was Muriel's sister Sheila. Muriel said, "You needn't tell me, I know Auntie Celia died". Sheila confirmed that thc dcath occurred at exactly 7.00 am in England, 11.00 pm in California. Sheila asked how Muriel knew. Muriel said, "She was here".

Muriel's sister Susan was Auntie Celia's Godchild. When Helen died, 4 ½ years ago, Susan immediately came here to comfort Muriel. They spent hours talking together, and I paid little attention until one day Muriel called to me to "come and hear what Susan has just told me". Susan repeated the story, which was about a very vivid "dream" she'd had shortly after Auntie Celia died.

Susan was standing at the bottom of Milsom Street in Bath, England, a street of very high-class stores. The day was a very pleasant sunny day, and she saw Auntie Celia approaching her, looking young and very healthy, and smiling. She passed within a few feet, and continued on, looking back and smiling until the scene disappeared. Susan said that she could not move. Her feet seemed stuck in mud. This happened just 200 yards from Northumberland Passage and seemed a parallel experience to mine.

Chapter 44 - Summer 2006

This summer started very warm with record temperatures, but has cooled down a bit now (mid-July). As related at the end of the last chapter, Muriel's sister passed away and Muriel is still in England until next Monday, 17th July, and this gives me the opportunity to get ahead with this writing. Every day, Muriel is taken out driving by one or other of her sisters and goes to a different sister or brother each night for dinner. The next problem for her will be getting into her clothes.

Some months ago, Kirk, Helen's husband, who is a sergeant in the California Highway Patrol was called out to go to the aid of a lady who was being chased in her car by an ex-boyfriend who was shooting at her with an AK47. There was a newspaper report of the incident. A few details were left out of the story, such as the fact that Kirk had some bullet fragments in his arms and shoulder, caused by bullets breaking up and flying around when hitting the metal of his car. There was only one window of the car not shattered, and the rear seat was a mass of shredded stuffing. The car apparently was a write-off. How Kirk was not hit is a miracle. Apparently, the criminal had recently come out of prison and was on parole. Now he will probably spend the rest of his life locked away.

Following this, Kirk has had many awards, but the main one was described in a newspaper article, where he was named International Trooper of the Year. Our two grandsons, Andrew, 16, and Matthew 14, had a wonderful time during the visit to Washington for one award ceremony. Also, Kirk was presented with an award in Sacramento, by Arnold Schwarzenegger, the governor of California. Whilst in the governor's office, the boys were allowed to examine the sword used by Arnold in the film "Conan", in which he starred.

We are determined to pick our life up, and to this end, we have just booked an eight day cruise to the Mexican Riviera, to places like Cabo San Lucas, Puerto Vallarta, Ixtapa and Acapulco. We have done this trip before, but it is very cheap, and we are trying to get Kirk and our grandsons to come with us. At this time I am awaiting his confirmation that he will come, or at least let the boys come with us. They would have to miss 4 days of school, unfortunately.

We are also making plans for a trip to England next spring 2007, with our son David and his wife Susan. Susan has never visited England, and has had to live with all of us who frequently talk about it, something she has not experienced. She is very excited.

On another subject, my eldest sister, Christine has had a hip replacement operation. She had it done before, but apparently the pins loosened, and it had to be re-done. Hopefully it will help her back problem, and reduce the total pain which she has suffered for many years.

Our church pastor retired a few weeks ago, and last Sunday was the first Sunday for our new man. He did very well and appeared younger than I expected. There are fears that he is going to rock the boat a bit as he has a reputation for being a bit progressive, advocating new ideas. The rumor is that the mother church has charged him with bringing in lots of younger people, which may shake up some of the older folks. Also, our choir director resigned, (long overdue). There is a search going on. Lots of changes. We'll have to wait and see.

I'm sure I mentioned in earlier chapters that we left our old church, Torrey Pines Christian Church, (that we attended for 30 years), because of the nasty lady who was the choir director. Well, finally they got rid of her because she couldn't get on with the recently new pastor. Surprise, surprise. It should have happened 5 years ago. If things don't turn out too well at our current church, I may well go back to the old church. We have already been asked by one old friend from there, to return. Muriel is not too happy at the prospect, but this may change if she becomes uncomfortable with our new pastor.

Today, in early August, we have booked the cruise mentioned above. Kirk cannot go because he cannot get time off, but Andrew and Matthew can go. They are very excited. I have asked them to get Kirk to check into this again as I know they would like him along.

Now it is early September 2006, and we have accepted an invitation from old friends, originally neighbors in Santa Monica, George, and Anna. They have houses in Westlake Village, a few miles north of Los Angeles, and one in Trinidad, Northern California, about 100 miles from the Oregon border. We drove to Trinidad, a distance of approx. 816 miles.

We arrived at 8.15 pm after 12 and a quarter hours of driving. We knew that the house was out in the countryside, and traversed the last quarter of a mile of bumpy road, admiring the trees, and the beautiful countryside there. They have 8 acres of mixed redwood trees and grassy areas. It is truly like a park. George cultivates a large vegetable garden, surrounded by 6-foot fencing to keep the deer out. He produces large amounts of beautiful vegetables.

The first thing when we arrived was meeting their pit bull. Muriel is not comfortable around any dog, and this one looked quite ominous. However, it turned out to be more scared of us than we were of the dog. Muriel soon realized that it was no problem.

Apparently, Anna likes to visit Trinidad, a town of 340 people, but she doesn't like to spend all her time there. George, on the other hand, loves it, and is reluctant to leave, so for years, Anna has traveled the world quite a bit with a hiker group, whilst George's most recent passport expired in 1983. He hasn't been anywhere for many years.

Trinidad is a tiny village on the coast, and very picturesque. It is one of our favorite places that we remember from our several trips up and down the California and Oregon coasts. We never dreamed that George and Anna would have a place there. There is one store, one gas station, and a couple of restaurants. They have the cutest tiny harbor tucked up against a small headland.

We mentioned our upcoming cruise, and Anna wanted to go also, so after some arm-twisting, we got George to book the trip for them. Then we scurried around for them to get photos taken and the passport application sent in. Their two sons could not believe that their father had agreed to go

We stayed for 9 days in Trinidad and had a wonderful time. Anna joined us for the journey back on the 10th of September, and we delivered her to Westlake Village to stay with their eldest son whose wife was due to give birth. Anna will stay for 3-weeks, and take care of their other child and assist when the new baby comes. We were due to come back home on the 12th of September, but Anna was asked to get to Westlake early, as the baby was expected early.

It is early October and I can report that the baby mentioned above was born on 9/28/06, about 2 1/2 weeks late. Anna was due to go back to Trinidad on 10/1/06 but has had to stay on a bit.

Chapter 45 - Cruise to Mexican Riviera

The cruise is just 4 days away (14th November). We bought black suits, white shirts, black shoes, and socks for Helen's sons, and we're hoping to get them to wear bow ties and cummerbunds. They don't want to wear bow ties, but maybe they will change their minds when we get ready for the formal dinner evening.

A few days before the cruise, I was able to get a top-of-the-line laptop computer for $398. Anna has expressed an ambition to write her life story (like this), and also wanted a computer, so I bought an extra one for her.

On the cruise, the boys were able to watch some of their DVD's on my new computer.

It is now 9th February 2007, and an opportunity to continue this story. The cruise was wonderful, and the boys enjoyed it enormously. Anna and George came along and seemed to enjoy it. I took 287 photographs on the trip, and the boys are eating in half of them. Since then, Andrew has grown to be about an inch taller than me. I must have shrunk a bit as he is only 6ft 4". I used to be that tall.

Anna & George came here after Thanksgiving for a few days, and I was able to give Anna a few pointers on computers. She didn't remember too well, but she has to work it out for herself like I did. Whilst they were with us we found that Anna doesn't like living in Trinidad, and George does, so there is a bit of a tug-of-war going on. It sounds like Anna is going for a walking tour in Hawaii in early March, then she says that she is going to live in Santa Monica from 1st May. We'll have to wait and see.

George is planning his garden for the season, so it seems he will be there for another year. I must say that Trinidad is beautiful to visit but offers no place to live. There is nothing there except trees and hills, with virtually no life or services close by.

We have booked our trip to England for 19th April, returning on 6th May 2007. We will stay with Joy's cousin, Tony, near London, for about 5 days, then go to Bath to tour around the west of England. When we come back home, we will leave for a car trip to Mount Rushmore on around 15th May. Muriel has always wanted to go there, and we find that if we plan it we are more likely to do it whereas we tend to put off things if we haven't planned it ahead and named a definite date.

Surprise, surprise. We have put the house on the market, sort of. We have a sign outside, and some brochures, but no price. In 2 weeks, 63 brochures have been taken. My son Nick has a real estate license and has his name on the sign. There have been a few inquiries but nothing that seems terribly serious. We have time, and may not find a buyer for years. We will continue here as we are in no real hurry.

Grandson Michael arrived in California a week or so ago. He is the one who stayed with us for about 9 months a year ago. With him was Leta, his old girlfriend. Apparently, they got married on 15th January. He has signed up for the National Guard for 6 years. I believe this is the very best thing for him as he appears to not have the self-discipline and "stick to it ness" that he needs. They plan to have a more formal wedding at some point in the future, and by the Ocean, so that probably means California.

We came by a piece of news at Kirk's house the other day when we were visiting Helen's boys. There was a photo of Kirk and a lady, and I asked Matthew if the lady was his Dad's girlfriend. He said it was.

Some months ago, we told Kirk that we didn't expect him to stay single all his life, and we are pleased that his loneliness is relieved somewhat. Apparently, the lady sometimes does the boys' laundry and I'm sure she does other things for them. Kirk does seem happier, which is good for all concerned.

Chapter 46 - Troubles in Paradise

As you may have picked up earlier when I was updating my conversations with Helen, her sons are not happy. They are suffering from a bit of jealousy over their father's new live-in girlfriend. They have done a complete turnaround from supporting him in everything, to hating him and their life in Hemet. Andrew, 18 next December 2007, says he is leaving home as soon as he can. We go to see them tomorrow and expect to hear more complaints as their father and girlfriend have gone away for a few days leaving them home alone in the care of their other grandmother.

We asked them to talk to their father about their perceived problem, and they apparently did, and he yelled at them to the point that they were reduced to tears. They talked to their other grandmother with a view to her talking to her son, but she won't say anything. We hesitate to say anything as we could easily upset him to the point that he won't let them see us.

Matthew, Helen's 16-year-old, has never driven a vehicle. Andrew, the eldest, regularly drove the truck on the property from the age of 12. He got his license at 16. During our last visit 10 days ago, Matthew, for the first time, drove our car along the dirt road. He was always very scared of doing this, but afterward, he said he really enjoyed it and found it easy. Since then, Andrew has encouraged Matthew to drive his car along the dirt road on their way home from school. We want to encourage independence for the boys, but unfortunately, the law has changed and Matthew will not be able to get a license until he is 18. Andrew drove at 16, just before the law was changed.

Later contacts with the boys resulted in Andrew actually asking us if he could come and live with us. He wants to attend Carlsbad High School and Mira Costa Community College, which is 5 ½ miles from our house. He apparently hates schools in Hemet. He said that they are full of Mexican gangs and drugs.

Andrew's best friend, Josh, has a tough life with a nasty mother and a step-father. He has daily regular jobs and has to work all day Saturdays before he can go out. Andrew sometimes helps him, but then on occasions, she won't let him go, apparently just out of nastiness. Now, Josh wants to come and live with us. Consequently, we have withdrawn the sale of our house, as we may need the space. We go again tomorrow to visit them.

Chapter 47 - Early Summer 2007

Unfortunately, this has turned into a sort of diary, because I write this as it happens, or soon after. This was something I wanted to avoid, but it appears there is no other way to do it.

Andrew and Matthew finally did follow our advice and sat their father down and had a serious talk with him. He took note of their problem and has been spending more time with the boys. They have gone fishing together the last two Saturdays. The boys say that the girlfriend is nice to them and does their laundry and cooks food. I have met her twice and she seems very nice. Hopefully, this situation has been resolved.

As planned and mentioned earlier, my son David, his wife Susan, Muriel, and I went to England on the 19th of May. We arrived on the 20th to gray skies, but no rain. We went through immigration and customs and picked up the car with no complications, but had to find our way from the Hertz rental place to the motorway (M25) which circles London. We needed to go around the northern loop, but could not get to it even though we could see it. Finally, we went west on the M4 (east/west) and turned around and were able to get to the M25 going in the right direction. We were going to Muriel's cousin Tony's house in Basildon, on the east side of London. For those who don't know, London Heathrow Airport is on the west side of London.

We had very detailed instructions to get to Tony and his wife Pauline's house which depended on us getting off an off-ramp and looping around to go under the motorway but could not find our way. We took an hour to finally get to our destination.

The next day, a Saturday, Tony drove us into and around London, and we saw some of the sights, returning late afternoon. There was a dinner party arranged and we met Roger and his wife Jean, (Roger is son of Tony's older sister, Muriel's cousin Sybil), Tony's son Steve, his wife Debbie, and two nice and well-behaved children, Sam and Laura.

Roger and Jean are very keen wine fanciers, belong to a club, and have a basement devoted to storing wine. Not my cup of tea, but everybody to their own opinions. Roger and Jean will probably be coming to see us in the near future, also, since our visit, Steve and Debbie seem keen to come also. They may come with Tony and Pauline, who have been here many times.

The next day, Sunday, we went to nearby Leeds Castle. Muriel and I have been there before but had to go for David and Susan's sake. The only outstanding item was the cost to go in, $32 each. This was to be the trend for all the places we visited. I decided after that I would not pay these exorbitant costs. The weather had turned beautiful, however, but not warm by California standards. Susan was enthralled.

The next day, Monday, I stayed at Tony's house and read a book whilst the others went back to London.

We had to leave for Bath on the Tuesday, about 160 miles away. On the way, we stopped at Windsor Castle. I stayed in the car and read and slept while the others went in without me. My back was bothering me as I had walked too much around Leeds Castle. Not only that, as expected it was about $35 each to go in.

The exit from the motorway for Bath is about 10 miles from the city and is at a much higher elevation. The road into the city drops steadily, with a parallel deep valley on the north side. This provides a panorama of a distant patchwork of green fields all the way. Susan and David became a bit emotional. David was returning to the place of his birth and Susan was overcome by the view. We first went to Beechen Cliff, which allows a magnificent view of one of the most beautiful cities in England, Bath. By now, Susan's eyes were wide with what she had seen so far.

Muriel's brother Paul and his wife Karen, have a large house and we were staying with them for the rest of our trip. We arrived early evening and Karen went out to buy fish and chips, English style.

The following day, Muriel and I met with Muriels's co-workers from the telephone exchange, and we entertained them for lunch. In the meanwhile, David and Susan walked around the town and then came back to where we were to meet us. They were loaded with food shopping. David loves pickled onions and many other food items only found in England. He was flushed with the excitement of the stuff he had bought. We went back to the supermarket and bought more food items before going home in the early afternoon. We had bought beer and fizzy English lemonade and introduced Susan to Shandy, a mix of beer and lemonade. She loved it. Up until now, she had loved everything.

Susan has a cousin who has never been to England but spouts about the terrible English food. Susan now thinks English food is wonderful as do we. I believe that the bad reputation that English food bears, comes from GIs in England during war-time when there were terrible shortages, and food was poor.

We had many invitations, met all of Muriel's relatives, and generally had a marvelous time. David drove most of the time which gave him lots of good experience with the roads, for use in later visits. Susan was amazed at the narrow roads and said she would never drive in England. It can be a bit scary, but you get used to it. Side mirrors on the cars are all spring-loaded so that they don't break off but spring back after being hit. On the trip before this one, we had our mirrors twanged twice.

Our leaving Bath was not without sadness. Susan was somewhat distressed and didn't want to leave. It was a Sunday morning and very early for the trip back to London airport, and the weather was misty and cloudy with some drizzle, the first bad weather experienced over the whole trip. Later we heard that it had started raining after we left and continued for most of the following week. The flight back was wonderful. The Boeing 747 with 450 seats only had 100 passengers and we were able to stretch out over a number of seats. We made the trip from Los Angeles to Carlsbad in record time. It was good to be back.

David took 1,850 pictures. I took 187 pictures and about 40 minutes of video. A very successful trip, followed by a good time looking at the pictures.

Chapter 48 - Summer 2007, A Scare

In July, we heard some disturbing news. Muriel's mother, at 96, was short of breath and taken to hospital. Apparently, she had been coughing for some time, about a year. However, she hadn't coughed during our recent visit.

She was taken to the doctor and x-rayed, and a shadow was found on a lung, but it was not thought to be much.

Within a day of her getting into the hospital, she was found to have fluid on her lung, and she appeared to be sinking. In fact, she was not expected to survive the weekend, but survive she did. After about 3 weeks on oxygen, and other treatment, I suppose antibiotics, she was almost back to normal. It seems most likely that she will go to a residential care facility, just a mile from Muriel's brother's house.

In the meantime, Muriel was ready to rush to England at a minute's notice, but as soon as the emergency was past, we were able to resume our plan to go and pay a visit to our son Peter in Tennessee, which we did. The timing was based on the fact that Peter said he would be ready to start finishing the sheetrock (wallboard) in a house he was re-building. Our purpose was to help him with this phase as it is comparatively easy and light work but needs some skill. I enjoy this part of the construction. Not only that, I can do some of this whilst sitting on a chair with wheels, which saves my back, which is getting worse. I have to get serious and seek a permanent cure. This was in August 2007.

On the day we arrived in Nashville, the temperature was around 100 degrees, and it stayed this way for the next 12 days, the whole time we were there. Also, as is normal, the sheetrock had not been done. Due to one problem after another, the project was behind.

We started work by driving 20 miles through rural countryside with Peter's truck, pulling a trailer, to pick up a load of sheetrock. It was a relief to be in the air-conditioning in the truck instead of in the house with no air-conditioning. It took us about three hours round trip to get a load of 40 sheets. The temperature in the house, with the sun on the roof, must have been 110 or 115 degrees, and it was always a shock to return to it. In all, we did 3 trips with the truck and trailer to get enough sheetrock to finish the job.

It was now September, and Peter was sounding a bit down with all the work still to be done at the house, so we went back again for 12 days. I sat in a small seat with wheels and wired up 60 or so electrical boxes, some with 3 or 4 switches. Peter confirmed later that every outlet and switch worked properly.

Since our return, my back is worse. The work in Tennessee didn't help it at all. I have an appointment with an orthopedic surgeon in a couple of days with a view to discussing my options. Recently, I have run into a second person who had a successful operation for the same problem, so it is likely that I will undergo this operation.

At the start of the school summer holiday, we told Helen's 2 sons that we would take them somewhere on a trip, but they seemed to lack enthusiasm for anything, so we told them to make up their minds and let us know. They never did and they start back to school shortly, so their opportunity is gone along with our opportunity to have a summer vacation.

Their father has bought a new huge boat. It is about the maximum size that will go on a trailer. It must be over 30 feet long and uses about a gallon of gas per mile. They go sea fishing almost every weekend.

Chapter 49 - Christmas 2007 Is Over

It is 29th of December 2007, and Christmas is over. Christmases are just not the same as they were when I was younger and our children were small. Part of the problem is due to the fact that there is no Boxing Day celebration in the USA, and that means if you sleep later on Christmas day you might miss Christmas completely.

So much has happened since I last wrote. Muriel's mother died on 15th October, at the age of 96 after a brief bout of pneumonia. Muriel feels that it was time and a happy release. Some weeks later, I asked Helen, "Is your grandmother there with you?" She said, "Yes, and she's glad to be back". I'm not certain what this means. I am just reporting what I hear.

Muriel, my son Christopher, his wife and both daughters, David, his wife, and Peter, all went to England for the funeral. There were at least 60 that went back to Muriel's brother Paul's house afterward, and there were more at the graveside, so she had a good send-off.

I know I spoke before about my back problem, and it got so bad that I went back to the back surgeon of the group I had seen before, and he said casually, "I think I can fix you up with a little operation, so think about it and let me know if you want to go ahead". I didn't have to think about it so one day in early October, I went to the hospital at 11.00 am, and into the operating room at noon. The last thing I remember was 12.05 pm and I woke up around 4.00 pm after a 2 ½ hour operation. I needed to go to the bathroom and I got up and walked there without pain for the first time in several years. I left the hospital at about 5.45 pm and came home. It was a miraculous cure and I was back almost to normal in a day or so. I still have some slight other problems with my back, but they are minor in comparison.

Whilst in Tennessee last August (you remember it was extremely hot), Muriel apparently had a hemorrhage in her left eye. She was sent, on an emergency basis, to a retina specialist who prescribed pressure-reducing eye drops followed by many checkup visits. The eye pressure got higher, and in December she got an injection into the eyeball, which seemed to work. In the meantime, her vision in that eye went almost to nothing but did start to come back after the injection. The rest of the treatment was for a laser operation directed at the back of the eye. Since then, her eyesight has continued to improve, but she has to use eye-drops several times a day, at least for the foreseeable future.

You will remember that Helen's husband received many awards for the shootout, well only two weeks ago he was called to Washington to receive from President Bush, along with 4 other law enforcement and firemen, a medal of valor. The country's highest civilian honor. He is the most decorated California Highway Patrol Officer ever.

About a month ago Muriel and I discussed our future moves, and we decided that this house of 12 bedrooms and 11 bathrooms is just too much house for us and that we should move toward fixing all the things which had been neglected during my bad knees and bad back time, so we made me a job list. It had 38 items on it and I started work. As of today, I have completed 25 jobs, but the list has grown to a total of 56 jobs, which means that there are still 31 jobs to be done. We are adding jobs almost as fast as I can do them, but I am gaining. There is bound to be a time when new jobs will be showing up more slowly. We are hopeful that we can put the house on the market in April or May 2008.

It is now early May 2008, and our plan to put the house on the market has been delayed until 2009. We have accomplished some of our plans to clean the house up, but not nearly enough. In the meantime, we gave in to Muriel's long-term wish to visit the Epcot Center in Orlando, Florida. Peter and his girlfriend Anne decided that they wanted to go also, and so they met us there.

The Epcot Center was a complete disaster as far as we were concerned. It cost $72 each to go in and for very little. There were a couple of rides, one of which cost us 45 minutes to wait, and then it was just the international houses spread around a lake. I cannot understand what all the fuss is about. It was a complete disappointment.

We saw my sister Daphne and Bert who live near Orlando, and after a day or so we drove to Panama City in northern Florida. Peter's main objective in going to Florida was to look at sailboats. He has this hankering to buy a boat of around 50 feet, live on it, and sail around. He'd heard that there were many boats for sale in Panama City, the result of the hurricane Katrina. We looked but didn't find anything of interest to him. After a couple of days in Panama City, we left for the drive to Peter's house in Leipers Fork, Tennessee. For a few days, we did a bit of work on Peter's basement, putting a wall down the center of his basement garage with a view to making it into a couple of rooms behind the double garage.

We'd only been back a week or so when Peter's girlfriend Ann asked Muriel to go back and help her with an estate sale that she was holding, so one month to the day after our return, we went back to Tennessee. I spent 2 weeks finishing sheetrock for the basement rooms, and Muriel spent the time on the estate sale. I think we have decided on no more trips to Tennessee. It is just too tiring.

The week before we arrived in Tennessee, Peter's horse gave birth to a baby colt. He is very large and grew a lot while we were there. At first, he was a bit scared of Peter, but soon got friendlier and even sucked on his fingers.

As of today, it is sad to relate that Peter and Anne have had a monstrous fight and we doubt that it can be patched up. Their plans to come out to California in late June are probably cancelled, but maybe Peter will come alone. My sister Rosemary, her husband, and her daughter were planning on coming from Woodland Hills, to see them, and we were to have one of our sing-alongs whilst they were here. We'll have to wait and see.

Chapter 50 - Mid-Summer 2008

It is July and we had the sing-along a few days back. We are still eating the leftover food. It was very successful, and everybody enjoyed it.

Peter did not come to visit, and neither did my sister Rosemary. Her husband finally got talked into having the hip replacement that he needed, and during the pre-operation physical he was found to have a heart artery 70% blocked, so instead he had a stent inserted, and he was not too well. In the meantime, I talked Peter into adding two rooms to his now 1 bedroom house, and he is in the middle of it today. This is the house that was filled with mold, and it had 3 bedrooms and 1 bathroom. He tore the inside out and redesigned it, but it was my opinion that a 1bedroom house had little value. He finally agreed.

His plan is to sail the world when the addition is complete. To this end, he has bought a 43-foot sloop which is on blocks in Boston. When he finishes this house he will rent it out and travel to Boston and get his boat in the water. Then he will sail south to Savannah. He intends to make that his home port as it is about the closest to where all his property is in Tennessee.

Peter has talked to Anne many times, but there is no sign of them patching up their differences. The baby horse is now doing well. When we were there, we noticed that one of his front knees was a bit swollen. We told Peter this and finally, he had to get a vet, and a 6 weeks anti-biotic course was started. Finally, the drug had an effect, but it is thought that it caused the horse to lose patches of fur, but it is now growing back. This young horse is extremely friendly and follows Peter around like a little dog. He is very large, and a thoroughbred, with an excellent personality, which apparently makes him worth a lot of money.

On the home front, there is little news. I mentioned Muriel's eye problems before; she is now healed after many trips to doctors, and many painful treatments. Apparently, she came close to some serious problems.

Helen's husband Kirk got married to his girlfriend, and the boys were not happy. To our horror, Andrew, the eldest boy, who just graduated from High School, signed up for the army and flew to Fort Knox to start his training last week. His reasons showed us that he was completely disillusioned with where they lived, Hemet, and didn't want to go on to school, and was angry that his father refused to help with any education expenses. We feel quite badly about it as we, or mostly me, feel that we let him down by not providing some solutions for him. Hopefully, it will turn out OK.

Our grandson, Michael, Peter's eldest son, got married about a year ago. His wife, for whom nobody has much regard, is pregnant with what is our first great-grandchild. Michael is in the Missouri National Guard and only signed up on the understanding that he would not go to Iraq. In December, he goes to Iraq. Daniel, my son David's youngest, is getting married in November to a lovely young lady. He has just completed fireman's school and is looking for a job as a fireman, and working as an EMT until he gets a fire department job. Shane, his older step-brother is getting married in October. Shane is a deputy sheriff.

We have booked a trip to England for this Christmas, staying for a day or so with Muriel's cousin Tony in London and then with Muriel's brother Paul in Bath. After Christmas we will go on a coach trip to Scotland, returning to California mid-January. We will no doubt feel the cold, but we have warm clothes.

I know I have mentioned the fact that we feel that we should give up this big house. I am tired of the continuous maintenance, and we have so much money tied up which we can make good use of, just enjoying life. Did I mention that we have in the past, rented rooms to some marines from the local camp? We have decided that we will not replace them as they leave, and we are down to the last two. I have finally convinced Muriel that she must get serious about clearing out our accumulation of "stuff". We spent half a day two months ago, and that was it. Tomorrow, she has agreed that we will start in a serious manner. I hope so. I told her that if we leave it too long, it could get to be too much for us, or become the problem for one of us.

Since writing the above paragraph, about 3 weeks ago, we have made great strides in clearing out years of accumulated "stuff", and I have great hopes that this progress will continue. By the way, I just read through this chapter, and I have to report that our plan to visit Mount Rushmore, as mentioned earlier, did not happen. I finally convinced Muriel that a round trip of about 2800 miles was a long way for something which we could see from travel photographs. Not only that, friends have told us that it isn't really too spectacular.

It is October 30th, 2008, the last marine is moving out at this very moment, and the house will be ours again. The rooms have had lots of damage on which I am working. It will take months, but it will get done. This is taking priority over the clean-up of our accumulated "stuff". We have one large room where I have placed all items of which we can dispose. You can hardly get into the room and walk around, and still lots to be collected up. We have had loads already taken by San Diego Rescue Mission and Disabled Veterans group.

In the meantime, on 8th of November, my son Peter has a tenant moving into the house he rebuilt. He has no home now, but he created a large basement under the two rooms he added and has all his "stuff" stored there. He has bought a 29-foot diesel motor home and at this moment is loading it up with all the necessary items, cutlery, kitchen utensils, linens, clothes, tools etc. etc. that he will need in the motor home and on the boat. He has been trying to sell his horses and has some interest, but nothing firm yet. David, (Peter's youngest son) is accompanying Peter on the 150-mile trip to the boat, near Boston, and then they will start to work on it. First, it has to have the bottom painted with epoxy paint, but the paint can only be used above 40 degrees, and this temperature has to be exceeded for at least 12 hours. The temperature "high" in Boston yesterday was 47 degrees, so there may be a delay. If he gets a long delay, he may have to give up on launching until the spring and come to California for the winter. At this time, we will travel back with him and help with the transfer of the boat from New England to a warmer home port.

We attended the wedding of Shane, my son David's second stepson, and in 10 days we will attend the wedding of David's son, Daniel.

We get regular letters from Andrew, our daughter Helen's eldest son, who joined the army some time back. He will be going to Texas in the next month or so when his job training is complete.

Chapter 51 - Spring 2009

So many things have happened in the last few months. Peter was unable to get his boat into the water last year, before everything froze up, and came to stay with us. He is booked on a flight back to Tennessee on 15th April, then will pick up his motor home and go to Boston to his boat. Although, he plans to sail about a bit, the boat will probably end up in Savannah Georgia. A school friend is going with him for about 8 weeks. We may go to drive his motor home to wherever he plans to end up.

Our trip to the UK for Christmas was OK. Muriel enjoyed it, but I was very disappointed. We took a 5-day bus tour to Scotland after Christmas, and it was cold and dark and not too good in my estimation, but Muriel appeared to enjoy it as we went with Muriel's cousin and two sisters. I had forgotten how dark the winter days are. At midday, the sun is at about 35 degrees above the horizon. At 3.30 pm the light is starting to fade.

A pleasant surprise when we returned. Peter, who stayed at the house when were away, bought us a 42-inch TV to replace our old 55-inch TV which was suffering from an over-heating component that causes it to lose the picture after a while. I don't understand why this happened as we have only had it for 23 years without any problems.

A huge shock was finding out that Andrew (Helen's son), got married to the girlfriend we met briefly at his High school graduation dinner.

I don't think I mentioned earlier that Peter's son Michael is now a father of a baby boy, making Peter a grandfather and us, great-grandparents. Michael is in Iraq and Andrew has been in Afghanistan for about 10 days. He will be going to his assigned station in a couple of days. We received an email from him just now, the first communication since he left. He received his final training in Texas and they got an apartment and now his wife is there alone. We call her every Sunday as we feel very sorry for her having no family around her. She is only 19 years old. They came to see us just before Andrew left for Afghanistan.

I have carpal tunnel syndrome at the moment so I am typing with my left hand only.

You will remember that we got rid of the marine room renters; well a friend asked us to rent a room to a nice young lady that they knew, and so we did rent her a room. It has worked out so well, that we have now rented another room to a young Chinese lady. Up until now, we barely know they are in the house, not like the Marines, who were constant problems. One of the rooms rented by a marine, used to be our den, and with a wood-burning stove which we had removed. I found the stove and chimney, and to my surprise, after 20 years, found the back plate which covers the fireplace. I had it put together in an hour. The only problem was that the stove was rusty, so I wire-brushed it and sprayed it with barbeque paint. It smelled pretty bad at first. After a couple of hot fires, however, the smell left. We now have a lovely additional winter living room which is so warm with the stove going. The stove only uses about 4 small pieces of wood for a whole evening of heat. It also is a very attractive room. Somehow, I think we are destined to stay in this house for a few more years, especially in view of the decline in house prices.

As I may have mentioned before, the area in Tennessee where Peter lived and owns property is a country district where every house has a complete field to itself, with a long winding driveway. There are few people and not much going on. I believe that the cost of living is comparatively low. Well, Peter has met up with old friends here in California and has a nice girlfriend. He is very busy all the time, and increasingly appears to be comfortable here. The only problem is that berths for his boat are very, very expensive like everything else. Also, there is a 9-year waiting list at the local harbor. With regard to the girlfriend, she has two children and is tied to staying here, which doesn't fit in with Peter's plans at all. Have to wait and see what happens.

Chapter 52 - May 2009

The weather is warmer now, averaging 68/69 deg. F in the day.

Our son Peter has been back in New England working on his boat for about 6 or 7 weeks. As I'm sure I've said before, the boat was out of the water on blocks for 6 years, until 10 days ago, when the high tide came. The boat is 43ft long and 13 tons, and the local bay barely has enough depth of water to float the boat. Peter had about 20 minutes of high tide to get the boat in the water and out of the bay. Apparently, the boat scraped along, barely making it over some sand bars, but he finally reached deeper water. He has fixed a number of problems, and at this time he has to fix the lights and transmission. The forward gear stopped working after he arrived at the mooring where the boat is staying. He will be ready to sail in a week or so. He has an ad out to sell his motor home, and will live on the boat if it gets sold.

On a personal note, the single lady that I introduced to Peter, at our church, when he arrived back last December, has visited the boat, and it seems that they are working toward them both going on a sailing trip together. He seems very happy about it, so we are pleased about it. However, he is still planning to end up in California one way or another.

On the home front, I have been working hard around the house, mainly aimed at cleaning up our stuff. I have transferred everything from a sort of temporary lean-to, which I call the workshop, into what is called the "tractor garage", with the intent to tear the workshop down. However, with the prospect of Peter bringing mountains of his stuff here, I will leave it standing.

Grandson Andrew, 19 years old, in Afghanistan with the army, is said to be coming home next month, in June. He has only been there about 3 months. Apparently, his unit had been there for months before he got there. He received a promotion within the first couple of months.

His younger brother, Matthew, who has always been a sedentary TV/computer games enthusiast, suddenly signed up for track at school. He specialized in the pole vault and seemed to do quite well. He has grown, and his appetite is much better with all the exercise he's been getting. His father still has not arranged for him to get driving lessons and he will be 18 in a few months. Andrew got his full license at 16.

Muriel is recovering from Bronchitis, and 5 weeks ago I had an operation on my right hand for Carpal Tunnel Syndrome.

As of the 1st June 2009, Peter set sail south, a week ago, and ran into 7-foot seas and a 50 mph headwind. In a whole day of sailing, they traveled 20 miles and finally took refuge at a small island where they were tossed about all night, being thrown out of their beds and getting little sleep. They discussed the situation and decided to return to the starting point, where they unloaded the boat into the motor home and drove to Tennessee where Peter had some jobs he wanted to take care of.

At the time of writing the above, Matthew is now completing online the requirements for his driving permit.

Footnote: In reading the past few chapters, I find that many plans involving Peter never did come to pass. Various circumstances caused many changes to Peter's and consequently our plans.

Chapter 53 - Change of Lifelong Dream

Peter must have had a really bad time on that trip sailing south. He completed the work needed in Tennessee and drove his motor home to San Diego on his own, and put the boat on Craig's list for sale. I believe his change of heart and lifelong dream is through a combination of exhaustion, the bad sailing experience, and frustration with his old school friend who exhibited some terrible behavior toward the end of the sailing experience. Peter is here now, and at some point, he will probably return to Tennessee for the rest of his personal belongings, which includes a truck and an SUV. We will probably go with him and help on driving vehicles back, but who knows. We've changed plans a few times lately. Here again, we seem to be putting off our own plans.

Good news, Andrew, Helen's eldest, is arriving back in Texas this coming Tuesday (mid-June 2009). He has been in the army almost a year now and has about 2 years to go. We hear that Michael has seen some action in Iraq involving some enemy deaths.

In about 10 days our sons, wives, and some of the grandchildren and wives are going on a 3-day camping trip with us. Muriel and I will occupy Peter's motor home and the rest will be in tents. We will be up at around 6000 feet in the San Bernadino Mountains, and it could be very cold. We are not using our old motor home as Peter's is more luxurious. Apparently, Kirk, Carol, and Matthew will be paying us a visit at the campsite.

In late June 2009, many of the families who could make it, went on the above-mentioned three-day camping trip to the mountains above Riverside California. This trip was organized by my son Nicholas. We all came home safely. During the camp-out we had visitors. Several coyotes, a bear, and a mountain lion, actually showed up at the campground.

13 of us went, including our son David & wife Susan, 2 of their sons, Shane and Daniel, with wives Teresa (pregnant with great-grandchild) and Erin, Teresa's daughter, Deneice, my other son Nick and wife Karen, Peter and girlfriend Amy, and of course, Muriel and me. On Saturday, Kirk, Helen's husband arrived with his new wife Carol, and our grandson Matthew. On Sunday, Peter's school friend Mark and girlfriend came for a visit. (They live nearby). Unfortunately, our eldest son Christopher and his wife Mary and 2 daughters, and David's eldest son Scott could not make the trip. Helen's eldest son Andrew, just back from Afghanistan, is in Texas and couldn't make it either. Muriel and I stayed in Peter's motor home, but all the rest were in tents.

We were at 6500 ft., with little patches of snow on the surrounding mountains which had to be 8000 to 10,000 ft. high, but it was comfortably warm. David and Nick provided most of the fantastic food and did most of the cooking. For example, the last day's breakfast menu included bacon, scrambled eggs, sausage, fried tomatoes and onions, fried potato slices, waffles, grits, hash browns, coffee, and tea, but that was all. David was the head cook assisted by Nick and his wife Karen. We had huge campfires every night and told stories, while David kept us going with hot chocolate or cappuccino and homemade cookies. David's daughter-in-law, Erin made "smores", toasting the marshmallows to order. The step-daughter of David's other son, Shane, Deneice (16), had an oil painting session with me, but it still has to be finished as we ran out of time and energy. By the way, Deneice qualifies as our eldest great-granddaughter.

At the nearby lake, Jenks Lake, we all went fishing, but only a couple of little ones were caught from the bank by Erin. Nick, in his float tube, caught 18 trout on Saturday, and David and Nick caught more on Sunday, but the count escapes me. We all had fish or hamburgers for dinner Sunday evening. We demolished a bottle of Crown Royal with multiple cans of 7-up, and about 10 bottles of Dos Equis beer, some in the form of shandy (beer and 7-up, one of the favorite women's drink in summer in England), plus most of a bottle of "already mixed" Pina colada. This group did very well for a group that hardly ever drinks.

The trip was absolutely wonderful, and notable for the fact that there were no mishaps or squabbles which is amazing when you consider that everyone there was of a strong personality with minds of their own. We thank God for this wonderful opportunity, and for taking care of us all, and bringing us back safely. We were only home for 24 hours when Nick sent out an email inviting all the family to a barbecue sometime in July.

Chapter 54 - Bit of Bad Luck

I had several new chapters written, but neglected to save them in a permanent form, and then had a computer problem and lost the lot. At least it won't be rewritten like a diary. It is now March 2010, and I am going to have a difficult task to reconstruct the missing chapters.

Since that family camping trip last year, our son David's son, (our grandson Shane), has become a father. His wife, Teresa, gave birth to a boy last October. This makes great-grandchild number 3. Shane's wife has a daughter from a previous marriage. Peter's son has a 15-month-old son also, and we have just heard that they are pregnant again. As I reported earlier, grandson Andrew got married some time back, and now he just reported that his wife, Marisol is pregnant, making potentially, great-grandchild number 5. Andrew has been stationed at Ft Hood in Texas since his return from Afghanistan last year.

Peter is still with us, and his plans have completely changed. He did not find a buyer for his boat, and now he has decided that he wants it here in California. To that end he has bought a 45-foot trailer which he has spent 2 months modifying, to transport his boat. He has contracted with a boat transporter company to bring the boat from New England to California on their trailer, where they will transfer it to his trailer. Then he plans to bring it to our house and do some remodeling to bring it up to perfect condition. He cannot get a berth in the local harbor (Oceanside), for a couple of years. He is on the waiting list.

Before the boat arrives here, he has to get an area of our dirt, down by the road, bulldozed to allow the boat trailer to curve into our driveway. Peter has a friend who owns a bulldozer, but he had no tires on the bulldozer trailer, so Peter bought them and had them fitted. There are so many parts to the plan that it is very likely to run into some snags.

In January 2000, we heard from the US Immigration Department that Muriel's brother Paul's application for immigration for him, his wife, and two children, had been accepted, with Muriel as Petitioner and Sponsor. Last December 2009, 10 years later, we heard that the application had been forwarded to the National Visa Center for action. The action includes us paying fees and Paul filling out several lots of forms with photos and copies of passports, and police reports, etc. etc. It has been 2 ½ months of constant letters, emails, and phone calls to England. We have internet, and Paul doesn't, so the National Visa Center takes the easy way out and corresponds through us. However, I think we are getting near the end now. Paul still has to fill out forms we downloaded and gather lots of information together. However, as of today Paul still has not received the package we mailed to him a week ago. The last set of forms clearly stated that a child who has reached 21 years cannot enter the US under the visa application in question. Unfortunately, Paul's daughter is 21 this coming August. She was 11 when the application was made. Hopefully, Paul will get a move on with his latest part. I can now understand why it needs a lawyer to do this work. I cannot foresee anybody who doesn't speak English, being able to do this without help.

I've had a bad few months with a strange problem with my throat. Several doctor visits and several courses of a variety of medicines have had no effect. Finally, it appears that I have a "nodule" on my thyroid which is close to my larynx, causing discomfort when I sing. I had a biopsy a couple of days ago to establish the status of it and will get the result in a day or so. I am a little tired of it as I have had it for at least 6 months. Also, the cost of ineffective drugs has reached several hundred plus the travel and doctors' charges.

I am optimistic that it is about to get solved. I may still have to have a minor operation to have it removed. This is a later note, the nodule turned out to be nothing, not cancerous.

For once, we have had a lot of rain which should help with the drought conditions we've had for the past few years. We are only a bit above what is normal, but hopefully, we will get more before we reach April when the rain normally stops until November. Our grass which was yellow due to watering restrictions, is now very green and lush except we have had a gopher problem with piles of dirt. However, in the last few days, Peter has sat with my rifle and killed 3 of them. In the last 24 hours, we have had no more piles of dirt.

To bring you up to speed on my conversations with daughter Helen, I've had 2, of what I believe are significant contacts in the last few months which are worth reporting. (I have daily little exchanges which are little more than "hellos").

I have been following Glenn Beck, a political commentator on Fox cable news channel. He has been exposing corruption in the government and in Obama's White House administration. The subject on the day in question was the Democratic health care bill which seemed almost certain to pass, and during an advertisement, I got up to go to the bathroom. Out of the blue I heard Helen clearly say, "You're worried about this health care thing aren't you"? I said that I was, and her immediate answer was, "It won't fly". At the time I felt she must be wrong as the Democrats had a majority and the bill seemed a certainty. Now, months later, it has died, but there has been squabbling over changes and new ideas and rewrites, etc. It is possible that some form of health care reform may get through, but not anything like the old bill which was an expensive monstrosity.

The other significant contact was some weeks after the above. I was watching some birds flying and I thought to ask Helen a question. I said, "Helen, can you fly"? Her immediate answer was, "No, but I can float". This brings to mind the facts reported by those who have had near death experiences. (We know 2 people who have had this experience). Most of them have reported that they have floated up above their bodies and looked down and watched resuscitation efforts, or have seen items stored high up above their normal area of vision. I continually receive bits of information like this which in themselves are not complete proof, but enough to make me wonder and they tend to confirm that I am talking to Helen.

Chapter 55 - Something New

As you know, our house is very large and wonderfully comfortable except for one shortcoming. It is all electric. No gas. It does not have any central heating or cooling. Cooling is not a problem as we are on a hill overlooking the ocean, and it only gets uncomfortably hot on about 2 or three days per year, and then we get into the pool. Each room has its own individual electric heater. The only problem is that to adequately heat each room that we might use, costs hundreds of dollars per month.

We decided to buy a second slow combustion stove, or in Americanese, a wood-burning stove. We have plenty of wood, but we have been burning through it at a tremendous rate in our open fireplace (with glass doors and a blower) for very little heat. So off we went to visit local fireplace equipment and hardware stores and found the prices of stoves to be from around $1400 to well over $2000. This dampened our enthusiasm somewhat, so we decided to look on the internet. Right away I found better prices and eventually bought a very adequate stove for around $500 which included shipment from Virginia

It took about a month to arrive, and it turned out to be exactly what we wanted, but HEAVY. Peter and his son David, got it up the stairs after we spent half an hour uncrating it. The plan was to install it in front of the fireplace with a metal plate over the fireplace opening and run a chimney through the plate. However, due to the fireplace height restriction, I had to cut 3" off the stove's legs, which put the wood floor underneath it at risk for overheating. The next move was to find some asbestos-type sheeting for insulation. We went back to the fireplace store and they had what they called "hearths". These consisted of a rectangular sheet of some hard insulating material with a top surface of floor tiles. We did see some similar insulating sheets at Home Depot, and with the addition of a few tiles, I could have made one for $25. However, Muriel fell in love with one hearth and so we bought it for $470. I couldn't believe the high price and also that Muriel wanted to buy it. However, it looks nice and works well.

The performance of this stove is staggering. For those who don't know, the whole point of having a slow-combustion stove is to restrict the air going through it and up the chimney, taking all the warm air from the room and the heat from the fire. The best efficiency is gained when the wood burns in a charcoal-like state without flames. After the new smell burned off, one evening it was going well, and I closed off all air, and the damper. Even then, the temperature in the room was maintained above 84 degrees F for many hours with no wood added, and this is in a large room 30 feet by 26 feet with 6 windows. Since then I have installed a sliding shut-off plate to cover the built-in air holes, and use only short pieces of wood to keep the fire small. Now, with logs cut in half, we can keep very comfortably warm with three pieces of wood per evening. One morning we found the stove still hot with one piece of wood glowing like charcoal. I believe that with logs cut in half, we have enough wood for the next 5 years. Now it is March and getting warmer every day so we are not lighting too many fires.

Chapter 56 - Something for Posterity

The purpose of this book, (for want of a better name to call it), is to record things the way they were during the lifetime of us, Brian and Muriel Walters, at least for our descendants. Our children and some grandchildren are aware of this writing, but we have little control over how many descendants will actually read it or even get to see it.

I (Brian) personally feel that as time goes on, we in the USA have more and more of everything, but somehow this leads to less and less appreciation, which causes a situation where the more we get, the more we seem to be unhappy. By reading this and getting some feel for the way things were years ago, hopefully, the reader may get a better sense of the wonderful standard of living that is available to us in this day and age. You notice that I say "available to us". It is not automatic. It still must be earned.

Bearing in mind that the main purpose of this writing is to record the way things were, we feel that one of the subjects that should be recorded is an English Christmas as spent in England in 1930s and 1940s when we were growing up. This is from a time when you made your own fun. There was no TV, no computer games, and there was no spare money to buy toys and go places. Food was strictly rationed as you have already learned. In some ways, people were much happier and content with less.

A Typical Old fashioned English Christmas as remembered by Muriel and Brian Walters.

Christmas starts on Christmas Eve with parties at work in the afternoon, with pastries, snack foods, and a few alcoholic drinks for which everybody has contributed a small amount of money on a weekly basis. Usually, we would leave work early and then go to a party at a friend's or relative's house. Christmas Eve church services are held in most churches. Christmas day starts with opening presents, and a good English breakfast of sausages, bacon, eggs, fried tomatoes, and fried bread (in bacon fat). Christmas Day was the day for some families to go to church in the morning. Church bells are heard all over the town. Christmas dinner was held at a late lunchtime, around 1.00 to 3.00 pm mostly with immediate family only. This meal consists of roasted goose, (goose was the old traditionally preferred item) or chicken or turkey, roast potatoes, Brussels sprouts, carrots, parsnips, stuffing, cauliflower, roasted onions, gravy, etc., followed by Christmas pudding with custard, or brandy sauce. Hidden in the Christmas pudding were some silver coins, and you had to chew carefully, but you always hoped you'd get one. The Christmas pudding would have brandy (French) poured over it in the kitchen and it would be brought to the table in flames. Unfortunately, US brandy doesn't burn too well so we use Scotch.

At 5.00 to 6.00 pm would be the Christmas tea-time for the family, including an occasional aunt, uncle, and cousin, etc. Food would be Christmas cake, trifle, jello, blanc-mange, mince pies, fancy biscuits and very fancy individual tarts and other pastries. Jello and blanc-mange were made in molds like rabbits, or crowns, etc. Christmas Crackers were on the table by each place setting, either for dinner or Christmas tea. They were pulled with the next person, and they always contained a party hat, a tiny prize, and a motto that was read out to all. For those who don't know about Christmas crackers, they are made with a 1 ½" by 3" cylinder of cardboard to hold the contents (above), and wrapped in 8" wide. Gaily decorated crepe paper which is tied to each end of the cardboard (to keep the contents inside). Included is a dual offset strip of thick paper with s spot of some explosive on one side and a patch of sandpaper on the other. When the crackers are pulled, the sandpaper ignites the explosive making a loud crack noise, and the crepe paper splits and spills the contents.

The rest of the day was spent with the party hats on. The Christmas cake was a rich fruit cake with a layer of marzipan, covered by a layer of royal icing, (hard icing), on which would be winter snow scenes, with tiny figures of Santa Clause, or skaters, with little trees and animals, sprigs of holly, and writing like "Merry Christmas" etc. The cake always had a traditional frill around it with "Holly" and "Merry Christmas" etc. on it. Supper, with just the family, would follow at about 9.00 pm and consist of cold meats like tongue, ham, and beef, some of the dinner bird, pickled onions, chutney, piccalilli, pickled beetroot (beets), cheese, sausage rolls, cheese straws, and mince pies.

The next day, 26th December, was called "Boxing Day". It was the day for getting up a bit late, not doing much work, and eating what was left over from the previous day and food as listed below. It was the day for big parties with all the family and friends going to one family member's house at about midday, or early afternoon. The rest of the day was spent eating, drinking, and playing party games such as those listed below. By the end of Boxing Day, the Christmas cake, the Christmas pudding, the jello, and blanc-mange, etc. were nearly all gone. It is a mystery how we managed to eat all the food that was prepared. Boxing Day got its name from the fact that in real olden times, it was common to hold boxing matches as a popular pastime.

Typical Games for Boxing Day

Passing the orange	Marmalade Cat
Musical parcel	Chi Chi - Fortunes
Kissing The Blarney	Pitch the penny
Clothes Pin Drop	Murder
Flap the fish	Consequences
Hypnotism	Trivia Questions contests
Jerry the donkey	When the moon comes over the mountain

And many more from our party game book.

Passing the orange is done without hands, but by gripping the orange between the chin and shoulder and passing it to the next person in a circle. If it is dropped that person or persons are out. The winner is the last person in.

The musical parcel requires a small prize which is wrapped in many, many layers of wrapping, and it is passed around a circle to music. When the music stops, the person holding it can start to unwrap but must pass it on as soon as the music starts again. The winner is the person who unwraps the final wrapping.

Kissing the Blarney requires a volunteer with hairy forearms and one other male person. A few other volunteers, preferably women, who don't know the game, are sent out of the room. All other party attendees are watching. One volunteer is brought back into the room and is offered the chance to kiss the Blarney Stone blindfolded and gain all knowledge. Once blindfolded the victim is encouraged to bend to hip height and is guided to kiss the hairy forearm. Immediately the victim is shocked and tears off the blindfold to see the other male zipping up his trousers and fastening his belt or braces. The antics of the kisser, rubbing their mouth etc., amuse the audience to no end.

Clothes Pin Drop requires a chair, a jam jar, and 5 or 6 clothes pins. The jar is placed on the floor, a few inches behind the chair's back, and each person gets to kneel on the chair, with wrists resting on the top of the chair's back. The object is to drop the clothes pins into the jar. The winner is the one who can get the most pins in.

Flap The Fish is a game for a number of people, with fish shapes cut out of newspaper, and with ping pong paddles. The objective is a race to get the fish to a finishing point first, by flapping away at the fish with the paddle. This is a favorite game for younger party-goers. At this point, I would like to include a story about the time when a whole bunch of our young grandchildren were involved in this game. We were holding elimination heats. I was in the last heat, just to amuse the kids. From its hiding place under the couch, I pulled out my huge newspaper fish and a paddle-shaped implement that was 2 feet across. There were cries of protest from the grandchildren and a huge argument about the fact that there were no rules about this "and they could also use bigger paddles if they had them" etc. We had great fun.

Hypnotism is a game where a couple of unfortunate victims who don't know the game, are taken advantage of for the amusement of the rest. A saucer is secretly prepared by holding a lighted candle a couple of inches below it, leaving a layer of soot. The victim is told to stand in front of the "hypnotist," and look into his eyes and follow instructions, then he is given the sooty saucer to hold. The hypnotist holds a clean saucer and instructs the victim to do what he does. The victim is told to touch the bottom of the saucer with one finger without taking their eyes off the hypnotist and is shown how to run the finger across their face, making black streaks. This is highly amusing to all onlookers, but a bit cruel for the victim who should always be a good sport.

Marmalade Cat calls for all players to sit in a circle, and each person in turn, has to make a statement "A Marmalade Cat is an. . . . ." , adding an adjective that describes the cat, such as "admirable cat," or the "Marmalade Cat is an awful cat" and so on until one participant cannot come up with an answer. He is out, and the next person goes to "B" adjectives. The last one is the winner.

Chi Chi Fortunes is a Chinese game using a container of small flattened sticks. Each stick has a "fortune" printed on it. The container is held at about 45 degrees and shaken and gradually a stick works its way out. The first one to fall is your fortune. It is pleasant and fun but not too exciting.

Pitch The Penny is exactly what it sounds like. A saucer is placed 8 or 10 feet away and each person tries to toss some pennies into the saucer. Mostly they bounce out. The winner is the person who gets the most to stay in the saucer.

Murder is similar to hide and go seek, except it is played by adults, and takes place in the house after dark. All lights are turned off, usually at the main fuse box. The "murderer" gives the others a certain time to hide before he starts to hunt. Even before the hunt starts, people are creeping around and bumping into each other, and little giggles and screams erupt. It usually ends in a riotous manner. I have one funny story to add. I was about 7 years old, and the Second World War was in full swing, and I was always very nervous that a bad German soldier would suddenly appear. We were at my Auntie Dorothy's house for Boxing Day, with all the relatives. The game was Murder. I was too young and too nervous to play, so I was made to sit on one end of the couch in the dark by myself. My mother's brother, Uncle Ron, had to work late. He was always the life and soul of the party but was not able to arrive until a bit later. The game was on, and I was very scared, but eventually, the game ended, and the lights were turned on. Everybody came back into the room to find Uncle Ron, sitting on the other end of the couch. He had arrived and realized what was going on and crept into the house and sat down. If he had sat on the other end of the couch he would have sat on me, I would have died of fright.

Consequences is a game where all participants are issued with a strip of paper and pencil. The paper is usually about 4 inches wide. It starts off by the leader asking questions and the others writing in fictitious answers. When each answer is written, the paper is folded over, covering the answer, and the papers are rotated to the next person. The first question requires the name of a famous person or other party-goer. The next question is another famous person or party-goer. Then a location, followed by an activity. Then the consequence, and finally, what the world said. At the end, the papers are read out, and go something like this, except that they aren't all as nice:

"President Bush met Mother Theresa on an island in Chicago. They got drunk, and had 14 cats, and the world said, "Eat more rice." Most readings are very funny.

Jerry the donkey needs a volunteer who knows the game, 6 foot length of rope, a bed sheet, and an old chamber pot (popularly called a Jerry, which insulting name was applied to Germans during WWII). The volunteer gets under the sheet on his knees, and holds the chamber pot with the rope tied to the handle. An unsuspecting victim is brought into the room and asked to pull on the rope and lead "Jerry" across the room. When a couple of yards are traveled the volunteer under the sheet lets go of the pot, and it comes out from under the sheet to howls of laughter from the onlookers.

When the moon comes over the mountain is another game where a sheet is held vertically by two volunteers, and a victim is brought into the darkened room. The moon is a flashlight traversing and shining on the sheet in a horizontal trajectory from about 6” away. The victim is on the other side of the sheet and is to bend down and from 6” to 12” away follow the moon. The person in charge drones on about what a nice moonlit night it is, then as the moon gets halfway, starts talking about how it is getting stormy and looks like rain etc., until the flashlight gets to the end of the sheet. At this time somebody throws a wet or dampened sponge in the face of the victim, again to howls of laughter from the onlookers. Care should be taken as some victims may not like this activity.

Christmas Day and Boxing Day Food in addition to normal Christmas Day Dinner etc

Sausage Rolls	Mincemeat (fruit) tarts
Cocktail Sausages	Cheese straws
Chips & dips	Trifle
Nuts	Ham
Veg tray	Cheeses
Pickled Beets	Wassail
Chutney/pickles	Egg Nog

Explanations of some of the English items are:

Sausage rolls are made from small English sausages or small rolls of sausage meat, wrapped with flaky pastry. English sausage meat is different from any other that I have experienced. I can’t imagine them being so good with any other sausage meat.

Beets are well known in America, but in England, they are served sliced and pickled in strong English vinegar. English vinegar is so strong and tart that it can give you an ache in your lower jaw, but it makes the beets wonderful.

Chutney/Pickles are quite a large part of English food. Chutney is made from various chopped vegetables and fruits from green tomatoes to cauliflower to mangoes, to apples, and soaked in strong vinegar, with brown sugar, and spices. The only pickles you’ll ever see are pickled onions or gherkins (baby cucumbers about 1 ½” long).

Mincemeat Tarts are concave pastry discs containing sweet fruity mincemeat, not minced beef. Sometimes they have lids.

Cheese Straws are 1” by 3” pieces of pastry into which shredded cheese has been mixed. The strongest cheese gets the best results.

Trifle is a multi-layer dessert made in a large deep bowl. The first layer is plain Madeira cake slices over which is poured red jello and sliced strawberries or raspberries. The next layer is custard. Now this is English custard, which has no American equivalent, however, vanilla pudding is the closest substitute. On the top of this is a layer of real whipped cream, over which is spread grated chocolate.

Wassail is basically hot apple cider (slightly alcoholic) with cinnamon, cloves, and slices of orange. Served hot.

Sherry and port are commonly the preferred libations.

Chapter 57 - Excitement Mounts

Peter's boat was picked up yesterday from the boatyard in Mattapoisett, near Boston, where it has been stored for years except for the brief period when he had in the water for the aborted sailing south to Florida. It will be transferred to another boatyard where it will be lifted onto a boat trailer tomorrow for the trip to California.

In the meantime, since last writing, the trailer that Peter has been modifying is now residing at the side of our house, where it has had further modification and some painting. In order for the trailer to get here Peter had a small tractor move dirt to make a wider entrance to our driveway so that the trailer could curve into it. His friend who promised that he would do the job in exchange for the new tires on his tractor-trailer, made some excuses, so Peter couldn't wait and made other arrangements. This "friend" is not too popular now, and owes Peter for the tires.

The boat will arrive from New England in a week and then we will go through another bunch of gyrations. The boat will be delivered to the local boatyard in Oceanside where it will be lifted off. Then the cross-country driver will drop his trailer and come to our house to pick up Peter's trailer. He will then take it to the boatyard for the boat to be loaded, and then deliver it to our house. We have to keep our fingers crossed that the modifications made to Peter's trailer will fit the boat. We will take cutting tools and other equipment in case changes are needed.

For the trailer transfer day, our sons Christopher, Nicholas, Peter and his son David, myself, and the long-distance driver will be available. There are eight posts/pads to be adjusted to support the boat, plus webbing straps to be stretched between them to prevent the supports from splaying outwards. Then the masts have to be placed in the slings that Peter has made. The two masts are 50 feet long and possibly weigh as much as 600 pounds each, so many hands are needed to move them. The chances that it will go smoothly are not high, but it has gone without a hitch up until now, except that we lost some Jade bushes when the trailer was first delivered to our house. We think that the driver couldn't see or he was drunk.

Tomorrow, Tuesday, is the big day. The boat should have been here today, Monday, but there were hold-ups in Arkansas for road repairs, and Arizona will not allow wide loads on their roads at the weekend, so the boat sat for two days on the Arizona border.

The last few days have been spent sanding and painting the trailer, and we went through a routine of measuring and re-checking. We had a bit of a scare. The keel is 3 feet 2 inches from the bottom up to the body of the boat. For some reason, we mentally carried the measurement as 32 inches, (a difference of 5 inches) which made some of the trailer modifications incorrect. We soon discovered the mistake after a few horrifying minutes.

We have loaded up tools, electrical cables, and power saws for any on-the-spot "mods". We may have to move and adjust the heights of support pads and add wood blocks where necessary. The trailer was here in California, and the boat was in the Boston area, 3000 miles away.

Peter modified the trailer based on measurements sent to him by somebody in the Boston area that he employed for that purpose. We are keeping our fingers crossed.

The boat has arrived, and the changeover to Peter's trailer went without a hitch, and we have been working on sanding wooden parts of the boat to make it look good. There is a lot to do, but it will be worth it.

At this time, Peter is in Tennessee, working on some things that need fixing with his houses. They have catastrophic flooding there but luckily none of Peter's houses have any problems. His main reason for being there is to pack up all his tools and some furniture and bring it here to California. To this end, he bought a 36-foot moving van and it is here, parked out front of our house. He bought it to drive it back for his belongings, but then he worked out the cost of driving it there and back. He found it was cheaper to fly him and his son David and rent a truck there, so now he will use his van for storage when the rented truck arrives.

We have booked a 14-day cruise out of Los Angeles, to all the Hawaiian islands for November of this year.

Chapter 58 - 75th Birthday in 2010, The End

I will be 75 in a week, and Muriel will be 76 in 3 weeks. This book covers ¾ of a century and a lot of history has accumulated in that time. We have covered many miles and experienced a great deal of what our world has to offer. Muriel and I have lived through a most exciting time with some amazing developments in technology, which I'm sure will continue.

Our remarkable life has had only one real blemish, the loss of our beloved daughter, Helen. Otherwise, we have been blessed beyond measure. We have always tried to live honestly and worked hard, and given our best and there is no doubt that it has paid off. We are amongst the most fortunate of people, starting off in less than wonderful circumstances and living in the middle of the worst war the world has ever known, and have reached the Promised Land in Southern California. Our life is very comfortable, surrounded by 4 loving children, their spouses and grandchildren, not forgetting a number of small great-grandchildren. We love our house of 35 years. It is large and gives views of mountains in the east (back), and the Pacific Ocean in the west, (front). We have good friends, and good health, although we should get more exercise and lose a bit of weight. We believe that our unfortunate start allows us to appreciate what we now have, more than is normal.

I suppose our story has to have an end at some point, for instance, like now, or it will end in the middle of a chapter when I suddenly get too old to continue. Maybe we should end it now and say goodbye, and if I feel inclined to add to it as things happen, then I will do so.

As I've said before, this is written mainly so that our descendants can learn the way it was in a personal way and not as a history book. We will have little control of who reads this in the future, but we hope you have enjoyed reading about us and our lives, and even more, we hope that it will help you to fully appreciate what you have. May God bless you as He has always blessed us.

Muriel and Brian Walters.

Chapter 59 - Continuation

I had some doubts that I could end it early, and several noteworthy things have happened since, so I will continue until I can no longer do it. It may well just end in the middle of a chapter at some future point.

About a month ago, we received the news that son David's step-granddaughter, (Shane's stepdaughter), Denise, was in the hospital. They were due to go to Hawaii for a vacation, but Denise became unwell the night before, and they took her to the emergency hospital. There they were told that it seemed that she had a serious problem.

It turned out that she had a 2" diameter tumor growing inside her heart, and it would have to be removed. Two days later she had open heart surgery, which took place on a Wednesday. All went well, and she was sent home on the following Saturday, just 3 days later. It seemed a little soon to us, but amazingly she appeared to be fine.

We were invited to go to see her on the following Monday. She was asleep when we arrived, but in a few minutes, she appeared all dressed and ready for the world. The tumor was found to be non-malignant. She has got stronger and starts back to school this coming Monday, just 4 or 5 weeks after the operation.

Another item of importance is that daughter Helen's eldest son Andrew is due to go to Iraq between the 20th and 23rd of August 2010. Unfortunately, his wife was due to give birth on the 22nd of August, and it was possible that he would miss the birth. We were working on a plan to go to visit him in Texas before his leaving, and possibly also to see the baby. However, he came to California on his own 2 weeks ago, which saved us a trip. He returned to Texas a week ago, and almost immediately his wife started labor pains. They had a baby daughter on 11th August, 11 days early. (As you probably know, late-term pregnant ladies are not allowed to fly, so Andrew came alone).

Andrew arrived back in Texas on the 10th, called us around midday on the 11th to announce the birth, and shortly thereafter I called my sister Christine to give her the news. She runs a prayer group and likes all the news. I put the phone down after the call, and almost immediately, a music box in the form of an angel, which has been on the shelf behind my chair, started to play. This music box angel has been on that shelf for maybe 15 years and has not been wound or played for many years, and we certainly haven't heard it play for many years also. Both Muriel and I were very surprised to hear it start playing all on its own. Just after this, I said to Helen that she was now a grandmother. She said that she had heard. I assumed she heard me tell my sister. I asked her if she caused the music box to play and she said, "Yes, wasn't it good"? This is just one more unexplained strange occurrence, and I am more convinced than ever that we are closely surrounded by our departed loved ones.

Bad news. My sister Christine's husband Bill, fell down their stairs a couple of months ago, breaking his collar bone, and an arm bone, and was generally banged up. He was in hospital for over a month. During this time, Christine fell in the bedroom and went to hospital. She was in for about 3 weeks. They are in their 80's. They have now moved to a senior care establishment, but 2 days ago, I learned that Bill was back in hospital with a serious bladder infection and loss of balance. It doesn't sound good. We have talked about driving to Vancouver (Canada) to see them "as soon as the kids went back to school", but put it off because we were possibly going to Texas. At this point, we hope that a trip to Vancouver does not become a trip of necessity.

In the meantime, our son Peter's boat, parked alongside our house, is in the process of being completely renovated inside and out. The whole inside and outside have been sanded, and the teak decking has been removed. At this time the deck is in the process of being recovered and waterproofed with an epoxy coating. Apparently, this is the modern way. The inside wood is now in the process of being finished with varnish and clear epoxy. Peter is not satisfied with the main engine, a 70 hp Perkins diesel, and will either rebuild it or replace it with a larger engine. Also, he has to install a 120-volt AC diesel generator, to which he has added a 12-volt DC alternator. The boat should look beautiful and be worth a fortune when completed.

Muriel's brother Paul has visited the US embassy in London, and he will get his visa soon. He estimates that he will arrive in the USA early in 2011.

On Sunday 8th August 2010, we held at our house the annual summer garden party for our choir. About 45 signed up, but only about 35 showed up. I had erected 5 tarps for sunshades and put out 7 tables and 50 chairs. All preparation, including cleanup of the garden and pool area, took almost 2 weeks. We had two small refrigerators out, one with beer and the other with soft drinks with wine on top of one and bottled water on the other. We were way overbought, and we had lots of everything left over. It got very cool in the early evening and people left early. In my opinion, the party was a disappointment, but most people seemed to appreciate the effort. It took me until the Friday after to clear up everything, and we were both exhausted. Chances are that we won't be expected or asked to do another, and we certainly won't volunteer again.

Grandson Daniel, David's son, has just finished a 10 months course to become a paramedic, (which cost him $10,000). He passed the mandatory examination, so now he can start looking for a job as a fireman, but it won't be easy. Most cities etc. are laying off lots of employees in an effort to cut costs.

We just heard that Muriel's sister Susan will be visiting us in November, arriving the day we get back from a 15-day Hawaii cruise. That's not true now. We heard this morning at 6.30 am from Susan that her health insurance for the trip will cost $2000. She cancelled, but then almost immediately we heard that Susan found cheaper insurance and IS coming. Can't keep up with it.

Chapter 60 - 18 months Have Gone By.

Yes, more bad luck. 5 pages have disappeared from my computer which were not backed up, so I have 18 months to catch up. Susan did come for a visit, and Andrew, daughter Helen's eldest son, came home OK from Iraq, and then was sent to Afghanistan which he survived OK. Peter is still working on his boat but has taken a couple of months off as he got married to Gayle 3 months ago, another sailing enthusiast. He bought a house and has spent the time re-doing lots of parts of the house until it is like spanking new. Of course, he has moved out of our house, but left all his stuff that is stored outside and most of the stuff in the house. He will be back on the boat in the next few weeks. His son David is living here and has to do 10 hours work for us per month to pay his rent.

We've bought a more modern motor home, a 29-foot "Minnie Winnie" Winnebago. It has a bedroom at the back and you don't have to climb up a ladder to get into bed, which is one of Joy's pet peeves about the old one. Hopefully, we will sell the old one soon. This year, 2012, we hope to do a bit of traveling in spite of the cost of gasoline, around $4.30 per gallon.

Sad news from Canada. My eldest sister Christine's husband Bill finally died as a result of the fall on the stairs mentioned earlier, and about 13 months ago. Probably, as a result of the stress of Bill's illness, and dealing with Bill's business affairs, Christine had a massive stroke, which left her with movement only in her left arm. She lost her speech capability, but has recovered that partially, and can respond with, sometimes, two or three words. We call her twice a week to make sure she knows we are thinking of her. In the meantime, John, Christine's only son, had a flu-like illness for three months, probably due to the stress of the whole situation, and at the same time, his wife was seriously ill in the hospital. He was also in the middle of divorcing her as she was an extreme alcoholic. She died just before the divorce was final.

Andrew, my daughter Helen's eldest son is leaving the army in about a year. His daughter is about 20 months old and one of the cutest little girls we've ever seen. She is friendly almost immediately you meet her with smiles all the time.

We heard just the other day, that Andrew's wife is pregnant again which is a disappointment considering the fact that he will be joining the workforce without much training in anything. With a young baby and a toddler, it will be a bit more difficult for them.

As you read earlier, Muriel's brother Paul and his wife have kept their immigration status alive by visiting us several times. At first, they were working on the big house they lived in, and now that is sold they are working on other properties they own. When you have to wait 12 ½ years for immigration, you have to go on with your life, and that is what they did.

Finally, they expect to arrive for good in September of this year. In the meantime, Katie, their daughter, is living with us. She and her brother Richard came over in the summer last year for a couple of months. Katie had graduated from university, but Richard had to go back for his last year. Whilst here, Katie found a job and stayed. Since then Richard found himself a job in London after graduation, so he may well be left behind.

Chapter 61 - Visit from Helen

Yes, really.

I've had some health problems lately. This year has not been good. I started out the year with bronchitis in Jan/Feb and followed up a month later with a shingle as opposed to shingles. I had one main lesion just above my right eyebrow. I had a tiny one on my right eyelid, but it was small. I recovered very quickly.

Early in May I developed a very serious prostate infection and had injections and a course of anti-biotic pills for 25 days. I was just feeling a bit stronger when I realized that my pulse rate was going wild with every little exertion. I struggled with this for a week, thinking that it was due to the antibiotics, but finally contacted our doctor who sent me to Emergency. They found I had blood clots in both lungs and I spent a week in hospital on blood thinners, with blood thinners to be taken for at least the next 6 months.

One morning, whilst in hospital, my phone rang. It was Muriel and our cleaning lady, Elsa, who has come to us every Tuesday for the last 13 years. She'd got to know our daughter Helen very well when Helen came with her boys to visit us.

Muriel sounded very emotional on the phone, and said, "Listen to what Elsa has to say". They were on a speakerphone. Elsa was crying and said that she was vacuuming in our living room and somebody brushed past her. She said that she felt the clothing brush her. She looked around and to her surprise she saw Helen standing just 2 feet from her, looking out of the front window at the ocean. In a surprise, she called Helen's name but got no response, then she ran to get Muriel who was in the kitchen. Seconds later, Helen was gone.

I questioned Elsa. Her own daughter was killed in a car accident about a year ago, so I asked if it could have been her daughter. She said that her daughter was short and this person was a tall white lady in a white gown. She was very familiar with Helen and knew for certain it was her. Helen was 5 ft. 9 inches tall. Interesting fact, Elsa saw Helen AND felt her clothing brush her.

Strange thing, for several days after I didn't seem able to contact Helen, and I began to think that perhaps this visit was a goodbye visit. However, after a few more days I was able to speak to her again as normal.

I had been out of the hospital for over a week and felt that I would never get back to normal. I didn't seem to be getting my strength back, but suddenly, I was back to normal. I had taken the last of the anti-biotic pills 2 days before this sudden improvement.

I was looking on the internet to find out about a home-type machine for checking my blood rather than going to the doctor every week or so, and I was shocked to find that there was a warning about drug interaction when my blood thinning drug was taken at the same time as the anti-biotic I was taking. It took 2 days without the antibiotic for me to get back to normal. The 2 drugs were prescribed by 2 separate doctors. The antibiotic is Ciprofloxacin, and the blood thinner is Coumadin or its other name, Warfarin.

When I was young I remember the invention of a wonderful new rat poison, Warfarin, which killed rats by thinning their blood, causing their blood vessels to leak. Little did I think that I would be taking it eventually.

Now back to other things. Peter got married about 4 or 5 months ago and bought a house in Oceanside on which he spent 2 months fixing it up to like new. He moved out of our house but didn't take any of his stuff. Now he is back to working on the boat which must be nearing completion. However, some of the woodwork which had been finished is showing signs of wear and will have to be redone.

Peter and wife Gayle have booked a rental sailboat in Greece and will be going in October, along with Muriel's brother Paul. Paul has rented sailboats in Greece several times and talked Peter into going this time also. Funny thing, the cost is per person not per boat so Peter and Paul will have separate boats without additional cost. As a result of this, Paul and Karen will not arrive in the USA until after the sailing vacation is over. In the meantime, Paul's son Richard will start work in London and will not be coming at all. Their daughter Katie who has lived with us for the past year is going to England for a visit. It started out as a trip to attend Richard's graduation from university, but she will miss that. It is my firm belief that she will not want to come back, and also there is a risk that the whole family will stay now that Richard will be staying in England.

By the way, I got a machine for checking my blood levels. It works, but it is a bit difficult to operate and takes a couple of goes to make it work correctly. I think it takes practice, and I will get it right soon.

I am continuing to strengthen after my stint in hospital, and I am practically back to normal although I do feel that I don't have the stamina that I had. Or maybe I am feeling my age a bit.

There is something important to record; another strange happening involving Helen.

I was making 8 invitations for a tea party and was printing 2 per sheet on card stock. Then I had to make a total of 32 cuts with a razor knife and metal ruler, to cut them from the sheets. I remember that when done I wrapped them in a sheet of regular paper. I was to take them to choir practice on Thursday to give to the lady who needed them, but I couldn't find them, so I decided to take them to the lady on the following Saturday. On Friday we looked for them for 2 hours, covering the whole house and the cars, but they weren't found. Muriel suggested I ask Helen about it, but for some reason, I could not seem to get a response from her.

Finally, I decided I would have to reprint, but suddenly Helen's voice said, "They are in the kitchen". We searched the kitchen high and low, but there was no sign of them. I reprinted them and proceeded to cut the invitations to size in the kitchen using the back of a large plastic cutting board, a razor knife, and a metal ruler. When the new batch were cut to size I swept the off-cuts towards me and reached for the kitchen garbage can into which I would scrape them. At that second the thought hit me that I may have swept the original invitations away with the scrap. I looked into the bottom of the garbage can and . . . . . there they were, all wrapped up nice and clean, and in the kitchen as Helen said. Again Helen was able to make her continuing presence felt.

Tomorrow we fly to Vancouver to visit my sister Christine. She has been paralyzed for two and a half years. We will be in Vancouver for three days and then we get on board MM Westerdam (Holland American line). For a 4-day cruise home to San Diego.

More news today. Paul and Karen, our "would-be" immigrant relatives from England, advised us that they are arriving on 20th December for a 2-week stay. Also coming is their son Richard (Katie's brother), who now works in London. Actually, Richard will return after a week as he can't get any more time off from his new job. If you remember he, graduated from college a couple of months ago.

Paul and Karen are on the final stretch. They have almost finished refurbishing their last house and will put it on the market. Then they will be able to come and stay permanently, hopefully about April 2013.

Chapter 62 - Finally, Vancouver.

On 26th September 2012, we left for the long postponed trip to Vancouver to see my sister Christine.

We flew by Air Canada direct from San Diego to Vancouver on a small plane with 4 across and two jet engines. We arrived 20 minutes early, then lined up for about an hour and a half to get through customs and immigration. Apparently, 3 planes arrived at the same time. When we finally got to the inspector, we were still at the end of the line as no more planes had arrived.

We booked a car with Budget because they advertised that they were the only ones in the airport. Lies. They were in the airport parking structure along with all the others, and it was most confusing if you followed the signs. We walked up and down with the luggage and finally found them.

We had our Tom Tom satellite navigation device which led us about 20 miles straight to the hotel, and we took it easy for the rest of the day after having a roast beef dinner next door to the hotel, for $5.00 each. Tom Tom was wonderful except for one evening. We came out of a restaurant at about 9.45 pm, and started to drive as usual. However, Tom Tom, which usually starts giving instructions immediately, stayed silent. It was displaying "no signal". I had a rough idea in which direction to go and we eventually found the main road which led to the hotel, and we made it back OK. All the way back, Muriel had kept trying to get the Tom Tom going but got no response. Inside the hotel, I turned it on and immediately got 7 satellites.

We were pleasantly surprised to find Christine in much better shape than expected. Her son John said that she is still paralyzed the same, but otherwise much better than she was. I saw photos of her a year or so ago and she was bedridden and she seemed pretty sick. Now she was sitting in a wheelchair with her hair done nicely and with make-up.

We spent about 3 hours a day with her for the 3 days that we were in Vancouver. We talked to her and got a few smiles and I showed her photos of our kids etc. on my laptop, which she seemed to enjoy. Her companion brought tea, and Christine started pointing and mumbling indicating that she wanted tea also. I passed her a cup and she sipped it and then said "Hot". I took it from her then she spied a brownie and indicated that she wanted some. She broke off a piece and put it into her mouth and chewed it. Then she had more tea, and a dreadful thought occurred to me. Was she allowed to eat and drink as she is being fed by a stomach tube? I hurried out to find a nurse, and asked if Christine was allowed tea and brownie? This was panic station. Nurses rushed to Christine, but she was fine, which may work out well. Apparently, she will be tested to see if she can now handle food and drink by mouth.

We spent a good time with John, my nephew, and met his current girlfriend who seemed very nice. He is used to not having relatives around as he has only one uncle in Canada who he hasn't seen for many years. He seems to regard our family as his only relatives. We invited him to our house for Christmas and he was very excited although understandably reluctant to leave his mother at Christmas time. He offered any of us the use of his condo in Whistler, a ski resort north of Vancouver. Apparently, he fondly remembers visits to California and the time we took him to stay with us in the mountains where we went every year after Christmas.

It is my opinion that he has not had a happy life without brothers and sisters and close-by relatives. He said that Christmas was always a lonely time spent with him and his parents alone. Also, without going into details, my sister, his mother, appears to have been a bit of a tartar.

The return trip was by a 4-day cruise to San Diego, which was uneventful, and we arrived home at about 10.30 am. I always notice how you are treated like royalty at the start of a cruise, and they can't wait to get you off at the end of a cruise. We were met by our son David. There were no problems or emergencies at the house. Our other son Peter and his wife Gayle are in England for a week before going on to Greece for a week's sailing, so we immediately called them to see how it was going. Everything was fine. I asked Helen if we did right in visiting Christine, she said, "It was good you went when you did".

A bit of good news, our 7th great grandchild, was born on 11th of October 2012 to Grandson Andrew, (son of our daughter Helen), and wife Marisol, and a daughter, Sophia, weighing in at 7lb 3ozs. She had a couple of health problems but they cleared up and she came home on the 17th of October. In the meantime, Andrew, who is getting out of the army this coming January, looks like he has been accepted for the Killeen, Texas, police. He has passed all the examinations and tests and should be starting the police academy in January. We have been very worried about the fact that he has a wife and 2 children, and he will need a job, and this came exactly on time. Let's hope all goes well for him.

Chapter 63 - Sad and Other News

On the 16th November 2012, at 5 pm, we received a call from John, son of my sister Christine, to say that she was in the hospital with more pneumonia. This was her third bout in the 2 years during which she has been paralyzed. I asked daughter Helen about her prognosis, and she said, "We will be seeing her soon". At 11.30 pm that evening John called to say that Christine had died 10 minutes before.

I still cannot feel any sadness. Christine had suffered many years with a debilitating back problem, followed by 2 years of paralysis. When I asked Helen how Christine was on the "other side", she answered, "She is hopping around like a 2-year-old". I can well understand this happening after so many years of restricted mobility. We have asked John to join us for Christmas along with 26 of his California relatives who will be with us.

On another front, after 3 months of wrangling with a bank and mortgage company. My son Peter finally bought the house next door to the house he bought about a year ago after he got re-married. Both houses have large backyards facing a lake, and he intends to add a 1600-square-foot "granny flat" to each house. This should put him in a comfortable position with his 4 additional rental properties in Tennessee.

Unfortunately, the additional house requires about 2 months of refurbishing to make it habitable. I have been fixing numerous holes in the walls for Peter. It seems the previous occupants punched the walls for something to do. The place is so dirty, all carpets and other floor coverings are being removed along with baseboards. Several windows need to be replaced, and it will have to be thoroughly cleaned and then painted throughout. Peter got this house at way below market price so he will not lose. Peter's work on the boat has been put on hold in favor of these other projects.

Daniel, son of our son David, passed his paramedic exam after about 3 years of waiting due to some mix-up over his practical internship. Thank goodness it is over now. However, there are not too many jobs going currently due to budget cuts by local governments.

Over the past 6 or 8 months I have been working on creating a small apartment in one unoccupied wing of the house. I thought I must have mentioned it before, but can't find it so at the risk of repeating myself, I can now say that it was completed and is occupied by a very suitable lady who apparently loves the apartment and the location with the view of the ocean. I love the rent that we are receiving, so everybody is happy.

On a sort of connected subject, Peter our youngest son, has expressed his interest in acquiring our house and eventually turning it into several separate apartments. He also would like to have all his brothers in those apartments, but that is a little bit in the future. Also, he contemplates us sub-dividing our nearly 1-acre lot and building a superior class house in the front. Our house is about 80 yards from the road on the high point of the lot allowing a low-profile house to be built in front without impacting the ocean view too much.

Christmas 2012 has just passed. We had 26 for dinner, including our children, most of our grandchildren, and some great-grandchildren. Also Muriel's brother Paul, his wife Karen and son Richard, and of course, their daughter Katie who lives with us. A good time was had by all.

Chapter 64 - Now February 2013, Start of an Era

This year may well be a year of construction. Surprise, surprise, Paul, Joy's brother, called the other day to say that he has bought the empty lot right next door to our lot. He intends to build a house on it. Muriel said to him "I assume you will live with us while you build". He answered that he wanted to do this if it was OK. Of course, she told him, it was OK. He expects to complete work on his current house within about 2 months then he has to sell it and emigrate finally to the USA. This could be within 3 or 4 months.

As a result of this, and my liking for the extra rent we are receiving, I think we will build up on the small one-storey apartment that I recently created. With this addition, Paul and Karen will be able to occupy a complete 3-bedroom apartment without sharing with us. When they vacate it, we will close off some doors and put in outside stairs, and create another small separate apartment.

In addition, my son Peter will soon be starting construction of the first "granny flat" in the back garden of his latest house, the modification and upgrade of which will hopefully be completed in about two months.

My other son Nicholas, Muriel, and I went to reconnoiter a possible camping site for a family camping trip in the next month or so when it gets a bit warmer. We went to Lake Hemet which is one of my favorite places. We found the water level had dropped so low that the water edge was about a hundred yards from our favorite camp site which was formerly right next to the water. The nightly cost is now exorbitant, and Nick has found a less expensive state camp site just up the road, so this is where we will propose the next family affair.

Now, a few weeks later, we have booked 4 camp sites just about 300 yards from the entrance to Lake Hemet. It is called Hurkey Creek Park. Up until now 12 of our family are signed up to go on Friday the 26th of April for 2 days, returning Sunday midday. Fishing on Lake Hemet will be about a mile away as we have to go to the dam end of the lake, beyond the campground. It is on Federal land. Nick and I checked it out and while we were there we saw a 16-inch trout pulled out, and this was the fourth one caught by this angler. We will have our motor home, my son Nick's trailer, and my son David will use the trailer of a neighbor. Others will sleep in trucks/campers, SUV's, and tents.

Last Wednesday, we went to Hemet to see Helen's eldest son, Andrew's wife and children. Alison, 2 ½, and the new baby Sophia, 4 months old. They live in Texas. We last saw Alison when she was about 20 months old, but she remembered us, and called Muriel "Grandma" right away. She is a real cutie and bright as a button. Andrew is in the Killeen, Texas Police Academy. He was one of 13 chosen out of 250 applicants for the positions.

After seeing the children we drove up to the mountains to do a second check on Hurkey Creek Park. It was after that, we made the booking.

A couple of Fridays ago, I was going out to take a friend to have an X-ray on his chest and a scan of his brain. He had suffered what is, to me, a mental breakdown. I forgot to take my cell phone, so I returned after, about 100 yards down the road to hear Muriel speaking on it. Our son David's wife had called to say that David had been in a car accident. There had been a deluge of rain and his tiny two-seater car had hydro-planed along the freeway, hitting two cars, and demolishing his own car. She said he was in hospital with a broken wrist and severe chest and abdomen bruising. He was expected to be discharged in the afternoon. I was driving my friend because his wife was undergoing a long-planned serious back operation at the time of the X-ray and scan.

Muriel called to our other sons to tell them about David, and found out that son Nick was at home in bed as a result of a minor surgery the day before and didn't tell us to save us worrying about him.

After I returned from the X-ray and scan visit with my friend, we went to see David at home, and his son Daniel and wife Erin also called in to see him. Whilst there, Erin had a phone call to say that her grandmother, with whom she had lived for many years, was expected to die within 12 to 24 hours. At 5.05 pm another call came to say that the grandmother was dead.

Luckily, David's broken wrist turned out to be a chipped bone, but 2 ½ weeks later, he is still in pain from the bruising received. Nick has completely recovered from his ordeal and is back to a regular working schedule. That day was a day that we don't want to repeat.

After 4 ½ weeks, David went to his doctor to have a new caste put on his wrist, but the Dr. said it had pretty well healed already, and a new cast was not necessary. He is going to work on a limited basis, but still has pain and is restricted on what he can do.

We are just back from the Hurkey Creek family camping trip. The camp site was beautiful and the day temperature and weather was perfect. However, the first night was cold, as expected, and one of our number went home later in the day. My son Nick tried the fishing at the nearby Lake Hemet but with no success. Otherwise, we had a great time.

Unfortunately, Muriel is down with pneumonia, and she feels it is due to the cold night when we were away.

I have to relate an unfortunate occurrence on the trip. We left home just after 11.00 am with a view to getting there early. We were to meet up with Nick and Karen with their new trailer, in the parking lot of Home Depot. On the way to them, we heard some really loud "thumping" from the back end of the motor home. We stopped at the side of the road to investigate but could see nothing wrong. We continued and met with Nick and I decided that I would do a thorough check. One of the tires on the inside of a rear set of wheels seemed shinier than the others. A large part of the tread had gone and I was looking at the metal of the radial tire. We called for somebody to comer and put on the spare which took 2 ½ hours. In the meantime, Nick had found a tire company that had the correct size tire and we retraced our steps back to Oceanside. We left there, with our new tire on, at 3.40 pm and arrived at Hurkey Creek Park at 4.45 pm.

On the way back, we were just getting on the freeway for the last 3 miles, when the steering felt wobbly. Within the next few yards, there was a loud bang and a front tire burst. We called the same company for help and they said it would be 30 minutes, but within 10 minutes a large tow truck pulled up behind us and the man got on with putting on the spare. In about 15 minutes another tow truck stopped. It was the one I'd called. Apparently, the first truck was part of a free service provided by the state for helping stranded motorists. The service was free which saved us $115.

Tomorrow I am getting 5 new tires to put on the motor home. Several of the tire people said that the tires, although only about ¼ worn were 10 years old which is why they blew up. I didn't know that tires get old.

It looks as if my son Peter has sold at a nice profit, the first house he bought in Oceanside about 18 months ago. He has been refurbishing it since then. The escrow closes in the next day or so.

While he was living there he bought the house next door to him, and has been upgrading it also and is now living in it. He intends to build the famous Granny Flat in this backyard as it is much bigger than that of the first house. After that, he is committed to finishing his boat which is still alongside our house. In this new backyard, he has a 32-foot motor home (just bought), his 34-foot removal van which was at our house, plus a small tractor to which he is adding a backhoe and a shovel/bulldozer attachment. Also he has a 9-foot utility trailer, which he uses to transport his tractor. However, after he puts on all the attachments, it will need a much larger trailer.

After the Granny Flat, he says he going to build a house on our front lot which we've agreed to sell him.

We have recently started collecting succulents and cactus plants. Muriel is tired of having to water plants in the back yard so this may ease the watering problem. I am amazed at how fast these succulents grow if they are kept moist. We have had lots of flowers on them already, and have been able to propagate some and give them away.

Two items of good news, one is that my son Christopher's daughter, Chelsea, is getting married on January 4th next, 2014. The other is that David's son Daniel's wife is pregnant with great-grandchild number 8.

A bit of sad news this morning, my cousin David Simmonds, who lives in England got word to me that his wife Tina died this afternoon (England time). She was diagnosed 5 weeks ago with pancreatic, liver, and lung cancer.

Chapter 65 - Many Changes

Many changes have taken place since the last writing. Chelsea's wedding took place last weekend. From things we heard it promised to be a strange affair, but it turned out to be excellent, but the weather was cool and it was outside. We dressed for the coolness, but it still shortened an otherwise happy time. Chelsea and her husband Tony will eventually live in Texas, close to Andrew, our daughter's eldest son.

Peter has not done any more work on the boat alongside our house. In fact, he has bought another 44-foot sailboat and will transport it to his backyard for some work, and then he will probably sell it.

In the meantime, he has discovered a new purpose in life. Apparently, there are many foreclosed lower-level houses and apartment buildings for sale by banks in Tennessee, and Peter has set up his eldest son Michael to find suitable properties and buy them. In the last 3 weeks, he has bought 7 properties at very favorable prices and has 3 workers who are re-painting and generally fixing up. Peter plans to sell for profit and then continue buying as a business for his sons to operate.

Peter's other plan, to build a granny flat in his backyard, is still on and moving slowly. Sewer and water lines are laid, and he has truss quotes and plans in the process. This building will consist of 3 garages with a complete living area on the second floor. As you know he has a tractor and fitted it with a backhoe and bucket/bulldozer in front, and this is what he used to bury his newly installed service pipes for the new building. Recently he bought a larger tractor as he found that the old one is a bit small for the work he plans.

We went out to lunch a couple of weeks ago, and on the way back, with no previous thoughts or plans about it, we stopped and in 15 minutes, decided to buy this tiny new car. Our other 3 cars take approx. $55 to fill with gas. This car takes about $25 to fill up. Although it is very small, it has plenty of room for 4 passengers, and up until now, with less than 1000 miles on the clock, it is getting 30 miles to the gallon around town. I reckon it will do at least 37 miles to the gallon on a long trip. One of the displays indicates miles per gallon, and for the couple of times, we've taken it on the freeway. At freeway speeds, it runs between 40 and 55 miles per gallon.

This past Christmas, we were expecting Muriel's brother and wife to arrive from England and stay permanently in the USA. It is 2 ½ years since they received their immigration visas, but they are in the process of selling their last property in England. They have a buyer, but the sale is not complete, so they had to go back 3 days ago. They now threaten to come permanently in about 3 or 4 months but I wrote the same thing back in January 2011. Their daughter, Katie, who has lived with us for about 2 years, has now bought a house and will be moving out in the next few days. Our grandson, David who has lived with us for about 2 years, is going back to Tennessee at the end of the week to take on the work that his elder brother, Michael, was doing for Peter. Michael has to go on a nine-day training course. He is still in the Tennessee National Guard. Bob, Peter's friend who has been renting a room from us for a couple of years, is planning to get married this May (2014), and move out. However, he just told us he has bought a house and will be leaving us in the next month, so we will have an empty house except for Muriel and me and the lady in the separate little apartment.

In the meantime, we have contracted to have a solar electric system installed. Our electricity bill has been getting completely out of control and there are more cost increases coming. We hope it works out for us. Unfortunately, the large tree that has occupied a central position immediately in front of the house, largely blocking a view of the ocean, casts a shadow on our roof in midafternoon. This would affect the efficiency of the new solar system and it has had to be removed. We have a mountain of foliage and large logs to be dealt with. I spent two mornings tidying up and moving two massive piles of foliage from the parking area. It was really heavy work and I found that a couple of hours at it was enough for me. I am becoming aware that my age, nearly 79, is showing. As a bonus, the clouds of dust and yellow pollen have caused me some considerable discomfort with sneezing and itchy eyes, etc. All that remains is to dispose of the tree foliage. Peter bought a shredder, and one of his workers is coming this week to start work with it.

We go to Las Vegas tomorrow with our son David. He has customers to see and wants company, so we will stay there for a couple of days. His wife Susan, needs to stay home as their son (our grandson) Daniel's wife is close to giving birth to our eighth great-grandchild and Susan will look after their two-year-old, Jade. They say it is another girl.

Chapter 66 - A Girl It Was.

Ellie Caroline was born early in the morning weighing in at 7lbs, 14ozs. She is a very happy child who hardly ever cries. She makes great-grandchild number 8 and David's 4th grandchild. This was closely followed by a remarkable happening.

David's eldest stepson, Scott, was divorced about 12 years ago and has never remarried. He has brought many different girlfriends to family gatherings, but none of them have become permanent.

Some weeks ago, an old girlfriend came to see Scott to announce that she had a 1-year-old son and that he was the father. Apparently, her current boyfriend had doubts about the paternity and had a paternity test which proved him to be not the father.

Scott's immediate response was that he had not seen the girl for 2 years and could not be the father. After some discussion, Scott decided to have a test and found that he was indeed the father. David gained another grandchild and we, another great-grandchild.

Our solar system is working fine. We are producing about the same amount as we are using. We had our first bill from SDG&E, the power company, and instead of our usual $300 bill, we had a credit of $31.

Peter's boat was moved from our house to his backyard. He now has a slip at the Oceanside harbor, but he has to have his boat in the water by the end of the month or lose the slip. It is still not ready but it is close, so I don't know what he is going to do if they don't give him an extension. He has already waited 4 ¼ years for the slip.

Later, it turned out that Peter applied for an extension and he was granted an extra 30 days. He has to have the boat in the water by 1st July.

Paul and Karen and their son Richard arrive in 4 weeks, early June, but Paul and Richard will return to England after 10 days. Paul still has not completed work on properties in England but is leaving Karen here so I sort of believe him when he says he will come back to stay in September this year. Their daughter Katie who used to live with us got engaged to Nate, and they are planning the wedding in England for July next year, 2015.

Just to re-cap, Katie is doing well in her new house, our grandson David who lived with us is still in Tennessee, and Bob has moved into the house he bought. We went to his wedding in Palm Desert last weekend.

Grandson Matthew went to Marine boot camp 2 months ago, his older brother Andrew, a policeman in Killeen Texas, is coming to San Diego for Matthew's graduation, and is going for a test with the San Diego Police. The graduation is in one week and we will go to the camp in San

Diego this coming Thursday and Friday, then to his father's house on Saturday for a welcome home party for Matthew.

In the meantime, granddaughter Chelsea, daughter of son Christopher, who got married last January, has gone to live in Austin, Texas where her husband's parents live. They are old and infirm, so he wants to be near them. Chelsea's older sister Lauren has a boyfriend named Fred and they are talking about marriage. Just today, I heard that my son Peter's daughter Kerri is also talking about marriage.

My back problems have been increasing. I have just got over almost 2 months of sciatica, so it was decided that I should get some professional advice. I have stenosis, arthritis swelling which is putting pressure on the nerves in my back. I am scheduled to have a little operation to remove the swelling in about a month. We have so much going on that I cannot think about it at present. I had a similar operation about 7 years ago, and it solved the problem.

We went to 2 days of graduating ceremonies at the marine camp in San Diego for our grandson Matthew. The next day, Saturday, we attended a party for Matthew in Hemet and were greeted by a fire caused by electrical wires being brought down by a localized mini tornado. This happened alongside the dirt road a quarter of a mile from Matthew's home. There is only one dirt road in or out, and we were a bit nervous but drove on down the road. We stopped to film the action. A helicopter was dropping water and a twin-engine plane was dropping fire retardant and flying low right over us. The fire was only covering about an acre, but flames were at least 12 or 14 feet high. After about half an hour, the flames were virtually out.

The "month" mentioned 2 paras. above is over and gone. 2 weeks ago I had my back operation which was scheduled for 3 ½ hours, but actually took 6 ½ hours. Apparently, the old operation where they installed an "X stop", a plastic spacer to keep the bones apart, caused all sorts of problems and left lots of scar tissue which had to be removed. Already, after 2 weeks, I have less pain, and I am hopeful that I will be much better for the operation.

Chapter 67 - In The Water At Last

Peter's boat finally entered the water after the most amazing series of mishaps and stupid mistakes. The epoxy paint which costs hundreds of dollars a gallon, arrived damaged, and then the wrong color. To cap it all, the people doing the painting made the most elementary mistakes, and it had to be done over in several places. The normal cost to paint a boat of this size is around $35,000, which I can well understand after seeing the problems Peter had.

Peter continues to work on the boat in the slip. He has one of the masts set up and is working on the sails.

I was just reading what I wrote back in February 2013 and saw that Paul was about to come to the US permanently. Here we are in September of 2014 and he is due to arrive finally in November. In the meantime, Karen, Paul's wife arrived 3 months ago, living with us until a month ago when she bought a house in Oceanside, about 10 miles away, and close to sons David, Nick, and Peter. Apparently, Paul has almost finished fixing up houses. Katie, their daughter, is making plans for her wedding to Nate, to take place in England in July of 2015. Muriel is planning to go, but I'm not too enthusiastic about it and will probably stay home.

It is November 26th and Paul did arrive 2 weeks ago. They held a housewarming party to which all the family was invited. Karen, Paul's wife, arrived in June and bought the house a couple of months ago.

Michael, Peter's eldest son, had a new baby named Raphael Brian, just a couple of weeks ago. This is great-grandchild number 10. Number 11 is due to be born in April 2015 to Andrew and Marisol. Andrew is the eldest son of our daughter, Helen. Andrew is a policeman living in Killeen, Texas and in January he is coming here to take a test for the California Highway Patrol.

The test did not take place as the Killeen police would not let him have the time off to come to California. He now plans to apply to the San Diego police as he has heard that they are adding police recruits.

Andrew came (in January 2015) for the tests and interview with San Diego police, and passed OK as expected. He is awaiting their call. We have offered him and his wife and 2 children (soon to be 3) the use of our lower floor which is completely unoccupied. There are 3 bedrooms, a den, a dining room, 2 bathrooms, 3 half bathrooms, a huge living room, a kitchen, a breakfast room, and a laundry room. It is fully furnished so Andrew is looking into storage for his furniture. It will be nice to have them here.

My son Nicholas and his wife Karen, are a bit dissatisfied with California. Nick lives for fishing and hunting and he feels that it is too expensive and not enough of it in California. So, he decided to check out Tennessee and he and Karen flew back there a month ago. However, they decided it was not for them. It just happens that they were there in the coldest period they have had for years, so this may have had something to do with their decision. In two weeks they are flying to Idaho to have a look around to see if that fits their needs. I doubt they will beat California.

Paul and Karen have really settled in. They have bought a large trailer and a diesel truck to pull it and are going off camping this weekend. Apparently Karen has been saving money for years just for a trailer.

I just read the last few chapters and I spoke of the period of probable construction projects coming up. Well, none of them have taken place. Paul has settled in to his house in Oceanside and is showing no signs of building in the lot next door. Peter has apparently lost some of his enthusiasm for building a granny flat in the back garden, and I am not ready to go ahead with my proposed building, so we are at a standstill.

Peter has changed his priorities and may be making some surprising moves very soon, but there is no point in explaining them as he changes from week to week. His boat is close to being completed and his new plans include making more use of his boat and his motorhome.

Chapter 68 - An Amazing Story

I spent 15 minutes looking back for an earlier mention of this story and can find nothing. I started writing this book about 25 years ago, and can't remember what I wrote in the early days, so I will start this saga from the beginning. If some of this is a repeat, please forgive me. At least we now have answers.

When Muriel was very young, she remembers being known as Muriel Joy Sanderson, and then she remembers her name being changed to Newton. She also remembers being present at an adoption proceeding involving her. She asked her mother about it and why sheets and other linens were embroidered with the letters SSS. She pieced together the fact that there was some mystery in her past. An old aunt who had maybe imbibed a little too much, eventually told her that her real father was named Sidney Smith Sanderson and that he was in the British Navy. Muriel could not get any more information from her mother.

A few years later, when Muriel and I met, she related this information to me. This was shortly before we were married. I worked at the Admiralty (British Navy administration) and told a workmate about it. Strange coincidence number one was, he said that his wife's sister worked in the Admiralty too, and kept all the records of all navy personnel going back to the beginning of the British Navy. Coincidence number two. He said he would talk to her. The next day he arranged for us to look at the records which were kept in a locked room just 40 feet from where I worked. It could have been at any of the dozens of Admiralty facilities anywhere in Britain. Coincidences number three.

We crept into this huge storage room filled with ping pong size tables loaded with 5 x 8 inch cards. In no time we found him. The card contained addresses and the fact that he currently had 3 children, John, David, and Wendy. Diagonally, written in pencil was "new address, 7 Teign View Place, Teignmouth Devon". There was also a much more complete file which I was not allowed to see.

I went to Muriel full of this information, but to my surprise, she wanted nothing to do with it. She was frightened of contacting her father. But two days later I saw a newspaper ad for a special one-day excursion by rail to Teignmouth, and reluctantly Muriel agreed to go there with me. A cheap day excursion to Teignmouth at that moment in time was coincidence number four. We went there a week later.

We found our way to 7 Teign View Place to the alley behind the house, and I could see over the 6-foot fence a woman beating a doormat. We were reluctant to speak to her in case she was unaware of her husbands' previous marriage.

A small boy of about 10 or 11, came along the alley and I asked him if he knew Mr. Sanderson in number 7. He said, "Yes, he's my uncle but he's moved away". "Uncle", coincidence number five. We were disappointed, but the boy said. "I can take you to where he moved". He led us up the alley across a road and an empty lot and pointed out a motorbike parked outside a house. He said, "Mr. Sanderson lives there, that's his motorbike".

I knocked on the door which was answered by a stocky man in shirt sleeves. I asked, "Are you Mr. Sanderson"? He said no, he wasn't, and that Mr. Sanderson was his brother in law, but was not available. Apparently, he'd gone off to London and was working for Sankey, a large civil engineering company. We got the impression that there had been a problem. He didn't know any address for him. I asked him if he or his sister were aware that he had been married previously. He said he did know it. I pointed out Muriel who was standing shaking with fright across the road. I told him that Muriel was Mr. Sanderson's daughter. I called Muriel across and we talked a while but there was no way we could do more. We gave up and went back home. After this, I wanted to write to Sankey but Muriel was against it. It remained shelved, still haunting me. However, I've never quite understood why we didn't think to inquire more about Muriel's siblings at that time.

When our youngest son Peter was about 25, he spoke to me expressing the fact that he wanted to know more about his ancestors, namely Muriel's father. I wrote to the Admiralty giving all the information I had, and requested Mr. Sanderson's whereabouts, knowing he had been in the navy a long time and would have received a pension. Two months later a reply came saying they could not reveal information on Navy personnel. A dead end. However, the situation continued to haunt me with feelings that this should have been brought to a conclusion by at least making contact with Muriel's siblings.

In recent years, Sidney Smith Sanderson who was born in 1911, was very likely deceased, but where were his children, John, David, and Wendy? I have brought this subject up to Muriel regularly, and as recently as two months before writing this, but Muriel always discouraged any action to find them. But a week ago Muriel's brother, Paul visited us and used my laptop to look up the registrar's information on his parents and aunts, etc. This sparked my renewed interest, and the next day, unknown to Muriel, I started looking for Teignmouth births, etc. I found nothing after hours of looking, so I turned to several "People Finders" etc., and could not find anybody close to Teignmouth with the Sanderson name. If the name had come up they would normally want money for the phone number etc. but there seemed to be no record. I started searching for British Telecom records, but again found nothing on Sanderson in the Teignmouth area of Devon. I was about to give up about 3 hours into this when another page for British Telecom popped up on the screen. I don't recall any action of mine which caused this to happen, but here it was just sitting on the screen.

It was the last page I was going to look at. I was giving up. I typed in David Sanderson, thinking that Wendy would probably have married and have a different name. Up came "D M Sanderson" followed by "Wendy Sanderson", and to my complete surprise, the phone numbers and addresses were included, which is most unusual. I was feeling shaky and very excited. This was the first positive occurrence to date. I wondered if the D stood for David. I called Muriel and said that I was going to phone. She was terrified and begged me to not call. I picked up the phone several times, then put it down several times, whilst discussing it with Muriel. Finally, she agreed that she had no real reason for not calling, and nothing would be lost. I dialed the number with shaking hands. A man answered. I nervously asked, "Are you David Sanderson"? When he said, "Yes", I nearly dropped the phone. With quaking voice, I explained I was looking for somebody and would he mind telling me if his father's name was Sidney Smith Sanderson. There was a moment of complete silence, then with his voice rising in pitch he said, "Yes". With violent tingles running up and down my spine, and the sudden knowledge that I had found "them", I asked the unnecessary question, "Do you have siblings named John and Wendy". His voice was again rising in pitch with nervousness when he said, "Yes". Another pregnant pause. I said, "I am your brother-in-law, and I'm married to your half-sister". I'm sure he had put two and two together already because he immediately said, "We've been looking for you for 50 years".

I think we were both in shock for a few moments, but we talked for several minutes which revealed the fact that they knew of our visit to Teignmouth 60 years ago, but couldn't find us as they didn't know Joy's name.

Reading this does not describe the level of excitement. It was only then that I realized the depth of my lifelong disappointment at Muriel not wanting to investigate this to completion and find her siblings. I asked Muriel to at least say hello to her brother. She refused. She was in shock as were both David and I. Muriel was as white as a whitewashed wall. I talked to David on speaker a bit more with Muriel listening and asked Muriel again to say hello. Then she took the phone and had an emotional talk with him for 20 minutes. The call ended. We had Wendy's phone number and dialed it. It was busy. David had immediately called her. We waited 15 minutes and called again, and got Wendy. Muriel and Wendy spoke like sisters do, for about 50 minutes. It was now 10.00 pm in England. Wendy couldn't find John's phone number, but we had got email addresses from David for all three of them, so I emailed John for his phone number. He replied and we called John the next day. His first words were, "We've wanted to contact you for 50 years since you came to Teignmouth". Muriel and her new siblings are now over the moon and exceedingly happy at the result and Muriel doesn't really know now why she was so scared. The lesson for me is to go ahead and do what you think is right. I could have found these relatives many years ago. We are all getting close to an age where we may not be able to visit much longer.

Since then, we have exchanged many phone calls, photographs, family trees, etc. by email. Muriel goes to England next week for niece Katie's wedding which was planned months ago. John, David, and Wendy will drive from Teignmouth to Wellow to meet up with Muriel. In about 3 months, (October) they plan to come to California to meet all the family here. John is 74, David is 71 and Wendy is 68. John was 14 when we visited Teignmouth. We cannot understand why we neglected to ask about Muriel's siblings at that time. Everybody is now excited beyond words.

The most mysterious parts of this are the fact that we are in our eighties and Muriel is not likely to go to England again. This was a last chance. Also, it is weird the way the page came up on my computer without me doing anything. Previous British Telecom pages didn't find the Sanderson name, "no record". Also, the greatest coincidence is that I worked with somebody who had a way into Admiralty records, (a closely guarded secret) without which we would have known nothing. I see, for sure, the hand of God in all this.

Since writing the above, it now seems almost certain that the small boy we spoke to in the alley was Muriel's half-brother David. Muriel's eldest new brother now says that there were no 10 or 11-year-old nephews (boys) in the family, except for David who was 11 at the time.

When we asked the boy for Mr. Sanderson, we now think the boy was thinking we wanted his uncle who lived with them. The motorcycle belonged to him and not to Muriel's father, but the boy said it was Mr. Sanderson's. The boy's name was Sanderson, as was his brother's, sister's, and mother's, and we think the boy assumed his uncle's name was Sanderson also. I gave the boy 2 shillings for helping us. If we hadn't met the boy, (coincidence number six) we may never have found the new address. The mysteries don't stop.

Most relatives and friends have read the above or heard a verbal account of this incredible story, and express great happiness for Muriel. Although everybody loves the story, I appear to be the most excited except for Muriel's new sister, Wendy who is also very happy to have a big sister. She's 68 and never had a sister before, but always wanted one.

I believe my high level of excitement is due to the fact that for 60 years I fought (for want of a better word) with Muriel about this. I wanted to know, and she was too scared to pursue it. Scared of what, she didn't know but she knew she was scared. As I said above, I brought the subject up with Muriel as recently as two months ago, a couple of weeks before we finally made contact.

I hesitate to dilute this fantastic story with more commentary, but a few words are warranted. As of this date, June 23rd, 2015, the latest is that the new relatives, John and wife Sue, David and wife Hilary, and sister Wendy will meet with Muriel in 3 days in Wellow near Bath where Muriel is staying with our eldest son Christopher, his wife and 2 daughters, Muriel's cousin Tony and wife. They have rented "The Wagon House", a part of Weavers Farm in Wellow, a small village near Bath.

I've looked at it on Google Earth, and the place appears to be actually the farm wagon house, converted to vacation living accommodation. It is directly across the road from the local village pub, "The Fox And Badger". Next Wednesday, Muriel is entertaining 16 friends she knew when she worked as a long-distance telephone operator when she left school at 16 years of age.

Muriel has a cell phone in England with her, and we have spoken every day whilst she was traveling around. However, since arriving in Wellow 2 days ago we have not had contact. It is a small village out in the "boonies", beyond cell phone coverage. I knew that Muriel intended to take her new relatives for lunch at the Pub across the road from where they are staying, so I called the Pub and was lucky enough to catch Muriel there. I found the Pub on Google Earth, and could just make out the name, "Fox and Badger". The meeting between Muriel and her new relatives occurred on schedule, and it turned out to be a very emotional time. Muriel's comment was, "They are lovely people".

I allowed time for the relatives to drive the 80 miles home and called them to get their reaction. They all said similar things such as "Muriel is lovely" (she is), "We had an emotionally tiring time" and "Yes we are definitely coming to California". Apparently, they were not frightened off by Muriel. Muriel will be home in 10 days.

With the prospect of the "new" family coming to visit us in about 3 months or less, there are a few things we must work on around the house, and a few things we must buy. When Muriel arrives home from the trip to England, we will create a list.

With regard to long trips with them, we plan as a minimum to take them to Las Vegas and the Grand Canyon, Hoover Dam, and on the way back, visit a few places such as Oak Creek Canyon and Sedona, very picturesque, then Jerome, a quaint old copper mining town perched on the side of a mountain and gradually slipping down.

For local trips and day trips, we will do all the sights in San Diego and go to Hollywood etc.

Muriel has arrived home, tired but happy. We called John, her new eldest brother, and he said he has zeroed in on some good fares, leaving England on 7th October and returning about 19 days later. We warned him that if we are to do a long trip, it will require many hours in a car. He seemed to feel that was not a problem, so we are at a "go" point. John was worried about getting from the airport to Carlsbad, and we allayed his fears saying we would be happy to collect them regardless of the time of their arrival.

My son Nick is staying with us for about 6 days as his house is sold and he is out of it, but can't leave until he gets his money. Also, he will be towing his house trailer with his truck and a friend will drive his SUV pulling his 17-foot boat, but suddenly his SUV has developed a mechanical problem and it is being fixed. He will be leaving this coming Saturday, 11th July 2015.

Nick, Karen, and the vehicles arrived in Middleton, Idaho on the 13th of July. His new house was in fine condition.

Now to the next big change in our lives. Tomorrow, Saturday 1st August, a 16-foot Pod storage container arrives at our house, ordered by Andrew, our daughter's eldest son. A rented truck will be loading up in Texas with Andrew's belongings and it will be driven here by Kirk, Andrew's father. Hopefully, Andrew, Marisol, his wife, and three children will drive their two vehicles and all should arrive either this Sunday or Monday depending on traffic and how fast the truck goes.

Finally, after 6 months of tests and 3 flights from Texas to San Diego, the police department called Andrew last week to tell him that he is hired by San Diego police and he is needed here by 7th August for indoctrination and to start the police academy on the 20th of August. They gave him about 10 days to resign and move to San Diego, which sounds ridiculous when it took 6 months to go through the hiring process.

Chapter 69 - The Family Visit is Soon Over and Life Goes On

Muriel's "other" family, all 5, arrived as planned on the 7th of October 2015. We picked up a rental Toyota Sienna 7-seat van at about 2.00 pm, and left for the airport an hour later. After some parking problems, we got to the point where we could watch for them coming out of the tunnel from Immigration and Customs, and there they were. Eldest brother John, 74, and his wife Sue, Brother David, 71, and his wife Hilary, and sister Wendy, 68. We got all the luggage into the van OK, which was a worry of mine, and we were off to Carlsbad.

I had not met any of them before. You may recall that they traveled from their homes to meet Muriel on her summer visit to England. They seemed very nice friendly people, although a little nervous, which is understandable.

We had prepared a very busy schedule, and for the next 19 days, we had something planned nearly every day. Total miles driven were around 2,400. We went to Las Vegas for 2 nights then on to Grand Canyon and Flagstaff, then Laughlin Nevada, and home. We traveled all over San Diego County seeing most of the many spectacular attractions. On another day we went to Lake Hemet and a picturesque small mountain town, Idyllwild. For some reason, they all particularly loved the scenery and the wildness of Lake Hemet. The weather was perfect and it was just us, the squirrels, and the birds.

We had a dinner party at home for them to meet our three sons living in the area, and played a filmed recording of a message from our son Nick who has moved to Idaho. We had a sing-along for the visitors to meet friends, and took them to a Bunko party at a friend's house. We took them to a band concert in which some of our friends performed. Peter took them sailing which they loved.

Another day we went to Hollywood, and walked Hollywood Boulevard, photographing the brass stars and the foot and handprints set in the pavement in front of the Chinese theater. Wendy, in particular, was enthralled by this. It was a lifelong dream for her. To my surprise, the visitors loved our Carlsbad beaches. They all live in seaside towns, and so I assumed that beaches would be of no interest to them. They liked to walk, and they walked to and along the beaches for hours.

The visitors expressed gratitude for the trip arranged for them in words such as a "dream trip", and "far beyond their wildest expectations". We were invited to stay with John and his wife Sue if we went to England.

For the whole trip, the weather was spectacular, although a little warm in places. Everything went exactly to plan and timetable and there were no problems at all which is incredible when you consider the miles and the number of people involved.

In the meantime, grandson Andrew, his wife, and 3 children have settled in downstairs, and Andrew is more than 2 months into the San Diego Police Academy and seems to be doing very well. He feels that his Killeen Texas police experience has been helpful to him. His 2 daughters are lovely and I enjoy them very much. Their son is only about 6 months old and just getting a bit more interesting.

Peter will finally drive his motor home back to Tennessee and spend 5 months doing work on his more recently acquired properties. This work was supposed to be done by his two sons, but David, the youngest, walked out on it and went to Colorado to live near his mother, Luanne. Michael has continued with the work, but I fear he has little experience and has been floundering and not getting too much done, although he apparently made a good job of preparing one house for sale. In the meantime, David has done well in Colorado and enjoys his job, which is maintenance at a very large apartment complex. He will shortly move into his own apartment.

Some news. Daniel, son of our son, David, and his wife Erin announce that they expect their third child in 2016. This will make great-grandchild number 12.

Earlier, I mentioned Lauren, the eldest daughter of son Christopher, and the talk of getting married to Fred. This has now solidified and they will tie the knot on 15th of May 2016.

Grandson Matthew, a marine, will be shipped off to Japan next month, for 7 months. Returning mid-2016.

The Wheels of God Grind Slowly But Exceeding Fine. We've all heard this expression or one like it. Well, today we heard a story which made us stop and think. Probably about 20 years ago, our daughter Helen had a problem with a neighbor, a small-town lawyer, who sued her because it was alleged she separated fighting kids rather roughly. His kid was a troublemaker. This situation caused Helen some grief, and she was ordered to pay something like $3000. Sometime later, the wife met Helen in the street and she tearfully apologized profusely. The lawyer husband was recognized locally as a sleazy operator, and soon after, was disbarred from practicing law.

Shortly thereafter, the wife divorced him, and she eventually married a man who is the tenant of Helen's original house in Hemet, still owned by Helen's husband.

Recently, the ex-lawyer was crossing the road in Hemet when a car came along and hit him, killing him. This is not remarkable in itself, except for the fact that it happened on 10th November just a few days ago.

Why is this remarkable? The 10th of November is Helen's birthday. A fitting end to a bad person.

I realize that this is not a truly Christian attitude, but it makes you think of God's words as reported in the bible, "vengeance is mine" sayeth the Lord. Also, the fact that it happened on Helen's birthday, looks almost like a gesture to Helen.

Son Peter has decided to sell his house in Oceanside in order to finance modifications and upgrades on his properties in Tennessee. There is no doubt that Tennessee is the place for rental properties. The cost of houses is about half the cost in California, but rents are about the same.

Peter will move his huge motor home to our side yard and live in it temporarily when he returns, and as needed, will drive it back to Tennessee and live in it whilst doing the necessary work. He has got permission to park a boat and his tractor on the empty lot next door, which belongs to Paul, Muriel's brother.

We can easily run electricity, water, house telephone, TV cable, and a sewer line to our side yard. In the meantime, Peter is delivering his many potted plants, mostly succulents, to our backyard.

Almost as soon as I wrote the above three paragraphs, Peter did his usual and changed his mind. He says he will now rent his house out. By doing this, he can store all his boats and other equipment in a separate part of the huge backyard. A separate storage part is already fenced off.

Andrew just graduated from the police academy last week, and we went there to cheer him on. The class graduating was about 70 to 80 officers. After they had all received their badges and sat down there were some special awards for extra special good performance during the 6 months course.

The first award up was for the best at fast emergency driving. The recipient was. . . . Andrew VanOrsdel!!! He sat down after the award, and there was another award, I don't remember what. The third award was for the best shooter. . . . Andrew VanOrsdel again. There were a few more special awards, maybe 3 more, and the ceremony ended. We were so proud. 3 of his friends, police officers, flew from Killeen to be present at the graduation. One of them was a training officer. He said that Andrew was the first of his trainees ever in Killeen to whom he awarded 100%.

On the following Friday Andrew and his wife held a party in our back yard to which about 35 family and friends came.

Andrew has now resumed normal police work and does 4 days (of nights) of 10 hours, then gets 3 days off. After 3 months they change to another shift like 5.00 am to 3.00 pm, 4 days a week and 3 off. He is now in a different area with more activity, and he likes it better than the previous area where there was not much activity.

At long last, Muriel and I fulfilled a promise we made to our son Nick and Karen last year, which was to go and visit them in Middleton Idaho. We left on a Sunday morning and drove about 550 miles through California to Reno, Nevada, where we stayed in a motel. We were so tired we just ate a few snacks we'd brought with us and went to bed at about 7.00 pm. The next day we had breakfast at Denny's restaurant and drove on. Unknown to us, we had to cross a high plateau at about 5000 feet.

The sky turned black and it started to snow. To my horror, I noticed that the outside thermometer on the car showed 32 deg. F. I switched it to Centigrade which confirmed my worst fears and showed 0 deg. C. We were seeing an occasional other vehicle but very little traffic. We were traveling at about 80 mph in order to get to Nick's that evening. Along the center of the road, and at the side, there was about an inch of what looked like slush with wet pavement where the vehicles traveled. Everything else was white. I think it was too cold to melt but the road was too warm to freeze completely.

After 2 hours of this, the road started to slope down, and the temperature rose to 35 deg. F. However, after half an hour the road rose again and we went through the same thing for an hour, after which the sun came out and the road dropped to a lower elevation. We were worried by visions of us being lost in a blizzard.

Our GPS unit worked perfectly and we arrived at Nick's house at about 4.30 pm.

The house was on a road of similar houses, with large rear gardens with a culvert about twenty feet from the back fence. Probably 3 to 4 feet of water was gushing along at a fast pace. Apparently, all the local houses had this. The whole area is covered with these irrigation channels. It is a very rural area, very flat with fields and irrigation channels on both sides of most roads.

Near the back fence of Nick's garden is a small box containing a water supply; free water for irrigation. Nick is in the process of planting a vegetable garden. He has created some little channels between rows and he puts a hose at the slightly higher end and turns it on.

The house has 5 bedrooms and 3 bathrooms and costs about a third of local California houses of the same size.

We had a good time, with them and the two dogs. They have mountains east and west of them. We drove around a bit and saw the foothills to the east, and the river which runs through the area. There seems to be water running everywhere.

For the return journey, we decided to go through Utah, via Salt Lake City and Las Vegas. Driving SE from Middleton through Boise, we found the roads to be excellent and this continued all the way through Utah. We finally stopped at Cedar City in southern Utah after 617 miles.

It was a beautiful journey with snow-covered mountains all down the east side of the road. I didn't want to stop in Cedar City, but Muriel seemed tired.

The next morning we left at about 8.30 am and drove 168 miles to Las Vegas where Muriel wanted to stop and hit the slot machines. We went into Circus Circus as we know our way around. Muriel put $20 into a machine and lost a couple of dollars so she moved and stayed at the next machine for almost 2 ½ hours. She got down to her last $3 and had a big win of $13, and she agreed it was time to stop. We left around 12.30 pm and got home in 4 ¼ hours for the 315 miles.

Overall it was an excellent trip and we thoroughly enjoyed it. We've decided we must do more like this.

Lauren, granddaughter, and eldest daughter of my son Christopher, got married last Sunday. It was held in San Diego Botanical Gardens a few miles from home. It was a beautiful setting with great accommodations, with many large trees, and plants and shrubs from all over the world. We first went to the area for the wedding ceremony and took our seats. It was surrounded by large shade trees, with a flowery bridal arch at the front. At the rear was a small building where the bride and 3 bridesmaids dressed.

When the wedding began the bride, etc. came down the steps and paraded down the aisle to the bridal arch to join the groom. Officiating at the wedding was our number 2 son David. He'd got a license from the county government to do this, which he did very well. In fact, he did so well that another granddaughter asked David to perform the ceremony at her wedding next year. Following the marriage ceremony, we were invited to walk a few steps to another area with an outdoor bar. Following this we were invited to take a few more steps to where there were many tables and chairs set up and food was provided. It was a lovely day except it got a bit cool later in the day.

Fred, the young man that Lauren married seems a very gentle soul, but apparently is a little tougher than he appears. He has had a good influence on her.

As usual, Peter has changed his mind again and is not selling his house in Oceanside after all. I don't know why I report Peter's plans as they change almost as soon as they are made. I will just report when his plans come to pass. At the time of writing some weeks later, Peter has rented his house and is living in his motor home in the extended backyard. He leaves for Tennessee in about 3 weeks in his motor home, and it sounds like he is expecting to be gone several months. He will tow his SUV filled with tools for the work he has to accomplish.

I believe I omitted to report that grandson Daniel's (son of our son David) wife gave birth to a son and named him Cole David. This makes a brother for their two daughters.

You probably have guessed I am fascinated by what I see as mysterious. I believe that another mystery recently occurred.

When I was about 10 years old, as reported at the beginning of this story, I passed the "scholarship" exam and was sent to the City of Bath Boys' School. Going to this special school was a real privilege. It was here that I met David Gane, affectionately known as Gaffer because of his habit of trying to help people too much. We were great friends for many years. Later, after leaving school, we drifted apart and I heard he had been transferred out of Bath. He worked for the gas board, a national quasi-government company. This gas was coal gas during our time in Britain, but later it became a natural gas company after the discovery of North Sea oil and gas.

After my success in finding Muriel's "other" family, and long after they returned from their visit to California, I set out to find my old friend Gaffer.

I started looking at Bath, thinking he may have retired to his old hometown. I found no record, but I had an idea of another town to which he may have moved but with no success. Gaffer was the same age as me, now 81 years old. I didn't even know if he was still alive. I had a bright idea. Gaffer had an older brother named Ron who most likely was still living in Bath. I found Ron immediately and made a call. There was no answer but British Telecom provides an answering recording, but I didn't leave a message. Apparently, they do leave a recording saying that there was a call, and they invite the recipient to hit a button to call back.

An hour later I got a call from Ron and he remembered me, but he went ballistic when he realized he had made an overseas call to California. After he calmed down, we talked. Apparently, Gaffer's wife died a couple of years ago, and he was on his own except for 3 children in the area. Ron gave me Gaffer's phone number and I made the call. (I sent 5 pounds to Ron to reimburse him for the phone call). A croaky voice answered Gaffer's phone. It was Gaffer and he had just come out of hospital after a heart attack which had put him there, but he had caught an infection which kept him in hospital for 6 weeks. Also, it had affected his voice which was little more than a croaky whisper. He was very happy to talk to me but talking was difficult for him. He seemed quite lonely so I said I would call him every few weeks, and I invited him to come to California for a visit. This perked him up enormously. I called again 2 weeks later, and we had a nice chat (still croaky), which he seemed to enjoy. He was scheduled to go into the hospital a week later for a little op. on his voice, so I said I would call in about 2 weeks to see how he was doing.

2 weeks later I called but got no answer, so I called again a week later, thinking his original hospital stay may have been extended. Still no answer. I called Ron, and Ron told me the bad news. Gaffer had died during his second hospital stay. I am so pleased that I got to talk to Gaffer before he went. What was the strange thing prompting me to find him at that exact moment, just in time? It strikes me as very mysterious.

A little bit of interesting news is that our daughter's younger son Matthew, who is in the Marines, and as last reported above, being posted to Japan, was transferred to a navy warship which was sent on a virtual world cruise. He went to India, Sri Lanka, Thailand, Singapore, Hawaii, and several other places. He tends to be secretive and doesn't want to tell too many secrets. Now, about 6 months later, he is home in Virginia but is going to be transferred and he is hopeful that he will get to Camp Pendleton, just about 10 miles from here.

I am working hard on finding cheap fares to England. Muriel wants to go so we are aiming for a trip in middle to late September. (Found the cheap fare, $817 round trip, and booked it for 7th September, returning on 3rd October).

My son Peter left California a few days back, traveling in his 43-foot motor home to Tennessee to complete the work on his houses that his sons should have done.

A third of the way there a front tire blew out at 65 miles per hour. Luckily they swerved onto the dirt with no real damage except a piece of the tire made a hole in the floor. However, he decided to replace the front 2 tires at $1500 for the pair. Later on, he decided to replace the back 4 at $3000. The tires are huge long-distance truck tires.

It is 1st August 2016, and Richard, son of Muriel's brother Paul has just arrived to take up permanent residence in the USA, seventeen years after they first applied to emigrate. Richard stayed on in England for a while to pursue some of his own interests.

Now, on 12th of October 2016, our 26-day visit to England has been over for a week. We are still adjusting to the time change, waking up in the middle of the night. During the trip, we visited most of Muriel's sisters, and we drove to Minehead and stayed 4 days with Joy's newfound brother John and his wife Susan. The first day there we drove 80 miles to Teignmouth, the home of Wendy and David, the other members of her "new" family. In Minehead, we met for the first time, several new nieces and nephews, all very nice people. Whilst there I contracted bronchitis and had to go to a hospital to get some antibiotics. Chances are that we will not see any of this side of Muriel's family again unless they make the effort to come here.

This trip will definitely be our last to England. We found it very tiring, and the driving and parking is impossible. Driving in England is not for sissies or nervous unconfident drivers.

Interesting fact, the flight to England took only 8½ hours instead of the normal 10 1/2 hours. We were on a Boeing 787 called the Dreamliner. We hit ground speeds of 710 mph. There was lots of knee room, a first for me. We were on the same plane returning home but it took 10 hours 50 minutes, and seemed to go on forever.

Matthew has got his permanent posting from Virginia. He is coming to Camp Pendleton, just 9 or 10 miles from us. He wants to get an apartment, and we told him he can stay with us until he finds one. He will be arriving around the middle of December. Also, Peter says he is flying back to California on the 7th of December, staying with us, so we will have a full house for a while.

A very good bonus of Matthew returning to Camp Pendleton is that the camp occupies about 10 miles of coast, and relatives of those assigned to the camp can stay on the beaches in RVs. We don't know any details, but we can't wait for the chance to drive 10 miles to get a piece of beach all to ourselves.

Our son Peter arrives in 2 weeks, on 7th of December, and Matthew, Helen's younger son, arrives around mid-December. Also, my son Nick, living in Idaho, is thinking of driving here for Christmas.

NEWS FLASH. We have just learned that Marisol, wife of Andrew (our daughter Helen's eldest son who lives downstairs) is a couple of months pregnant, making this their fourth child and our 13th great-grandchild. Sadly, this development has them talking about returning to live in Texas as the cost of living, houses, etc., is so high in California. They say they can buy a nice house in a good neighborhood for about half the price of a California home. Also, they have to buy a bigger car as they will have 4 children who will need car seats, according to California law. Their current vehicles aren't big enough. Also, Andrew feels that the San Diego police are a cold bunch and aren't friendly like they are in Killeen Texas. I believe what he says. The San Diego police chief is a skinny woman with a high pitched raspy voice, who doesn't exude the vibes of a real leader. I would believe that they have morale problems. Marisol has just started working for Apple, and apparently, she can get a transfer to Austin, Texas, which is about 20 miles from Killeen where Andrew used to work. He is hoping to get back to the same city. He currently travels about 28 miles each way.

Almost before the above paragraph was written and within 24 hours, Matthew, on the way to the Marine camp near us, called to say that his wife Karla, is also pregnant with number 14 great-grandchild. He is now looking for an apartment near here.

Unfortunately, Peter's booking to fly to California on 7th December didn't materialize. His flight got fouled up and the airline wanted 3 times the price so he cancelled the idea. Nick was unable to come due to a state examination being scheduled for 22nd December. He felt that he didn't have enough time as his prospective employer wanted him to start work soon after. We spent Christmas Day with Joy's brother and family. The latest information is that Peter and his wife arrive in San Diego on 7th of January. We'll see if this really happens as Peter's plans rarely come about. This time it may though because he has a possible buyer for one of his boats, and needs to meet up with him.

Further to the above, after Nick spent weeks preparing for the "new" job, his would-be supervisor met with him and Nick found out that the job had been completely misrepresented by the Personnel department. Nick is considering legal action to recover his costs and work on exams, etc. and a missed trip to California for Christmas.

One Sunday, just before Christmas, Muriel became unwell in the middle of the church service. She felt weak and faint with severe pains in her right arm, plus cold sweats, and classic heart attack symptoms. She recovered a bit but we went straight to the hospital. She was given every test available and kept overnight. The result was that they found nothing. Her heart is perfect with no artery narrowing or blockages. She came home the next day.

As a result, she has become very ambitious. She has already had me contact the whole family with a view to having next Christmas at our house when previously she felt unable to handle visitors and large parties. We have even arranged a sing-along for a future weekend.

Peter finally showed up in California on the 8th of February, and is currently working on disposing of some of his millions of possessions or "stuff". It seems to me that he gets rid of "stuff" and then buys more. I'm glad it is his problem. He has a mountain of his stuff stored at our house which he has to eventually dispose of.

Because of our last few years of drought, we were unable to keep our pool in operation, and it had to be emptied. Well, with the record rainfall we have received this winter, I am pumping out the 2 feet of rainwater which has been collected and will clean and fill it ready for the summer.

I finally got to see a neurological back surgeon last week with the hope of getting my back improved. I've been told that arthritis is putting pressure on my sciatic nerve causing continuous sciatica. I thought he would scrape away the arthritis to relieve the pressure, but he said it can be relieved by injections. So this is what will happen. I'm currently awaiting insurance to give the go-ahead. Note. Written sometime later. The final recommendation is that I should have 8 therapy sessions and that should help the situation. It helped about 30% as long as I do the exercises every day. It certainly is no cure but it seems as if I have to live with it.

Big announcement yesterday. We went to Muriel's brother Paul's house for dinner and were the first to be told that their daughter Katie and husband Nate are expecting their first child in 7 months. You may remember that Katie was the first to arrive in the USA after the family received their immigration visas, and she lived with us for 2 years. She became almost like a daughter. They have just bought a house in addition to the condominium that Katie bought a couple of years ago. She and Nate have lived in Paul's small separate apartment for about 2 years.

Update on our daughter's sons: The eldest one Andrew, currently in the San Diego Police, a little happier nowadays and they are planning to rent a house or apartment in Escondido, about 15 miles inland. His wife, (5 months pregnant) has a job in Escondido which she loves, and housing is cheaper and it is about the same distance for Andrew to drive to the SD police department. Matthew, the younger son now lives in Temecula, about 20 miles from us.

Now, four months later than the above paragraph, the baby is due or even overdue but not here yet. Andrew has been looking at houses to buy but found nothing yet. It seems there is a shortage of houses and too many buyers.

News Flash. One day later than the above paragraph, on 4th June, Sawyer Andrew VanOrsdel was born at 7.57 am, weighing in at 8lbs 15oz.

As previously reported, Matthew and his wife announced about 5 months ago that they are expecting also. It will be a girl, due in about 2 months.

We have just returned from having dinner with our two sons and wives living in California. This was to celebrate Muriel's 83rd birthday. We learned at that dinner that our eldest son's youngest daughter, Chelsea is also pregnant. This will be great-grandchild number 15. No doubt this will spur their eldest daughter into action. There seems to be a rush this year for new babies.

Within 2 weeks of the baby's birth, Andrew had his offer for a house accepted and they expect to move from our house in about 3 weeks, around mid-July. Immediately we advertised for a tenant for the small apartment attached to the front of the house, (not the part that Andrew occupied), and within 15 minutes of the ad being put in Craig's List, we had a call and later a visit and we had a month's rent in hand. I'm busy doing a couple of upkeep things. It has been empty for a year.

A week ago, a great-granddaughter, number 14 great grandchild, (Victoria Joy VanOrsdel) was born to Helen's son Matthew and wife Karla. She was 8 days late and as sometimes happens with late babies, she inhaled some of the amniotic fluid, which sometimes contains the baby's fecal matter. She has been in intensive care for a week and is improving and is expected to make a full recovery.

Exactly as I forecast above, Our eldest son's daughter, Lauren, has just announced that she is pregnant with number 16 great-grandchild, sex unknown at this time, due in February 2018.

Keri, our youngest son's daughter got married a month ago in Denver, so there is potential for many more great-grandchildren. Our son David officiated.

Victoria Joy was released from ICU after 17 days and the word is, no residual problems.

At long last, after many months, one of Peter's 43-foot boat has been sold and the money has been paid. It is in the water in Peter's boat slip in Oceanside Harbor. Some months back he found a buyer for the other boat, actually 44 feet long, which has been on blocks in the back garden of his house here in Oceanside. The buyer was supposed to pay him $1500 a month and to pay it to me during Peter's absence in Tennessee. Well, it turned out that his payments averaged about $600 a month, and after paying about $5,500 he decided to give up on it. By prior written agreement he was not due any money back upon default and had done lots of work and bought lots of equipment for it including a new mast. He is the second would-be buyer to go through this. The first one paid $7500 before backing out. We think the size of the boat scares these people, and it takes some months for reality to sink in.

About a month ago, on a Tuesday morning, our phone rang at about 8.30 am. (Note the time). It was a call from an ex-daughter-in-law, Peter's first wife. She re-married and is divorced again, and lives alone in Denver (at 5000 feet plus elevation). She had terrible abdominal pains in the middle of the previous night and drove herself to a local hospital in the first snow storm of the winter. They operated immediately for appendicitis, and sent her home at 9.00 am, just before she called us. I remember the time when appendicitis meant a week in the hospital.

Within minutes of us getting off the phone, it rang again. It was our eldest son reporting that his eldest daughter (about 4 months pregnant) was about to have surgery in order to try to save the baby. (The surgery worked after a tense few days).

Almost immediately, we heard that Katie, our pregnant niece was in hospital, as her water had broken. Now she was not due for a couple of weeks. However, the baby was born normally with no problems.

Another phone call was from Peter, reporting that he'd just returned from having his dog put down. The dog had been unwell. It was not yet 9.30 am. All these things had happened in less than an hour. The rest of the day was uneventful.

We can foresee a need for more vehicles in the family in the near future, so we bought a new car. Around this time of the year, prices seem to be lower. We looked at Kia first as they have a 100,000 miles warranty. I feel it doesn't matter if the car is not too reliable if there is a good warranty. (We had considered buying a Toyota due to their reputation for reliability). We walked into the Kia dealership and there was the exact car we wanted and marked with a price $7000 less than the equivalent Toyota we had investigated. It was ours in no time. We could not pass the price up. Now we have a beautiful new Kia Forte. The color is called Titanium Brown. It looks black most of the time but is a dark red with the sun on it. When we told our son Peter, our family mechanic/car expert, he was very excited. He feels that Kia cars are excellent. Also, a friend has had one for many years and a relative in England has one. They both think highly of them. We have 3 cars again with the problem of deciding which one to use every time we go out. We look at it as a Christmas present to ourselves.

We are coming to the end of 2017, so I shall probably close this chapter soon and start another chapter. Christmas is just 2 weeks away, and we expect about 19 for Christmas dinner, all organized by our son David, who loves to cook, etc. We still have to get the house ready and then take everything down after. We still have lots to do.

Just before closing this chapter, I must report the birth on 17th January 2018, of number 16 great-grandchild, a daughter, to granddaughter Lauren, daughter of our eldest son Christopher. The baby is named Selah, and was 3 weeks early and weighed 7 pounds 11 ounces.

Chapter 70 - A New Year 2018

There seems to be little that is worthwhile reporting in the near future. No pregnancies, little travel contemplated except we are probably driving to Idaho to see our son Nicholas in several months, and Muriel has booked a trip to England in November for her sister's 70th birthday.

Did I say "no pregnancies"? Our daughter's younger son Matthew just reported that his wife is pregnant again and due in October. Their first child was born last August.

Bad news. Christopher had a hip replacement due to an old injury when he was a teenager. He recovered normally. My son David reported that he has prostate cancer. He chose to have it removed which took place with little trouble except he had some heart irregularity afterward. His later results show no recurrence of cancer to date

10 days ago, my son Peter went to a hospital emergency room with violent pains in his lower chest. A "mass" was said to be the cause. It was not attached to any organs, and a biopsy was not done because immediate removal was recommended. It had not spread to other areas. As I write, Peter is in the middle of the operation in a hospital in Tennessee. Of course, we hope it is non-malignant, but we will have to wait and see. Peter is told that recovery will be long and he shouldn't work for 3/4 months.

Update on the proposed trip to Idaho. Due to so many visitors, Nick and Karen were a bit overloaded and begged for relief from visitors so we agreed to delay our visit to next spring. It seems like everybody is worried about the decline of California and eager to check out other places to live, and Idaho seems to be one of them. We have firmed up our visit leaving for Idaho on 22nd April 2019.

Great news. Just got a phone call to say Peter's operation is over, went perfectly and Dr. thought it looked benign, but pathology will take a week. This is the best news we could expect.

Further examination showed no malignancy.

Grandson Matthew's baby boy, Benjamin, number 17 great-grandchild, was born with no abnormalities.

Muriel arrived in England this morning for her 16 days visit. Going to England in mid-November is not a smart move, but it is what she wanted to do. I hope it works out OK.

Muriel returns in two days and I'm still surviving OK. Just today, Peter says he may be able to get here by Christmas, but we won't hold our breath. Peter's plans rarely work out.

Peter's recovery is not going too well but the doctor says everything is OK,

Chapter 71 - 2019, Another Year

It is now late March 2019, and Peter is still not fully recovered but is struggling with shortness of breath. The doctors say it could take him nine months to fully recover. It seems that every time he sees a doctor, they extend his recovery time. He is still unable to travel. He is coming up to 6 months now.

Our plan is still in motion to drive to Idaho in about a month.

Muriel's eyes have become a problem over the last 6 months. She apparently is suffering from macular degeneration, and now cannot drive, or walk around in a store without guidance.

The eye injections she has been receiving have made no improvement despite our cost (after Medicare and supplemental insurance) of $630 per month. However, over the last few weeks, she has been getting another injection and suddenly her sight is improving a little bit but not enough to drive. The doctor says she should continue to see improvement.

An unhappy situation arose. Our choir director chose some unfortunate music. Over a 4 week period, he had us sing 3 Sunday morning anthems in Latin, and at the next Thursday practice, he had us practice a Russian piece to be sung in Russian with the Russian alphabet. As you probably know, they do not use the same alphabetical letters as we do. Mostly choir directors come from the ranks of university professors, and it is my contention that they think in terms of high-brow, and weird new-fangled type music as if to provide an atmosphere showing how smart they are.

However, in 54 years of singing in church choirs, I have learned that the average churchgoer likes pretty, tunes in English with a generous sprinkling of well-known "oldie" type songs. One wise lady said she wanted "a sermon in the song".

I loudly complained and was met with an angry response. It festered and got a bit worse with emails flying back and forth. I finally left the choir. Muriel continued. In the meantime, a choir concert was planned, and slips of paper were handed out to the congregation and choir asking for input on favorite anthems to be sung at the concert.

The choir performed the chosen eight favorites and it was a resounding success. Guess what; the 8 chosen favorites were old well know anthems and all in English, proving me right. I'm not sure that the lesson will stick. I pointed out this lesson to the choir director who accepted it to some extent, and we settled our differences. I returned to the choir for the next Sunday, and the choir director remarked that he heard my contribution and it was good. Now everything seemed OK and I looked forward to continuing as normal.

However, one busybody choir member of the bass section, took it upon himself to email me to say how he was on a church committee, and importantly advising me on how I was graciously allowed to have a second chance with the choir. Now this is completely the reverse of my reading of the situation. Two years ago there were 14 basses in the choir. Currently, at best, we have 6 basses including me. The week before Easter this year, during the time when I was not singing, there were three basses. I am the strongest bass, and the only male capable of singing solos. So I feel I am the gracious one in going back to the choir. I think he wanted me to know how important he was.

My response to this person's email was immediate and angry asking him who did he think he was getting involved when the problem was solved. I also asked who told him he could sing. (He has no idea of singing. He is atrocious). I also pointed out that he was a stuffy pompous no-account light-weight, and I would no longer sing with people like him so now I'm out of the choir again.

An incredible thing just happened, providing proof positive that I really do talk to Helen our dear departed daughter.

In two days' time, we plan to drive to Idaho to see Nick, our third son. Today, I drove Muriel to the hairdresser for a perm and called in to the local drug store to pick up extra pills for the time we are away. Time to pay, but I didn't have my wallet in my pocket. I said I would come back, and went a few yards to the hairdresser and got the money from Muriel. I drove home confident that I would find my wallet somewhere at home.

I first looked around in the car I drove, but no luck. I spent the next hour and twenty minutes looking in every conceivable place including all three cars, in the pockets of clothes I'd worn for the previous couple of days, under chests of drawers, and under the bed. I turned my armchair upside down and inside out, but no wallet.

One of the first things I had done when I first arrived home was to ask Helen where my wallet was. She said, "In one of the cars" which is why I looked in the car I'd been driving, a second time.

I was beginning to think in terms of canceling credit cards and our trip to Idaho, but Helen was becoming more insistent about me looking in a car. Then she changed the message to me looking in the Toyota which was the car I drove to the hairdresser today. I had already checked twice getting down on my knees on the ground beside the driver's seat to no avail. I put Helen off saying that I would look when I got the call to pick up Muriel. This didn't seem to satisfy her, so reluctantly I took a flashlight with me for a third look in the Toyota. I moved the car so that I could open the door widely, and there it was, the wallet sitting on the floor leaning against the side of the driver's seat. When I was on my knees, fishing around under the driver's seat, my nose was within 6 inches of the wallet. It was very very obvious, so I cannot think why I didn't see it immediately when I came out of the drug store when I gave just a cursory look as I got in to drive home.

I can't believe that I'd missed the wallet in several searches when it was very obvious. I believe it wasn't there in my previous searches. I am reminded of another time when a diamond was missing (to our eyes), but It suddenly appeared. Could it be that these are lessons in faith? I must admit that I have, many times, felt that my contact with Helen is possibly not real but all coming from my mind in spite of several occasions when I have had irrefutable proof that my contact with her is real.

I think this is the final proof and I belief my contact with Helen is more real now. I think that her repeated insistence that I go and check the Toyota "now" is the clinching factor.

We have been in Idaho for about a week, and drive home tomorrow via Reno and through California. That route is about 915 miles. We came here via Salt Lake City and Utah, but I discovered it is 200 miles longer that way. However, the new car, (I say new, we've had it 17 months. but it only has 2500 miles on the clock) appears to fly.

The speed limit in Nevada and Utah is 80 miles per hour. We kept speeding up to 100 mph without realizing it. Our average speed for the first day out was 80.75 mph including a stop for the toilet and one for gas. We covered 646 miles that day. The computer in the car said we were averaging an incredible 46 miles per gallon, and at one point it went to 47 mpg. A really amazing car.

We took with us 15 new canvases and a selection of paintbrushes and tools, and a set of oil paints. This was because Nick's wife Karen, who has shown some artistic talent, expressed her interest in doing some painting with me. While we were there, with my help, she painted an excellent first-try painting. Hopefully, she will continue. However my main objective is to get my son Nick into painting, and he also made his first attempt and almost completed his first painting. Nick, the father of our grandson artist Robbie, has shown talent in drawing, sculpting and a variety of other artistic endeavors, and combined with his wild life interests, I would like to see him get into wild life painting.

While on the subject, I just called him. Unfortunately, he was out hunting with friends, (it is Memorial Day). I was calling to say that I expect him to start by painting a trout or something similar. I spoke to Karen who told me he plans to start by painting a rainbow trout. Great minds etc. etc.

We had a great time in Idaho. Our journeys showed beautiful scenery, snow-covered mountains in Idaho, and all the way on both routes.

It is about 9 weeks since we got back from Idaho and it has been routine, except for the fact that we have experienced several house problems. The first thing was the fact that we had no hot water, then the house phones wouldn't work, then we had a toilet problem which I am still working on (almost done, but I only put in an hour at a time. Had to rebuild the floor). The exhaust fan failed in the toilet we use. There were several other small problems which I can't remember but I have worked continually and still more to do as we are expecting an influx of visitors.

Andrew, our daughter's eldest son, lives with us and is getting divorced and now has his 4 children here every other weekend. They are hard work but he has no alternative, and we want to support him. He wants to maintain custody for after the divorce.

Now, it is 6 months later than the above paragraph, Andrew has moved out and is living with his girlfriend and has the children visit there, so we don't see them much.

Chapter 72 - 5 days before 2020 dawns.

I haven't mentioned this before, but I used to write humorous poems or rhymes. I read some to my sister Daphne who laughed her head off and insisted that they should be recorded and not lost. I have decided that I should have a chapter devoted to them, and they are following.

Mother made some dumplings, they came out just like lead,
We only needed one a day to keep us all well-fed.
She also made some cakes one day and gave our Dad a pair,
On the way to work he got a flat and used one as a spare,
This spare gave a bumpy ride, this cake tire that was mother's
It didn't matter very much, it outlasted all the others.
Mother's in production now and giving all it takes,
Her tires are well thought of and selling like hotcakes.

We've heard a tale of Mother's cakes outlasting rubber tires,
She also thinks her toffee stretched would make piano wires,
Now Mother's research chemist is studying the case
For Mother's home-cooked pancakes, shoe leather to replace.
The only problems so far, the research chemist found,
When someone's walking very fast they make a squelching sound,
These shoes, they tend to pick up leaves which isn't very wise,
And leave great sticky footprints which will attract the flies.
This is a tricky problem, a cure must be found,
The shoes are quite attractive, construction very sound.
But now they have the answer, the problem is now gone,
Pour in less pancake syrup before you put them on.

Madame Maria Dallas, diva of renown
This prima donna singer had squeezed into her gown
The diet she should be upon she didn't want to hear
She huffed and puffed and sweated to get into her gear.
Her face grew red with effort as higher up she sang,
She strained to hit the high notes and hit them with a bang,
She hit the really highest note and made the rafters ring,
Her elastic couldn't stand the strain and gave up with a ping.
Her dress came down around her knees, it really was a chuckle,
It almost would have fallen off, except caught on a buckle.
The diva sang, the audience cheered in spite of this great blooper,
All persons there that night agreed she really was a trooper.

I wrote a number of rhymes for use in the church choir concerts. Some of them are below.

It's tough to be an alto at SDUMC, (San Dieguito United Methodist Church)
They sit before the basses who lack humility,
The basses drop their music, they whisper funny jokes,
They're generally annoying those lovely alto folks.
They blow their noses, cough and sneeze, and also sometimes sigh and wheeze,
Their big boots shuffle to and fro, they need big boots for singing low.
In spite of all these tales of woe, the basses will not have to go,
From all we see it does appear they have a friend that we all fear.
Bass Jesus holds them very dear. God in his wisdom says hear, hear.

Those awful basses in our choir, they really are a pill,
They murder every song they sing and make the choir ill,
The choir director tries so hard to keep the choir together,
The basses just go on their way and watch him hardly ever.
They act as if they own the choir which makes some people cry,
They think the tenors should be changed to basses who sing high,
They say sopranos sound like cats, the altos sound like dogs,
The rest of us, we all agree the basses sound like frogs.
No angel choir will have them with all this bad behavior,
They'll be the lowly janitors for God our heavenly savior,
And clean the harps and trumpets and groom the angel's wings,
And shine each tenor's halo so it glitters when he sings,
So if this fate reported, the basses would prevent,
Forgiveness should be asked for and then they should repent,
And pray to God almighty, our heavenly protector,
Who in his wisdom maybe will make them choir directors.

I went fishing one fine day to catch a trout of two,
I asked a friend to come along but he said no can do,
He also said "Don't throw them back, please save them all for me",
I asked him if he planned to eat a couple for his tea.
He answered "No I have a plan to smoke them all tonight".
I said "A fish stuck in your mouth will make you quite a sight.
Not only that the smell they'll make is like a garbage can,
You really should smoke cigarettes like any other man".

My friend said "Wow a great idea, I'll think this over dinner,
A cigarette that's made from fish could really be a winner,
Some people will smoke anything and love them with a passion"
Fish cigarettes outrageously have now become a fashion.
No cancer will you get from these or lung or heart disease,
You will be chased by all the cats and catch a lot of fleas,
The other great advantage of having these great smokes,
They are a source of protein and very good for folks.
If ever you are hungry your butts are there to eat,
Your own fresh smoked creation will really be a treat.

(Scott is the choir Director)
Our Scott, he works so very hard, he's always in a pother,
You hold him down in one place and he pops up in another;
So what to do to slow him down is really quite a chore.
The only thing that's left to us is nail him to the floor.
He comes to church so very early every single Sunday,
By half past eight he's done enough to last at least till Monday,
He loves the music, Latin too, which makes poor Brian crazy,
These languages take effort and Brian's just too lazy.
What we all fear, it's getting, near, a summer trip is planned,
He'll come back home with big ideas and Brian will be banned.
It is so sad to see him go, but nothing else will suit,
He will say no to foreign words, himself he'd rather shoot.

Sopranos are a lucky bunch, they really are some winners,
They're in a place of honor sitting right up by the tenors,
How fortunate it is to be so very very near
The golden tonsilled tenors singing grandly in their ear.
They also sit by Sharon who at the organ plays,
And add to that Johns face they see on Sunday when he prays.
Now Scott is looking sternly, can reach them with his swatter,
Especially when they're singing wrong instead of what they oughter.
We love them all and need their help and overlook their errors,
We say this in humility because we know they're terrors,
It's fear that they instill in us, especially the basses
Please keep them calm and lovely with their usual smiling faces.

I tried today so very hard for something nice to say,
About our tenor singers who show up every day,
They always sing their hearts out, God bless their cotton socks,
In spite of rotten basses who give them lots of knocks.
The choir director in his wisdom, favors tenors most,
The basses they don't sing so well, that's maybe why they boast.
They get their music upside down, or start on the wrong page,
Not only this, their eyes are bad all due to extreme age.
They can't stand up they can't sit down they cannot walk up stairs,
Their joints are stiff, they're either bald or covered with white hairs.
The tenors on the other hand are handsome, young and spritely,
To anyone who hears this trash they know I lie thrice nightly.

Now young Ron Zehr, a master bass, tries very hard to lead,
A very tough assignment as they're going fast to seed,
We think that someone's spelling is really up a tree,
Bass should be spelled correctly as B-A-S and E.
Now Scott has come to join us to raise our standard levels,
With basses he is working hard to exorcise the devils,
And young Fred Zerlaut singing hard a perfect tune he makes,
The basses so much off the note, "keep quiet for all our sakes."
I've heard it very often said that wouldn't it be fine
If music could be written without the basses line.

Ferdinand Gorilla and his buddy Sammy Snake
After ballet practice went fishing on the lake,
They fished and fished and had some fun, but didn't see the day was done,
The night grew dark, the wind got chill, but on the lake they stayed until
Of fishing they had gained their fill.
Unknown to them their oars had drifted, but Sammy with a brain was gifted,
He knew exactly what to do, and filled his lungs with air anew.
Lead tenor in the choir was he, fame was his for his high C,
He let out such a high pitched HELP, all the dogs began to yelp,
The lights were turned on all around, they knew whence came this high pitched sound,
The police chief and the fire brigade were all called out to give their aid,
The choir director and the basses all stepped forth to take their places
In the rescue boat they rowed, at the tiller 1st bass toad.
The rowing stroke by choir director, encouraged by police inspector,

Maintained a moderate 4/4, which pulled them fast away from shore.

And then brought rescue boat alongside, a tow line with a knot was tied,

And soon the group was at the pier, a crowd of friends let out a cheer.

The rescue mission now was done, which everyone agreed was fun,

The choir director reviewed the case, promoted Sam to noble bass.

*The first 6 lines and the last 2 lines are from an old English rhyme. The rest is my original.

A mother to her kittens said come listen now to me.

Your pa and I have both agreed to have some friends to tea,

Hurry up and wash yourselves and put your whiskers straight,

Then scurry off to tell the guests be here at half past eight.

But tell them not to venture out if bad or stormy weather

But if it's fine upon the roof we all will meet together.

Now Ma and Pa sopranos were and all their friends were too,

The choir they belonged to met mostly at the zoo,

Where cheetahs sang the high notes with all the other cats,

And next came alto wildebeests in various sharps and flats.

The tenor line hyenas sang, they really were a treat,

Their voices carried wonderfully and had a marvelous beat.

The grand and noble elephants with low melodious noise

Made heaven seem much closer with all its love and joys.

The choir director somewhat short, the whole group couldn't see,

To solve this nasty problem she had to climb a tree.

The organist, an octopus, needed all her fingers,

With white notes, black notes, pedals and staying with the singers.
Now back to Ma and Pa and friends, their party had some tea,
And then they sang a song or two with happiness and glee.
Nearby an old man sleeping was awakened by the racket,
Got out of bed, put on his shoes and then put on a jacket.
He got a water hose in hand and sprayed them from the spout.
Ere he retired one thing is sure, there were no cats about.

Basil, eager for a raise, keen to get his bosses praise,
Leapt smartly forth to light cigar, but couldn't reach, it was too far,
The boss leaned forward to the flame, just as Basil did the same,
The flame it met the bosses beard, ignited it and we all feared
The bosses' wrath which we all knew would soon make Basil black and blue.
Now Basil, careless with a hose, alas he broke the bosses nose.
The boss now soaked from head to toe, let out the loudest wail of woe.
He chased poor Basil down the hall, letting out an awful bawl,
The boss now sprinting, water streaming, Basil running fast and screaming.
Across the parking lot they ran, dodging truck and car and van,
Into the street now went the chase, the boss now flagging losing pace,
Fear driven Basil, running faster, face as white as alabaster,
Local dogs joined in the fun and soon the cats were on the run,
And some small boy's intent on strife added fear to Basil's life,
Yelling, howling barking screeching, the chase the corner now is reaching.
The chase continued o'er the hill, the last we've heard he's running still.

Young Ted he was a singer, but no ambition he,
Tried hard to be a tenor but couldn't hit high C.
He strained and strained, went red of face, but couldn't make the grade,
Sometimes he got so very close but then his voice would fade.
One day he met this wise old bass who said life isn't fair,
If singing higher's what you want then stand up on a chair.

One day God said to Jesus let's make a super race,
We'll make them tall and handsome and call them noble bass.
Now treat the others kindly said Jesus to the basses,
You must remember always they are the lesser races.
The basses from their lofty heights must thank God for the rest,
Without the lesser beings how could they be the best.

The alien craft swooped low and fast, causing a wind storm as it passed,
Two alien flyer's noses twitched, they smelled some English fish and chips.
Two noses each the aliens boasted, their favorite food, fish fried or roasted.
From ten thousand meters, their twin set of beakers,
Picked up the scent for these fried fish seekers,
They followed the trail to their favorite fare which sent them descending down through the air
The alien craft maneuvered to stop, alongside the local fish and chip shop.
2 fish, 6 penn'oth of chips to go, paid with an alien I U O. (alien IOU)
Riding home was fat Rupert MacTupper holding his favorite fish and chip supper.
He suddenley saw with the greatest of fear the alien craft that was hovering near,
He fell off his bike all due to shock, and banged up his nose upon a big rock.

He fell right upon his fried fish and chips and crushed it quite flat with his overweight hips

Poor Rupert stood up all shaky and pale, and letting out a terrified wail,

Then sprinted away with fear driven speed, and left a wet trail, maybe he peed..

The aliens beamed up their chosen repast, flew up and away from the place real fast

The word spread abroad in the stratosphere, space fish and chip shops soon appear.

"Cash only" is the space shop's way, no IUO's will do today.

Chapter 73 - Pandemic.

We are in the middle of the Coronavirus pandemic of 2020. We at the 6th day of 15 days of (state imposed) being house-bound to try to slow down the infection rate. The rate is still going up. We don't know what the future holds.

Chapter 74 - Pandemic – a new experience.

The Coronavirus is starting to loosen its grip. Numbers are plateauing, and people needing hospital treatment are declining. The rule is to stay home, and if you have to go out, stay 6 feet away from people, and wear a mask. This seems to be paying off. The streets are deserted and freeways are running at full speed with no traffic jams. There is talk that the President is planning to re-open the country and allow some people to return to work in the next few weeks.

The government is giving everybody $1,200 to help cover the costs of not working. Unemployment was down to 3 ½% but now it is around 25%. Each person on unemployment benefit receives an extra $600 per week, all in order to get cash into the economy. Unfortunately, this pandemic has put the brakes on the strongest economy ever known on this planet, and it will not recover immediately as it will take time to get up to speed. I just hope that it will not affect President Trump's chances at the next election in a few months. If a Democrat wins, the country is finished.

Deaths to date are around 25,000 in the USA. We are told that a vaccine is 15 to 18 months away. There are many drugs for treatment being tested, but results for these are some months away. It is my opinion that we are going to have this for many months. By the way, we just received our $2,400.

It has been quiet lately. We now have 19 great-grandchildren, but last week our granddaughter, Lauren, daughter of our eldest son, Christopher, announced she is pregnant with a boy. She has a 2-year-old daughter. Also, we heard that Holly, the daughter of Gayle, our son Peter's wife, is also pregnant. We count all members of the family, like through marriage as "ours", which will bring us up to 20 great-grandchildren.

A few weeks later, the Covid deaths in USA are approaching 60,000 but infection rates are down and people are starting to rebel against staying home and staying away from other people. Several counties are going to court to get the restrictions removed, so I believe the numbers are not going to decrease. We will continue to be cautious. However, we have been shopping 3 times and are going again tomorrow.

My son David has a shopping list for us and he will get it in about 3 days.

Funny thing, influenza deaths which normally run at a rate of 20,000 to 40,000 each winter, are going down. There was a report that for one week, flu deaths were 3,500, and succeeding Week were 1400, then 700, then 140. It is likely, in my opinion that some flu deaths are called Covid 19 deaths and even Covid 19 deaths are declining.

Some good news, Peter's eldest son Michael, who has been in Afghanistan for several years, flying drones, has completed his first few weeks of training to become an airline pilot. He is already a certified helicopter pilot for two helicopter categories, so he is going to be a very experienced flyer.

Covid 19 deaths are around 95,000, and there are lots of relaxation of restrictions. We are following our own common sense awareness of this problem. We have been shopping many times, and we seem to be lucky in getting recently disinfected shopping carts (still wet handles), and Muriel touches nothing, When we get back to the car, I put the shopping in the trunk, then use my hand sanitizer before getting into the car.

A couple of days ago, when I was looking at my funny poems, which are included earlier in this book, it struck me that I may have left out something I wrote a few years ago. Our choir was planning a concert based on romantic and funny stuff, and at an earlier concert I had sung a very funny song called "The Hippopotamus Song". It tells of hippos falling in love and wallowing in mud etc. For this later concert, I wrote new words and called it "The Piggly Song" which is about pigs falling in love and wallowing in mud, but with a shocking twist. It uses the same tune and chorus words.

The original Hippo song was written by Flanders and Swan who were famous 50 years ago, as writers of very funny songs. I have a book of their songs.

The piggly song words are given below:

One morning in summer-time young Percival Pig, decided his fortune to follow,

The story he'd heard was that over the hill was a muddy and marvelous wallow.

The sight that he saw when he looked down the hill, a beautiful piggly maid.

His high tenor squealing roused amorous feelings, she joined in his love serenade.

Chorus

Mud, mud glorious mud, there's nothing quite like it for cooling the blood,

So follow me, follow, down to the hollow and there let us wallow in glorious mud.

They wallowed in mud for the next several hours then joined by her Mother and Pa.

Her Pa said "your intent is so very clear, but forget it and go on your way.

My daughter is pure and not likely to sin, I won't let you tempt her to stay,

We go on vacation, a lovely location, a big truck will take us today.

Chorus

Our handsome young hero, the pig of this song, so sad as he sat in the muck,

He waved his goodbyes to his beautiful maid as she trotted along to the truck.

With horror he saw through the tears in his eyes, the words on the side of the van.

"T. Jones Esq." pork meat supplier, bacon and pork pies and ham".

Chorus

Young Percy was angered to think of her fate, and rushed to the side of the road.

He raised a cacophony of deafening squeals, now joined by the vehicle's load.

With 42 porkers all joining the song, a thunderous chorus ensued,

The driver took fright like a bat in the night and ran like a rabbit pursued.

Chorus

The doors were all opened, the pigs came to see, the words on the side of the van,

Young Percy was greeted with cheering and glee for thwarting the pig farmers plan.

Permission was given to Percival Pig, the romance it moved right along.

The wedding was blessed by 300 guests and everyone joined in this song,

Chorus (final)

Chapter 75 - Pandemic & Surprise

Sadly, mostly due to younger people who flout the rules, party, and get together, the number of Covid cases is rising.

However, the first vaccine is likely to be available within 3 weeks with 2 more companies a week behind.

We are told that vaccinations could take place by Christmas, just 3 ½ weeks away. The three companies involved have produced many millions of doses of the vaccines on the expectation that their vaccines will pass the Federal Drug Administration's testing. This could start the recovery, although it will take many months to see a decrease in Covid cases but there is light at the end of the tunnel.

There is an extremely serious subject on which I haven't touched. USA had an election to vote for the President, and also Representatives and Senators.

Donald Trump has done a marvelous job as President although you would never know it from the grossly left-leaning media. He has been under attack for the whole of his 4-year term with impeachment attempts on everything from Russian collaboration to lying and treason, etc. Every one of these impeachment exercises failed because they were all contrived from nothing.

The result of the election showed that Joe (Joke) Biden won, but there is so much evidence of corruption by the left, that there appears to be a possibility that the election results could be overturned. For example, one county sent out 1.8 million mail-in ballots and counted 2.5 ballots being returned and the excess all had votes for Biden, and this is just one example of the treachery of the left. Another blatant example, several counties closed up counting at approximately 11.00 pm. The count watches were ushered out with Trump being as much as 600,000 votes ahead, and then the count was apparently resumed without the count watchers, and Biden was declared the winner. This actually occurred in several places indicating collusion and a pre-planned activity. There are dozens of reports of count watchers, (required by law) being made to stand as much as 30 feet away, and I actually saw a small video of the watchers being put on the other side of a wall of windows and then huge pieces of cardboard being placed against the windows. This is completely unlawful. Whistle-blowers in the thousands have come forward and given affidavits of criminal wrong-doing under oath with the penalty of perjury if false information is given. However, if the election is over-turned as it should be, there is likely to be war in the streets.

Chapter 76 - Vaccines Arrive

Today is the shortest day of the year. It is 21st December 2020, and Pfizer vaccinations have been going on all week, and starting tomorrow, the vaccines made by Moderna will begin.

I recently was told that I had lymphoma and that it was moving slowly and I could get treatment or just ignore it. Apparently, it is not critical and should respond well to the treatment, which is a course of chemotherapy. I have had the first treatment and will go again in 24 days and will continue this schedule for about 6 months. I feel fine after the first go-around. Hope it continues.

Two medical workers related to our nephew Richard, told me yesterday, that lymphoma is the best one to have if you have cancer. Today a friend told Joy that her brother had the same thing about 10 years ago and had the treatment, and has been fine ever since. All good news in the face of bad.

The two medical workers were at our house yesterday participating in a surprise for us, instigated by the afore mention nephew Richard. He is the son of Muriel's brother Paul and his wife Karen.

Both of Paul's children are kind and thoughtful and good to us. They are ever very conscious of the fact that we sponsored their immigration to the USA from England. They have both met partners here and are very happy.

This marvelous surprise started with the arrival of 10 people outside our house in our paved parking area.

The first hint was noise, and we looked out to see all these people unloading chairs and tables, all dressed in Christmas clothing. Richard had brought his keyboard and song sheets for Christmas songs, and we were escorted out to join them in a Christmas sing-along with regular refills of egg nog. Richard played the keyboard. It was bright and sunny and around 70 degrees F.

Those in attendance were of course, Richard and his fiancée Meghan, Paul's daughter Katie and husband plus her 2 children. Paul and Karen and Meghan's brother and parents and grandparents. The persons employed in the medical field are Meghan and her mother. Both of them work as physiotherapists.

Both Muriel and I had our first (of 2 recommended) Covid 19 vaccine shots about a week ago. We had no ill effects, and hope this applies to our second shot due in 3 weeks. Some people have had a bad reaction. For example, Erin, wife of grandson Daniel, had to spend a day in bed after her second shot.

Here's an amusing story. As you know, our whole downstairs is unoccupied, and I've teased Muriel's brother's wife Karen by asking her when she is moving in. Karen and Muriel's brother Paul live in a country district nearby and have a house on 5 acres. It is a bit off the beaten track and has all the normal wildlife, like snakes and coyotes, etc. Anyway, Karen is not a lover of this type of thing and has wished to move for some time.

About a month ago, a friend of our grandson, Daniel, decided he wanted to move his trailer. He is divorced and uses it to house his 2 children for a weekend every 2 weeks. Part of a divorce agreement. He lives with his girlfriend in Carlsbad with no room for the children. The nearest trailer park is in Escondido, about 20 miles away. We agreed to him moving his trailer to our lot, and then he wanted to use the downstairs for showers and toilet, to which we agreed.

At about the same time, Karen got Paul to agree to put their house on the market but Paul felt it would not sell, or not for a long time. It is possible that our empty downstairs entered into their thinking, bearing in mind that they own the empty lot next door to us, and intend to build on it.

To everybody's surprise, they had about 12 buyers view their house within the first week, and several offers resulted. The best offer was a cash offer with a 25-day escrow, which meant they had to move pretty fast, literally.

We had no knowledge of this until about the time of them receiving offers, and I made a remark to Karen that we had committed to the trailer family for the downstairs.

A few days later, the trailer family decide that they didn't need to use the downstairs as there was a sewer cleanout just down the slope from the trailer, with water and electricity available close by. They ran a sewer line to the clean-out and now they are set up.

I told Karen that the downstairs was now available, and there was no visible reaction, but almost immediately we got into a discussion about them moving into our downstairs. I think everybody said "Phew". They will be moving in the next 2 weeks.

They are all moved in now and in the middle of finding places for all their possessions.

Paul is in the middle of "tax time" and is working from about 5.30 am to about 7.30 pm, so has no time for anything other than working, sleeping, and eating.

We had our second Covid vaccination on Sunday 3/7/2021 in Oceanside.

By now, we have 19 great-grandchildren, and number 20 is due in 6 weeks. However, there have been some problems such as a few labor pains. The latest news is that the baby is hanging in there for now.

The baby, a boy, was born on 5/6/2021, 4 days late. He weighed in at 9lbs 13ozs.

Chapter 77 - Disappointment and Good News

Six months after moving into our lower floor, Muriel's brother, Paul, and wife, Karen, announced that they are moving out of our house. They have bought a house in Fallbrook, about 20 miles northeast of our location. A coolness toward us has developed recently, and we don't know what we have done, and we have no choice but to ignore it and carry on normally. Karen has made a few calls etc. and invited us to dinner at their new house, and I suspect she is confused about the problem also.

About a week ago, I had a phone call from the cancer doctor who told me that the Lymphoma had gone! This is after about 9 months of treatment. However, I still have some unusual blood levels which will have to be watched with regular blood tests. Deep down, I have doubts that I ever had Lymphoma, as I was told that whatever I had was slight, and very difficult to diagnose. Whatever I have, my treatment costs Medicare about $520,000. In spite of having Medicare, I pay extra for supplemental insurance, and on top of that, my additional cost to date is around $12,000. I drove 1,600 miles for treatments, and my blood numbers are the same as they were before any treatment. The medical profession is not backward in collecting revenue.

We went to Paul and Karen's house for dinner. It is 21 miles from our house and up some winding hilly roads. It is a nice modern house on about a couple of acres of land. The visit started off with what I felt was quietness by Paul, but within a few minutes everything became normal and we had an excellent dinner and a generally nice visit. Maybe we were imagining a problem.

Muriel had some bad news recently. Her brother John, about 3 weeks ago, was diagnosed with pancreatic cancer which had spread to his liver. He was given less than 2 weeks to live. He died about 10 days later.

And soon after, her sister Sheila died in England of cancer of the throat, after a few months of illness and treatment.

Unfortunately, Brother John who has lived about a mile from us for the last 25 years, chose to be of a personality that made him difficult for people to get along with him. He hated being small and apparently tried to equalize by aggression. We sponsored him, his wife, and his 4 children to emigrate to USA many years ago, and housed them initially until such time that I was not willing to tolerate his stupid and aggressive behavior any longer. The fact that he only came up to my shoulder did not help him. Three of his four children are lovely people. The other one appears to be trying to emulate his father. We've had very little contact with them as has Paul, Muriel's younger brother. You don't get to choose your relatives.

Chapter 78 - Sad News.

Shortly thereafter, Muriel's favorite cousin Tony, 91, was put in hospital, and died within a couple of weeks.

A month ago, Mary, wife of Muriel's brother John, passed away while visiting England. She was about 78.

Karla's family lives in Temecula, 50 miles N.E. of us, and it is likely she will move back to California which will mean that Matthew will be transferred to Camp Pendleton, our local marine camp, but we will have to wait and see. Apparently, the divorce will be final some months after Matthew leaves the military, planned for April of 2023

Some encouraging news, Andrew, Matthew's older brother who was divorced about 4 years ago, got remarried back on 3rd of September this year (2022). He married a wonderful young lady, named Krista, who has one son about the same age as Andrew's eldest son.

Between them, they have 5 children, and Krista treats them all the same, and they all love her.

Chapter 79 - Catch up.

It is near the end of 2022, and there has not been much happening. Grandson Matthew, as previously reported, has chosen to leave the military as of early next April. His divorce is still in process and set to happen about the time of Matthews's departure from the Marines. He has a job opportunity with a police dept. in some small town in Idaho, and a better opportunity with a government nuclear facility, also in Idaho. He chooses Idaho as his best friend and my son Nicholas (Matthews uncle) lives there. He is hoping to get custody of his 2 children in his divorce, otherwise he will have to travel to S. California to see them.

Muriel and I are still soldiering on as usual, but we are definitely feeling our age. Muriel's eyesight is virtually gone but she is brave and tries to live normally. Of course, it puts a load on me which is OK as I am capable of doing what is necessary.

We recently rented our unoccupied downstairs to a divorced man, and as usual he wanted his son and girlfriend to move in after the fact. This is OK as he seemed to find the rent a little bit beyond him and the son's contribution seems to help. I'm a bit worried about the cost of electricity as our 25 solar panels cannot provide enough "juice" for a large number of people.

We are suffering under a completely inept government who are closing down all fossil fuel industries like oil and coal, and expect everything to go on as usual with only solar and wind sources which are 20 to 30 years away from producing enough.

Inflation is running at about 8.3% according to government sources, but gas and food prices are up as much as 50%. Happily, the recent election changed control of the House of Representatives, and we are expecting some improvement. The whole of USA has been ruined in the last 2 years, a feat which is unbelievable.

It is some weeks since I wrote the above, and we are having second thoughts about driving to Tennesee. The street crime all across the US, has risen to dangerous levels and we feel that strange gas stations, hotels, and parking lots, etc. have become dangerous places. We should fly in spite of the problems of getting to and from airports, lining up for extra checking of my metal knees, and renting a car. However, yesterday, we had an unfortunate exchange with Peter who reacted strangely and violently to my talking about the weather, so any trip or us moving is in question. Peter has a tendency to fly of the handle for completely weird things. We have unfortunately had serious bad reactions for unknown reasons from him before. The real truth is that we really have very little faith in his stability and very little interest in moving to Tennessee. California is getting to be a crazy place but it doesn't affect us too much. One example of the crazy stuff going on is a proposal by the California legislature to ban gas stoves for cooking. They want to only have electric vehicles, and then they announced that people could not charge their vehicles between certain hours due to shortage of electricity. Apparently, some pick-up trucks take 4 days to charge on the normal home battery chargers. Weird hey? Makes no sense does it. We like California weather in spite of the problems.

I was encouraged by friends in the choir to send an email to the new choir director regarding my returning. I did this but received no reply. I believe she talked to the (snake) church minister who advised her to not answer. Now I don't feel guilty any more.

We were invited to our nephew Richard's house for Christmas day, which ended in a sing-along. It was there that I found out that my singing was not like it was, but by the end of the evening it was coming back. I have done no singing for about a year. Richard is son of Muriel's brother, Paul.

One exciting bit of news, Andrew, eldest son of our dear departed daughter, and brother of Matthew, tells us that he and Krista are expecting our 22nd great grandchild. Apparently, it is a boy. I believe I may have overlooked a couple of births of great-grandchildren. Oh well, I think I do OK for an 88 year old.

Guess what, now, some months later, Andrew, Krista, the 4 children from Andrew's first marriage, Krista's son and the NEW BABY (10 days old), are coming to visit us in 2 days.

We are very excited as all 5 older children are very well behaved and lovely.

I have to apply for a new 5 year driving license before my birthday on 23rd May this year and I'm a bit worried that I may fail the eye-sight test. My results 5 years ago were a bit questionable and I only squeaked through. So I went to see an eye doctor to find out if my eyes were OK. I don't wear glasses except my $2 reading glasses

He did all the tests and announced that I had cataracts, and he could only give me a "pass" for one year.

That seemed no good so I decided to have a go at the DMV's eye test, and to my great delight, I passed, then I passed the knowledge test easily and I walked out with a new 5 year license, good until my 93rd birthday. This is very important as Joy cannot see to drive and we need to be able to get about or we have to employ somebody to do the shopping, etc.

Chapter 80 - More News.

California is getting to be a crazy place but it doesn't affect us too much. One example of the crazy stuff going on is a proposal by the California legislature to ban gas stoves for cooking. They want to only have electric vehicles, and then they announced that people could not charge their vehicles between certain hours due to shortage of electricity. Apparently, some pick-up trucks take 4 days to charge on the normal home battery chargers. Weird, Makes no sense, does it. We like California weather in spite of the problems.

Three weeks ago, we were shocked to hear that Jacquie, aged 59, only daughter of my 94 year old sister Brenda, was found dead in a hotel room. Five days ago, Clair, my son Peter's ex father-in-law, our church minister from our long time church, Torry Pines Christian Church, died after a long illness. Just two days ago, my sister Brenda was found to be non-responsive and died minutes later. We are hoping this is the end of this sad period, although everybody around us is getting very old. Our recent annual physical showed that Muriel and I are in both in normal health for our age, thank you God.

Christmas 2022 has come and gone and we are in early January 2023. We went back to our old church for their Christmas performance of the Messiah. The choir had a surprisingly good turnout. 28 people showed up. Normal for a Sunday has been about 20 or 21. A few years ago, the choir had as many as 38 on Sunday, and as many as 50 for special performances.

I have felt a little guilty as I sit and watch them on the TV every Sunday morning, knowing that I still have the same powerful male voice that I've had for seventy years or so.

Chapter 81 - The end.

Recently, I have experienced problems with my computer. It duplicates paragraphs, and moves them around and completely fouls up in places, making it difficult to continue. This is the end as I'm tired of checking and rechecking for these problems, and I will print and send out this last part of the story to our sons, Christopher, David, Nicholas, Peter and to Andrew, (eldest son of our deceased daughter Helen). These people already have parts 1 thru 10 in print in a 3-ring binder, with instructions to make this record available to their interested descendants.

I have enjoyed writing this epistle over the last 25 years. I believe I have found the most pleasure reading about our earlier recollections. It is possible that my readers are not as excited as I am and may find it boring. I've tried very hard to not make this like a diary, but unfortunately, the later part of this record has become a little bit like that. I apologize. I also apologize for the numerous places where I duplicate some facts by recording upcoming plans and then recording them as actual happenings.

As you can tell, we have had a very fortunate and marvelous life in a world where dramatic progress and changes have occurred in human progress. I remember when horses were an important means of power for goods delivery vehicles. We lived long before TV and when not everybody had a radio for news and entertainment, and when home telephones were rare. Dick Tracy's wrist watch communicators were a dream, but today they are real.

We are very grateful to God for our wonderful life. He has protected us and our family from nearly everything bad, and we are surrounded with dozens of wonderful friends and family members. We pray that this continues.

Muriel Joy, my wife of 68 years, has been a wonderful woman, mother, and friend. We are both 88 years of age now and still enjoying life, THANK YOU GOD.

Love and Blessings to you all and goodbye from us both.

Brian John, and Muriel Joy Walters.

Carlsbad, California, USA 5/29/2023

Made in the USA
Las Vegas, NV
22 September 2023

77954702R00216